Korczyna Memorial Book

Translation of
Korczyna: Sefer Zikaron

Original Yiddish Book Edited by
Morris Zucker and Isaac Wasserstrom
New York, 1967

Project Coordinator and Translator:

William Leibner

Editor: Phyllis Kramer

Published by JewishGen

An Affiliate of the Museum of Jewish Heritage - A Living Memorial to the Holocaust
New York

Korczyna Memorial Book
Translation of Korczyna: Sefer Zikaron

First Printing: March 2014, Adar Sheni' 5774
Second Printing: March 2019, Adar II 5779

Project Coordinator and Translator: William Leibner
Editor: Phyllis Kramer
Layout: Joel Alpert
Image Editor: Jan R. Fine and Joel Alpert
Cover Design: Rachel Kolokoff Hopper
Publicity: Sandra Hirschhorn

Published by JewishGen, Inc.
An Affiliate of the Museum of Jewish Heritage
A Living Memorial to the Holocaust
36 Battery Place, New York, NY 10280

The mission of the JewishGen organization is to produce a translation of the original work and we cannot verify the accuracy of statements or alter facts cited.

Printed in the United States of America by Lightning Source, Inc.

Library of Congress Control Number (LCCN): 2013957648
ISBN: 978-1-939561-13-8 (hard cover: 332 pages, alk. paper)

Cover photographs courtesy of Baruch Akselrad.
Background of cover photographs courtesy of Rachel Kolokoff Hopper.

Front cover image has this written on it:

ביתו פתוח מימי עלומיו
עד זקנה ושיבה לתמוך
נפשות עניים. בשלחנו סמוך
דכים מרודים קרובים ורחוקים
יתומים להשיא בעזרתו רבקים
טוב חלקו הוא בו בשחקים
הרבני הנדיב מ' יוסף בענדיט
אקסילראד במ' יהודא ז"ל
נ' זקן ושבע ימים ובעושר

Increasingly and from afar speak of his charity,
His home was open from his youth
until his old age, to support the
poor. At his table ate the downtrodden from near and far,
unwed orphans to be married off with his assistance.
Good is portion here and in the heaven.
Our teacher the generous Yosef Bendit Akselrad, the son of
the late Yehudah of blessed memory.
He passed away an elderly and wealthy man.

May his soul be bound with the bonds of eternal life

(partially damaged)

Notes: It is believed that the bottom line and a half of the tombstone are missing.

The first letter of each word on the first line spells "Yosef." The rest of the first letters downward spell "Benidit."

Deciphering and translation was by Dovid Shatz.

JewishGen and the Yizkor-Books-in-Print Project

This book has been published by the **Yizkor-Books-in-Print Project,** as part of the **Yizkor Book Project** of **JewishGen, Inc**.

JewishGen, Inc. is a non-profit organization founded in 1987 as a resource for Jewish genealogy. Its website [www.jewishgen.org] serves as an international clearinghouse and resource center to assist individuals who are researching the history of their Jewish families and the places where they lived. JewishGen provides databases, facilitates discussion groups, and coordinates projects relating to Jewish genealogy and the history of the Jewish people. In 2003, JewishGen became an affiliate of the **Museum of Jewish Heritage - A Living Memorial to the Holocaust** in New York.

The **JewishGen Yizkor Book Project** was organized to make more widely known the existence of Yizkor (Memorial) Books written by survivors and former residents of various Jewish communities throughout the world. Later, volunteers connected to the different destroyed communities began cooperating to have these books translated from the original language—usually Hebrew or Yiddish—into English, thus enabling a wider audience to have access to the valuable information contained within them. As each chapter of these books was translated, it was posted on the JewishGen website and made available to the general public.

The **Yizkor-Books-in-Print Project** began in 2011 as an initiative to print and publish Yizkor Books that had been fully translated, so that hard copies would be available for purchase by the descendants of these communities and also by scholars, universities, synagogues, libraries, and museums.

These Yizkor books have been produced almost entirely through the volunteer effort of researchers from around the world, assisted by donations from private individuals. The books are printed and sold at near cost, so as to make them as affordable as possible. Our goal is to make this important genre of Jewish literature and history available in English in book form, so that people can have the personal histories of their ancestral towns on their bookshelves for themselves and for their children and grandchildren.

A list of all published translated Yizkor Books can be found at:
http://www.jewishgen.org/Yizkor/ybip.html

Lance Ackerfeld, Yizkor Book Project Manager

Joel Alpert, Yizkor-Book-in-Print Project Coordinator

JewishGen
Yizkor Book Project

This book is presented by the
Yizkor Books in Print Project
Project Coordinator: Joel Alpert

Part of the
Yizkor Books Project of JewishGen, Inc.
Project Manager: Lance Ackerfeld

These books have been produced solely through volunteer effort
of individuals from around the world. The books are printed and
sold at near cost, so as to make them as affordable as possible.

Our goal is to make this history and important genre of Jewish
literature available in English in book form so that people can have
the near-personal histories of their ancestral towns on their bookshelves for themselves and for their children and grandchildren.

Any donations to the Yizkor Books Project are appreciated.

Please send donations to:
Yizkor Book Project
JewishGen
36 Battery Place
New York, NY 10280

JewishGen, Inc. is an affiliate of the
Museum of Jewish Heritage
A Living Memorial to the Holocaust

Korczyna: Sefer Zikaron

Korczyna Memorial Book

Original Book

Written in Yiddish

Assembled and edited by

Morris Zucker and Isaac Wasserstrom

Published by the Members of the Korczyner Relief Committee in 1967 in New York, USA

This is a translation from: *Korczyna; sefer zikaron* (Korczyna) Memorial Book of a Jewish Town whose People were destroyed by the Germans in World War II), New York, 1967 (Hebrew and Yiddish, 495 pages)

Original Yiddish page

קאָרטשין

(קאָרטשינא)

ספר זכרון

געדענק־בוך

פֿון אַ ייִדיש שטעטל, וואָס די דייטשן, די מערדער ימ״ש
האָבן אומגעבראַכט, אין דער צייט פֿון דער צווייטער
וועלט־מלחמה, מיטוואָך דעם 12טן אויגוסט 1942
כ״ט אב — תש״ב

◄■►

אַרויסגעגעבן פֿון קאָרטשינער יזכור-בוך קאָמיטעט

ניו-יאָרק, תשכ״ז — 1967

From the Original Yizkor Book

KORCZYNA

MEMORIAL BOOK

OF

A Jewish town whose people were
destroyed by the Germans in World War II
August 12, 1942 — the 29th day of Av — 5702.

Printed in the United States of America

NEW YORK 1967

Translation of previous Yiddish page

From Original Yizkor Book

יזכּור־בּוך

קארטשין

ערשטער טייל

◆

פֿון

יצחק ענגלאַרד־װאַסערשטראַם

און אַנדערע

Translation of the Title Page of Original Yizkor Book

Memorial Book
KORCZYN

FIRST PART

FROM
Itahak Englard-Wasserstrum

AND OTHERS

From Original Yizkor Book

Printed in the United States of America
BALSHON PRINTING AND OFFSET CO.
480 SUTTER AVENUE   BROOKLYN, N. Y. 11207

Korczyna is located at:

49°43' North Latitude, 21°49' East Longitude
178 mi SSE of Warszawa
24 miles SSW of Rzeszów
3 miles NNE of Krosno
Also near Jaslo and Galicia, Poland

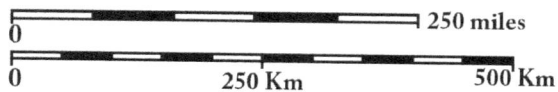

POLAND - Current Borders

Geopolitical Information:

Alternate names for the town are: Korycin [Polish], Kartchin [Yiddish], Korytsin [Russian], Karitchin

Time Period	Town	District	Province	Country
Before WWI (c. 1900):	Korytsin	Sokolka	Grodno	Russian Empire
Between the wars (c. 1930):	Korycin	Sokółka	Białystok	Poland
After WWII (c. 1950):	Korycin			Poland
Today (c. 2000):	Korycin			Poland

Nearby Jewish Communities:

Krosno 3 miles SSW
Jasienica Rosielna 6 miles ENE
Jedlicze 7 miles W
Domaradz 8 miles NE
Brzozów 9 miles E
Rymanów 9 miles SSE
Strzyżów 10 miles N
Niebylec 11 miles NNE
Dukla 12 miles SSW
Frysztak 12 miles NW
Zarszyn 13 miles SE
Nowy Żmigród 14 miles WSW
Jasło 16 miles W
Osiek Jasielski 16 miles WSW
Czudec 16 miles N
Błażowa 17 miles NE
Wielopole Skrzyńskie 18 miles NNW
Jaśliska 18 miles S
Kołaczyce 18 miles WNW
Bukowsko 20 miles SE
Tyczyn 20 miles NNE
Dynów 20 miles ENE
Sanok 20 miles ESE
Zgłobień 21 miles N

Brzostek 21 miles WNW
Wisłok Wielki 23 miles SSE
Nižný Komárnik, Slovakia 24 miles SSW
Jawornik Polski 24 miles ENE
Zabratówka 24 miles NE
Zagórz 24 miles SE
Rzeszów 24 miles NNE
Ropczyce 25 miles NNW
Sędziszów Małopolski 25 miles NNW
Jodłowa 25 miles WNW
Biecz 25 miles W
Čertižné, Slovakia 25 miles S
Szczawne 26 miles SSE
Dubiecko 26 miles ENE
Tyrawa Wołoska 26 miles ESE
Habura, Slovakia 27 miles S
Ladomirová, Slovakia 28 miles SSW
Pilzno 29 miles NW
Lesko 29 miles SE
Dębica 29 miles NW
Bircza 29 miles E
Gorlice 29 miles W
Siedleczka 30 miles NE

Note to the Reader:

Please note that all references within the text of the book to page numbers, refer to the page numbers of the original Yizkor Book.

Dedication and Acknowledgements for the Translation

The book is dedicated to the Leibner family that lived and died in Korczyn with the entire Jewish community of the hamlet. A small vibrant shtetl that lived for generations was wiped out by brutal killers for no other reason than "they were Jews." The Jews have disappeared from Korczyn and so did almost all of their traces, except for the cemetery. This book is a reminder or "*matzevah*" for this community.

Special thanks are in order for Meyer Denn who helped with the translation and other materials relating to Korczyn. He even provided me with the original Yiddish book of Korczyn that was used in translating the book.

First we'd like to thank Larry "Bulldog" Freund for his tireless work in shaping the translation of the manuscript into book format. Rachel Barkai, Director of Commemoration and Public Relations, Yad Vashem; Dr. Robert Rozette, Director of Yad Vashem library; Rachel Cohen, Secretary of Yad Vashem Library; to Mimi Ash at the Yad Vashem Media Center in Jerusalem; Yad Vashem staff at the various research stations in Jerusalem.

Many thanks to Phyllis Kramer who edited the translation in spite of her busy work schedule with JewishGen, especially with the Korczyna and Krosno websites. Her gracious offer to permit the use of all the pertinent materials was sincerely appreciated.

Many thanks are in order to my wife, Claudette Leibner, who created the ambiance that resulted in this work.

Special thanks to the National Yiddish Book Center in Amherst, Massachusetts and the New York Public Library for supplying the high resolution images used in this book.

Our sincere appreciation to Morris Zucker and Isaac Wasserstrom for their permission to publish this material.

Importantly we must also thank Rabbi Edward Boraz of Dartmouth College Hillel, who with students from the college restored the Jewish Cemetery of Korczyn in 2012, as part of Project Preservation. They provided the list of headstones in the cemetery that appears in this book.

Joel Alpert deserves the greatest mitzvah for his dedication and hard work in transforming written material into permanent books that stand tall as tombstones for the communities that no longer exist.

William Leibner
November 2013, Jerusalem, Israel

A Short History of the Hamlet of Korczyna

KORCZYNA was originally settled by German colonists; the name itself is a corruption of the German words *"Kot Schelne"*- pretty swamp. The area then contained many swamps.The Poles mispronounced the words and eventually called it Korczyna and the Jews called it Korczyn. The early settlement dates to the 13th century. By the 15th century the well established feudal community of Korczyna received municipal status under the Magdenburg rules. The hamlet established fairs and trade markets that attracted sellers and buyers from the area that was basically an agricultural region.

Korczyna provided residence to Jews who lived and traded in the area but were forbidden to reside in many places, namely in Krosno, 5 kilometers from Korczyna. We know little about the early Jewish life in Korczyna but we know that in the XVII century the hamlet already had a synagogue and a cemetery that provided burial services to the Jews in the area. In 1784, Korczyna already had 80 Jews that established a well-run community or " Kahal" that provided religious and social services to the local Jews and the Jews living in the vicinity. area. According to Jerzy Potocki, a Polish historian of the region, the Jewish population increased to 209 Jews in 1824, and in 1900 the population totaled 1209 souls. This number would steadily decline and prior to World War II Korczyna nearly 786 Jews and about 50-60 Jewish families in nearby villages.

The Jews dealt primarily in petty commerce, crafts such as tailoring, shoe mending, glass and peddling. An important source of income for the Jewish community was the market place in town with all the stands, and the markets and fairs in nearby towns, notably Krosno. Weaving, tanning and the wine industries provided jobs to the local population.

Korczyna had a few well to do merchants in wood, forest, grain and fruits. The city also had a few cloth spinning facilities, which provided employment to local Jews. The situation changed radically with the Austrian Imperial abolishment of the need for a special permit to move from place to place. In addition, great opportunities opened for the local Jews with the industrial boom in the city of Krosno, where oil was discovered and the railroad linked the city to the rest of the country. Jews began to leave Korczyna in large numbers for nearby Krosno or Jaslo as well as emigrating to Germany and the USA The Jewish population in town steadily declined.

The Jewish Kehillah was well organized and had administrative control over a large area that contained many localities including Krosno or Kros as it is called in Yiddish. The Jewish community was predominantly Hassidic mainly followers of Belz and Dzikow. Ach of these groups had their own synagogue, Korczyna of course had a regular synagogue e and the "Beit amidrash" or study ceter was also used as a synagogue. The rabbis of the town were provided by the Rubin family, which was related to the Hassidic courts of Ropshitz and Lejansk. The last rabbi of the town was Rabbi Eliyahu Rubin who perished with the entire Jewish community in the Shoah.

Alexander Bendit was the last leader of the Jewish community in Korczyn. The community had several voluntary associations to help the sick, the needy, and the poor. The community also had a mutual bank that granted free interest loans to the needy merchants. The first Zionist club opened in 1905 and gathered momentum following WWI with 68 shekel-paying members. The war started on September 1, 1939, Friday, 17 days in Elul, tartzat. Nearby Krosno was immediately bombarded since it had a military airfield and industrial plants. The Germans entered Korczyna on September 9, 1939. The Germans soon left the city but made sporadic raids to grab Jewish workers for all sorts of work details. Then, on December 1939, the order was issued that all Jews must wear arm bands and Jewish stores must be marked. In January of 1940, the Judenrat was created headed by Oscar Rubin and his assistant Yehezkel Lewitman. Both had lived in Germany and spoke fluent German. The Judenrat created a Jewish police to enforce the tax laws that were imposed on all Jewish residents of the town. The council became a tool in the hands of the Germans who ruled it with an iron hand and did everything in their power to pauperize the Jewish community. The council provided cheap Jewish labor for the Germans. It also provided shelter and food for Jewish refugees from Lodz, Krosno and other cities. A J.S.S. (Jewish Self Help) committee was established that opened a public kitchen that distributed meals to the needy. Then, all Jewish stores were closed in June of 1941. The Gestapo constantly harassed Jews and frequently killed them on the flimsiest of pretexts. Each day seemed to bring a new edict aimed at harming Jews.

Finally, in July of 1942, an order was issued to all Jews inhabiting villages near Korczyna to move immediately to the hamlet. On August 12th, 1942, all the Jews were ordered to assemble in the market place where the selection took place. The old, sick and the infirm were trucked to Wola Jajnicza, near Korczyna, and shot. The women and children were sent by truck to Krosno. All men were forced to run on foot to Krosno. In the market place of Krosno, the Jews of Korczyna waited two days until they were sent to the death camp of Belzec where most of them perished.

The Jewish community of Korczyna was thus obliterated. Hundreds of years of Jewish life was destroyed within a very brief period of time for no reason except the fact that they were Jews. No Jewish trace was left in Korczyna except for the old Jewish cemetery. Since the Jews of Korczyna have no grave or gravestone, we memorialize them through the pages of the translated Yizkor book.

May they rest eternally wherever they are buried.

Pour out Thy wrath

Upon the Germans, the Nazis,   שפוך חמתך

That knew Thee not   על הגרמנים הנאצים

And upon those that call not   אשר לא ידעוך

Upon Thy name: ואשר בשמך לא קראו

For they have eaten Jacob   כי אכלו את יעקב

And laid waste his dwelling.   ואת נוהו השמו

Pour out Thy fury upon them   שפך עליהם זעמך

And may the kindling of Thine   וחרון אפך ישיגם

Anger overtake them   תרדף באף ותשמידם

Pursue them with anger   מתחת שמי ד׳.

And destroy them from

Under God's skies.

Introduction to the Translation of the Korczyna Yizkor Book

Dear Reader,

What can one say that will begin to express the sadness and pain related by the authors and compilers of the Korczyner Yizkor Book. In 1967, as the last generation to carry the memory of *shtetl* life before the *"churban"* (destruction) began to pass from the scene, they hurried to document for future generations the story of their beloved hometown of Korczyna (pronounced Kortcheen in Yiddish). Most of the authors of this book had left Korczyna long before the Holocaust, settling in such disparate places as the United States, Canada, Sweden, Austria, South America, and Israel, must have felt that the common language of Yiddish would be the logical language through which to pass on their stories. They obviously did not have the foresight to understand that Yiddish would soon be a language reserved for the *bays medrash* (House of Study) of the great Chassidic yeshivas, not the lingua franca of their progeny. This miscalculation led this book for consignment to attics, Holocaust sections in unused libraries, bookshelves of academic institutions and second-hand Yiddish bookstores for the next 35 years.

I inherited this book from my grandfather, Yosef Yehudah (Joe) Denn *z"l* (of blessed memory), a son of Korczyna, upon his death in 1981. Being able to read Hebrew but not Yiddish, I painstakingly went through the book word-by-word, page-by-page, looking for references to our family's name. It soon became clear to me what a valuable treasure trove of information the book held for those of us who were so fascinated with the lives of our loved ones who lived and died in this shtetl. Using the book as a starting place, I subsequently traveled to Korczyna four times between 1983 and 2008, visiting the cemetery, the town hall, and elderly Christian neighbors to see what remains.

When I met Bill Leibner in Jerusalem in 1997 to discuss our common roots in Korczyna, he expressed a desire to translate the entire book. He painstakingly completed this project with great love and attention to detail. As a result, you hold in your hands the fruit of his labor. It is the fulfillment of the dream of its original writers and compilers: to keep the memory of their beloved community and the holy souls who lived and died there alive and memorialize the martyrs whose blood cries out to us from the dust of its streets, the neighboring forests, the ghettos and the camps, may they be avenged.

Lastly, we must express appreciation to Rabbi Edward Boraz, who together with a group of his university students from Dartmouth College, undertook the holy work of returning to Korczyna in the summer of 2012 to clean, restore, renovate and re-dedicate the old Jewish cemetery. With over 400 stones hidden in thick vegetation, each stone was located, re-set into the ground, photographed, epitaph transcribed and translated for an eternal memory, the concrete gate surrounding the cemetery repaired and a new iron gate replaced the old deteriorated gate that once protected it from vandals. He and his students should be blessed with all good things for their selfless deeds and *chesed shel emet* (kindness to those who cannot repay their act).

Meyer Denn
Dallas, Texas
August 20, 2013/Elul 13, 5773

Family Notes

Table of Contents

[Page 11]

A statement from the publishers of the Korczyner memorial book

There is a statement in the Talmud that says: "Rabbi Yossi said that he never contradicted his friends. I know that I am not a cohen but if my friends insist that I go and bless the congregation, I would do it (Sabbath 115)".

We know that we don't have the necessary literary skills to create a fitting memorial but the remnants of the Jewish community of Korczyn demand that we undertake the task in spite of the fact that we are not priests (cohens) or writers. Of course we can ask whether any professional or literary writer can do justice to the Jewish destruction in our times. The object of the memorial book is not to create a literary or historical masterpiece but to create a memorial, a tombstone in the memory of our fathers, our mothers, our brothers, our sisters and our children from Korczyn that were innocently killed by the Germans. The object of the memorial is that the children and their children should read and especially see the book in order to remember what the Germans did to our community. The future generations must remember that there once existed a Jewish community in Korczyn that consisted of 786 people who lead a simple and pious life. In 1942, the Germans cleared the Jews from the entire area about 800 into the ghetto of Korczyn and then destroyed the entire Jewish community of about 1600 people.

This deed can't be forgotten. It must be memorialized for eternity. Perhaps the future generations will be able to see in the German defeat some consolation as the German philosopher Nietzsche stated: 'A token revenge is better than none'. May their memory be erased forever.

[Page 13]

Pour out thy wrath (passage based on the Haggadah of Passover)

Upon the Germans, the Nazis
That knew Thee not
And upon those that call not
Upon Thy name:
For they have eaten Jacob
And laid waste his dwelling,

Pour out Thy fury upon them
And may the kindling of Thine
Anger overtake them
Pursue them with anger
And destroy them from
Under God's skies.

[Page 15]

Introduction

A Yizkor book is dedicated to the memory of a township that the Germans, meanest killers in history, destroyed. It is a vocal protest against the senseless slaughter while the world stood by in resigned silence and watched the destruction of innocent and hopeless men, women and children. Hundreds of Jewish townships and villages were wiped off the map without leaving a trace or survivor that could write a Yizkor book for the place.

Most of European Jewry was destroyed. Why does each city or hamlet publishes its own Yizkor book. This was a national catastrophe and not some local event. Why don't we create a national monument that will serve as an eternal memorial to the great Jewish tragedy, something that will be observed and kept by the entire Jewish people for generations to come. Each Jewish tragic event in history is immortalized. We express our sorrow for the destruction of the Temple for about 1900 years. The sorrow lasts from the seventeen day of Tamus (Jewish month) to the ninth day of Av (Jewish month). For 2400 years we abstain from eating on the fast of Esther and enjoy the holiday of Purim that destroyed the evil plans of Hamman to kill the Jews. For 1800 years we mourn the death of the 24000 students of Rabbi Akiva who died as a result of an epidemic or revolt directed at the Romans. We don't shave and marry on the days of the Omer (between Pessach and Shavuot).

Can't the holocaust where hundreds of communities were destroyed compare with the dying of Rabbi Akiva's students. Were the rabbis, talmudic scholars and yeshiva students of these communities less important than the yeshiva of Rabbi Akiva. Where are the present day religious leaders, the orthodox leaders and the leaders of the secular Jewish world. About postmortems in Israel, the streets of America are constantly alarmed. We see big warning signs about these events. Even marches to the United Nations are organized. Where is the big protest for the killing of the 6 million Jews. Why can't we create a special day to memorialize the destruction of European Jewry that would be observed by all the Jews.

[Page 17]

Yizkor Book: Korczyn - First Part
by Itzhak Englard Wasserstrom and others

[Page 19-22]

יצחק ענגלאַרד־װאַסערשטראָם

Itzhak Englard-Wasserstrom

The Hamlet

The name of the hamlet is Korczyna and Jews called it Korczyn. We don't remember whether we studied it in school or read a history book to the effect that the name supposedly stems from the fact that there were once many German settles in the area and they called it Kot Sheine (pretty swamp) for the many swamps in the area. The Poles mispronounced the name and called it Korczyna. The township is centrally located in Galicia along the railway line to Krosno or Kros as the Jews called it. Westward, Korczyn is 5 kilometers from Krosno, 21 kilometers from Jaslo and 200 kilometers from Krakow. Eastward, Korczyn is 15 kilometers from the spa resort of Iwonicz, 40 kilometers from Sanok, 80 kilometers from Przemysl and 200 kilometers from Lwow (Lemberg or Lviv). The following villages belonged administratively to Korczyn: Kombornia, Kroscienko, Iskozinia, Wenglowka and Adzikan. Even Krosno once belonged to the Jewish community of Korczyn until it received permission in 1901 to create its own kehilla administration.

The township consisted of a square that was called the market or the ringplace and several small streets: the Mangel street, the beth hamidrash (study center) street, the street to the old post office, the street to the Kombornia road, the street to the Krosner road (Goszciniec). The market measured about 1000 x 700 square meters. Most of the homes were built around the square and had one floor except for seven taller buildings. Most homes had stores in front facing the market while the family lived in the rear.

The taller buildings had windows facing the market. In a corner of the market, was the study street, which lead to a smaller square that was called the moon square since Jews blessed the moon each month there. According to the Jewish Encyclopedia (Yevreiska Encyclopedia) published in Russian in St. Petersburg in 1909, volume 9, page 777 (see YIVO, NY), Korczyna had a Jewish population of 1026 in 1900.

In 1939, the population of Korczyn consisted of 6000 people, amongst them were 786 Jewish residents in the township and 50-60 Jews lived in the nearby villages. The Christian population, exclusively Poles, lived around the township. Four Christian families lived in Korczyn proper. The entire center of the township was Jewish and 99% of all the stores were Jewish owned. The Jews built the township.

Street leading to the study center.
Nachman Leibish Reich's house on the right and Mendel Rubin's house on the left.

The center of Korczyn

The last house on this street belonged to Mrs. Godel Gutwein. Today the place serves as a slaughterhouse. The man in the picture is Yaacov Fessel a great grandson of hers. He took the picture while visiting Korczyn in June of 1963.

[Page 23-24]

When did Jewish life begin in Korczyn?

We don't know when the first Jews arrive in Korczyn or when the Jewish community started to function. All Jewish community or kehilla documents were ceased by the Germans in 1942 or were destroyed. The municipal documents were not placed at our disposal. We base our book on the stories told by the old-timers of Korczyn and the tombstones of the old cemetery, especially the first row, which reveals a tombstone, dated 1701 (tasa). This would indicate the existence of Jewish families as well as a community in the 17th century. Thus, we can safely assume that the Jewish community is at least 300 years old. The area belonged to the feudal family of Szepticki in the days of the Polish kingdom. With the partition of Poland in 1772 between Russia, Prussia and Austria, Korczyn fell under the hegemony of Austria.

Today the town is devoid of Jews or Jewish traces except for the cemetery that indicates that there once existed a Jewish community in Korczyn.

All our enemies opened their mouths at us
Fear and death reached us
Waste and destruction is our lot
My eyes shed rivulets of tears
Upon the destruction of my people
The stream of tears can't be stopped
(Job, aprt 3, pp 46-49) freely translated by **William Leibner**

[Page 25]

The Kehilla or Jewish community administration

Under Austrian law, there was a Jewish community leadership that was responsible for the affairs of Jewish communal life. The leadership consisted of several people (we don't know the exact number) and a presiding officer. Only people that paid taxes voted for the kehilla leadership. Thus, only the well to do and the merchants played a dominant role in the elections. The latter, well advertised in advance were held in the beth hamidrash or at the home of the well to do. On occasion the leadership of the kehilla was selected by the head of the area office (starosta) if there was bitter dissension or lack of decision.

In 1919, with the establishment of an independent Poland, the government passed a law regarding Jewish community affairs. According to this law, the kehilla leadership was to consist of eight duly elected members who in turn elect the leader of the kehilla by majority vote. The rabbi of the community is automatically a member of the leadership and has full voting rights. The elections must be secret, general and proportional. Every man aged 21 had the right to vote. Every person that collected 20 signatures of eligible voters could stand for election. Each list of candidates had to have eight names and 20 signatures of eligible voters. The leadership was elected for a term of four years following which new elections had to be called.

[Page 26-28]

The activities of the public and the elections

The kehilla leadership was primarily responsible for the religious needs of the Jewish inhabitants such as the maintenance of the beth hamidrash and the public baths, flour for matzoth on Passover, the salaries of the rabbi, the shochet (ritual slaughterer), and the Shamash (custodian of the synagogue) etc. The leadership had no other functions. To maintain all these expenses, the kehilla levied a tax on ritual slaughtering that is if someone wanted to kill a chicken or slaughter a cow, they had to buy a ticket from the kehilla office. The kehilla also imposed taxes on the Jewish inhabitants of the town. These taxes had the force of law and could be collected through the official administration if the parties refused to pay. All these incomes barely covered the budget of the kehilla. This caused many a headache to the head of the kehilla especially if the rabbi or the shochet did not get their salary on time or belonged or sympathized with the opposition in the kehilla leadership. No one could then envy the members of the board, nor were many people interested in the job. Most stayed away not wanting to get involved. Thus, the same board continued to function for many years and many terms. Until suddenly someone demanded elections for the kehilla.

The community emerged from the so-called trance and everybody became interested in elections even those that could not vote. Political fever seized the town. The rabbi wanted a new board where he would have greater sway, why the urgency, nobody knew.

In our township as in most Galician towns, the rabbis were related to famous rabbis and the job went from father to son. Nobody even thought of changing or that there was a need for a change. The rabbi's job consisted of answering questions concerning religious laws, judicial arbitration andmaking the flour mill kosher for Pessah so that matzoth could be baked for the community. That was the extent of his job, ample time for political life. Factions soon formed, issues were created, each side tried to show strength and wisdom. The fight was especially difficult in a small community where there were about 200 eligible voters. Four electoral lists appeared for the election of the kehilla leadership. The elections cost a great deal of money, votes were expensive, bribes had to be given to the prince of the locality and to the local administrator of the area or strarosta in order to keep things fair.

The prince could create all kinds of problems if he was paid the right sum of money. He could cancel a list on technicalities, postpone elections, or delay the transfer of administration to the newly elected leadership. Thus, the contenders would pay various sums so that the prince would stay out of the race. Each list of candidates made appeals for contributions. The economic situations was difficult, people barely met their needs, to buy clothing or shoes for children was a hardship but to contribute to the election fund was a must. How could one permit for so and so to become the leader of the kehilla, here is another fifty zlotys for your campaign.

Brief, it was a regular election campaign, ads, speeches, rallies and even promises of paradise. Hassidic lists promised paradise for those that will vote for them and not for the reform lists. Elections similar to the ones in the big cities and one can even compare them to the American elections. All sides lost, only the prince made money by keeping out of the way. We must stress that the elections did not create eternal animosities or hatred between the contending parties. It was more a sporting event than a real fight. The campaign did awake the lethargic community from its slumber, people began to talk, to think. The blood circulation increased and affected the sclerotic organizations of the community. A bit of reawakening did take place in the township.

[Page 29-30]

Rabbis

We don't know when the Jewish community of Korczyn selected the first rabbi or his name. We do know however that in the first half of the 19th century, the rabbi of Korczyn was Shmuel Aaron Rubin, author of the scholarly book "Beth Aaron ". We think that this rabbi was the great grand father of the rabbi Shmuel Aaron of New York. The latter called himself "Der Moreh Derech" (The Guide) and established the institution called " Anshei Maamad Ubeith Vaad Lehahamim" (A religious institution) located in the Lower East side, on Henry St. NYC. With the death of Rabbi Shmuel Aaron Rubin, Rabbi Shmuel Rubin became rabbi of Korczyn. He was a father in law to the Sziniver Rabbi, Rabbi Yehezkel Halbershtam, author of the book "Words of Yehezkel ". Shmuel Rubin's son, Asher became the rabbi with the passing of his father in 1901. Rabbi Asher Rubin passed away in 1932 and was succeeded by his son Mordechai Eliezar Rubin who died two years later due to pneumonia. His brother, Eliyahu was appointed Rabbi of Korczyn.

The Germans killed the rabbi, his wife and their six children aged 6-14.

We see the tombstones of Rabbi Asher Rubin and Rabbi Mordechai EliezarRubin at the cemetery of Korczyn. Yaacov Itzhac Fessel of Sweden took the picture in June of 1963.]

[Page 31-32]

Synagogues

We know practically nothing about the synagogues prior to the 20th century. We describe here the synagogue, the study center (beth hamidrash) and other places of worship from 1901 until the destruction of the Jewish community. The last study center was built in 1901 mainly due the initiative of the then leader of the kehilla, Mr. Meshulem Akselrad. The study center was beautifully decorated, the ceiling and walls were covered with painted scenes created by an artist. All this work was encouraged by Mr. Haim Den also referred to as Haimel Broider.

When the synagogue was built nobody knows. The synagogue, the study center and the prayer house called Yad Harutzim formed one building complex from the exterior. The complex was situated on 200 square meters and had one entrance. In the hall there were three doors: one facing south led to the study center, one facing north led to the Yad Harutzim synagogue and the last one facing east led to the synagogue proper. Little is known about the latter, it was never finished. It had red brick walls and a roof. The ceiling and the walls were never painted and it had no floor. It had simple wooden tables and benches and a simple holy arc. We don't even know who exactly prayed in this synagogue.

During WWI, the entrance to the building complex and the roof of the synagogue burned down since they were built of wood. Only the walls of the synagogue remained standing. It could no longer be used as a worship place and served as a place for the blessing of the moon (each Hebrew month is blessed) and for bridal canopies for weddings. The entrance to the study center was rebuilt through the erection of an additional building that led through the women section of the old synagogue. The Yad Harutzim synagogue was established in 1930-1931 in this addition.

On Sabbath and Holidays there was also prayers in the house of Mendel Schroit until 1919. There were also regular prayers held for many years at the home of Mendel Gleicher. There was a small congregation of Dzikower Hassidim that prayed at the home of Israel Meir Dorschowitz and a similar congregation of Belzer Hassidim that prayed at the home of Nachman Leibish Reich. These congregations disappeared with time.

[Page 33-34]

The Beth Hamidrash

In a township like Korczyn, the entire Jewish communal life revolved in and around the beth hamidrash. Naturally, the place was foremost a holy place where Jews prayed and studied torah. The beth hamidrash was never closed, the doors remained open from 5 AM to midnight. The walls of the beth hamidrash soaked up the prayers of the congregants as well as the chants of the students who sat and studied holy texts. The place was drenched in tears that were shed in supplication by our mothers and fathers demanding divine assistance with health, income and family protection and continuation. The sounds of supplication still rings in our ears as women would enter the beth hamidrash and literally scream for divine intervention on behalf of a sick husband or child. We all shed tears and looked as the women would frequently open the holy arc and kiss the torah and ask for divine pity and protection.

The beth hamidrash was a holy place but contrary to a synagogue was also a community hall. All meetings and assemblies were held there. The sale for the purchase of flour for Passover was held there, the discussions regarding the maintenance of the public bath was debated there, a candidate for Parliament spoke there and large group meetings were held there. After the Minha and Maariv services or in the middle of the day, one could see people light up a cigarette and discuss with friends and neighbors topics of interest. The Shamash of the beth hamidrash had a little candy store in a corner where you could buy cigarettes, cookies, chocolate, apples, pears, soda etc.

People that wanted to meet someone or hear the latest gossip would come to the beth hamidrash, not necessarily to pray. Here was the place to release your sorrows or worries and listen to other people and to other problems. You realized that you were not the only one with problems. The beth hamidrash was a sort of social club for the individual as well as for the collective Jewish community.

The beth hamidrash is no longer a teeming center of activity, there are no Jews in Korczyn. It serves as a warehouse. The eternal light that lit for ages is gone and so are the Jews, our parents, brothers, sisters and small children. Don't forget that the Germans performed this heinous crime.

The economic situation and jobs of the Korczyner Jews

Old people told a story that once upon a time Jews could not celebrate Purim since they could not give donations for the poor because there were no poor people in Korczyn.(Tradition has it that on Purim it is a mitzvah to give gifts to the poor). This was about a hundred and fifty years ago when Korczyn was the center of the area and nearby Krosno had no Jewish residents to speak of. With the settlement of Jews in Kros, the commercial life of the city developed rapidly and inversely caused the decline of economic opportunities in Korczyn. The economic base of the Jewish community steadily declined. The hamlet had plenty of poor people, as a matter of fact, it had more takers than givers. Thus there was no problem celebrating the Purim holiday.

In this chapter we are describing the Jewish economic situation of Korczyn prior to WWI, between the wars, WWII and the destruction of the Jewish community. Korczyn had no railway station but Krosno, seven kilometers away, had one. Everything had to be transported by horse and carriage. The township had no industry or large commercial enterprises. Most Jews engaged in small trade that provided the surrounding peasant population with their needs. The farmers sold their products in town and bought all their needs. There were textile stores for clothing material, haberdasheries, leather goods, metal, paint, chalk, cement, glass, pots and pans, food, beer, liquor and two tobacco stores. Until WWI, Jews owned all stores except for two grocery stores. There were Jews who were not involved in commerce, they were watchmakers, bakers, butchers, coachmen, tailors, seamstresses, porters and glaziers The glaziers carried their wares in a box on their back and went from village to village to fix windows. Most of artisans and petty traders could not afford to eat meat every day, they barely provided milk for their children. Poor storekeepers ate a piece of chicken only on Saturday or Holiday or if they were sick. To consume a quarter of a chicken was a rare deed. A chicken had to provide food for the Friday night and Saturday meals for the entire family of 6-8 people. With each bite of meat came a piece of hallah to satisfy the hunger. Bread and potatoes were the main food staples of the families. For breakfast, bread with a thin spread of butter, coffee or chicory with a drop of milk. Eggs, cheese, marmalade were only served in the richer homes. For lunch, potato soup, potatoes with butter milk, dough with beans, and other meatless dishes. Pastry was only consumed at a wedding, a bar mitzvah, or a Brit. Nobody would eat pastry on a simple day, even well to do people would abstain from showing off fearful of an evil eye. A piece of sponge cake was a luxury.

[Page 37-38]

The economic situation and jobs of the Korczyner Jews following World War I

Following wars, the general public is hungry for things that they could not obtain during the war years, people buy everything, and there is prosperity. The same thing happened in Korczyn. Business flourished, everybody was in business: shoemakers, tailors, shochtim, cantors, coachmen, butchers, teachers in heders, their assistants and even people that never dealt in commerce. You did not need experience for what you bought today you sold the next day with a nice profit. Everything was in demand: soap, candles, paper, shoelaces, you name it. In special demand were the materials for clothing where small fortunes were made. Every home had a corner set aside for merchandise that was sold wholesale. No store or agent, the goods went from hand to hand.

A Korczyner Jew would travel to Kros, or Rymanow, or Sanok (Sunik in Yiddish), or Nowy Sadz (Zanz in Yiddish) and buy merchandise. A week later, the salesman from Krosno, Rymanow, Sanok or Nowy Sadz would come to Korczyn and repurchase the merchandise at a higher price. A week later, the merchant of Korczyn would again travel to look for merchandise and pay more money for the same merchandise he sold last week. Everybody made money, everybody had bundles of paper money, everybody lived way above their means and people counted their money that grew by the day. Yesterday's nobody was today a millionaire. Money was constantly printed but merchandise became scarce. What you purchased this week, was more expensive next week, in short, a galloping inflation.

The bubble burst, the money became valueless. Those that had merchandise in stock were left with value. Those that only had paper money were wiped out overnight. Time moved on and with it came some sort of normalcy. People slowly returned to their previous positions. The shoemakers and the tailors returned to their workshops, the butcher to the butcher store, the coachmen to the horses and the coach, the shochet and the cantor to their work, the teacher and his assistant to the heder. Some remained grocery men or storekeepers. The main source of income for the storekeepers and the merchants returned to be the market. Friday was market day in Korczyn and Monday was in Krosno. On Friday, hundreds of peasants would arrive from the surrounding areas and park their carriages in the market place. They sold their goods and spent their money in stores, bars and food stores.

Monday morning, all merchants of Korczyn with exception of food and metal merchants left for the Krosno market in order to sell their wares. The rest of the week, the merchants sat at the entrance of their stores and waited for customers or talked politics with their neighbors. After WWI, tobacco licenses for stores were granted to war invalids, one of them was a Jew by the name of Haim Wolf Koref. Two non-Jewish food stores and some bars opened up. The rest of the commerce in Korczyn was in Jewish hands. Korczyn had two restaurants owned by Aaron Blank and Wolf Gleicher where one could eat a meal. There were also grain merchants and forest merchants. The city had a vinegar factory owned by Yosef Holloshitz and a soda factory owned by Haim Eliyahu Kaufman. There were also merchants that purchased the entire egg or butter production of a farmer and resold it wholesale to the city. There were merchants that would purchase an entire apple orchard while the fruit was still on the tree and then sell the picked apples to big city fruit dealers. This business was seasonal and the biggest apple dealer was Wolf Kirschner.

There were also haulers and suppliers. The latter provided the merchants with items that could only be obtained in the big cities. These suppliers would come around take the orders and then bring the merchandise. The main supplier for merchandise of Krakow was Israel Margoles and the one for Tarnow was Simha Bezenshtock. The haulers transported merchandise from and to the railway and saw to it that the goods were tended to. The leader in the field was Leibele Schiff. With the exception of a few well to do Jews, most of the Jewish population in Korczyn barely existed for the economic situation was very difficult. They worried about income and a dowry for daughters if they had, without a dowry it was almost impossible to marry a daughter. Many a person grayed before their time due to these worries.

The first attempts to produce lines were made in 1935-1936. Jewish entrepreneurs would give polish spinners the materials and the latter would produce beautiful tablecloths, towels, kerchiefs and different lines in various shapes and different qualities. The items we pretty and nice and attracted attention throughout Poland. Korczyn had a linen industry prior to WWI but it was somewhat backward and lacked incentive. Jews entered the field in 1935-6 and gave it the necessary push and it soon reached markets throughout Poland. Korczyn had four large spinners where the items were pressed and stretched into shape. Three of the spinners used horsepower and one used engine power. Four Jewish families drew their income from the spinners. The main dealers in the industry were the following families: Lezer, Pinter, Reich, Willner, Dym, Rubin and Weber. There were also a few other families that did not deal directly with the linen production. Most of the families that dealt with the linen industry and its services made a nice living and some even prospered.

Acording to unofficial reports, the following families were considered wealthy in the years between 1850-1914: Wele Rapport, Naphtali Raab and his descendants called Raabes, Mendel Schroit, Moshe Rothenberg, Meshulem Akselrad, Mendel Gleicher and Mendel Rubin. These were well to do people and lived accordingly. Some of them lost their place and their fortune during WWI and others took their place. But the newcomers never measure up to the old established families. We can safely say, that a garment operator in NYC lives nicer, more comfortable, more secure, dresses better, enjoys more luxuries, feels safer economically that the rich Jew of Korczyn after WWI.

[Page 41-42]

The spiritual and cultural life of Korczyn since the second half of the 19th century to the outbreak of World War II

During the second half of the 19th century the culture of the Jewish of Korczyn during the period consisted of studying the torah, the shulhan aruch (codex of Jewish orthodox customs), and living the life of a Hassid. Their life was based not only on the ethical and moral teachings of the principles of the halacha (religious law) in accordance with the torah and the talmudic sages but on the wisdom of the sages. 100 years ago, Jews of Korczyn did not subscribe to general studies. Reading a non-religious book was considered profanity and even negation of religion. One could almost be considered a non-believer. In those days, you could not find a Jewish home in Korczyn with a general book, even in homes of non-scholars. Ordinary people would have at home books like moral preaching, stories of saints such as "Praises of the Baal Shem Tov", "Stories from grandfather Spoler" and Sefer Hayashar-the Right Book".

Children were not sent to regular schools. When the ordinances were issued for compulsory education, parents would pay the doctors two kronen Austrian money (to get notes stating that the children were sick and needed to stay home). Rudimentary writing and reading skills as well as some basic knowledge of the local language were acquired through the pages of the book "The Letter Writer". Basically the parents wanted that their children should be raised as torah scholars, even the rich wanted their children to be known for their torah learning. The Jews of Korczyn did not about things outside their community and furthermore were not interested. No newspaper reached the township, Reading a paper was considered a waste of time, which could be better, used to study the Talmud. Besides, there was always the fear that the written material will tend to weaken the religious base of the reader and slowly weaken the entire religious foundation that was built for generations to give sustenance and strength to the religious Jewish way of life.

A small illustration of the mental attitude of the time: the event took place in the second half of the previous century. One morning, Fishel Mener entered the study center and shouted to the effect that there was a fire in the house of Naphtali Raab. People stopped the prayers and run to save the house. To their astonishment, they saw no fire or smoke. They returned to the study center and Fishel Mener is still talking about the fire. The congregates try to calm him by telling him that there is no fire but Fishel Mener continues to scream that there is a fire. Then he admits to the congregants that he saw Zishe Beck, Naphtali's son-in-law, read a paper. This he considered a serious fire.

[Page 43-44]

The first years of the present century

With the beginning of the present century, young boys and fellows sat in the study center and studied Talmud from dawn to dusk. Quietly or surreptitiously they also studied non-religious materials. Besides dealing with the sea of Talmudic knowledge they also delved into the secular world of knowledge, especially Hebrew and Yiddish literature. The parents did not only object to their children reading Jewish history books by Prof. Gretz but also general books on Jewish topics. Even books dealing with the philosophical implications of Job were considered smacking of enlightenment, which was forbidden. Even very pious Jews avoided reading such material for fear of being labeled religious doubters. Nobody was caught red handed reading books or newspapers but rumors were afloat. Perhaps a parent spotted his children reading secretly such material but he would not divulge it. But the place was small and no secret can last forever and it soon became apparent that people were reading the "Lemberger Togblat" (Yiddish daily newspaper published in Lemberg or Lviv or Lwow), first secretly and then publicly. Amongst this circle of readers, we can describe Haim Levi Tzeiger. He was a Talmudic scholar and a very pious Jew. He studied not only religious texts but also other Hebrew texts. Rumors had it that he sympathized with the idea of returning to Zion, in other words he was a Zionist sympathizer.

Haim Levi had a long beard and curled peyot (side curls) that no barber ever touched. He wore a long caftan, a black velvet hat and under it a black velvet kippah, a long woolen talit katan (leibtzudekel) with the fringes hanging on the sides and a pair of boots on his feet. Shoes represented modernity or progress in Korczyn. Haim Levi thus incorporated torah, faith, and self respect. Others young men, not of the scholastic caliber of Haim Levi, also dressed in the traditional Hassidic garb. No fellow would dare wear a jacket or a simple hat. Some of these young men created in Korczyn in 1909-1910 the first Zionist group called „Halutz" The town went berserk, who were these hoodlums? Who were these non-believers? Others identified them as Zionists.

A Zionist to an old Korczyner Jew was a non-believer, a denier of the articles of faith. They all implied that Haim Levi Tzeiger had a hand in the development of this apostasy. They even implied that the name of Halutz stands for the name of Haim Levi Tzeiger. The fact that he never entered the place or gave support to the group did not squash the rumors. The club continued to function and provided lessons in Talmud, bible, Hebrew, Hebrew literature and the concept of Love of Zion. The club was limited to men.

[Page 45-47]

The period following World War I

During WWI, the Austrian army drafted all men from the age of 17 to 50. Many men never left Korczyn in their lifetime, suddenly they met people from different cultures who were exposed to the modern way of life. Korczyn was occupied by the Russian army, which caused many Jews to flee to Hungary, Bohemia, Moravia and Austria proper. The war and the migrations caused great upheavals in the life style of Korczyn. Young people started to dress in modern fashion. Yeshiva students who studied in the beth hamidrash started to wear regular hats, they trimmed their beards and peyot and began to read newspapers and general books.

Parents began to look for son-in-laws that had acquired some general education. Brides to be were also required to have some general rudimentary education. Parents wanted their children to read and understand a Polish newspaper as a way to insure their ability to exist in the world. For the competition for survival became fierce with each day. The Polish Prime Minister, Skladowski urged the Poles to fight the Jewish predominance in the field of commerce. He urged the Polish masses to move to the cities and open stores in order to compete with the Jews. The masses did not move but enough Poles took the advice and moved to the cities and competed with the Jewish merchants. The latter suffered hardships and some even folded. Daily economic existence became harsher with the time.

The parents realized that their children must be educated and trained to cope with the new threats if they were to survive. They could no longer isolate their children and expect them to survive on their own in the contemporary era. One had to know how to speak to a client, one had to learn some manners, one had to learn how to explain finances, briefly, and one had to get an education. As the mishna (Talmud) says "It is nice to study torah and respect as long as it enables one to earn a living" (loosely translated by the translator). Parents started to send their children to public schools. There were no yeshivas in Galicia that combined religious and secular education.

Korczyn had a sizable number of highly self-educated students that were mostly former yeshiva students. They formed the literary backbone of Jewish life in the city. The average Jewish person hardly played a role in the cultural life of the hamlet. The Warsaw Yiddish daily paper "Heint" also published a weekly literary issue called "Der Weltspiegel" (The World Mirror). This publication invited writers to write short stories on the theme of Jewish life, about 1929. The first prize was to be 100 zlotys, the second price 50 zlotys and the third prize 25 zlotys. Prominent authors wrote short stories for the newspaper.

Second prize was awarded to a former Korczyner yeshiva student for his short story "The Auction" based on the annual matzo flour sale held in the beth hamidrash of Korczyn. (Each community had to provide matzoth for the poor people. So the community held auctions as to who would provide more matzoth for less money). The author was the talented Yossef Weber who combined torah knowledge with human decency. He also wrote the short story "The Fisherman". Both stories appear in the Yizkor book.

The youth that was not attracted to the synagogue, dressed modern and formed a variety of organizations and clubs such as the Zionist organization, the Hashomer, Betar and a library. Both genders participated in these activities. They even organized theater performances and dance events that did not get the support of the parents. Still, the Jewish population did not desecrate publicly the Sabbath. Most young people wore hats or headgear. Organizations like "Aguda" or "Mizrahi" (religious Zionist organizations did not exist in Korczyn).

[Page 48-49]

Jewish life hundred years ago in Korczyn

A hundred years ago, a Hassidic Jew (and who was not a Hassidic Jew in Korczyn in those days) wore a beard and peyot, a long black overcoat (capote) to the ankles with side pockets. No split in the back which would indicate modern dress. A black velvet hat and a black velvet kippah or yarmulka under the hat but not completely covered by the hat.(People could see that he was wearing a kippah under the hat). A loose belt or a gartel would tie the coat around his waist. The belt would always be carried even during prayers. Saturday and holidays, all married men wore a streimel (fur hat). Even the coachmen took his horses to drink on Shabbat in his streimel. A newlywed carried his streimel for the entire first week after the marriage. Everybody wore boots, or shoes without laces that were considered modern.

Women wore very long dresses and had to pick up the dress if it rained or in order not to sweep the dust. All married women had their heads shaved and wore a kerchief. On Saturday, they wore silk kerchiefs. Under the kerchief, there were special combs to give the kerchief some shape. Well to do women carried on Sabbath or holidays above the head kerchief, headbands that contained pearls or diamonds. No married women wore her own hair. This was considered an outrage and bordered on lewdness. Even sheitels or wigs were not worn in Korczyn.

Many women maintained the family while the husband studied in the beth hamidrash. Frequently the tasks in the family were divided, the mother provided the income, prepared the food, kept the house and worried about all the needs of the present while the father studied and worried about the heavenly future for the family. Her sole concern was that after she passes from this world she should be next to her saintly husband. These men were called in Korczyn after the name of their wife, for example: Hersh Miriam's, that is Hersh the husband of Miriam, or Itsche Blimele's, that is Itsche the husband of Blime. Wives that remained at home or took care of the house were refereed to as Malka Zalman Leibs, that is Malka the wife of Zalman Leib, or Feige Hersh Yankel's, that is Feige the wife of Hersh Yankel, or Haitsche Israel Itsche's.

Nobody was called in Korczyn by his or her family name. Everybody, men and women, were called by their Yiddish first name and the father's name, for example: Yidel (Yehuda) Gedle's: Idel the son of Gedles, Haim Wolf Yankele 's: Haim the son of Wolf Yankel, Haitsche Israel Itsche: Haya the daughter of Israel Itsche. The custom of calling people by their family name started with the end of WWI. And was proceeded by mister, or misses. People were referred as you unless they were officials or married, then they were referred as you in the polite form.

[Page 50]

Friendly relations

From Rosh Hodesh Elul until after Yom Kippur, every Jew walked the streets of Korczyn with trepidation and hoped to be inscribed in the book of the living. Everybody hoped that his prayers for health, income, and peace for himself, his family and for all of Israel would be accepted. Everybody tried to be on good terms with everybody else and if someone did something to offend somebody, he would try to make it up to him by every means at his disposal in order to get his pardon. Thus friendship was restored.. The old-timers always complained about the present day people who did not take things seriously. Once Jews loved each other and shared their joys and sorrows but today it was different. When a merchant failed in Korczyn once, people used to collect money and put him back in business. They used to refer to Korczyn as the small Israel.

When somebody had a visitor on Sabbath or Holiday, people used to send gifts to the house: a cake, fruits, beer. A child would bring the items and indicate that this was for the guest and the father would soon arrive.

Indeed, the family would arrive and spent time. When somebody married, the shamash (care taker of the beth hamidrash) would go from house to house and invite the people to come to the reception.

[Page 51]

Sickness

When someone was seriously sick, the Jews in town were worried about him. He was on their mind and everybody went to visit the sick person and people tried to help him with everything that they could, whether financial or medical help. If money was needed to bring a specialist from Krakow, then a collection was made and the money was available, to save a person meant saving a whole world.

Perhaps this attitude was once prevalent, certainly this was not the case in our times. We can't report of such wonderful relations between people.

[Page 51]

Sabbath

Who can describe a Sabbath in Korczyn in those days. An entire town rests, absolute standstill. All stores closed all traffic at a standstill. The town is wrapped around in a blanket of silence, a majestic silence of sorts that reign in the city. Jews go to the mikve (ritual bath) before their prayers.. Jews review the parshat hashavua (section of the torah reading for the Sabbath), or hum the talmudic tunes or sing the songs of Sabbath meal. All these tones float from the open windows to the market area. The restful Sabbath afternoon sleep gave everybody the feeling of a restful day. Mordchai Schiff from Jerusalem states that a Sabbath in Korczyn can't be compared to one in Bnei Brak of today.

[Page 52]

Parental respect

In those days, the father was the patriarch of the family in all respects and his word was law. One couldn't joke about a father's statement or ignore it. His words almost had the sanctity of one of the commandments. Respect for a father was the highest compliment one paid to his parents. A son would never think of taking his father's seat at the table in his absence. A personal story comes to mind that we ourselves witnessed. Ber Den owned one room where he and his five children lived. When his mother, Malka, the wife of Zalman Leib, was very sick , he took his mother to his one room and took care of all her needs. All this was done in one room. Ber gave his bed to his mother and he slept on the floor. When his mother wetted the bed, Ber would clean the bed, wash her, take her out for fresh air and bring her back to a clean bed. Everybody saw that it was done with sincerity and kindness. His face showed a certain happiness that indicated to everybody that he was happy to do to something for his mother.

[Page 52-55]

Marriages

A matchmaker arranged marriages in most of Galician townships. Social status, financial status, family status played important roles. A merchant or an innkeeper was on a higher scale than the Hebrew teacher in the heder. In the USA, a Hebrew teacher is an important person and frequently referred to as rabbi, teacher and has lots of prestige. In the little towns of Eastern Europe, the Hebrew teacher was regarded as a non-achiever, someone without ambition or drive, incapable of earning a living. someone that merely existed but happened to know a little of religion. Thus, the Hebrew teacher was usually a poor person in the town. A textile merchant or a metal dealer would not consent to the marriage of his children with those of the melamed or Hebrew teacher, even if the latter 's children were individually more capable or smarter than their counterpart. Still in did not matter, since the father's occupation placed the children in a particular class. Love did not exist in Korczyn a 100 years ago. If a marriage resulted as a result of love, the parents would not divulge it for it was considered in poor taste. Dating was considered a lewd business even if the parties came from respectable homes. Places like Korczyn, where the children knew each other from birth and grew up together, parents tried to marry them with children from out of town. To stand and talk to a girl in Korczyn was unheard of. To ask a girl on a date was madness. The matchmaker arranged marriages. The matchmaker did not invest money into his business, all he had to invest was time and effort which the Jews of Korczyn had plenty. He negotiated once or twice. If he failed, there was no loss on his part. If he succeeded to bring the girl and to boy together, he made money. There were plenty of matchmakers, everybody tried their hand at the game. The going rate was usually 5% of the dowry. There was almost something intriguing about marrying somebody from an other place. Yankel the matchmaker comes to Meshulem and brings a special proposal, a beautiful bride, plenty of family prestige, has all the niceties, something special. Or he has a scholar, a fine man, great potential, comes from a nice family etc.. If things moved correctly, the mother of the future groom would travel to see the future bride and the father of the bride would travel to see future groom and interview him. If both sides agreed to the match, a temporary agreement or tenaim were signed.. The parents wished each other mazal tov and set the date for the wedding.

The bride and the groom would not meet each other until the day of the huppah. More modern couples would arrange to meet half way between the township prior the wedding day. The meeting was always arranged and never between the groom and the bride but in the company of others. Both young people were usually so excited and nervous and had practically nothing to say to each other. The parents of the couple would agree to the terms and a plate was broken when an agreement was reached. On returning to his place, the future groom would search someone to write for him a scholarly letter to his would be in laws. They of course would show the letter to everybody in their town. The bride would try to find someone that could write a nice Yiddish letter to her in laws that would be shown to everybody. Both sides tried to impress the people with the wonderful match that was arranged.

[Page 55-56]

Problems marrying children

To marry children were very difficult at all times and even the Talmud says that to arrange a marriage is as difficult as crossing the Red Sea. This, what is difficult for the Almighty is certainly no easy task for the simple parent. To marry a child, especially a daughter with limited substances was no easy task. Prior to the destruction of European Jewry, the economic situation of the Jews was getting worse since the opportunities for commerce were constantly shrinking. Yet, this was the base of Jewish existence in Eastern Europe. So to marry children became a real problem. There was also a tradition that a girl has to be provided with a dowry. If she had no dowry, her chances of marriage were very limited. A thousand dollars of dowry was considered a poor dowry. Young men had no professions or trades. They could not get jobs even as janitors since the Poles would not let them enter the factories. So the only thing left to do was commerce as their fathers or relatives did. But commerce requires money and this is where the dowry came into play. If the parents of the girl had money, then there was no problem. However, if there was no dowry, the problem became acute. The standard of living was also high, young couples did not want to live with their parents, and they wanted their own flats of 2-3 rooms, which were very high, since few new buildings were built in the small town. Indeed, the problem of marrying a daughter prior to WWII became a serious situation for poor parents.

[Page 56-58]

Similar situations in the past

A hundred years ago, it was also difficult to marry children but not to the extent of today. A young men had nothing to worry, even a poor fellow, as long as could sit and study a bit of torah. As the saying of the period was, studying torah was the best business. The father of a girl practically bought the fellow as a son-in-law. He bought him all the clothes that consisted of silk overcoat or bekeshe, a silk under coat or halat and a streimel or fur hat for Sabbath. He also purchased a regular overcoat for daily use, three pair of hard slacks, 5-6 shirts, a velvet black hat and a pair of boots or shoes. As a dowry, the father promised to provide 200-300 silver thaler (Austrian money) and a flat was no problem. The father gave the young couple their sleeping corner in the apartment. The father, mother and the children moved to the kitchen. The latter were huge by comparison with today's kitchen. One bed was placed in one corner of the kitchen and the other bed in the other corner of the kitchen. Between the beds, they placed a big table and chairs where the family ate. Benches that were seating places during the day, were pushed together at night and served as beds for the children. If more room was needed, a child could sleep with the father or mother, or begs filled with straw were placed on the floor at night and removed in the daytime Income was no problem, for the young family ate with the rest of the family. All that was needed was an extra setting. The mother could always increase the amount of soup, or bread by adding some boiled potatoes in the dough. The bread tasted just as fine and lasted longer. The father would go to Naphtali Raab, or Moshe Rothenberg, or someone else and vouch for the merchandise that would be granted to the young couple. They would take the merchandise and place it in a corner in the kitchen. The merchandise would be displayed Friday at the market in Korczyn or Monday at the market in Kros. The couple would pay up their debts and pocket the profit for they had no expenses. Rent was free, food was eaten with the family, his or hers, and clothing was hardly purchased after the wedding.

Everything was fixed, repaired and repatched. The shoes, boots and pants were constantly fixed. Even if the pants were patched, it did not present a big problem since the overcoat covered it. With time and savings, the young couple moved into their own place. There was no dining room or living room sets, or wall to wall carpets. The young family followed the pattern of their parents. The style was primitive and simple, the bare necessities of life. They had little and needed even less. Their life style was easygoing, happier, less worrisome and warmer than the present generation. This generation is richer in material well being. It lives on a higher economic, social and cultural level but lacks feeling and spirituality. Raw materialism corrupts the heart and soul of man.

[Page 59-60]

Relations between Jew and non-Jew prior to World War I

Friendships never existed between the two groups. Jews never met Christians. They existed in different worlds that did not relate to each other culturally or socially. Everything separated these two groups: religion, culture, language and clothing. The Jew in the small town dressed completely different from the non-Jew. He also lived differently and talked differently that is Yiddish. The Jew and the Christian met only when they needed to sell or to buy something. Jewish and non-Jewish children did not mingle. Jewish children did not attend regular public school in those days. Most of the non-Jewish families lived several kilometers from the city with the exception of two poor Christian families. The majority of the Christian population at the time consisted of peasants, hardly a literate person amongst them. The only people that could read were the priest, the teacher of the public school, the doctor and the pharmacist and they all came from different areas of Poland. The local farming population did not believe in educating their children. The peasants as a group were not ant-Semitic, although some hated Jews due to their religious beliefs that the Jews killed their Lord. On occasion a Polish youngster would scream at the sight of a Jew that all Jews should go to Palestine or that Jews are like Russians. But in general Jews lived in peace with their Christian neighbors. There are no records to the effect that a Korczyner Jew was ever physically attacked for being Jewish by the Christian neighbors. In 1919, when Poland celebrated its independence with beating Jews or tossing them out of running trains, or pogroms of one sort or another, the city of Korczyn remained calm. The nearby city of Kros witnessed a full-fledged attack on Jewish stores and stalls in the market since it took place on the traditional market day of Monday. Korczyn remained quiet. The mayor, Michael Miensowicz and some of the influential Poles of the city visited the homes of some of the agitators and warned them not to start "celebrations" or trouble in Korczyn. With the exception of some broken windows in the home of the Rothenberg family, the Korczyn Jewish community spent a few fearful days.

[Page 61-63]

Relations between Jew and non-Jew following WWI

With the proclamation of Polish independence in 1919, relations between Jews and Christians changed overnight in Korczyn. Under the Austrian administration, the number of Jewish officials in Galicia exceeded the number of non-Jewish officials. Most of the judges in the courts and high school teachers were Jewish. They were assimilated Jews and sometimes even hid the Jewish ancestry but they did not preach ant-Semitic diatribe to their students. All these Jewish officials were summarily retired or fired with Polish independence and their positions granted to Christian Poles, many of whom were fanatic anti-Semites. Polish high school history teachers taught their students that Polish Jews were not part of Poland but a foreign element. An element that is unreliable and interested in creating a state within a state, in other words a Jewish state within Poland. The Jews of course were responsible for the economic crisis in Poland since they controlled the commerce of the country. All the capital was concentrated in Jewish hands. The economic solution was very simple, get rid of the foreign element that is the Jews and replace them with Poles. The latter will assume the positions held by the Jews as well as their financial possessions. For the wealth was accumulated in dealing with Poles. These simplistic solutions were offered to the Polish student body that steadily grew. Many farmers now sent their children to school and they absorbed this anti-Jewish poison, which intensified with time. Polish youth developed a hatred to the Jew and especially to the Jewish trader and merchant. Polish high schools graduated thousands of students who could not get jobs nor could their parents afford to send them to university that was very expensive. As a result, many high school students returned to the farms and sat at home, doing nothing for it was below the dignity of high school student to work on the land. With the government slogans that Poles should enter the field of commerce, many of these students decided with the help of their parents and the government to enter business. They knew how to read, write and mathematics. They could also appeal to the Pole to buy from his own kind instead of from the Jew. Some Polish farmers bought homes in Korczyn for their educated sons from Jews that were leaving town. The Poles immediately opened stores. The stores proved to be a failure. The Polish peasant ignored the government slogans and preferred to shop in the Jewish stores where he could handle the merchandise, bargain with the merchant, offer a very low price, walk out of the store and return later and offer a higher bid for the merchandise. These tactics could not be performed in a Polish owned store. The Polish owner started with a higher mark up, did not permit the handling of the merchandise, was not crazy about bargaining and other antics of the market. At the Jewish store, credit was extended and re-extended while in non-Jewish owned stores the customers did not want to barrow for fear of not being able to pay on time and have their name ridiculed. The Jewish store owner spoke to his client softer and more businesslike than the Polish owner who had very little sales experience or merchandising knowledge.

The new Polish storekeepers soon realized that their dreams of wealth were evaporating, they closed the stores and joined the ranks of the educated unemployed elements who spread anti-Jewish poison through the country. All these slogans and proclamations that were issued by the government and the press merely encouraged more anti-Semitism.

[Page 64-66]

Aaron, he is the crisis

In the thirties of the present century, when Hitlerism ruled Germany and sent an overflow of anti-Semitic poison across the borders, the Polish anti-Semites even tried to exceed their neighbor's deeds. Jewish students were forced to sit on the left side at the high schools and universities. Jewish female students were flushed with water hoses or their faces scarred. Polish students picketed Jewish stores and urged Poles not to buy there. This poison even reached Korczyn. There were no attacks on Jews or pickets in front of Jewish stores but the feeling of hatred was there. The feeling that if they could do away with the Jews of the town they would gladly do it. Slogans to the effect that Hitler is on the march were frequently heard and provoked laughter. The elder generation of farmers did not buy readily the political anti-Semitism. He was mainly interested in his farm and the local affairs. He dealt with the Jew for generations and was rather satisfied. But all around him, everybody talked and wrote about the economic crisis and the Jew was behind it all. Even the simple farmer started to think that there must be some truth if everybody says that the Jew is responsible for the economic crisis and that the Jew acquired a fortune on account of dealing with the farmer. The latter did not know how, he knew that every item was more expensive in the Polish owned store than in the Jewish store. But the papers stated that all the houses were Jewish owned. Something must be going on that only the intelligent Poles understood. The farmer was told how hard he works while the Jew stands in the store and does nothing. But the Jew lives much better than the farmer. The Jew can afford to buy a rooster that the farmer can't afford to eat it since he must sell it to the Jew. A great majority of Jewish traders barely had enough bread for their family let alone meat. The Polish farmer always had food for his family, be it wheat, potatoes or other produce. The trader was constantly manipulating, twisting and turning to make ends meet. His entire possessions did not match the worth of the farm or the implements. The constant worries of payments and credits were a constant companion of the trader. Yet, everybody pointed at the fact that he purchased a rooster for Sabbath. When the farmer came to town on Sunday to church. He saw all the posters calling him to come and hear the speeches about the economic crisis, the causes and the solution. In 1936, two schoolteachers, Stecz and Urbanek, in Korczyn staged a school play in the municipal auditorium. Both teachers were natives of the nearby hamlet of Gosztiniec. The players were children aged 10-12. The play begins, the curtains part, on the stage we see a council of children debating the economic crisis. Suddenly, a child dressed as a Jew appears on the stage. Another child shouts and points at Aaron, he is the crisis. He is the walking crisis. Another child states that he will kill Aaron, this will merely solve one problem. You have to remember that we have three and half million such problems in Poland states another student.

[Page 67-70]

The Destruction By Itzhak Englard-Wasserstrom

From the day W.W.II started until the Germans appeared in Korczyn and the destruction and liquidation of the Jewish community of the town

About the destruction, the pains and the disappearance of Korczyn On reaching this section of the book about the destruction of the Jewish population of Korczyn, I am totally mesmerized. Many times I sat down to write the section but was unable to write a line. The blood begins to circulate much faster and the heart beat increases, the nerves are tense, I sit in stupor and think. What a terrible tragedy has occurred to our people. The Germans killed millions of helpless Jewish men, women and children and nothing happened. In Genesis, section Vayera, we are told that the people of Sodom were mean and sinful and that is the reason why G-d destroyed the city.

The various biblical descriptions of the evil deeds of Sodom can't even begin to compare with the deeds of the German murderers. The people of Sodom were practically saints in comparison to the Germans. Yet the latter were not destroyed or wiped off the face of the earth, on the contrary, they became richer and fatter in spite of all the cruelties they committed. The world continues its course, the Germans are accepted in society of men, Jewish merchants buy and Jewish customers purchase German products. Jewish survivors go on with life as though nothing happened. Religious Jews feel insulted when they don't get the right aliyah in the synagogue, the less religious organise parties and bar-mitzvahs with music and dancing. Everybody in his own way is deeply involved in acquiring more luxuries as though no great tragedy took place.

We mourn the destruction of the temple for three weeks but the destruction of hundreds of Jewish communities where millions of our fathers, mothers and children were killed is not mourned even for three hours by the Jewish world. Today, 25 years after the great tragedy, what is the purpose of retelling the tragedy and am I capable of telling the story in my humble way. Will I be able to transmit the pain, the degradation, the hunger and the various deaths suffered by the victims. Even if I had the literary skill of Job and was able to write a masterpiece, who would be interested, who would care to listen and what influence would such book have.

I would like to describe in the next chapters in a chronological sequence the life of the Jewish community of Korczyn from the day the war started to the day that the Germans erased the community.

[Page 71-72]

The outbreak of the war

Friday, the first of September, 1939, 17 days in the Jewish month of Elul, Tarzat, the war started. The same afternoon, German planes bombed the airfield and the rubber factory, Wudeta, in Krosno. We in Korczyn, saw the smoke columns of the burning factory that was located near the Krosno railway station. Fear struck everybody. Orders were issued to darken all windows. Jews were even afraid to go to the beth hamidrash for Friday night prayers. The radio stations did not give clear indications. The German radio interviewed Polish prisoners of war who described terrible events. The Polish radio interviewed German prisoners of war who stated that Germany was in total darkness and there was fear that Poland will destroy Germany.

The Polish government ordered the call up of all reserve units by means of posters, radio announcements and other available means. Total confusion seemed to be the order of the day. For the government was not prepared for such massive draft and had no ability to absorb all these men. The German attacked an ill-prepared country for war, namely Poland. By Monday, the fourth day of the war, it was obvious that the Germans are advancing very rapidly, government offices began packing in haste and leaving town, Polish retreating soldiers began to appear in the streets of Korczyn. They were totally disorganized and did not know where to go. Tuesday, columns of refugees, Jews and non-Jews, passed through the township-heading east. The Polish government ordered all men to head East. The merchants took the merchandise from their stores during the night and hid it. The panic was growing from minute to minute. The burning question was what to do, to stay or leave Korczyn. Where do you go with your family or can you stay and face the Germans.

The Germans will never kill anyone, they will take Jews to work said Korczyner Jewish who lived in Germany and supposedly knew the Germans. Germany ejected in 1936 most of the Jews of Korczyn that lived in Germany and they returned to their native hamlet. These people, the children of Haim Eichorn, the son of Moshe Lewitman and others remained in Korczyn. Very few Jews left Korczyn for Eastern Galicia and later for Russia. There were seven families: Mendel Rubin, Naphtali Dym, Avraham Lezer, Aisik Lezer, Yehezkel Pinter and Shlomo Horowitz. There were also a few individuals: Arie Dym, Mendel Rosenman, Zishe Grin, Mendel Weinstein, Yantsche Koreff, Leibish Atlas and Mendel Holoshitz. Only the last two individual people returned home following the war. We know nothing about the other single people.

[Page 73]

The German entry

Friday evening, the 8th of September 1939, we heard nearby heavy shelling or artillery exchanges. Saturday morning everything was silent. All the people were in the shelters. About 11oclock in the morning we heard some rifle shots and then deadly silence interrupted by the noise of a German motorcycle patrol. The latter crossed the city in great haste and headed for the village of Kombornia.

The first days of German Occupation

An entire week passed since the motorcycle patrol passed the city and no Germans in town. The municipal office is closed. The voit, mayor, and the soltis, municipal head, left Korczyn. Only Preissner, the carpenter, who was the assistant soltis, remained in town but did not officiate. The hamlet looked like a ghost town, all offices were closed. Even the Poles did not come to town. A deadly silence prevailed in Korczyn.

[Page 74]

Jews must sweep the market and bury the burned animals

Friday afternoon, the 15th of September 1939, suddenly the assistant soltis, Preisner and the policeman of Korczyn appeared in the market place. The latter kept beating the drum that signaled to everybody that an important announcement would be made shortly. Indeed, Preisner informed the assembled crowd that the German military commander of Krosno has ordered that the Jews of Korczyn sweep the market place. He added that the Jews of Krosno did the same thing on Tuesday.

It was never established whether Preisner was ordered to do this job or he took the initiative on hearing the events in Krosno and decided to imitate the Germans. Nobody questioned him and there were no discussions. However, it seemed to give Preisner some satisfaction in denigrating the Jews since the cleaning job could have been done for five zlotys, about one dollar, or even less. Plenty of workers could have been found to do the job. On hearing the order, instinctively, the Jews took brooms and went to the market and swept it clean. Monday, the 18th of September, under the leadership of Tsheike the thief we marched to the village and were forced to remove the burned cattle from the stalls. The cattle were caught in the rifle fire that was heard in Korczyn some days ago. The job of removing partially burned carcasses of horses and cows was very unpleasant and the air was stifling.. The work was terrible and filthy but less denigrating than sweeping the market. Furthermore, it was supposed to prevent diseases. The work was also removed from the sight of onlookers for no one went to the village to see them work. The population of the farms had scattered, thus there were no spectators apart from Tsheike the thief.

[Page 75]

The first Rosh Hashana under German Occupation

Few Jews prayed Rosh Hashana at the beth hamidrash. There was fear of congregating in public places. It was also known that the Germans were grabbing Jews in Krosno to do dirty and useless work for the sole purpose of embarrassing them in front of the Poles. Besides, nobody was certain that the only purpose was work. The Germans grabbed every Jew and tossed them aboard trucks that left for unknown destinations. Until a mother or a wife saw their loved ones, they died many deaths.

Jews organized many small prayer places in private homes. Amongst them was: Shaul Frei, Eliezar Rubin who moved into the apartment of his brother, Mendel, who fled to East Galicia, Eliezar Raab and Nachman Leibush Reich. Most of the prayer places accommodated neighbors who would arrive surreptitiously to the prayers. Guards were posted to sound the alarm in case Germans approached the place. There was fear that the Germans may accuse the people of meeting illegally and harsh consequences would follow. At the first sound of alarm, the congregants could slip into their homes and disappear. The Germans did arrive with trucks to the beth hamidrash and caught whoever did not manage to escape. They tossed them aboard trucks and took them to work. The families of the arrested waited in anxiety all day until they were returned late that night.

[Page 76]

Refugees return

The Germans advanced very rapidly and within less than three weeks Poland was occupied. The Russians occupied Eastern Galicia until Sanok. The new border between Russia and Germany was the river San. The German Army intercepted many of the refugees on the roads of Poland and in panic they returned back home, to Western Galicia where they shared the fate of the rest of the Jewish community. The Jews that remained in the Eastern part of

Galicia that was now under Russian control were soon shipped to Siberia and other distant areas of the Russian Empire. The young and the strong managed to survive the hardships and survive the war.

The first victims in Dynow

The sad news reached us that in the city of Dynow, about 50 kilometers east of Korczyn, where there were many Jewish refugees from all across Poland, the German soldiers seized 170 Jews. They were shot and buried in a mass grave. It took a lot of influence and a great deal of money to get the permission of the German military commander to exhume the bodies and bring them to burial at the Jewish cemetery of Dinow. Amongst the victims were Avramtsche Gleicher, and his son, Yudel Gleicher. They were the son and grand son of Mendel Gleicher. They lived lately in Krosno. In the mass grave they found father and son arm in arm. The news created panic amongst all the Jews in town. All the doors were bolted Everybody feared the Germans and everybody made plans to escape if need be.

[Page 77-78]

German soldiers in town

At the end of September 1939, many German soldiers arrived in town. The Market Square was full of German military trucks. Poland was occupied and the German soldiers returned from the battlefields and on their way home stopped in Korczyn. Some units remained in town for a few days and left, other units took their place. Week after week, units came and went. The soldiers requisitioned homes and seized Jews to serve them as domestics. Each unit had its special demands and the Jews in town were frightened to death.

In December some units arrived for rest and remained until May 1940. These units erected many barracks in a large area known as the priest field, it stretched from the school to the Mangl or to the Michael Kirschner house. The Jews did sawing wood and unloading coal and all dirty work such as bringing water, peeling potatoes. The Jews were not paid but received a steady stream of beatings. With time the beatings stopped but the German supervisors insisted that all their workers must show daily for work even if the weather did not permit such activity. Even if a German supervisor granted a day off, another would soon appear and insist that they must show up for work and threatened and cajoled the poor Jews to go to work. The behavior of the German supervisors can only be described as beastly. The work that the Jews in Korczyn did for the German army saved them from being sent elsewhere to do similar work. At least they came home, ate with the family and slept at home. The Nazi chief supervisor for building the barracks appealed to the military area commander not to sent Jews from Korczyn to other areas since they were needed in town. Jews from Krosno were sent to other places like Fristik to work.

[Page 78]

The Germans convert the beth hamidrash into a stall for horses

The first German soldiers that stayed in the city were Austrians. There were plenty of stalls in the hamlet, the stall of Graff Szepticki, or the one of the priest and still other places. Instead they chose to place their horses in the beth hamidrash in order to profane the Jewish place of worship. The unit commandant lived with the pharmacist, a Jew. They were both talking when the soldiers appeared and told their lieutenant that they requisitioned the Jewish prayer hall and converted it into a stall for their horses. Everybody laughed, nobody knew that the pharmacist was a Jew.

[Page 78-79]

Anti-Jewish slogans on the walls and the sidewalk

In the morning, we parted the curtains slowly to see what was doing in the market place. We suddenly saw Nazi slogans to the effect-- out with the Jews, the Jews are human excrement. These slogans were painted on the fence of the church and the sidewalks. Soon we heard the noise of Germans soldiers bursting into Jewish homes to grab Jews for work. They needed their slaves to saw wood, bring water, wash floors and clean toilets. Everyone still remembers the day when there was no sewer system and the entire hamlet used the municipal toilet. This is the way, the German military toilet looked and we had to clean it.

[Page 79]
Young Poles shave peyot of Jews

Young Poles who lived near the city decided to visit the place and when they saw the treatment that the Jews received from the Germans, they decided to have some fun of their own. They would grab a Jew who was carrying water and shave his oarlock. The Germans and the Poles would laugh hysterically as a result of this prank. Luck had it that the Poles and the Germans could not communicate with each other. Furthermore, the Germans dislike Poles and frequently refer to them as Polish pigs. These young Poles were too dumb to understand that the Germans dislike the Poles and if they will win this war they will suppress and slaughter them just as they did in the past during the Middle Ages and the Hansa period.

[Page 80-81]

The German soldiers plunder the Jewish homes

Before the Germans entered the hamlet, all the merchants removed and hid their merchandise with the exception of the metal stores of Bunem Margoles and Itsche Rosshandler. We do not know whether the Germans had information or whether Poles informed but the fact remains that searches were constantly taking place. The Germans searched constantly Jewish homes not the Polish homes. When they found hidden merchandise, they confiscated the content and arrested the Jew for hiding his merchandise. Once the acting soltis, Preisner, escorted the German officers to the homes of merchants and insisted that they open their warehouses. The Jews responded that they were small merchants and their merchandise was sold out with the beginning of the war and they have been able to get new supplies. The Germans accepted this excuse.

The Germans continued to search but found nothing and concluded that there were no hidden merchandise. Preisner insisted that all merchandise should be made available to the local population since it had no clothing. The author of these lines addressed himself to Preisner and asked him whether the local population was already naked after two months of war. Was it not a fact that the Jewish population lacked bread, which was in abundance amongst the farms yet, you are not worried about the hungry Jews but rather about the so-called naked Polish farmers. He did not answer. The Germans did not understand the exchange since it was in Polish.

The Germans plundered the Jewish homes without the slightest guilt feeling. Worse than the Russian Cossacks who knew that they were doing bad things. The Germans did it with greater precision, thoroughness and punctuality than the Cossack ever dreamt of doing. The German stole whatever pleased him, be it a coat, a suit or even bed covers. The Russian Cossack knew that he was committing a crime and faced the danger of being spotted by an officer who could reprimand him. The German knew that this was not the case.

Most of the German soldiers that were stationed in Korczyn from December to May 1940 were from Western Silesia and some understood a bit of Polish and some even spoke the language. They mingled with the local population and soon found out where the Jewish merchants lived and where they could locate some of the hidden merchandise. They would enter a store and find it empty. They would then measure the inside walls as opposed to the outside walls or the attics as opposed to the roofs. They would break into rooms or walls under the slightest pretext. Once they found a hidden warehouse, they would be encouraged to continue their search.

When the soldiers found merchandise, they stole everything they could carry and then notified the local commander who would sent a truck to pick up the remains. The truck would transport the goods to Germany and the soldiers would carry the loot home on leave. Presently, the Germans are asking the Jewish survivors to provide them with the license numbers of the trucks that took their merchandise.

[Page 82-83]

The Germans arrest Lea Blank

Aaron Blank owned a tavern. He removed all the merchandise prior to the arrival of the Germans. He hid all the spirits and liquors. Behind his house there was a big garden where he had a bowling alley. He dug a hole behind the alley and stored there his merchandise. Apparently, his helper or a friend of the helper revealed the hiding place to the Germans. The latter entered the garden and dug up the merchandise. Aaron Blank and his son Meir Blank decided to hide. When the Germans did not find the owner, they arrested Lea Blank and locked her up in the prison of Krosno.

Lea Blank spent almost two weeks in the prison, until her young daughters, Miriam and Rivka Blank assembled a few thousand zlotys which was given to a Krosno person with good connections. They worked and she was freed and returned home to Korczyn. Meanwhile, Aron and Meir Blank escaped from the city crossed illegally the border to the Russian side. Aron Blank did not survive the war , he died in Russia but his son Meir survived the war. The Germans killed lea Blank and her daughters Miriam and Rivkah in August 1942, 29 days in Av, Tashab.

[Page 83]

Jews must wear the Star of David

At the end of December 1939, the German military command issued an order to the effect that all Jewish men and women must wear in the street a white arm band with a blue star of David on the right arm. The order was effective the next day. The German soldiers took advantage of the regulation and began to beat Jews who did not wear the band before the regulation went into effect. The Polish police decided to exploit the situation and they too saw an opportunity to blackmail Jews who did not wear the band. All Jewish stores had to display the star of David in their windows.

Contributions

At the beginning of January 1940, the newly appointed mayor Mermon called some Jewish influential leaders and told them that he had been summoned to the German chief of the area. The latter has informed him that he decided to impose a heavy contribution on the Jewish community. The mayor insisted that he told the German that the community consisted of poor people and will not be able to pay a large contribution. He managed to bargain down the contribution to 300 zlotys. We must add that the contribution was indeed small in comparison with the one of Krosno. The city had to make a contribution of 5000 zlotys

[Page 84-86]

The Judenrat

A week after the contribution was presented, the mayor informed the Jewish community that the Germans had ordered the creation of a Judenrat within 5 days. Each home was informed that a meeting will take place in the home of Itsche Rosshendler to discuss the matter of the Judenrat. The Jews had no choice but to obey the order. People also thought that it would serve the Jewish community to have somebody supervise the supply of labor to the Germans. Otherwise the latter grabbed Jews on the street whenever they needed workers. People that had good hiding places used them daily and avoided working for the Germans. Others were forced to appear daily for work; nobody volunteered to work for the Germans.

The Judenrat consisted of Oscar Rubin, a grandson of of Benyamin Rubin. Oscar was born in Germany. He was elected to be the head the Judenrat. His assistant was Yehezkel Lewitman who lived many years in Germany. The other members of the council were Mendel Halpern,, the son of Hertz, Eli Grin, Ber Erreich, Shlomo Horowitz, Naphtali Infeld and Yossef Weber. Most people thought that Oscar Rubin and Yehezkel Lewitman would help the community due their knowledge of the German language. They were soon proven dead wrong. The difference between the Judenrat and the kehilla leadership prior to the war was simple. The kehilla leaders worked for the interests of the Jewish community while the Judenrat had to work for the Germans.

The Judenrat collected monthly taxes from the Jewish population in order to meet the financial obligations of the council. Whoever did not pay on time his assessment, the Judenrat would send a Jewish policemen to collect an item of similar value to the amount owed. The item taken could have been a lamp, a blanket, a pillow or a suit. On occasion, the head of the Judenrat wrote out a complaint against someone for not paying his assessment as part of a sabotage scheme .The Germans did not need any further evidence to arrest the individual and throw him into the Krosno prison.. He was usually freed by the efforts of Moshe Kleiner, assistant Judenrat head of Krosno.. When the people in question went to thank Moshe Kleiner, he made the following blessing, blessed be the liberator of prisoners and the resurrected to life. Why the latter part of the blessing, Kleiner stated that the Germans would frequently shoot prisoners in order to make room for more detainees.

The head and the assistant head of the Judenrat exclusively ran the Judenrat. Oscar Rubin received a weekly salary and Yehezkel Lewitman ran the office. The other members of the council had no say or responsibilities. They joined the council in the hope that they will avoid the labor draft. Some of them later regretted being members of the council but it was too late. Perhaps some would have survived the war had they not been members of the council, for their need ended with the destruction of the Jewish community of Korczyn. The Judenrat employed two Jewish policemen: Mendel Halpern, the son of Yona, and Naphtali Kirschner, the son of Moshe. The latter was called the lord. We have to praise his behavior that was outstanding. He would always pre-warn the Jewish inhabitants of German or Polish police actions aimed at them. Thus, they could take some preventive measures. The other policeman used his position for his own interest and income. Naphtali Kirschner escaped, hid, survived the war and came to Israel. Mendel Halpern remained policeman to the last minute and perished with the community.

[Page 86-87]

The exiled from Lodz and refugees from other cities

In November of 1939, the Germans grabbed Jewish men and women on the streets of Lodz and shipped them to various towns and hamlets across Poland. Some of these Jews wound up in Krosno. The Judenrat of Krosno could not accommodate the entire transport of Jews and decided to send some of them to Korczyn. About 40 Jews of Lodz, mostly women and young girls, some of them still in their bathrobes, were put aboard horse drawn coaches and sent to Korczyn. It was a painful scene to watch these Jewish daughters torn from their homes. Men did not know where their wives wound up and parents did not know where their children were located. The Korczyner Jews received the refugees with open arms. Families volunteered to take one or two people into their home. The wealthier Jews from Lodz managed to reestablish contact with their families and slowly moved back to the city. Others found other places in Poland. The poorer families about 20 in number remained in Korczyn. They lived with local families until the end of 1940. Then, the flow of refugees increased since Jewish life in many big cities became very difficult. Jews from many towns like Krakow, Radom and others cities began to arrive in the smaller towns where life was still livable. Korczyn was no exception, and the Judenrat opened a public soup kitchen where the refugees and the poor local Jews received warm meals. The facility was located in the home of the Raab family, one of the warehouses was converted into a kitchen.

[Page 87]

The German asked to be paid for shooting a Jewish dog

The pharmacist in Korczyn was a Jew and he owned a beautiful dog. When the German discovered that the dog belonged to a Jew, he was outraged and whenever he saw the dog he went mad. Once, he could not control his emotions and when he saw the dog, he took his gun and shot the dog. He merely injured the dog which ran away. The enraged German charged into the pharmacy with the gun in his hand and demanded 50 zlotys for the bullet that he used up in shooting a Jewish dog. The pharmacist did not make an issue, he took the money from the till and handed it to the German.

[Page 87-88]

The Pharmacist

We have to mention the pharmacist in Korczyn who gave a great deal of charity and helped directly and indirectly many Jews in Korczyn. To poor families he gave the prescriptions for practically nothing. Some of these were very expensive since they were made in factories. He gave prescriptions even to hopeless people knowing that it would merely create the illusion of help. He helped financially needy families on a weekly basis. He once said that money has value only when you can enjoy it and since he can not enjoy it presently, may be other families will enjoy the money. He disappeared with the entire Jewish community. His name was Yaavov Levy, honor his memory.

[Page 88]

The Germans rip open the faces of Itsche Den and Avraham Itzhak Kanner

German soldiers caught in the street Israel Itsche Den nicknamed Broder and Avraham Itzhak Kanner nicknamed Peitash. They forced them aboard a truck that headed in the direction of the village of Kombornia. Late that night they returned on foot to Korczyn. Pieces of flesh were missing from their faces. The Germans stopped the truck and forced the Jews off it. They attached their beards and peyot to each other and forced them to run in different directions. Pieces of flesh and meat were torn from their faces as a result of these barbaric activities. The event took place in December of 1939.

[Page 89-90]

The Rabbi escapes from town

The quote from the book of Deuteronomy, chapter 32, line 25 states, death stalked in the streets and invaded the home, loose translation by the translator. The quote aptly describes the situation of Korczyn.

In the streets of Korczyn were many German soldiers who returned victorious from the battlefield. They were full of joy and drank with their victory over Poland. Their hatred to the Jews was beyond description, especially to a Jew that had a beard and peyot. Such a Jew took his life in his hand if he stepped out of his house. When the Germans spotted him, they chased him and ordered him to stand still. The poor Jew did not know whether he would be shot or merely photographed. Regardless of the final action, we can imagine the thoughts that run through the mind of the poor Jew. Fear also extended to the home, the Germans plundered Jewish homes. Fear became a daily reality.

To avoid humiliations, jeers and nasty remarks, the rabbi of Korczyn, Avraham Itzhak Kanner nicknamed Peitash wrapped a kerchief around the beard and his peyot in order to hide them. When a German would ask why the kerchief, the wife of the rabbi would state that the rabbi has dental problems. He looked comical and this was enough to attract German attention and to ridicule him. The rabbi had a father in law in Slovakia, a place called Welka Berezna. He decided to escape to his family in Slovakia where it was rumored that the Germans behaved a bit better than in Poland. The rabbi and his family rented a coach and secretly left Korczyn. They arrived in Slovakia just in time when the Slovakian Jews were being deported to Poland, about 1940. The rabbi and his family shared the lot of the Slovakian Jews. He wound up in the city of Lublin, Poland.

The rabbi suffered pain and hunger in Lublin. He appealed by letter, still permissible at the time, to the Jewish community of Korczyn. The letters were heart braking and asked for help to get him out of Lublin. But the Jewish community could not help him since nobody had contacts with Lublin nor did anybody have ideas how to organise such rescue. Brief, he could not hope for assistance except to escape by his own means. Apparently he could not escape and disappeared. We do not know the date of his death but it is a certainty that he disappeared a year before the destruction of the Jewish community of Korczyn, may his saintly soul be blessed.

[Page 90]

The death penalty for listening to the radio

The German commandant posted notices throughout the city ordering all the Jews to deliver their radios to the Germans. Listening to the radio or owning a radio became punishable by death. Most German orders were punishable by death.

[Page 90-92]

The ban on ritual slaughter and the shochet Moshe Leichtog

As early as February 1940, the Germans issued a ban on the ritual slaughter of animals. Thus if the slaughterer would kill a chicken he would be shot on the spot. The shochet in Korczyn was Moshe Leichtog, a son-in-law of the shochet Pinhas Yaacov Schiff. Moshe Leichtog ignored the ban and did slaughter animals so that Jews could eat a piece of meat. He did his work secretly in the homes of the owners of the chickens. The owners notified him and he would come, slaughter the chicken, cut the head. The last act was done to protect the shochet in case the Germans appeared they would not be able to tell whether the chicken was slaughtered or killed. We must add that the shochet did not do it for the money but for the sake of helping a Jew to eat meat on the Shabbat. We must understand that Moshe Leichtog risked his life every time he slaughtered a chicken. Chanah Leichtog, the wife of the shochet and her four children were killed with the destruction of the Jewish community of Korczyn.

Moshe Leichtog survived the action and was sent to Krosno to work. We worked together in the same group. We were busy demolishing a wall that was situated along the road leading to Korczyn, facing the house of Itsche David Weisner.

We were supposed to build a road through the garden of the church of the order of the Capuchins. This road would link directly Korczyn to the road leading to Rymanow without the need to circle the church grounds. The monks insisted we stop working. An order was issued to us to sit on the ground and await a decision. We sat on the ground of the church and awaited the order. This was exactly a week after the Jews of Korczyn were deported. As we sat on the ground, Yehezkel Shtein asked Moshe Leichtog to tell a story about a Jewish saint. He started to tell story after atory about Jewish saints and the miracles they performed. I was astounded to hear the stories, how could a person that lost everybody, tell the stories as though nothing happened. I was hopeless, bitter, lonely and amazed at the ability of Moshe Leichtog to overcome all the tragedies and tell stories about Jewish saints. I could understand some people like Yehezkel Shtein who still had his wife and children listening to these tales. But how could Moshe Leichtog ignore all reality and transport himself to another period of time. Yet he did it. Was this heroism or spiritual heroism, perhaps someone could explain it to me. I don't understand it. Yaacov Itzhak Fessel, a native of Korczyn, that lives today in Stockholm, Sweden states that with the liquidation of the ghetto of Krosno, Moshe Leichtog was sent to the ghetto of Rzeszow, Reishe in Yiddish. Nobody knows the whereabouts of Moshe Leichtog or his date of death. May this be his eternal memorial.

[Page 92-93]

Poles requisition Jewish apartments

Each un-shameful Pole could seize the apartment of a Jew if he so desired. What happend to the Jewish family that resided there was of no concern to anybody nor did anyone care. When a Pole wanted an apartment, he went to the owner and told him that he wanted his place, the Jewish owner had to consent. If he consented, the Pole may let him remain with his family in one room. If the Jew refused to consent, the Pole went to the official in charge of lodgings, a German. The latter gave him a written order to the effect that the Jew must vacate the place within 24 hours and surrender the place to the Pole. The Jewish family knew that they must leave the house, the apartment or things will get worse.

In Korczyn, the Christian families lived outside the city and near their fields. This is where they had their homes and barns. They were not interested in places away from their cowsheds or farms. But there were exceptions even in Korczyn. Tscheike thief's son went to Lea Blank and told her that he wanted the front of her house. Lea Blank was familiar with the situation and heard of similar instances in Krosno. She consented to his request and he permitted her to stay with her daughters in the back of the house. Jewish refugees from other cities occupied the second house of the family Blank.

[Page 94-95]

The Germans attack the Russians
Harsh edicts and serious troubles for Jews

Since May 1940, there were no German soldier in town. In comparison with other big cities and even small cities, life in Korczyn was relatively quiet. Suddenly, German soldiers appeared in May of 1941 but they did not stop in town, they marched in the direction of Kombornia and East. They did not march four abreast on the road but rather single file, one behind the other, similar to a bunch of geese. Small groups of 20-25 soldiers, their heads covered with grass or twigs. They did not carry weapons. Some trucks covered with green branches followed them. This process continued for days. The Jews in Korczyn glanced through the cracks in the windows and saw this funny process but nobody could explain what was taking place. Some tried to explain that the German was teaching their soldiers how to camouflage their movements from the view of planes. But Poland was destroyed, France was defeated and Europe was under German control. Against what enemy was Germany preparing to fight. That an imminent attack against Russia will be launched, nobody expected. Only in June of 1941, following thew attack on Russia, did we understand the reason for the funny marching of soldiers.

Some predicted that Russia would defeat Germany and preclude it from carrying out the harmful policies against the Jews. There were others that said that things might get worse. The evil one, Hitler, stated publicly in January of 1942, those that laughed stopped laughing: I will not rest until the last Jew disappears in Europe. The entire free world heard this on the radio or read it in the papers, if we read it in isolated Korczyn in the Krakower newspaper.

[Page 95-96]

Jews are not permitted to own stores

In June of 1941, the Germans ordered the Jews to surrender their stores to Christians. It was forbidden for Jews to have stores. In the township there were only three Jewish stores at the time: the pharmacy and the metal stores of Itstche Rosshendler and of Bunem Margolies. One day in June of 1941, German officials escorted a Pole of German origin to the pharmacy. The Pole was from Poznan, a Polish town, and he was a pharmacist. They told the Jewish owner to hand over the key and gave it to the Pole. They divided amongst themselves the cash from the till and told the owner to leave the place.

Itsche Rosshendler and Bunem Margolies did not wait for the visitors. The former decided to hand over the store to the son of the cook that was employed by the lord Szepticki. In this manner, did the Rosshendler family remain in their apartment and enjoyed some share in the profit of the store. For the new owner gave a portion of the profits to Itsche Rossenhendler. Bunem Margolies worked out a similar arrangement with Solecki.

[Page 96]

Jews are not allowed to read newspapers

At this period of time, the Germans issued an edict to the effect that Jews are forbidden to read newspapers. The newspaper vendors were told not to sell newspapers to Jews. Newspapers were sold in the store of Andzej Gonet. There was a Polish newspaper whose name we don't remember and a German paper from Krakow. No Jew went to buy officially a newspaper but if someone wanted to get a hold of a paper there was no problem.

[Page 96-97]

Jews must surrender all furs to the Germans or face death

In January of 1942, German officials arrived and demanded that the Jews surrender all fur coats and furs to the authorities within the day. They also informed everybody that they would search each and every house the for these items. Anybody that doesn't comply with thye order will be shot. There were rumors to the effect that in other towns Jews were caught and shot for this offense. In some instances the items were not even furs. One Jew had an old green hat that looked like fur but was not. He did not hide it nor did he bring to the Germans for fear that they will laugh at him. Anyway, the Germans found the hat and shot him. A similar incident was reported with a Jew that had a piece of fur sewn onto a sleeve. He did not consider it fur nor was it fur but the Germans shot him anyway. Obviously, the Germans were terrorizing the Jewish population and shooting Jews achieved this objective.

The Judenrat sent officials to everybody to warn them to surrender all furs or furry items within the day. The Jews responded and carried every item, even an old worn out shtreimel to the office of the Judenrat where the Germans received the merchandise. Two days later, the Germans started to search the homes. They went from door to door, they checked every hiding place but found nothing. Our town survived the event without casualties but endured plenty of anxiety. .

[Page 97]

Jews are forbidden to leave the hamlet

In March or April of 1942, the Germans ordered the Jews to stay within the hamlet. They posted signs indicating the limits of the Jewish area. Jews could walk to Godele Gutwein's house, to Herz Halpern's house, to the Mangel street, to the pharmacy and to Pszyslowski's house. A Jew caught outside this demarcated area faced death. .

[Page 97-98]

The Germans demand Jews for an execution

The event took place on a nice May day, the sun was shining and warming all the people outside. The Ringplace was full of Christian worshippers who came to attend Sunday service. Suddenly a great commotion, panic in Jewish homes. The Gestapo from Krosno arrived and demanded that the local Judenrat give them Jews to be killed. No reason or rhyme was offered, just a demand. The Judenrat gave in. They learned their lesson from the Krosno Judenrat that had a similar situation. Sometimes ago, the Gestapo demanded from the Krosno Judenrat Jews for killing. The Krosno Judenrat gave them a few mentally retarded Jews. The Korcziner Judenrat gave them Naphtali Pinzel, the dumb one, Jehudith Holloshicz, Yossef Maltz and Mrs. Korb, the wife of Yossef Korb.

The Polish auxiliary police escorted all of these Jews to the police headquarters. From here, they were taken one at a time to the field of the priest where the Gastapo shot them. The local Polish population looked at our misfortune, they saw how we were led to the slaughter. There would have been some consolation if the sky was cloudy or dark but no, it was a nice and clear day. The sun was shining and witnessing human brutality, the killing of helpless Jews.

[Page 98-99]

Mrs. Korb

Mrs. Korb was not mentally retarded or mentally sick. She was a beautiful woman, aged 27-28, in her prime. She originated from Jaslo and married to Korczyn. Her husband was Yossef Korb who originated from Jasznica but settled in Korczyn. Mrs. Korb with her two-year-old baby in her arms was led to the killing site. Why did the Judenrat surrender Mrs. Korb to the Gestapo. The Judenrat claimed that the Gestapo specifically asked for her. How did the Gestapo know about Mrs. Korb. We tried to unravel the mystery by pumping Mendel Halpern, the Judenrat Jewish policeman.

According to Halpern, The Gestapo insisted that Mrs. Korb be handed over to them. It seems that Mrs. Korb was in her youth a member of the communist party that resulted in a trial. From the records of this trial in Jaslo, the Gestapo supposedly established the present whereabouts of Mrs. Korb. Whether the claim is correct or not we do not know. Obviously, the Judenrat can not be accused in this instance of totally fabricating the story, for the Gestapo did come and demanded Jews for execution.

[Page 100-101]

The Gestapo returns to kill Jews

The event took place towards the end of July 1942, about two weeks before the total destruction of the Jewish community of Korczyn. Suddenly, about 6 PM, Jewish policeman from the Judenrat went from house to house and informed the people to stay at home after 7 PM, for the Gestapo was in town. The policeman also stated that any Jew found in the street after the curfew will be shot. The people were terrified, they had heard terrible stories about events that took place in nearby towns and did not know what to expect. The Jews were terror stricken and did exactly what they were told to do. But the fear of the unknown was on everybody's mind. Nobody slept that night, everybody tried to find a corner and concentrate with his inner thoughts. The Jews were all paralyzed with fear and resigned to the unknown.

The hours passed slowly, deadly silence at home and outside. The night seemed never ending. Suddenly at 2 AM, we heard heart-breaking sounds, the shrill voices affected us all. We were speechless and terrified by the terrifying sounds that penetrated the home. How we managed to overcome the fear is beyond my comprehension. But we overcame it. The cries and sobs continued.

They became louder with time, it lasted for hours. At 5 AM, I peeked through a crack in the rear gate of our place. I heard Yiddish speakers and decided to open the gate. I saw below in the street, Yankel Schprung and Getzil Schiff, I approached them and asked them why is Eidel, the daughter of Moshe Willner, so hysterical. They replied that her husband and her brother Feibush Willner were shot. The house of Moshe Willner was the third house from us, the walls in the house were about a half a meter thick. Yet, the sobbing sounds penetrated all the walls and gave the impression that the crier was next door. To this day, I hear the sounds of the crying.

Eidel married about a year before the war. Her husband was from East Galicia and when the war started, he and his brother-in-law decided to go to his native place until things settled. They remained there since it became part of Russia. With the German occupation of the area, they returned to Korczyn. They were merely two weeks in Korczyn prior to their execution. Eidel's husband was a scholar and a handsome man. The Germans brutally murdered both of them. The Germans also killed Moshe Epstein who I will describe later. I was later told that the Gestapo demanded all the Jews that returned from the Russian occupied area as well as the rabbi of Korczyn.

On this terrible night, the Germans took Moshe Epstein, Moshe Willner's son-in-law, Feibush Willner, Leibish Ritter, Yehoshua and Avraham Ringelheim. The last three had work permits since they worked for the Germans. They remained standing with their hands in the air and facing the wall the entire night until 4 am when they were dismissed.

[Page 102-104]

The Saint Moshe Epstein

Moshe Epstein was the son of the Rabbi of Nemirow and the son-in-law of Avraham Raab in Korczyn. Moshe Epstein was an excellent Talmudic scholar. When the rabbi of Korczyn was out of town for a period of time, Moshe Epstein took his place and answered all religious inquiries without charging fees. He was an intelligent, easy going person and an excellent conversationalist. He was offered many rabbinical positions but he refused since he preferred his independence. This situation changed during the German occupation. The family, especially the children, were hungry. He therefore decided to appeal indirectly to the Judenrat for help since he was officiating as Rabbi of Korczyn without pay. The regular rabbi, as mentioned earlier, had left town. The Judenrat decided to provide him with a few zlotys each week. I don't know the exact amount nor do I know whether the amount was sufficient to provide bread for his children. We know that the pharmacist also provided him with 10 zlotys each week.

Moshe Epstein had small infants. He was not an ordained rabbi and did not want to become one. When the Gestapo asked for the rabbi, the Judenrat could have said that the hamlet had no rabbi since the Korczyner rabbi had left town in 1939. Any Jew in the street would have backed up the statement. Nobody considered Moshe Epstein the rabbi of Korczyn and most people did not know that he received support from the Judenrat. It is possible that the members of the Judenrat were so terrified that they lost all sense of leadership or that the Jewish policeman, Mendel the bulldog, went and brought him to the Judenrat. Nobody knows precisely what happened. Moshe Epstein was shot by the Germans but not killed. He fell to the ground and remained there. The Germans assumed that he was dead and left the area. Later that night, Moshe Epstein picked himself up and headed for Yantsche Infeld's place, the son-in-law of Sara Gutwein, and hid there. The next morning, the murders spotted that a body was missing. Meanwhile, the Gestapo had returned to Krosno. A Polish policeman, a real Jew hater, went to the Judenrat and told them that he received an order from the Gestapo to the effect that the missing body is to be produced within four hours at the police office or 40 Jews will be shot. The Judenrat again lost their heads. For the Polish policeman could not do a thing without German permission. The Judenrat could have waited and seen whether the Gestapo did issue such an order. At most, they could have offered a bribe for Moshe Epstein in Krosno and possibly saved him. It doesn't make sense that the Gestapo would rely on a lowly Polish policeman to carry out its orders. The Judenrat decided to surrender Moshe Epstein. They found him at 7 AM and surrendered him to the polish policeman. Could it be that other people would have also lost their reasoning abilities under such conditions. The Judenrat told Moshe Epstein that the Germans would kill 40 Jews if he did not surrender himself. He said that he was willing to be the sacrificial lamb for the Jewish community. He asked to be buried with a knife that way he will be able to extract revenge on the Germans. Moshe Epstein was buried at the Jewish cemetery in Korczyn. A knife was placed in his coffin. No tombstone was erected for him. May these lines be his eternal memorial.

[Page 105-106]

Frightful news – entire Jewish communities destroyed

News reached us that in the big cities like Krakow, Tarnow, Reishe or Rzeszow and other big centers, terrible events were taking place. Thousands of Jews were shipped away from their place of residence and nobody knew where they were sent. The Germans registered Jews for work and during these registrations they shoot large numbers of Jews. Entire communities seem to be wiped out.

In July of 1942, the Germans chased the Jews from all the villages in the area and ordered them to Korczyn. Even the Jews from the village of Toraszowka which belonged administratively to Krosno were told to move to Korczyn. Some villages which belonged to Fristik, were also ordered to send their Jews to Korczyn. We also had several Jewish families from Krosno as well as Jewish families from Radom, Krakow and other cities that had previously arrived in Korczyn. The Germans concentrated all the Jews in one spot. Korczyn now had 800 Jewish refugees and about 800 local Jews. Thus the Jewish population consisted of about 1600 people. All Jewish refugees could not be accommodated in private homes, some were placed in abandoned stores and others in the study center. To look at these poor refugees was enough of an inducement to all the Jews to envy those that had died peacefully prior to the war.

[Page 106-107]

Edict, Jews must pay all their Polish state debts to the Germans, Jews forbidden to use electricity

In July of 1942, the Germans issued an edict to the effect that the Jews, not the Poles, must pay to the Germans all the taxes that they owed the Polish government. The same decree ordered the Jews to abstain from using electricity. A terrible hopelessness seized the Jewish community. People began to suspect a devilish German plan to extract all the money from them before they kill them. Some people tried to dismiss these evil thoughts and looked at the bright sight, maybe the Germans only want our money and not our souls. But then news items kept filtering into town about the disappearance of entire Jewish communities.

Entire Jewish transports from the big cities disappeared and nobody knew where they went. Was this the final solution, nobody wanted to believe. How could people believe that the Germans devised a plan to kill innocent women and children? The Jews self deluded themselves that here in Korczyn nothing will happen. Why is Korczyn an exception, nobody could answer that question. Everybody said that bad things are taking place in other areas but here nothing will happen. Our Germans are better than their Germans and besides the Germans need the Jewish workers. Therefore, they will not permit the destruction of the community. The Jews did not believe the Germans, but what was the alternative. The hope to rescue us was hopeless. Perhaps there is a chance, perhaps G-d will have mercy on us, and everybody wanted to believe.

bribed the Gestapo and received permits to go to work in the German factories. Others that lacked money or were incapable of working continued to hide in the attics of the ghetto or in other places. About three weeks later, the Gestapo came to the head of the Krosno Judenrat and told him that those Jews that did not report to the registration may now step forward and they will be issued work permits. All Jews can step forth to the Ghetto Square and they will be legally registered. They will not be harmed and issued personal warrantees as to their safety. The Jewish leaders in the ghetto believed these promises. Notices were posted urging the hidden Jews to step forth. Indeed about 200 Jews responded to these ads and showed up at the appointed date and place.

The Gestapo men received them pleasantly and acted very nice. When the stream of applicants stopped, the area was sealed. Trucks drove into the ghetto and the Jews were forced to board them. They drove the Jews to an unknown destination from where nobody returned. Only one person, Mendel Lindenberg, jumped from one of the trucks and it took him two days to return to the ghetto in Krosno. The ghetto in Krosno existed from the 10th of August 1942 to the 2nd of December 1942. On this date, the remaining Jews from the Krosner ghetto were transferred to the ghetto of Rzeszow or Reishe. Many Jews were killed during the transfer, notably the Krosner rabbi, Rabbi Samuel Fuhrer. The Germans knew that there were hidden Jews in the ghetto and searched everywhere. The Jews that they found were shot on the spot.

[Page 112-114]

The Liquidation of Korczyn

Tuesday, the 11th of August 1942, 28 days in the month of Av, Tashab, Korczyn received an order to the effect that all Jewish workers must proceed to their usual positions on Wednesday. The Jews of Korczyn assumed that it was a safe day, since every place that the Germans decided to liquidate the Jewish population, they ordered the Jewish workers to stay at home. This was the case of Krosno where the Jewish workers were ordered to stay at home on Monday, the day that the selection took place. The Jews of Korczyn were now certain that they were safe for the day. They had no illusions that they will avoid the fate of Krosno. But the will to survive was so strong that even a day more of living gave the people some illusory hope that had no realistic possibility except to convince themselves that today it will not happen.

Wednesday at 7 AM, the Jewish workers lined up four abreast and marched out of town to Krosno to work The entire town was there, the manner in which parents said goodbye to their sons, wives to their husbands, brothers to sisters, neighbors to neighbors are very painful to describe. The premonition of something terrible was in the air and sunk deep into the crowd when the column left town. At eleven o'clock we were told to stop working and were escorted to a barrack near the slaughterhouse, just opposite the bridge on the Wislok River that led to Korczyn. Soon we saw our disaster, trucks loaded with girls, mothers and children passed us by. Today was our destruction. Today is the end of Korczyn. In the evening, about five or six o'clock, we saw the Jews of Korczyn driven by the Germans. The screams and beatings were beyond description. We were then ordered to join the column. The leaders of the column were told to slow the pace and the rear was forced to run full force in that manner they fell on top of each other.

Pessah Kratzer, Haim Halpern's son in law, was covered with blood that oozed from the beatings that he received from the Gestapo men. The later continued to beat him since he did not wipe his face. Supposedly he wanted to create a bad image for Germany. He has nothing to wipe his face with. For this observation, Naphtali, the son of Shabtai Raab, received such a kick in the stomach that he fell to the floor and lost conscience until a second kick revived him. Pessah Kratzer continued to beg G-d to take his soul. Finally we arrived to the Targowice market place in Krosno. There on the ground were already seated the Jews from Jedlice and other places. We were ordered to join them. Soon a messenger from the German district office appeared and demanded that he be granted 70 workers from Korczyn that worked on road construction. They selected 70 men and escorted them to a table where a Gestapo man recorded their names. Motel Rosshendler announced that he wanted to rejoin the group on the floor. The Gestapo men kicked him in the direction of the seated Jews. The same thing was done to Leizer Den who also chose to side with the condemned to death.

When a third person tried to rejoin the group, the Gestapo man shouted at him and informed him that Germany needed workers and any further request to leave the labor crew would be considered an act of sabotage and the party would be shot on the spot. The labor crew of 68 workers, spared temporarily, was led away by an Ukrainian SS man. He led them through the SS ranks that hit the Jews with rifle butts or clubs while hurling insulting remarks to the Jews. The 68 Jewish workers were taken to the Krosner beth hamidrash or study center where they found other selected Jews that were sent there from other places. We spent the night in the study center and in the morning. a Jewish supervisor came and led all the workers into the ghetto of Krosno. From the 68 workers of Korczyn, only two survived the war, one is in New York and the other one is in Stockholm, Sweden.

[Page 117]

Parchments of the torah used as insteps in shoes and Talmud pages used as wrapping paper

The Korczyner Jews that survived the liquidation of the community were in the Krosner ghetto. They were divided into two groups that worked on the roads. One group worked along the Krosno-Rymanow highway and the second group worked along the Krosno-Korczyn highway. The second group saw the spiritual desecration. They saw entire sections of the torah scattered in the trenches and Poles cut sections and inserted them in their shoes. They also saw in stores large numbers of Talmud, shulhan aruch and other religious books being used as wrapping paper. Pages were torn from these books and used to wrap the purchased items.

[Page 118]

The saints, Wolf Kirschner and his twelve year-old son David Leib

On Wednesday, August 12th, 1942, 29 days in Av, tashab, when the Germans attacked the township and drove all the Jews to the market, Wolf Kirchner and his twelve year old son managed to escape through a rear entrance from their home and headed to the Jewish cemetery. They remained hidden the entire day and next day returned to their home to find that the entire Jewish community was gone. Not one single Jew remained in Korczyn. He saw no hope or possibility of survival and decided to commit suicide rather than to surrender to the German killers.

Wolf went to the attendant of the Jewish cemetery and paid him to dig a grave for him and his son next to his father's grave, Mechel Kirchner. He then instructed him to call the Polish police. When the latter arrived he found Wolf Kirschner and his son in the grave. The policeman shot both of them. May these lines serve as an eternal memorial.

On their grave stands a tombstone that was erected in Polish in 1946 by his sister in law. I think she lived in Canada. She sent money to the cemetery attendant to erect a tombstone. In 1950, Zishe Eichorn visited Korczyn and photographed the tombstone at the Jewish cemetery in Korczyn. I think that the date on the tombstone is incorrect, it should read August 14th, 1942. The inscription reads, here are buried the bodies Wolf Kirschner and his son David Leib. The German killers murdered them on August 15th, 1942 in Korczyna.

On the right is the tomb of Wolf Kirschner and on the left is
that of his 12 year old son David Wolf. Both murdered by the Germans.

[Page 120-121]

The saints Avraham Bezenshtock, his wife and children and Yochewed Schiff

Avraham Bezenshtock, his wife and children Dawid and Miriam avoided the fate of the local Jewish population on Wednesday, 29 days in Av, Tashab. They were hidden with a local farmer. With them in hiding were also Mordechai, Pearl and Schiff's daughter Yochewed. Their oldest son Simha was amongst the 68 workers that remained alive and worked in the Krosno ghetto. From here he went to work daily along the road. A neighbor discovered that Jews were being hidden and blackmailed the farmer and the Jewish family for money. The appetite increased with time and he constantly threatened to expose them to the Germans.

Simha Bezenshtock worked along the road and had an opportunity to meet people and arrange a new hiding place for his family. He concluded a deal with a farmer by the name of Weida from Padziamatche according to which, Avraham Bezenshtock, his wife, daughter Miriam and Yochewed Schiff will hide with a neighbor of Weida and Simha Bezenshtock, his brother Dawid and Yehezkel Lewitman who also worked on the road will hide with Weida. The 22nd of November, 1942, Simha Bezenshtock and Yehezkel Lewitman did not return to the ghetto of Krosno but went to their hiding place.

Weida had a weakness, he liked to pinch stuff that belonged to other farmers. Nobody knew whether he stole a rooster or a lamb but the farmer complained and Weida was arrested in March of 1943, seven months after the liquidation of the Jewish community of Korczyn. Weida's wife demanded that Simha and Dawid Bezenshtock and Yehezkel Lewitman leave the house. The hidden Jews refused to leave whereupon she went to the Polish police and reported the event. The police soon arrived at the farm and found it ablaze. Simha Bezenshtock and Yehezkel Lewitman decided to torch the farm and themselves rather that fall into the hands of the polish police. They lit a match to the straw that surrounded them in the attic and within moments the place was on fire. The neighbor of Weida saw what happened and killed all the Jews that hid in his place. To this day nobody knows where he buried the bodies of Avraham Bezenshtock, his wife Ethel Bezenshtock, their daughter Miriam and Yochewed Schiff. May these few lines serve as an eternal memorial to them.

[Page 122-123]

The Saint Israel Brener

Israel Brener lived in the village Domaradz situated about 16 kilometers from Korczyn. The village belonged administratively to the administration of Brzozow or Brezew in Yiddish. Simha Rubin the son of Mendel Rubin of Korczyn was the son in law of Israel Brener and lived in Domaradz. Israel Brenner was different from all the other Jewish farmers. He dressed like a hassid and was one in the full sense of the word. He wore a long coat, a velvet black hat, a long beard and long peyot. He studied torah, was very observant, gave charity and was very modest in his behavior. He owned a torah scroll that he kept in his house and the Jews from the area would come to his house on Saturday or holidays to pray. Shmuel Aron Rosshendler told the information you are about to read to us in the ghetto of Krosno after the destruction of the Jewish community of Korczyn. Shmuel Aron Rossenhedler was a member of the Judenrat of Krosno and in this capacity had contact with some of the Gestapo men. The Gestapo chief, Schmatzler in Krosno came to Shmuel Aron Rosshendler and told him the following event. Rosshendler, I am amazed, this is unbelievable. I went to liquidate the Jews of Dormatch. The order was that all Jews of Domaradz were to leave the village and head for Brzozow. I entered the house of the Jew Brener and told him that he had 2 hours to leave the village and he can take everything with him. When the Jew heard the announcement he went straight to the closet and took his torah scroll and left for Brzozow. Nothing else mattered. He took nothing from the house. The German repeated the words, such spiritual heroism. He took nothing except for the torah scroll. He was astonished by this spiritual heroism of the simple Jew. May these lines serve as an eternal memorial for him.

[Page 124]

The Krosner Rabbi, Moshele Twerski and his brother in law Naphtali Horowitz, Rabbi of Rozwadow

In the Krosner ghetto was the Krosner rabbi Moshe Twerski and his brother in law Naphtali Horowitz, rabbi of Rozwadow, as well as their wives. The Krosner rabbi was dressed sporty, his pants were tucked in the boots and he wore a kasket on his head. His face was clean shaven, no beard or peyot. The Rozwadower rabbi was dressed in similar fashion except that he had a big blond moustache which gave him the appearance of a country peasant. Each day they marched to their jobs with the rest of the workers. They worked in the laundry and cleaned German clothing. There are still today Jews that remember the Krosner and Rozwadoewr rabbis in their impressive appearance prior to the war. What a picture of contrast between than and now that they tried to pass themselves as two farmers going to work in the laundry. This event is rather small in comparison to the total Jewish picture of the time but it illustrates the situation of the Jewish plight when a rabbi has to hide his identity for fear of his life. We seem to forget the past rather easily. Yaacov Itzhak Fessel, today in Stockholm, Sweden, informs us that the rabbi of Krosno died of dysentery in the ghetto of Rzeszow.

[Page 125]

The Gestapo grabs Jewish children in the ghetto

The event took place in the middle of the month of September of 1942. The Gestapo surrounded the ghetto and grabbed Jewish children and threw them aboard trucks that left for an unknown destination, a place of no return.

Pisgah Kratzer arrested in the ghetto

Pessah Kratzer, Haim Halpern's son in law worked with the German construction firm Kirchof that worked along the road to Dukla. On a particular day in September of 1942, Pessah did not report to work. He remained in the ghetto. To his misfortune, a Gestapo man with the nickname of Von Daladier made his appearance in the ghetto. He was a beast, a killer, a murderer. He saw Pessah Kratzer and asked him what he was doing in the ghetto. Pessah answered that he worked outside chopping stones and was on his lunch break. The killer went outside and asked the foreman how many workers he has. The foreman told him that he had 17 workers. The Gestapo man counted the workers and saw he had 17 without Pessah Kratzer. He returned to the ghetto and found Pessah Kratzer and took him away and killed him. May this be his eternal tombstone.

Yanka, Yente Geller

Yanka Geller was an assistant in the pharmacy of Korczyn. She was a proud woman of 27 and stemmed from a Jewish traditional family in Stry. I think that Nathan Eck in Israel who works for Yad Vashem was her brother in law. When the Jews of Korczyn were rounded up, she managed to hide in the attic of the pharmacy. A week after the liquidation of Korczyn, Yanka reached the ghetto of Krosno. She mentioned that she had a possibility of reaching the city of Krakow with the help of a Christian woman, Mrs. Grabowiecz. The latter was to provide her with Aryan papers so that she could live as non-Jew. The next day she left the ghetto and to her misfortune was identified by the wife of a polish policeman from Korczyn, Mrs. Habrat. She denounced her to the Germans who arrested her and she disappeared.

[Page 127]

Why We Did Not Resist

All kinds of paper heroes are now asking all kinds of question as to why the Jews did not resist. They themselves sat in comfortable places and witnessed the killing of millions of people without a parallel in human history. They did nothing then but have now all sorts of questions such as why we did not resist. These so-called Jewish heroes instead of demanding explanations from the German killers are directing their questions to the victims. Why did they permit themselves to be led to the slaughter instead of dying a heroic death. This would have pleased many of the paper heroes. They of course did nothing when the news of the destruction of European Jewry reached them. Unlike Mordechai in the story of Purim, who went into the streets to alarm the Jews about the impending disaster. These people did nothing to protect their brethren who were being slaughtered by the millions. They slept and ate and enjoyed themselves. Such heroes could also be found amongst European Jews. There is no doubt that all Jews that fell under the German boot were to receive the same treatment regardless of place. Even American Jews had they been seized by the Germans would also been led to the slaughter just like the European Jews. With what means would they have opposed the German soldiers, a kitchen knife or a club against a loaded rifle. Maximum the soldier would receive a blow but in the process how many people would be killed. Who dared to take a step that would provide the Germans with an excuse to kill women, children and elderly people. Such decision could lead to the total destruction of the community. The German always used their psychological strategy, registration, selection etc. There was always a bit of hope and always some survivors.

All the Jewish communities in the area were liquidated within the same week thus eliminating any possibility of coordination. They did not even know the extent of the liquidation. Who was supposed to organize and where were the means of defense. The Jew in exile was never trained to die a hero's death; in their long history they acquired the training to die as martyrs. Furthermore, most of the Jewish youth was no longer in the communities but in German labor camps. The communities consisted primarily of Hassidic, religious elements, elderly people, women and children. The ability to shoot or stab with a knife they never acquired and the ability to produce weapons was beyond their dreams.

[Page 129]

Weissberger

In the oil fields of Wenglowka near Korczyn, was employed a manager, a Jew by the name of Karol Weissberger. He knew that he was a Jew but refused any contact with Jews and kept a distance from Jewish life. His only connection to Judaism was the fact that he was born to Jewish parents. During the liquidation of the Jewish community of Korczyn, the Germans did not bother with him. He was on friendly terms with some Gestapo men and even invited them for drinks to his home. They of course assured him that he should not be worried by the events in Korczyn since he has their protection.

In the winter of 1943, the Gestapo men came to Wenglowka to visit Weissberger. He invited them to eat and to drink. During the meal, one of the Gestapo men took Weissberger by the arm and led him to the next room as if to reveal a secret. There another Gestapo men shot him in the back. The wife and his two children were arrested.

Urbankowa, the convert

After the house of Dr. Pszislowski, a few steps further there was log cutting plant that belonged to a gentile by the name of Urbanek. The latter was a postal worker in Silesia or Poznan. There he met a Jewish woman who had a Jewish child from her previous marriage. Urbanek married her and they came to Korczyn about 1925. She had converted to his religion. In 1943, the Gestapo came and arrested Mrs. Urbanek and their son Zbiszek aged 15. They took them and they disappeared.

[Page 130]

The survivors of Korczyn after the liberation

With the end of the war, 15 men and one woman survived the German occupation and 11 men and 6 woman survived in Russia the war. These are all the survivors of the Jewish community of Korczyn. All our parents aged 50 and over were killed by the Germans on August 12, 1942 or 29 days in the month of Av, Tashab. The memorial day for our brothers and sisters is not known specifically but it can definitely be placed in the first ten days of the month of Elul, Tashab, 1942. They were forced to board the train that left the Krosno railway station on Friday, the 14th of August 1942, the first day of Elul, Tashab. The memorial day of those that perished in the concentrations camps is unknown.

[Page 131]

Yossele Reich – He perished in the death camp of Plaszow

Yossef was the only son of Nachman Leibish Reich and the grandson of Shaul Reich and the great grandson of Mendel Shroit. He was my best and most devoted friend. He was an imposing young men dressed in the hassidic garb. On Saturday, a silk caftan and a velvet hat. He dedicated his youth to the study of the torah and knowledge. In spite of the fact that he managed a linen factory, he also managed to find time to continue his studies of the torah and general knowledge. He was a pedant and besides mastery of the Polish language and culture was also at home in the Hebrew literature. He wrote many articles in Yiddish and Hebrew and published then in various literary publications.

Yossele was a logical thinker, a calm person, a human heart, a fine character and had excellent mannerisms. Those that came in contact with him or conversed with him were impressed with his straightwordness, his refinements, his good nature, his wisdom and friendship. His loss is a pity.

[Page 132-133]

In the Concentration Camp Duchacka Wola

Written by Yosselle Reich, delivered by Avraham Horowitz of New York. The poem describes the suffering and martyrdom of the Jewish inmates. The poem was loosely translated into English by William Leibner.

Refrain
Under the control of the eastern railway
Exist thousands of slaves in the camp
Of Duchacka Wola

Whether they get a bone
Or a very hard stone
It doesn't matter in
The nazi regime

They were brought here
By German murderers and Gestapo men
They were given strange clothes
But never received a free moment

Bayonets drove them
Into closed railway cars
In the spirit of the time
They were exhausted and unable to breath
Oh mighty God
Trusted defender, dear Father
Extinguish the fire of Hell
Finish our troubles

From the cruel whip
Of the German murderer Mr. Keil (Nazi supervisor)
Protect us, Oh Merciful
The persecuted children of Israel

Refrain
Under the control of the eastern railway
Exist thousands of slaves in the camp
of Duchacka Wola

[Page 134]

– empty –

[Page 135]

About the author of poem, this is how I feel

The publishers Israel Platner, the author of the poem, this how I feel, lived in Krosno and then emigrated. He is a known poet and wrote many interesting articles and poems on daily topics. His creations were frequently printed in the Jewish Journal of Toronto and other newspapers. He was highly praised by the famous writer, Haim Liberman. The author speaks about the Lublin Reservation and Boxes of Ashes in his poem. In comparison with the death camps of Auschwitz, Maydanek, and other hell holes where European Jewry was massacred, the Lublin Reservation and Boxes of Ashes are rather mild stuff and don't convey the true picture of the tragedy that befell the Jews of Europe.

We have to remember that the author wrote the poem in 1940 when the situation was grim for the Jews but not catastrophic. The German murderers did not yet build the death camps of Auschwitz and Maydanek and others.

At the request of the author, we publish the poem as it appeared in the newspapers in 1940.

[Page 136]

Statement from the author of the poem, this is how I feel

I composed the poem with a great deal of pain and tears. Within a matter of a few weeks, following the beginning of WWII, the poem was finished. It remained locked in the draw of the editor of the Toronto Jewish Journal until February 1940. Then the poem was published. It was then reprinted in other papers such as the Yiddishe Welt in Cleveland, Chicago Courier in Chicago and the Yiddishe Welt in Philadelphia. As to the question why I knew what was going on there while the other leaders did not know, this is my secret that picks at my brain and presses my heart.

[Page 137-139]

Israel Platner in Toronto, Canada

This is how I feel

If I had courage
I would do the following
Not withstanding the laughter of the cynics
That I would ignore
I would dress a black sack of coal
For the destruction of Polish Jewry
And walk in the streets and scream
That would attract the attention of the young and old
And even the infants would join
Everybody would ask what is going on
Then I would scream even louder
For I hear the dying pains
Those reach us here
From the valley of the death
Where the German murder and persecute
The children of Israel

Hear, Hear, the vulgar beastly laughter
That silences the innocent crying
Of the daughters of Jacob

Why doesn't mankind morn
Like a mourner in the thirty days of morning
Don't you see the Boxes of Ashes?
From the murdered saints

Wicked science
Rotten civilization
A big slaughterhouse you call
Lublin Reservation
Let my heart be torn to pieces
If I can't awaken the conscience of the world

Ha, Ha, Ha, cultural advancement
Why the need for encyclopedias
Who needs literature?
Let it all explode
With the full impact
Better scream at the murderer
Drop the axe

Close the laboratories
Who needs to split the atoms?
Children whose bellies are swollen from hunger
Try to keep them alive

If you men, rich or poor
Are able to sit in peace and do nothing
Listen to the radio at home
And their suffering you don't want to hear
Then, a flood may come and soon
To wipe out mankind
Let the animals remain in the forest
Let them stay alive for they are innocent
But the people, they are evil!

Loosely translated into English by William Leibner

[Page 140-141]

Holy tombstone in memory of the city of Korczyn

by Aron Atlas, grandson of Hirsh Halpern, lives in Jerusalem

Amongst the hundreds of small towns of Poland, Korczyn stood out by the large religious following and by the large number of religious students. The Jewish kehilla as many others, is no longer. The German murderer killed the Jews of Korczyn just as he did the other six million Jews. The wound is open and there is no cure. Tears keep rolling in spite of the fact that 25 years have elapsed.

The tears will not cease for the eyes see distances and they can see the township of Korczyn in the lowest degradation. The Jews that lived there are no longer. The eyes see the soil of Korczyn drenched in the blood of our parents, brothers, sisters and children. The Germans spilled their blood that run like water.

Just like their blood will never dry so will our tears continue to flow. The eternal eye will forever have a frozen tear as a reminder for the holy people that were killed by the Germans. We are not talking of plain blood but the blood of holy people who died as martyrs and extinguished the light of the Jewish community of Korczyn. It is our obligation not to forget the destruction and to keep it alive. To weep for our dear ones whose blood was spilled. But we don't know how to weep said the sages: when the temple was destroyed, God wept over the loss of his home, he asked, where are my children, where are my priests, where are my prophets, where are my followers. God said to the prophet Jeremiah, go and call Abraham, Isaac, Jacob, and Moses for they know how to weep.

Jeremiah went to the cave of the patriarchs and said to the fathers of the world. Arise. God is demanding your presence. They asked why? Jeremiah answered that he did not know and let them go at that. Jeremiah also invoked Ben Amram to appear before God. They all knew how to weep, how to express sorrow but we don't know how to weep.

[Page 142]

Our parents in Korczyn

The township of Korczyn had about 200 Jewish families. Korczyn was not a big or famous city, but it had a name as a place where there were religious scholars and learned men. We will mention Rabbi Shmuel Aron Rubin, the head of the judicial council and the author of the known book of halacha, the house of Aron, that deals with divorces. This rabbi was followed by Rabbi Shmuel Rubin, a grandson of the famous Rabbi of Rupszitz. He was also related to the famous hassidic rabbi of Shinive. The city contained many religious scholars and teachers. The Jews of Korczyn were tied to their religious traditions, they had mercy, they were good natured and they gave charity.

The Jews of Korczyn awakened the dawn by rushing to the synagogue with the talit and phylacteries in spite of the bitter cold that prevailed during the winter months. This one sat down next to a page of the talmud, the next one studied mishnayot, another one recited the psalms until they all joined in prayers. In the evening, the stores were closed and the Jews went to the beit hamidrash to pray the evening prayers and following the prayers, Jews again sat down to study religious texts.

Shabbath of our fathers in Korczyn

All days of the week we were looking forward to Saturday. On Friday we already felt the atmosphere of the Shabbath, especially in the area of the market since many women purchased their needs for Saturday. Friday was also the day when they barrowed money to cover the purchases for Saturday. They were not worried about the debts since it was for the Shabbath and they had full confidence that the almighty will provide. Even the rabbi's house was full of activities since the rabbi had to answer many questions regarding the kashrut of the chickens that were being slaughtered for Saturday.

Friday afternoon, the Shabbath sanctity descended on the township. Stores started closing and preparations were made for Saturday. With the lighting of the candles on Friday, the Shabbath atmosphere reigned in town. The woman that lit the candles felt the importance of their actions and prior to the actual lighting would set aside some charity reciting certain prayers. She would then light the candles and express her wish for health, income, respect from the children and some tears would descend her cheeks.

The eyes should have seen how the Jews of Korczyn leave their homes and head to the synagogue in their special attire. Not only the well to do dressed especially for the Shabbath but also the poorer Jew had special clothing for the Shabbath. Thus, rich and poor dressed alike for the Shabbath. The synagogue was lit with many candles and white tablecloths covered the tables. The cantor started the service by singing the first lines of the Friday night service.

Before the services were finished, people looked for guests for their Shabbat meal. Happy and gay did the Jews return from the service to their home, tall and erect they entered their residences. They looked forward to a day of rest and spiritual recharge from the weekdays. The feeling is beyond description. When he started to chant the Friday night songs at the table and the chants during the meals, he felt like a prince. The whole week, he was constantly rushed but on Friday night he sat and ate with regal dignity.

There was no Jewish home that did not have some singing during the meal. After the meal, some went back to the synagogue to study while others went to the house of the rabbi to listen to a torah sermon. Saturday, the service finished about noon. Again the family had a big meal and plenty of singing. Then the father examined the son as to what he studied during the week or sent the son to the heder to be tested. After the evening service, the congregants would eat in the synagogue and sing chants of praise to the merciful God. With the end of the Shabbath, the sexton would light a candle and the light would remind the congregants that the Shabbath has ended and another workweek is about to begin.

[Page 144-155]

The story about the destruction of my family and our township

by Zishe Eichorn, Jerusalem

Zishe Eichorn

My father, Chaim was like the other Jews in town. He raised his children to love the Jewish people. I have to thank him for helping shape my character and personal traits. In all my activities as a child and as an adult in my wanderings, I always followed his example of honesty and integrity. I never managed to obtain a high education, secular or religious, since the family could not afford it.

I was one of ten children in the family. I survived while all the brothers and sisters were killed, I have no explanation. I was not better or smarter than any of my brothers or sisters.

The Germans killed six of my brothers and sisters with their families that lived in Poland, 52 people in all, and my wife and our 3 children. All the Jews that were under German rule shared the same fate. The survivors of course first see their own tragedies and those of their nearest kin before drawing general conclusions. I always see my parents, Chaim and Braindel, my wife with the three children, my brothers and sisters with their families. They always remain in front of my eyes and I can never forget them for a moment. I always ask why did they deserve this fate but there is no answer. Sometimes I even ask myself why I survived, for what purpose. I saw many times the angel of death and on occasion even met him face to face but I survived. Whether I am better off alive than my dead relatives, that is another question. Apparently, it was my destiny to survive and memorialize them to the best of my ability in the old Jewish tradition. I have no other explanation.

I already published many articles in various papers that dealt with my experiences and those of my family as well as items pertaining to Korczyn.

But the sadness remains, no amount of writing will remove the destruction of my family and the community. Before the last deluge, I lived in Germany where I married and three children. When Hitler became ruler of Germany, we, the foreign born Jews, were his first victims. He sent us all across the Polish border. My family and my mother in law reached Bieletz in Poland where we remained for a period of time. With the invasion of Poland in 1939, we headed to Korczyn. 19 years we lived happily together, first in Germany and then in Poland.

The children were raised in the Jewish spirit. They blossomed and we enjoyed watching their growth. The entire family was united. In addition to our arrival, the family also received two brothers with their families and three sisters with their families and a recently acquired sister in law, all in all 52 people. The first place they went upon arrival to Korczyn was to our mother's place. She took charge of the situation and made room for all the members of the family. Her small two-room apartment with a kitchen was the extent of the place, yet she found room for everybody. During the division of Poland between Russia and Poland and the ensuing chaos, my son Berish, aged 17, and myself were caught on the Russian side of the divide. We were no longer free agents and wound up deep in Russia, in Siberia. During our long trips through this big country, my son died. I buried him, and during the first three days of morning, I greyed beyond recognition. Now I was left alone, no relative or kin. Only the illusion that somewhere in Poland someone from the family managed to survive. This dream kept me going from day to day. Finally, after all the terrible experiences, I returned to Poland with the hope of finding someone from the family. My first objective was to reach Korczyn and when I reached it, all my illusions were shattered. I had already a premonition on entering Poland when I saw entire areas that once had large Jewish populations, totally devoid of them. The Jews lived and worked here for generations and each succeeding generation added another ring to the chain. Suddenly, the whole process stopped, the entire Jewish population was mercilessly slaughtered except for a few miraculous survivors, including myself.

The previous neighbors were astonished to see me, for they had already divided the inheritance and suddenly a claimant appeared on the scene. The neighbors wanted to forget the whole history and suddenly a reminder of the past appeared. Very uncomfortable were the Polish neighbors that took our possessions. But they did not show remorse or ask for forgiveness, this they probably had obtained from the parish priest. Besides, all sins could be placed on the Germans.

I wanted to visit two places in Korczyn, the first was the water well of Korczyn that still existed and was near our place of residence and the cemetery where the Jews were buried prior to the destruction of the community. I tasted the water and it was so fresh, this taste reminded me of my youth when I stopped frequently here to quench my thirst. The taste remained in my mouth throughout all my wanderings. To date I do not know what happened next to me but apparently I fell asleep or fainted from exhaustion. For my entire life, from childhood to the present, passed in review. My mother tended to me and gave me some of her tasty dishes to eat. I do not know how long I was daydreaming but when I awakened. I was angry with myself for letting my guard down. After all, my neighbors could have killed me.

My second visit was at the cemetery that belonged to the Jewish community. So far nobody claimed it and it remained as it was surrounded by high cement wall that was built by the late Chaim Wolf Koref. This was the only place where former Korczyner Jewish residents could feel at home. Some of the neighbors informed me that my mother passed away three days before the community was liquidated and is buried at the cemetery. The old caretaker showed me my mother's gravesite and I was able to pour out all my sorrows. I spoke to my mother and told her that her son Zishe survived the war and survived Hitler and will erect a tombstone for her. While talking to her, I must have passed out for the next thing I felt water running down my face that the caretaker must have spilled when he saw my condition.

I then went from grave to grave, I found my father's grave and prayed there, I located my grandfathers - Yossef and Nuta Leibush and my grandmothers. I informed them that one of the family survived the war. I decided to erect a tombstone for my mother and left for Bielsko Biala where I stayed since I came from Russia. Here I ordered the tombstone and had my mother's name inscribed on it as well as other members of the family whose whereabouts nobody knows. I shipped the stone to Krosno where I rented a cart, there were no haulers at the time, and hired a Pole to help push the tombstone to Korczyn. The trip lasted three hours and a downpour caught us halfway but we had no place to stay so we continued in the rain.

[Page 148]

The cemetery of Korczyn

The entrance and the wall surrounding the cemetery of Korczyn that Chaim Wolf Koref built.

[Page 150]

Korczyna, dnia. 3. XI. 1948. r.

The tombstone for the Eichorn family in Korczyn

Three times I revisited Korczyn since I returned from Russia. I spent 5 nights in my old town and the only place I felt comfortable was at the morgue of the old Korczyner cemetery. It is strange, but I felt more at ease with the death people than the living neighbors. The fear that is instilled in us children about the cemetery disappeared. I was unable to sleep, so I commuted with all the souls that rested in this place. With the crack of dawn, I prayed at my father's grave and then visited the graves of my relatives, my mother and grand parents. I also recited some prayers at their graves.

[III]

In Korczyn, I suddenly felt an urge to gather information about the liquidation of the Jewish community in order to memorialize it. Two Poles from Korczyn- the caretaker of the Jewish cemetery and the caretaker of the general cemetery offered to guide me to the various burial grounds. Of course they were well paid and took me first to the general cemetery and showed me ditches surrounding the cemetery. These ditches contained the bodies of many people that the Germans killed. Then they led me to the mass grave of Jews along the road to Brezew. I would have liked to have brought all these bodies to Israel but this was beyond my ability. What happened to the other survivors of Korczyn, for the town had close to 1500 people prior to the destruction of the community. There is no answer to the question. Thus we have no alternative but to memorialize our victims amongst the 6 million saints in our own yizkor book. Even if we are unable to list all the people in Korczyn for lack of knowledge, at least they will be listed in spirit of Korczyn.

[IV]

It was a nice sunny Sunday, I was standing helpless, a stranger, a heavy heart, and watched the Poles rest on their holy day. Had it rained, it would have made me feel a bit happier. I approached the water fountain, I washed my hands and did not know what to wish for. Should Jewish life be resurrected here, no was my answer. I merely commuted with the Jewish generations that lived here and passed forever. They lived, suffered, and united passed on. May my tears join the tears of other Jews and expedite the arrival of the Messiah.

Now to the skimpy description of the community, of Korczyn.

[V]

The 15th Memorial Day 12/8/1956, 29 days in the month of Av, Tashtaz, was memorialized at Mount Zion in Jerusalem. Here the Korczyner and Krosner survivors erected a permanent tombstone in the Cave of the

Holocaust for the Jews killed in both communities. We also added a plaque naming the two communities along the wall that contained hundreds of localities. There were many participants from both towns. Each year, we have less and less participants. In 1959, no Krosner survivor was there and I was the only survivor of Korczyn, indeed very sad.

[VI]

Each year, the 10th day in the month of Tevet, the survivors meet in a hall in Tel Aviv to memorialize the victims. We remember the saints and our hearts cry when the cantor from Krosno recites the prayers for the death. In the hall, the survivors of Korczyn and Krosno meet and exchange the latest news. The names of our departed are also listed with the names of other communities. May their memory be eternal.

[VII]

Our well-known hassidic Jewish township was well known for the production of fine linens. The Jews traded the merchandise throughout Poland and the world and established its fine reputation. Very few survivors were left to tell or record the story.

A distant place, seven kilometers from the nearest railway station. Yet it had its share of poor people as well as those that came to beg from other places. Nobody left the township without a donation. The rich gave more but the simple people also gave in order to fulfill the deed of giving charity.

We remember the well to do families in town: Mendel Shroit, Shaul Reich, Elieazar and Avraham Rab, Chaim Dym, Mendel Gleicher, Hersh Yaacov Rosshendler, Shulem Akselrad, Moshe Rothenberg and many others. Later, their descendants continued to give charity and help the needy. Following WWI, the financial situations of some families changed but the tradition of charity continued. Who can forget the charitable work of Bashe Welke Reich, Sarah Gutwein and other women who helped the poor and needy. Our neighbor, the butcher Moshe Kirschner and his wife Ita set an example. They were not rich people but helped the poor in town with meat for the Shabbath and holidays. The artisans were happy when they could invite a poor person to their Friday night table. The town population lived a quiet life until the Germans destroyed the entire community. This period is very painful to describe

[VIII]

29 days in the month of Av, Tashab, at 8 AM, the township was surrounded by Germans, Ukrainians and Polish collaborators. They drove the Jews from their flats and those that procrastinated were shot on the spot. The Jews with their hasty assembled packages were driven to the market place. There they kept the entire day. They were not permitted to approach the two fountains to drink water. In the afternoon, the chief of the Gestapo arrived and selected the old, sick and weak people. He tapped these people on the head with his cane, the party was immediately grabbed by the henchmen and tossed into a waiting truck. When the truck was full, it left in the direction of Brezew where there were ditches prepared for their execution and burial. Thus, the Jewish population decreased with each truckload.

The Germans did not reveal their intentions. They told everybody that they are resettling the population. Few believed their statements. But who dared to challenge the armed forces that carried out these operations. Amongst the victims were my sister Hanah Pessel and her husband Shmuel, my sister Bluma and her husband Ephraim, my aunt Percze nee Katz, Moshe Dawid Fessel, Moshe Kirschner and his wife and many others.

With the removal of the old people, the rest of the Jewish population was lined up 5 abreast and marched to the railway station of Kros where two days later they were shipped to the Belzec death camp. Shlomo Firsichbaum and his wife refused to follow the crowd, he wrapped himself and his wife in his talit and uttered the word, Shema Israel. The Germans shot him on the spot Their only daughter and her husband, my brother, and their 3 children witnessed the whole scene. In the transport were also my wife Esther and our two children: Rivka aged 18 and Hanah aged 16, my brother Jacob and his wife and their 3 children, my sister Rikel and her husband and 2 children. Many other members of the family were on the train but it is impossible to list them all. The Polish population that lived in close proximity with the Jewish population and traded with it for generations, appeared soon in town with sacs and carts to haul off the goods left by the Jews.

Before I left Poland in March of 1950, I visited Korczyn for the last time. I noticed a page of the Talmud that I took for burial to Israel. This page represented the spiritual inheritance of the destroyed Jewish community. Of all the books in Korczyn, this page had the luck to be taken to the Holy Land for burial. Thus, I left my birthplace, a broken down lonely person, a survivor of Korczyn.

[Page 156-168]

Bashe Krawtchik

My experiences, the pains and sufferings I endured in the concentration camps.

By: Bashe Krawtchik nee Schiff, Bari, Italy

Bashe Krawtchik nee Schiff is the daughter of Haya Libe Mecheles, a grand daughter of Mechele Kresh, Getzel and a sister of Mordechai Schiff. She wrote a letter on July 1st 1947 from a displaced camp in Bari, Italy where she described the sufferings she underwent during the German occupation. The editors.

Dear friend Dawidowicz,

I am pleased to write to a dear friend of Korczyn about times gone by. You are probably curious as to the author of the letter. My brother Mordechai Schiff who is presently in Austria wrote me about you and told me that you are interested in my experiences during the war. I see no reason to deny your request and therefore decided to share my happy and painful thoughts of the period.

You may not know me, but you are very close since your mother Pearl Yente was a close friend of my mother's and they maintained excellent relations. I consider my story similar to the exit of the Jews from Egypt if not worse. I shall begin with the outbreak of the war in 1939 and finish in 1945. Three weeks following the outbreak of the war, the Germans occupied Poland. Their entry to the city was very tragic for us. The first ordinance was on Yom Kippur day and ordered all the Jews to fill all the earth holes around town. These holes had to be filled smoothly or the people would face death. This was their agenda for the day. Fasting since it was Yom Kippur, I joined other Jews. I took a spade and started to work as fast as I could. The German supervisors watched us and did not permit an instant of rest. Thus ended the first Yom Kippur under German occupation.

We returned home exhausted and tired from the heavy work. The slave work conditions continued daily, whether we cleaned the streets transferred goods from warehouses or unloaded coal from train cars. These working conditions lasted until 1941. Then started a series of edicts that culminated in the creation of the ghetto. How I suffered in the ghetto is beyond description and I am unable to describe it but am certain that other people described the living conditions of the ghetto. With the liquidation of the ghetto, living conditions became catastrophic. The word resettlement send electric shock waves through us. Each person draw his own picture of the resettlement process but to all of us it meant that the weak, the ill, the old and the children will be slaughtered, the strong and healthy will be sent to work. I was one of those selected to work.

I was assigned to a factory that produced electro-mechanical parts for the German army. I worked in the place for two years and saw only barbed wire and heavy machines. My workday consisted of 12 hours of hard work serving heavy machinery. The latter used all my energies since we had to fulfill the quota set by the taskmaster. If we failed to fulfill the quota, we were placed on the black list that meant death. One could be shot or torn apart by dogs trained to kill people. This was the death camp of Plaszow. I must have had supernatural powers to overcome all these sufferings for it is difficult for me to perceive how I survived. People that were not in the camps will never understand the horrors of these places. Following two years of hard exhausting labor beyond our abilities, we moved to another camp. We were constantly hungry since we were fed a half a liter of potato soup and a half a kilo of bread per day. The constant fear of the unknown made conditions worse. Rumors started that the Russian and American armies are approaching and we will be evacuated. We did not expect good things from the Germans and as long as they ruled we expected the worst. Suddenly, the day arrived and we were called to the roll call square or appel platz. I will describe for you the square. It was a big field surrounded with electric wires and each morning at six AM before we went to work, we were called to the square by a loudspeaker that uttered the words, roll call, out, out, faster, faster. The people lined up in rows of five and the SS man counted them. This procedure was repeated three times each day; before going to work, returning from work and before going to bed. If a person escaped or disappeared, twenty other inmates were shot. On this day, the group leader informed us that we are leaving the camp tonight and ordered us to leave everything behind in Plaszow. I thought to myself, sooner or later we were all going to die, others in the group said let them kill us here why bother to drag us to other places. Still others hoped to survive the war. We started to march and walked an entire day until we reached a railway station. The Germans screamed and shouted for us to enter the cattle train cars with the sealed windows. They counted up to a hundred and twenty people per train car. Then an SS man closed the door and told us to shut up. The entire train was packed with 120 people per car. Nobody knew where we were going. I still see the mother that died in the arms of her daughter for lack of water. She begged for water but nobody could provide her with the liquid. Nobody cried for the woman, as a matter of fact, some were envious of her situation. She was delivered and they still had to suffer.

The train rolled, we stood like mommies without being able to move, and there was no air. I mentioned to some people that I have a pocketknife and asked to get to the wall. The people moved and I finally reached the wall and began to loosen a board. I worked for some time and finally managed to open a sizable whole in the wall. We immediately saw barracks with their small lights. I screamed out, we are heading to Auschwitz. Hell broke loose, people screamed and shouted, the German guards threw stones at the car and ordered us to shout up. Twenty minutes later, the doors opened and we descended from the train and were counted. We lined up and marched like soldiers through the forest. We expected to be shot at any moment, why the delay, we are not far from the crematoria.

I saw the tall chimneys, taller than the ones in the factory. I smelled the smoke filled air that was rising to the sky. My God, did you forget your people of Israel. I asked many questions but nobody answered them. Is the world dumb to permit the murder of millions of innocent people. All of them asked for revenge but nobody listened. Should we resist but how, meanwhile we are paralyzed with fear. Then we heard the command that we will be showering tonight. As we approached the showers, I noticed a thick curtain that hang over the place and a guard at the entrance. I mentioned to my friend that I would ask the guard what was behind the curtain. She told me not to ask such question since he may shoot me. I was bold and asked and was told that there was a kindergarten behind the curtain. Now I was certain that I faced the gas chambers. The last road that lead to the end, no return, this was where thousands of adults and children were gassed.

We entered a long barrack without windows and remained there the entire night awaiting our verdict. In the morning we awakened to the screams of the guards. They rushed us to undress and forced us to pass in review before so called German doctors that examined us if we were fit to work. The strong ones were sent to the right that is to continue slave labor. The weak, sick and hopeless were sent to the left that is the to gas chambers. Every woman that had to pass the review of the murderers felt debased and violated but there was no choice. I was one of the lucky ones and chosen to continue to work. The next day we received a slice of bread. I had not eaten for two days and therefore swallowed the bread with one gulp as though it was a pill. My stomach was already accustomed to everything, grass, raw potatoes, a luxury in the camps, there were even fist fights over potato peels. Our new camp was Birkenau near Auschwitz. Here I remained three weeks under quarantine. Ten women slept on a platform of wood planks. There was no room to move or budge. The three weeks seemed like three years. We were forbidden to talk loud, we received 5 minutes of fresh air before going to sleep. This bit of fresh air kept me going for the next twenty-four hours. Whoever did not adapt to the conditions suffered. Suddenly, a group leader appeared, a real beast, and ordered all inmates to line up. He checked every person thoroughly and those that looked fit he sent to another barrack where they would continue to work. The others will be sent to the crematoria. I failed the test. I discussed the matter with a woman from Krakow and we decided to leave the barrack. When everybody was asleep, we jumped from the barrack and headed to the one that had received the survivors. We of course faced death if caught but that we already that sentence. We were all tattooed on the left hand and to today I still have the number that remains me of my bondage. It is Germany's shame and not mine, thus was memorialized the brown beast. A new order started in Auschwitz. We entered a big building and received wooden shoes. Here we started very heavy work. Going and coming to work we were escorted by a music band. We marched to the tune. Every direction was 10 kilometers. We chopped trees. Three women were given a tree and it had to be removed with the roots. The tools were heavy and the work was very difficult. We could not relax for a minute for the murders were standing next to us with their dogs. These dogs could tear apart a human being in a matter of minutes. I was lucky that I managed to avoid whippings but I was constantly afraid, cold and hungry. Thus, we worked 14 months at which time I was totally exhausted.

Now begins a complicated game, as the allies approached the camp we are sent further away. The Germans packed us into cattle cars and sent us to Bergen Belsen in Germany. Allied planes flew above us and bombed some cars but we escaped injury. We reached the camp and new problems started. Nothing mattered anymore. We were 300 women in a room all stretched out on the floor. The people were no longer people. Many nationalities were here:

Czechs, Belgians, Dutchman, Russians, Hungarians, and Poles. Ten women received one kilo of bread. I distributed the bread in our group. This was a trustful job since everybody was starving. I used a string to measure each portion so that it should be fair. We stayed in this place for 15 months.

There was no shortage of lice. Once a week we did not get food because we did not work. Decisions. The Germans were busy with their own situations and forgot to assign jobs. They did not forget to punish us though for their errors. Many of the inmates lost all hope and collapsed. Suddenly we were on the move again. Nobody knew where we were heading. We were driven over unmarked byways. We walked over fields and through forests. There was no rest, people fall by the wayside like flies. We were exhausted, hungry and fearful. Cold rains, strong winds worsened our condition. The Germans shot anybody that fell and did not get up at the count of three. The fast pace was beyond our ability. We started 1300 women and were now 800. We no longer feared death. At last we arrived at Selenau, deep in Germany. Here a typhoid epidemic broke loose. I was affected and managed to survive without medication. How I survived is beyond my comprehension. There was no medical help or medications. I exchanged my bread ration for some jam. For two weeks I ran a high temperature of 39-40 centigrade. How I managed to overcome the disease is a mystery. Every day, some dead bodies were carried out from the bunk. No sooner did I feel better, they rushed us to leave the camp. The Russians and the Americans were surrounding the Germans from everywhere but the latter were still preoccupied with us. We marched in the direction of Austria. Then they packed us into cattle trains and closed the doors. But the tracks were bombed and the train blocked. We sat in the train for 14 days until the tracks were fixed. The train rolled and reached Check Territory.

Then a miracle happened, a Check delegation came to the train and told the German guards that they brought food for the inmates. The Germans grabbed the best foods for them but let the inmates out of the train and lined them up. From sitting and lying, our feet were numb. We saw that the first inmates in line received a piece of white bread, a piece of salami, a piece of sugar, and a cup of soup. We began to cry from joy. Our hands trembled upon receiving the food. When my turn came, I kissed the bread and the Checks cried. They also whispered that they would have brought more but the Germans did not permit it. When I started to eat my food, I had terrible pain since my mouth was no longer accustomed to food. We constantly gulped and here we had food to chew. We will never forget the kind help of the Checks that saved that day hundreds of women by giving them some food. The same day the train rolled again. The allied armies continued their advances but we were still in German hands. The firing could be heard in the distance, bombs flew over the train but we continued to roll. Already three days we are squeezed together without food. I reminded myself that I saved a drop of salt in my bag, a luxury at the time. I licked the salt and took another lick and another lick. I said to myself stop it, save some for the next day and started to put it away. My neighbors saw that I had something and told me that nobody would survive another day. Better to distribute the item now while we can still enjoy it. I distributed the salt to everybody. Needless to say, I became thirsty and the thirst increased by the hour. Luck had it that it rained. Everybody tried to catch a few raindrops through the pores of the car in order to quench the thirst. The train dragged forever and finally we reached the death camp of Malthausen in Austria.

We were skin and bone, skeletons, nothing resembling human beings. We did not have the energy to talk. They led us to the showers. We knew that this was the end. But we had luck, the crematoria was full with Russian prisoners of war and other transports that were ahead of us. So they took us to a big warehouse where we awaited our turn. Here we met other women from various other nationalities also waiting their turn. We received pieces of bread that tasted like sawdust. We swelled up from the bread, the soup and the grass. Even this food is too good for you since tomorrow is your last day said an SS woman. So indoctrinated were the Germans that to the last minute they saw the Jew as their eternal enemy. But when the allies surrounded the camp, they disappeared like rats.

One beautiful morning at 6 AM, we suddenly noticed that the German guards disappeared. Nobody watched us, unbelievable. Slowly we hedged to the entrance gate and noticed that the guards were gone. We did not believe our eyes and began to run back and forth for joy. Next to us were the inmates that were not able to move, mere skeletons, dying people, a horrible picture. Those that had some mobility moved forward and saw in the distance a white flag. Now we must strengthen ourselves and perhaps take revenge I thought to myself. Then Russian and American soldiers appeared. It was the 6th of May 1945. They immediately gave us assistance such as food, medications, and vitamins. They disinfected us but for many of the inmates it was already too late. No medicine or doctor could have saved them. Even the transition from evil to good required some strength that some inmates no longer possessed. The fact that I survived, I considered a miracle.

Slowly, I regained my strength and decided to move to Italy in order to reach Palestine. Nothing was left for me in Poland where my family perished. Everything was destroyed except for Polish anti-Semitism. I am already here two years and we still have not returned to normalcy. We are still looking for a better tomorrow. We live here in a camp, which is not normal, but we are free. The Italian people are very sympathetic and friendly. It is a year since I married Mr. Krawtchik. He is also survivor, he stems originally from Lodz, Poland. We have no income since we can't work in Italy in spite of the fact that my husband has a good trade.

We greet you and send you our warm regards.

Signed, Bashe Krawtchik, Schiff

[Page 169-180]

Memories of Destroyed Korczyn
By: Yaacov Itzhak Fessel, Stockholm, Sweden

In memory of my father and teacher, Berish-Dov, my mother Alte Hanna Tzirel, my sisters Sarah, and Feige Rachel, my brother Gudel Asher, grandfathers Shimon Wolf-Zeev, and Eliezer Lipa, grandmothers Ethel and Leah. In memory to the inhabitants of Korczyn that were murdered by the German murderers. May God avenge their death. For them I weep and my eyes shed tears, Job section A, line 17.

Yaacov Itzhak Fessel

It is with a great deal of respect and reverence as well as pain that I write these few lines about Korczyn in the past and present.

Our lovely little town in Western Galicia was known as a Hassidic township. It was destroyed in a brutal manner in August of 1942 by the German murderers and their Ukrainian assistants. Through this yizkor book we pay homage and reminisce of the people and their saintly souls that were murdered as Jews. 25 years passed since the community of Korczyn ceased to exist, still before us are the personalities of yesterday. They are full of life and devoted to their tasks. We feel that they are with us, they speak and warn us not to forget. Remember what Amalek did to you is written in the Torah. And we are supposed to obey the commandments that were so dear to them. The Jewish towns and townships in eastern and western Galicia were full of beauty, morality, social awareness, religious tradition, and Hassidic in their following. Each community had its talmudic scholars, intelligentsia, leaders, rabbis with or without Hassidim, charity institutions, philanthropic associations, educational assistance groups, teacher institutes, medical facilities, religious institutions, community workers, study groups of holy texts and psalm reading groups etc. A chain of generations continued the traditions from generation to generation and forged the chain. Such communities were numbered in the thousands and Korczyn was one of them. The Germans wiped them out and erased their traces. Slowly, the personalities of Korczyn emerged from memory and passed in review, tending to their activities.

Eliyahu Rubin, the Korczyner rabbi and his sons walked to shul to conduct the mussaf or second half of the Rosh Hashana service. They prayed with such fervor that the entire community felt part of their prayers and hoped that the prayers reached their destination. My Talmud teacher and cantor, Zalkele with his white beard approached the stand and uttered loudly the word King from the High Holiday service. The entire congregation felt the vibrations.

In the aisle, we saw Simha Diller, the shamash of the temple. He provided all the candles for lighting the shul. On Saturday he never spoke but the holy tongue. Next in the aisles we saw the figures of my two teachers, Mordechai Rossdeitcher and the gemarrah teacher Motel Push, both teachers stressed the importance of good deeds, sincerity in praying and continuation of torah studying. Next we saw the two ritual slaughters of Korczyn; Yaacov Pinhas Schiff and Moshe Leichtog who made great efforts to provide the Jewish community with kosher meat.

There was no luck of social and religious institutions in our town. Some are listed; helping the sick, the Talmud torah association, and the mutual cooperative fund. The association to help marry poor girls, the burial society, the transportation committee, the shas study group, the mishnayot group, the psalm group, and the book purchasing group. There were also Zionist groups and institutions that worked for Palestine and other institutions. I must add the name of my teacher Dworah Engelhardt that taught me mathematics and spelling. How can we forget the great benefactors of Korczyn; Yossele Reich, Yossef Weber, Arie Dym, Avraham Raab, Haim Halpern, Hersh Elimelech Reck, Yehezkel Horowitz and Haim Wolf Koref. They were all killed without leaving a survivor. The only active person to survive was Itzhak Englard-Wasserstrum, the leader of the community. He lives in New York.

Facing me were my friends; Avraham Push, Dawid Kirzner, the children of Moshe Epstein, Moshe Kalb, Betzalel Yaacov Reck, Dawid Leib Leiner, Wolf Schiff and his sister, Avraham Zilberberg, Shmuel Aron Dan the son of Yaacov Dan, the daughters of Moshe Leichtog, the daughter of Moshe Roseman. The grandchildren of the Den family, Henie Pineles, the daughter of our neighbor Zissel Pese, Ita the daughter of our neighbor Moshe Ber, the children of Yeshayahu Margoles and dozens of boys and girls that I knew but don't remember their names. The Germans killed them all. The women were also active in the community social life and assisted their brothers and sisters in need. Amongst them; Beile Hendel Margoles, Roisele Dym, Dinale Kaufman, Sartsche Raab, Mindel Rothenberg, Lea Wilner, Lea Rachel Weinstein. Bashe Welke Reich, Hayale Schroit, our neighbor Tile Pasternak Braindel Rossdeitcher and many others that gave of themselves to assist a woman in delivery or help a sick person so that the family would rest a bit. We were all apprehensive about the catastrophic feeling that engulfed the Jews of Europe in general and especially us in Korczyn. Early in 1942, the Krosner Gestapo arrived and shot Moshe Epstein, Naphtali Pinzel, Yehudit Holloshits, Yossef Malz, Mrs. Korb, Moshe Willner's son and son-in-law and others. Their blood was spilled while we still entertained hopes that the merciful God will have pity on his people and will not permit the destruction of European Jewry including the one of Korczyn. The religious judicial representative, the dayan Moshe Epstein, survived the killing with a bullet in his body and managed to reach the house of Yantsche Infeld. But he was forced to surrender to the murderers for fear that they would kill other Jews.

Following the terrible tragedy that affected us all. Entire families, fathers and mothers, brothers and sisters, wives and husbands, grandfathers and grandmothers, aunts and uncles, cousins and small children were murdered so cruelly within a few days in the middle of the month of August of 1942.

The German murderers carried out the destruction, may their name be obliterated. We remained so to speak orphans without a father said the prophet Job. The pain and the suffering are horrendous. We can not forget the terrible Tisha B'av, ninth day in the month of Av, the day of the destruction of the Temple of our period. We saw the trucks filled with people heading to their doom. We worked at various jobs during these hot summer days of 1942 in Krosno. We then followed the road that the Korczyner Jews took to the railway station in Krosno and saw the bloodstains of our brothers and sisters along the road. At the railway station we too passed a selection and confessed to our creator since we felt that we can not separate from our families and must share their fate.

From the Krosno railway station we were led like orphans to the study center of Krosno. Nobody slept that night, we all cried and wept over the destruction of our community. The next morning, they escorted us into the ghetto that consisted of a few houses packed with people that received labor papers that extended their lives. From the study center, the Gestapo took adults and children that lacked labor papers and led them to the railway station where they joined the Jews from Korczyn and the surrounding areas.

My cousin, the daughter of Rachel Freifeld was amongst them. Here they all waited to be pushed into the railroad cars by the German murderers. The transport headed to the death camp of Belzec where they all perished. In the ghetto of Krosno there were a number of Jews from Korczyn that worked at various places, some were killed like the son in law of Haim Halpern and others. Children and those lacking labor papers were sent to their death. When we left the ghetto of Krosno around Chanukah, some people left the night before to hide in order to save themselves. The Germans searched the attics and shot everybody they found. Amongst those killed was I belief the rabbi of Krosno, Shmuel Fuhrer. They took us to the ghetto of Rzeszow or Reishe. We arrived on a frosty winter evening. The Jews of Korczyn and Krosno huddled together, and talked about the destruction that they witnessed. Soon, the Germans seized both sisters of Shmuel Aron Rubin who survived and lives in Israel, and Malia, the sister of the Malz brothers, now in Israel. They disappeared from the ghetto. The ghetto consisted of two sections, the west and the east. Both parts contained Jews from Korczyn. I met here Shmayahu Ber, Mendel the son in law of Mordechai Rossdeitcher, Matityahu Infeld, and Leibish Infeld. I think that I also met Shimon Ferber and his son Dawid. I saw Avraham Silberberg and his mother and father, the latter managed to take his family from the train station to the ghetto in Krosno. I also saw the shohet Moshe Leichtog who was the only slaughterer in the Reishe ghetto, Nissan Gutwein, Shmuel Rubin Avraham Frei and other Korczyner Jews whose names I do not recall. A dysentery epidemic started in the Reishe ghetto that caused the death of the rabbi of Krosno, Moshe Twersky, Leibish Infeld and possibly Shimon Ferber. They took me, Shmuel Rubin, Avraham Frei and others to the labor camp of Bierzatka where we worked at forestry, other Korczyner Jews still remained in the ghetto of Reishe. From the labor camp of Bierzatka we were led to the labor camp in Mielec. Here we worked in a plane factory. Shmuel Rubin and others were sent to another camp. Sometimes later, I was sent from the camp of Mielec to another camp in the area of Lublin. Avraham Frei remained in the camp of Mielec. I do not recall the names of the other Korczyner Jews in the camp of Mielec or Bierzatka. At the Plaszow death camp I met my relatives and the brothers Benyamin and Yossef Gutwein. I do not know where they were later sent. A Jew from Korczyn told me that my cousins Yaacov and Aron Rothenberg, Mendel Teller, Yossef Reich and others were shot or died of exhaustion. After I left the labor camp of Mielec I never met Jews from Korczyn until I was liberated in Bergen Belsen on April 15, 1945. Then I met Yacov Eisen who lives in Israel and his brother Shabtai who died a few days after his liberation by the British Army. On examining the great tragedy that struck our family, our people, we are stunned. Such dear and pious Jews that devoted their life to worship and charitable deeds should be so severely punished. The children who were so innocent should be murdered so cruelly by the German murderers during WWII, 1939-1945. Very difficult to perceive such deeds in a rational manner. Of course we can ask the question whether they deserved the fate but there is no answer. No other period in Jewish history witnessed the destruction of a third of the Jewish people in a short period of time. Was our generation so sinful that it merited such deadly penalty and if so, certainly the Messiah should have arrived for it is said in the Talmud that the Messiah will come when the generation is all evil or all good. I do not know whether there are many rationalizations that could provide a solid answer to the question.

The heart feels the deep pain of the great destruction that affected the Jews and especially our community of Korczyn. I do not think that any rationalizations will erase the tragedy in our hearts. Today, Korczyn is clean of Jews, the Poles live in their homes and run their business. The Sabbath of Korczyn is no longer a holy day, it is a simple workday. The study center was converted to a store. No more sounds of torah study or prayers. The Jews of Korczyn are no longer, they all perished because they were Jews. Their memory is still part of us. The once lovely little township of Korczyn has the appearance of an orphan, the houses yellowed with time, the grass grew in the streets, nature sheds tears for the hamlet. There is still a memorial in Korczyn to the Jewish community, the cemetery that remained untouched throughout time. Thanks to the efforts of Haim Wolf Koref who built a wall around the cemetery that preserved it from incursions. The Jews that the Gestapo shot were buried in a mass grave in the valley covered with grass. The grave is not marked. At the cemetery, is located the grave of Wolf Kirschner and his son Dawid who were caught after the Jewish liquidation and begged the Germans to shoot them. Of course the Germans obliged and shot them and they fell into their prepared grave. Relatives erected a tombstone after the war for them. There is also a tombstone for the Eichorn family erected by Zishe Eichorn who lives in Israel. Many tombstones stand erect while others lean to the ground. When I visited Korczyn in 1963, I recited the kaddish at the mass grave and at the cemetery for my relatives and the saints of Korczyn I also recited a prayer for those that their burial places are not known. Some of them are in the Jasienica forest while others are at the death camp of Belzec. My prayers were for the Jews of Korczyn and the surrounding areas that were murdered by the Germans in August of 1942 as well as for those that died in the ghettos and camps throughout Europe. Let the Yizkor book of Korczyn serve as a memorial to the Jews of Korczyn. Let the book be a remainder to the generations to come that there was a Jewish community of Korczyn. When a tombstone is written or chiseled, the Hebrew words, our crown has fallen is inscribed at the head of the tombstone. Let us remember these words for our yizkor book that is in memory for those that were killed by the German murderers, may their name be erased. May the Almighty avenge the innocent blood of the Jews of Korczyn and all the other Jews that were killed by the German hands. Furthermore I say to the Germans, may you be paid for the deeds that you performed against the Jewish people. We must remember the saints of Korczyn and may they rest their eternal slumber in the heavens. We must remember the spirit of Korczyn. It lives on through our daily deeds of living and reminiscing of Korczyn. Through the celebration of Jewish holidays and reading books. By contributing to a better tomorrow and supporting spiritually your children. By participating in the renewal of Jewish life in Israel and in guarding the great Korczyn tradition, the traditions of the Jewish people.

In memory to my family and relatives I suffer immensely when I have to write a tombstone of words for my family that perished because they were Jews. A family that stems from Eliezer Lipa. The father of the holy men of Elimelech from Lejansk and Zishe from Anipol. I remember my father, Berish, Dov, Fessel, the man of devotion and piety, his concentration in prayers and study, his simplicity and charitable nature. I remember when he used to get an alyah in the shul and stand before the torah, he felt as though the holy text was directed at him. Both my parents died as Jewish martyrs. My mother, Alte Hannah Tzirel, his companion for life, dedicated herself to charity, to assist the helpless with words or deeds. Both parents devoted themselves to the education of their children and to raise them in the Jewish spirit. My mother was a saint with a good heart.

My two younger sisters; Sarah and Feiga Rachel attended a religious girl school where they studied Jewish laws of the home. My young brother, Gedalia Asher went to heder and knew the prayers by heart. All these innocent children were murdered by Germans. My grandfather Shimon Wolf Rothenberg read the torah in the study center of Korczyn. He also used to conduct the services. My other grandfather, Eliezar Lipa Fessel that always saw to it that there was always a minian of Jews for services in the village where he was the torah reader and the cantor. The grandmothers, Etel Rothenberg and Lea Fessel, both good souls that helped secretly in order not to attract attention and not to embarrass the needy, May they be inscribed in the saintly book. I must not omit my aunts and uncles, cousins, close and distant relatives, neighbors and Jews of Korczyn that I knew so well; Hersh Haim Rothenberg and his family, Hersh Fessel and his family, Berish and Rachel Fessel from Antwerp and Eliyahu Fessel and his wife. Moshe Fessel shot in Yedlice, Tzirel Fessel, Hannah Fessel, Haitsche Fessel, Naphtali Fessel, Rachel Freifeld and her daughter. Yudel or Yehuda Gutwein and his family and Yantsche Infeld and family. The entire Gutwein family and the brothers Den with their family. One of the brothers thought me during the war the laws pertaining to phylacteries, Yaacov Den and his family, Nachum Schpitz that thought me Yidishkeit during the war. Finally my teachers, my friends and neighbors whose names I no longer remember. Their names should be entered in the Yizkor book so that they remain with us forever. They were all Jews that cared for other Jews and continued the Jewish tradition of Yiddishkeit. Their murder ended the long chain of Jewish life in Korczyn.

Their souls were extinguished through their murder. May God avenge the spilled blood.

[Page 181-190]

What I saw in Maidanek
By Michael Horowitz, Petach Tikvah, Israel

During 1966-1967 these lines were readied for print, gallons of ink have already been used to describe the destruction of European Jewry. What can I as a later comer to the scene add that is not already known. I can contribute to the memory of the community of Korczyn by describing the murder places that the murderers of the 20th century left behind. With their civilized manners and German ingenuity, they ensnared their victims to the threshold of the gas chambers where millions of people were asphyxiated. Many of the victims hoped for a last minute miracle that did not materialize. The German plan succeeded only too well, the Jews were led like sheep to the slaughter. If only the Jews had been pre-warned, many of them would have challenged the Germans and died fighting, killing the enemy as they were being killed. Some victims did challenge the masters but few in numbers. Most of the victims lacked the physical forces. They were already exhausted physically, spiritually and mentally. To some of them death represented deliverance.

In 1946, on my way home from Siberia where I spent the war years, I came face to face with the great tragedy. No science fiction writer could have written such a script. I met some survivors and traveled with them to Lublin and then to Maidanek, which is about six kilometers from the city. We went on foot to see the death factories where millions of people perished by German methods. The dispersed tombs, in fields and forests, represent thousands of people without a name or address. But in Maidanek there was no problem of finding someone, for all the Jews contributed to the sacrificial alter. At Maidanek, the Jew can shed tears for his entire community.

In terms of human conception, the entire generation that lived during the period regardless of nationality can be sad over the fact that such beasts grew in a part of the globe. These beasts can not even be compared to the wildest beasts in nature. But we suffered the most and did not even have the satisfaction of fighting back and who ever heard of killing women, old people and children. We boast about the progress of civilization that produced such monsters. Perhaps it would be better to reject all the scientific advances and return to the primitive state of nature. A nation of art and letters without a conscience should not exist. They should not be permitted to exist as Germans in the family of nations. If for some reason Germans have to mingle with other nations, they must erase their German name that is adorned with the sign of murder. That should be the verdict of the world and the guilt feeling of the Germans. The latter besmirched their nation forever.

The road to Maidanek was built with Jewish tears and sweat. The road is soaked with Jewish blood. Red bricks were used along the road that gave it a fine aesthetic appearance. Three years the road was built and those who fell by the wayside were killed by a bullet or other means. Those that survived neared the gas chambers each day until they entered them. But the road to the gas chambers was beautiful and it was used by thousands of victims in their final destination. The Germans saw to it that both sides of the road should have greenery trimmed to an even height. Everything was done with precision and order. Only when the victims reached the gas chambers did they understand the meaning of German precision. No slow minded person could have devised such devilish plan, only bright people could have devised and fulfilled the plan. The victims believed to the last moment that this was not their final moment. It took an evil genius to devise such a master plan of destruction.

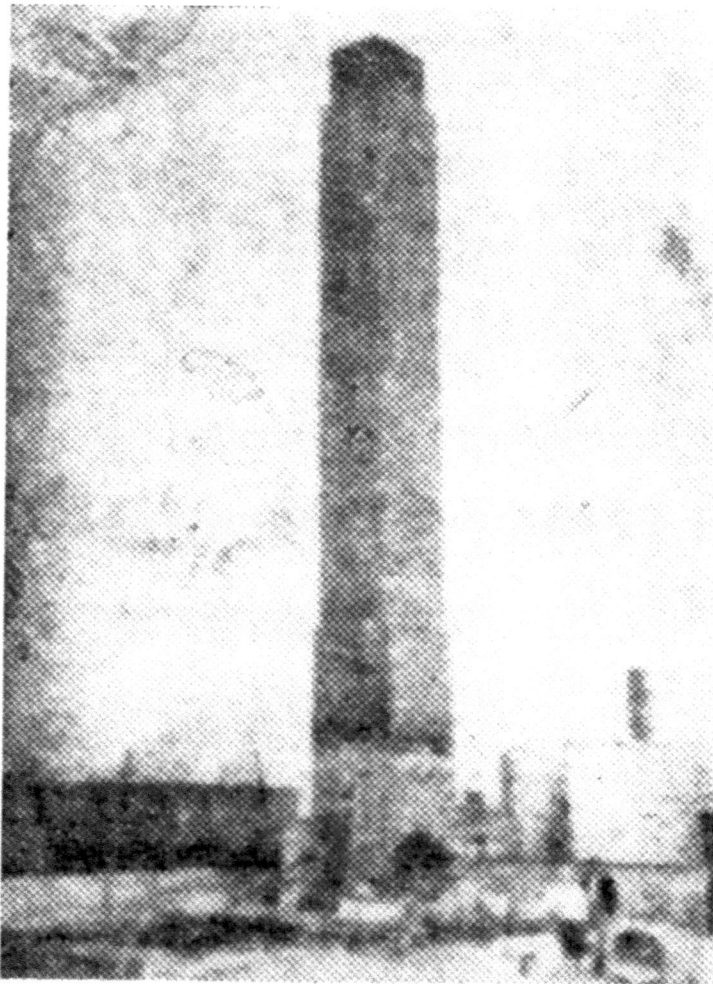

Picture. The chimney of the gas chamber in Maidanek

Maidanek consisted of showers and gas chambers that were connected. The death camp also contained about two hundred barracks arranged in symmetrical lines. The place resembled a spa center; everything was immaculate. Greenery everywhere, garden paths leading in all directions, all the hedges trimmed even. Only the chimneys of the gas chambers gave a fearful appearance to the place. To most victims it appeared as a transit camp for further travel to other labor camps. But the picture was totally different. Maidanek was a death camp. The transport of victims arrived before the showers and the people were asked to undress and to fold their clothing neatly in small piles. Those that balked at the order were forced to obey or were shot as warning to the others. The shower room was immense and accommodated several hundred people. When the room was full, the doors were closed and the water faucets were opened that sprinkled the people. Humidity was essential to the next step. Then, the bathers were driven to the gas chambers. The doors were sealed and cyclone gas entered the chamber through the water taps. Asphyxiation started immediately, the victims held on to their immediate neighbors and died in each other's arms. It took 18 minutes to asphyxiate the people. A German who stood outside the door that contained a small eyelet observed the entire process.

The asphyxiation finished, the rear door opened, and the bodies were removed. Slave workers performed the work. They untangled bodies that were entwined and frequently sprayed them with cold water to assist the separation. Bodies that were marked with red paint were placed in a special place. The others were transported directly to the crematoria and their ashes were buried. People received red paint on their back when the watchmen noticed that they swallowed valuable items on entering the showers. Following the gas chambers, the marked bodies were dissected in search for valuables. In one barrack, we saw a big concrete table and next to it a pile of human parts - hands, feet and heads. A Polish engineer explained the process of searching for gold, diamonds and valuables. The long table was the workbench for this gruesome work. Needless to add that the pile of human parts was left untouched by the Germans in their haste to escape from the allied armies. The human monument remained as was left by the Germans. The Polish engineer presented the following information as well as the previous information to us. To see the human monument was the most depressing sight and we were transported to the realm of unbelievable savagery. Of course, the human monument could not be kept forever on display since the human parts started to rot. The parts were buried in a mass grave where they found eternal rest. Gypsies, Poles, Russians and Jews were buried together so decided the Germans. Then there were no genocide laws, each country decided the fate of the conquered country as it pleased. No one cared what the rest of the world had to say. The Germans still defend themselves to today with the statement that they carried out higher orders. The religious order not to kill was unknown to them. Had the hungry Jews reacted to the same higher order, the Germans would have killed them much faster.

In a big hall, there is a display of 65,000 pair of shoes from children and adults. Men and women shoes, torn heel and sole in search of valuables. The children shoes evoked my sympathy. The shoes indicated the social status of the family. The mothers provided the children with the best shoes that they could afford. After all, the shoes represented the first steps of the child into the world. How many hopes and dreams the mothers dreamt for their children in the purchase of these shoes. The German saw a financial opportunity even here in the shoes. Another place contained toys of children. Balls, carriages, small and big dolls that the children played with until they were driven to the gas chambers where they existence was terminated. A mountain of glasses worn by all ages. Everything was sorted with German punctuality and in a civilized manner everything was recorded. There was no room for chaos or anarchy. Everything was recorded and alone condemned Germany for generations to come. Many of the records were destroyed but enough were left intact. Of course the Germans would have preferred that these documents vanish. So trials were staged and some condemnations handed down which made a mockery of justice. Killers of thousands received 5, 10, or 15 years jail sentence where conditions were livable. Nobody died during incarceration or suffered mistreatment at the hands of the jailers.

In a display cabinet, we saw passports and pictures of the victims from all of Europe. My ears and eyes heard and saw people fainted on recognizing members of their families in the pictures. The screams and shouts were heartbreaking, the pulling of hairs and hopelessness was beyond description. There was also a large bin that contained thousands of suits, Hassidic overcoats, coats or halats, velvet hats, velvet kippot and military uniforms of various European nations. There were also various camp uniforms with the star of David on the back, clothing that belonged to disabled people since they missed limbs and various Gypsy outfits that perished with the Jews. Perhaps the Germans intended to create an exotic museum to display these items and the people that wore them. The Germans were excellent researchers and would develop all kinds of theories about the development of the exposed items as well as the people that wore them. It would have never downed on the Germans that these people were superior to them in spirit. Fortunately, the Germans lost the war and we ceased to speculate about their intentions All the victims to Maidanek were ensnared with the slogan of resettlement in the East. All transport victims were always instructed to take with them the necessary personal items for the trip. Most of the victims took this as a sign of hope, otherwise, why bring toys. Some realized the situation towards the end but it was too late. Others continued to believe the Germans. They saw the showers as a hygienic necessity until a German grabbed a child and smashed the skull against a wall. Prior to the action, the German officer put on white gloves that were then cleaned with the uniform from the blood of the child. Of course Jewish slaves did the cleaning. But everything was done in a so-called civilized manner.

In the shower room we saw letters, postal cards, scraps of paper written in Yiddish, Polish and other languages. Most of them said goodbye to the survivors and some even mentioned items that they smuggled with them to the camp. One letter, addressed to the neighbor Raisel read: dear neighbor

Raisel, before we left the place, we gave all our jewelry and candelabras to the janitor Wroblewski so that he should give it to the gentiles that hid my son Mendele. Perhaps he will be the only survivor of our vast family. If you survive please tell everybody what happened so that the world would know. Stay happy if this is at all possible, your old and trusted friend Lea. There were other scraps that I had no time to read. It was difficult to believe that a third of the Jewish people were killed. We walked about Maidanek, cried and shed tears for our relatives that perished here. We felt the end of the world. We saw in every speck of dust the ashes of the victims and their holy souls that died with the words of Shema Israel, O hear Israel on their lips.

Yossef Weber
by Itzhak Englard Wasserschtrom

Yossef Weber was the son of Aron, nicknamed the Brezower, and Dinah Weber. Yossef Weber was a grandson of the Berezower rabbi, he was born and resided in the village of Berezow until the liquidation. In his youth he devoted himself to the study of the torah. He was raised in the hassidic spirit and dressed accordingly and managed his life in the Hassidic tradition. He was my second best friend. He was a lovely person and a fine soul. He never insulted a person and tried to avoid hurting people. He was always ready to help people and was liked by everybody. He personified Torah knowledge and respect for the individual. He was well read in religious matters and also had a fine general background . He had the artistic ability to describe types of people, scenes, pictures of daily life and the ability to write fine short stories.

The Warsaw Yiddish newspaper, Haint or Today, published a weekly humor edition called Der WeltSchpiegel or The World Mirror. This issue publicized a contest under the topic of shtetl life. The best story was guaranteed to be published and to receive a monetary prize. Many famous writers entered the contest. Yossef Weber received the second prize of 50 zloty for his story entitled The Auction. The story was published in the newspaper of Der Weltschpiegel, in 1929, issue number 45. He also published another short story in this paper entitled The Fisherman that was printed in 1930, number of issue 16. Both stories appeared in the collection of the Weltschpiegel stories and are on display at the YIVO Institute in New York. 25 years have passed and I still see my dear and unforgettable friend, Yossef Weber. The cursed Germans have killed this young literary talent in 1942

[Page 191-195]

Weltschpiegel No.45-1929 Our Literary Contest
Yossef Weber The Auction Entry No 31

[Translator. Most Jewish European communities baked matzoth for the local Jewish community. This involved the kehilla in the purchase of wheat or flour and in the sale of matzot. This was a large financial outlay for the kehilla. For provision had to be made to provide the poor people with matzoth for Pessah. Many of them could not afford matzoth. The price had to be set so that the well-to-do would help cover the cost of the production of matzoth. The kehilla covered the remainder of the bill. Thus the importance of the auction. The cheaper the price, the less the kehilla would have to outlay.]

The hamlet awaited with impatience but kindness the first bird that announced better or brighter days. The long winter was already on its way out. The smoked filled room blackened with fumes, the walls and ceiling torn, spiderwebs everywhere, water mixed with dust streams from the walls, the floor was covered with a thick coat of wet mud where planks disappeared. The small windows sealed with earth after the holiday of Succoth accumulated moisture and turned to a green slime. Through these windows the mud-covered rays of the outside tried to enter the house. The mist and the melting snow added a depressive feeling. The old worn clothes itched and scrapped the body. The hay of the mattresses was already rotten and spilled from the beds. The air in the room is stifling. Filth surrounded us. And the youth like all youth. How could we escape a bit from the room. But here was the holiday of Pessah knocking at the door.

The first day of the month of Adar, between the minha and maariv service, the shamash of the shul banged his bony hand on the table and announced in the name of the community that after the services there will be an auction for the Pessah flour. The announcement evoked a great deal of joy from the membership, a sort of holiday feeling swept through the air and warmed the entire shul. Happiness was written on all the faces. The hope for spring, flowers, grass and promenades was on everybody's mind. People started talking. It took a while until the congregation finished the maariv service and quieted down for business. The various shul activities like the mashnayot study group suspended the study program for the evening. Their tables emptied and orphaned this evening. The lamps in the area gleamed a bit weaker than other days. Here sat people in winter evenings, studied and frequently day dreamt. Young boys would spent entire evenings studying the talmud and often think of their future. Suddenly, the area was deserted.

The services finished, clusters of congregates formed to discuss the matter on hand, next to the door and near the stove stood the flour and wheat merchants. They discussed all kinds of possibilities and deals in order to form a cartel that would set the price and bid as a unit. All efforts to form a cartel failed and the merchants rushed home to bring money for the deposit that would be needed if they won the auction. Over there stood the jokers of the crowd and made fun of the way the business session was conducted. Meanwhile the shamash was very busy carrying messages back and forth and the merchants were very moody. Next to us stood a group of cheder boys and listed all the items that their parents would purchase for them for the Pessah holiday: new suits, shoes and hats. Their mouths salivated when they described the taste of the matzot and potato latkes. Profusion of words and noises and above us swept the smoke of cigarettes and pipes.

Suddenly, a loud noise was heard, the shamash banged the wooden hammer on a table and stood up on a bench in the corner of the eastern wall and towered above the congregation. His glazed eyes looked toward the ceiling and his head tilted to a side that gave him a saintly look. The yellow goat beard completed the picture. He announced that the auction has begun. The anticipation of the meeting grew by the minute. Haim, the biggest wheat merchant, moved to the big table covered with a green tablecloth. The movement was slow since there were many people and movement was difficult. The people were jealous as well as respectful of the position of Haim. On top of the table stood two candelabras with burning candles. At the head of the table sat the rabbi and next to him the head of the kehilla. A pen, paper, ink, and the seal of the kehilla were placed on the table. Along side of it sat the members of the kehilla board, their faces stern and serious. Haim reached the table and counted his deposit money. Meanwhile two other groups were formed and they sent their representatives to the table. The rabbi then spoke at length about the laws of kashruth, the laws pertaining to kosher wheat, the mashgichim or religious supervisors and the sacks containing the flour. The speech was followed by the leader of the kehilla who discussed the financial aspect of the purchase of the flour, the financial situation of the kehilla and so on.

Haim the wheat merchant looked askance at all the other merchants and chewed one wheat kernel after the other. He paced back and forth and seemed to talk to himself in an angry tone that the heavy gray black moustache prevented from hearing. His eyes half closed and his forehead deep in thought he seemed determined to move ahead. Indeed, he took several steps to the table and announced in his loud and husky voice ninety-four groshen or pennies. The audience began to murmur, the faces of the leaders indicated discomfort. Haim noticed the situation and stated that he could not do it cheaper. The leader of the community signaled to the shamash to start the auction. The latter immediately began in his melodious tone, ninety-four groshen for the first time and ninety-four groshen for the next time and. . . suddenly the audience protested vociferously, screams and shouts, a robbery, murder, so expensive, stop the auction, don't sell to the thief. He will make a fortune. Let the kehilla buy flour. We will bring flour from distant places. This community belongs in Chelm screamed a troublemaker. All other interested merchants added fuel to the incitement of the audience. No one should deal with this dishonest merchant, in all likelihood we will never get fine flour.

Haim was mad and stormed out of the shul, bunch of beggars, I will show you, he said to himself.

The hammer banged again, the congregational outbursts stopped, silence in the shul. The shamash voice intoned again, ninety groshen for the first time and the next time and. . . A stern look from the leader of the kehilla stopped the shamash in mid air. The latter read the message and pointed to his nose as if to say, I understood and his hand signaled that the bid would fail. The shamash started again the bid, ninety groshen for the first time and ninety groshen for the next time and to your health he added. The latter remark appealed to the religious people and the atmosphere of the shul calmed down. The audience loosened up and jokes and wisecracks started to make the rounds. The tension disappeared and joviality returned to the shul. Shlome, a happy Jew with a red nose and a potbelly rubbed his hands and slapped his nearby neighbors saying that happy days were here again. The Shamash's voice thundered again, eighty-five groshen for the first time and eighty five groshen for the next time and eighty five groshen for the first time. The audience that protested earlier so vociferously did it not out of stinginess but it did not want to be made a fool. The people knew that Haim was going to make money but they wanted it to be fair.

Haim was full of anger, a plague on you he said to himself, even if I have to add to the deal, I will add but the deal will be mine. He ran to the table and shouted eighty-three. The kehilla leader winked to the shamash to end the auction. The latter started, eighty-three groshen for the first time, eighty three groshen for the next time and eighty three groshen for the third time. Congratulations reb Haim.

[Page 196-202]

Weltschpiegel No.16-1930 Short story: The Fish Merchant by Yossef Weber

Yona was still a young man of about 35 but looked like 50. His red beard was drawn out, his peyot or sidecurls were balding and his hat was drawn over his eyes. His coat used to be brown before he was married. The coat was now torn from all sides and gaping holes exposed the body. He also wore a pair of worn boots and had a small pipe in his mouth. Neche was his wife. A small scrawny woman in spite of the fact that she wore a half a dozen dresses and kerchiefs that gave her the present appearance. She was an active woman, a real woman of valor. Her voice was somewhat masculine with a strong stress on the letter r. When she screamed or shouted, it sounded like a volcano. Yona was petrified of the voice as one is of a bomb. They had five children. The oldest was Henech, he was about eleven years old. He was shortsighted, always wore a big red scarf on his neck and wore an oversized pair of woman's shoes that he seemed to lose with each step.

The family had an income; of course there was always room for improvement. Yona had several jobs; he arose with dawn, prayed, took a slice of bread and placed in his pocket. He took a bag placed it under the arm, a shopping bag in his hand and set out for the village. There he bought whatever he saw fit: a rabbit, small furs, merchandise, an egg and sometimes even a chicken. He had a sad experience with chickens. He once purchased a chicken but it turned out to be a duck. His wife never let him forget the incident and nicknamed him the kwoke or duck. Yona felt badly about the incident and til today has regrets about the whole incident. Also Neche worked hard, she milked the cows and together with Henech sold milk to their customers and the remainder of the milk she converted to cheese and butter. These were all side jobs of the family. Yona's main business was the fish business for Shabbath. This should be recorded for future generations that Yona provided the Jews with fish for Shabbath.

Thursday, Yona assembled sweets and wrapped them in a clothe that he then slid down his boot. He took two big baskets and headed to the gentile Walente that controlled the river and the estate. The latter was a small person with a gray moustache. For years he sold Yona fish in spite of the many attempts to undermine the relationship. Walente has always been loyal and refused to be drawn into financial intrigues. He liked the Jew Yona, as a matter of fact, he sold fish to Yona's father. Yona was very important to Walente and in appreciation gave him some apples or dried prunes for Yona's children. Yona in turn let Walente smoke his pipe while they sat on the porch and talked about the hamlet and the economic situation. Yona was not a talker but out of necessity for his fish business sat and listened. Finally, Walente took his net and other items and headed to the river. Here he proved his skills. Hi filled the baskets with fish in a manner of minutes. Little fish, big fish and real big fish that he immediately assigned. This one will be for the rabbi, the other one for the kehilla leader and that over there for Itzhak. The baskets loaded, he said goodbye to Walente and rushed back home.

At home he started to work. One basket of fish went under the bed. He claimed that an abundance of fish lowered the price. Too many fish and I would have to give them away said Yona. This one basket would fetch enough money for both baskets and Yona was an experienced fish salesman. Yona picked up the basket with the fish and headed to the market. Neche followed him with two pails of fresh water and Henech rolled a box that would be a stand. Yona dunked the fish in the fresh water and displayed some of his merchandise on top of the box and the rest remained in the pails.. He selected the nicest fish for the rabbi and handed it to Neche to give it to rabbi Moshe. He also told Henech to take the next fish and bring it to rabbi Yekele. What, exclaimed Neche, the rabbi's wife is too sick to come and get her own fish, besides, she hasn't paid for last week's fish. Listen to what I tell you Henech. No screamed Neche, I will scratch your eyes if you dare to give them fish. Yona was speechless, pathetic, a beaten man. Neche continued to roar, wake up Yona and don't let them steal you blind. She grabbed the fish and headed to the rabbi's house. Only then did Yona regain his composure. He lit his pipe, wiped his nose with his sleeve and started to sell fish.

I can now reveal to you the secret of Yona's sales techniques. Yona lived in the Old World where there was an iron rule, fish for money. But the woman forced Yona to introduce the credit system as a result he never saw money, pennies chased pennies. People borrowed and did not pay so Yona had to collect debts and chase debtors. He even made a list of debtors, as was the custom amongst merchants. He himself did not understand the economic implications of the list since he rarely collected the debts. First, he never had the time since he was always busy, and second why bother people, if they have money they will pay otherwise what is the sense of pestering people. If a woman decided to weltch an account let it be on her conscience. The most important thing was quiet. He had enough of Neche's screams and Shouts, and as long as she did not know about the debtors he was pleased. Otherwise, she headed straight to the homes and demanded payment. Lucky that Neche could not read and therefore was unable to read the list of debtors.

Yona was ready for business and he was immediately surrounded with people. Screams and shouts, people shoved and pushed and Yona was totally confused. Woman with rolled up sleeves and uncombed Jews pulled and pushed Yona in all directions. He was unable to cope with the crowd around his stand. Braindel, a heavyset woman with dentures, searched in the pail of water and took out a big fish. She pulled Yona's coat and asked how much for the fish, Yona removed the pipe from his mouth, spit to the side, scratched his forehead as if he had to make a big decision and said eighteen sixers, Yona used the old expressions. Too much said Braindele, I will give you fifteen, come over there, and she disappeared. Fessel took a smaller fish and asked Yona for the price, Yona took the fish and said two guilden. You are not very intelligent said Fessel to Yona, Braindel's fish was twice the size and she only paid fifteen. Yona was angry and grabbed the fish and threw it into the pail. This is how I want it to be, the choice is yours. Fessel did not give in, she slowly picked up her fish from the pail and took another small fish and said to Yona, how much, thirteen sixers and finished. Yona loved this term. Please put me down for the sum. Yona pulled up from his boot a piece of wrapping paper, took a pencil and wetted the point. He then inscribed the debt.

Tzippe, Moshe's daughter, a woman with large face and birthmarks, blood-shot eyes, spoke in a raspy and supplicating tone of voice and always involved God in her conversation. She had a problem, namely, she had long arms that stole items under your nose if not watched. She also delivered blows if caught in the act. In the midst of all the hustle and bustle, Tzippe also decided to bargain. She took a small fish and in a trembling voice asked Yona for the price, Yona gave it. She protested and said to Yona, I will give you only forty. Yona refused to accept. No is no said Tzippe and placed herself squarely in front of the pail with fish. She then hunched over the pail and searched for another fish. Her blood shot eyes devoured the fish and her nostrils smelled the taste of the fish. Yona she said, what gives but Yona did not answer.

Tzippe turned around and headed away with the two fish under the apron. She would have succeeded if not for the angel in the person of Berl.

Berl was nicknamed the pointer or liar in the hamlet, He was a healthy person, very tall, a red neck and a well-grown beard. He wore a green cap that matched the green moss and a coat with a crown. This was a person without financial worries. His children emigrated to all corners of the globe and sent him money. He became involved in all community affairs. He knew who ate meat, who did not give a gift to the rabbi for Hanukkah, which girls danced with boys and who was in dire need. On market days, he promenaded through the market with his long cane. He inspected the prices of onions, ducks etc. Berele entered his nose into everybody's business and knew what was cooking in every pot in the hamlet. Even if his facts were not correct, he rounded them out, embellished them and completed the missing parts. This was his nature. Thursday when Yona arrived at the market, Berele also approached the fish stand but he took his time. He observed the entire scene with Tzippe and tried to protect Yona. He stood with one hand on the cane and the other on the side and called out to Yona, where are you looking. Tzippe just walked away with two fish. What did you say reb Berl, managed Tzippe to utter in amazement, such an accusation at a Jewish woman. I saw with my own eyes said Berl. You thief, you liar, join your criminal children. You shikse, you thief.

Suddenly Neche arrived on the scene, exhausted from the errands, she caught on what was taking place and without much ado pounced on Tzippe to look under the apron. You thief, you robber; You shikse, you spender... A word to a word and the two woman were at each others throat like chickens. They soon rolled on the ground, screaming, shouting, and pulling hair. Yona tried to make peace and stop the fighting. He said that it was a shame for woman to behave in this manner. Finally he separated them. They accused Berele of doing nothing to prevent the incident. Neche screamed and cried at Yona, they stole everything from us, from our hard work, they should only choke on their food. And you stood there and let them rob us blind. She grabbed two fish and ran. Slowly the fish were sold, the crowd in front of the stand dispersed. Only two small fish remained in the pail. Yona offered them to everybody for half the price but there were no takers. Yona reviewed his debtor sheet and returned it to the boot. Meanwhile children assembled and watched the small fish frolic in the water. Yona also enjoyed the scene until the children became boisterous and misbehaved. He then splashed some water or as he called it fish soup at them and they ran. The playful activities stopped when Neche returned and splashed the water from the pails. Yona took the baskets, Neche the pails and Henech started to roll the stand. With a great deal of noise they left the market and headed home.

[Translator: We translated the stories in a loose manner. Unfortunately, the Yiddish style and cohesiveness of the stories were somewhat lost in the translation. Still we hope that the readers will understand the essence and beauty of the stories.]

[Page 203]

Yizkor book - KORCZYN - Second part

Memories, personal experiences and life experiences by Moshe Zucker and others

[Page 205-206]

Moshe Zucker, President of the Korczyner Relief Society.

Moshe was born about 70 years ago in Korczyn. His father was Yidel and his mother Reisel. In those days, the family name was not used, a man was called by his first Jewish name and a woman by her first name. My mother was called Reisel Yidels, the daughter of Yidel and my father was Moshe, the son-in-law of Yidel. Moshe became an orphan at the age of three. He was the third child in the family of four children. Moshe was very talented. Already at the age of ten he created items that were displayed in the house. He also made flags for Simhat Torah, dreidels for Hanukkah and masks for Purim. The earnings enabled him to purchase items for himself such as a Talmudic book, or a biblical storybook that his mother was unable to purchase for him. Moshe created a panel with the word shaviti for the shul in Korczyn at the age of fourteen. Those in the know claimed that it was a piece of art.

He left his mother's poor home at the age of 16. The saying that from the poor children will emerge the torah scholars definitely applied to Moshe Zucker. Had he received a formal and artistic education he would have become an important painter or writer since was talented in both areas. Today, Moshe is an artistic painter. Apart from his attendance at cheder, he never visited a school. Yet, there is a lyricism in his work, be it painting or writing. The fact that he had no formal training, meant his talent was lost. I met him for the first time in 1949 in the USA. In spite of the fact that he left Korczyn about 60 years ago, he still has a warm feeling for the place. He also wrote although not professionally. He was the one who pushed for the Yizkor book. He always spoke of the hamlet as a sentimental and nostalgic place. He considered life in Korczyn ethical and honest. The Jewish survivors did not even dream of assembling a book. It was Moshe Zucker who developed the idea and slowly convinced us all that it was feasible and he slowly started to organize the activities and found the people to head them. Thus was created the Korczyner Yizkor book. Moshe Zucker was the force behind the project.

I admit that due to him I participated in creating the book. He never left the project until it was completed.

Itzhak Englard-Wasserstrum

[Page 207]

Personalities and types of people
by Moshe Zucker

Moshe Zucker

In this section I will present pictures of some people from our town that their memories were recorded in my memory. I beg of all the readers and survivors of Korczyn not to indulge in criticism as to why I chose some and excluded other people. There was no intention to offend people. But my abilities and my memory were limited and I did the best that I remembered. I tried to present an objective picture of Korczyn as I remembered it, sixty years ago. There was no intent to minimize or hurt people. However, if somebody finds fault or disapproves of the picture that I drew or thinks that I omitted certain important personalities, then the survivors have only themselves to blame. For they stood on the side line instead of giving a hand to the Yizkor book project.

[Page 208]

Wolf Rapport

Wolf or Wele Rapport was well to do and owned an estate near Korczyn. He led a princely life. He had three daughters and a son, Fishale. Wele Rapport lived to the ripe old age of 100 years. His son, Fishale, was raised in a princely manner and even rode horses, something unheard of in religious Korczyn. The daughters were named Pessel, Frumet and Mindel. Wolf Rapport stemmed from a famous family and he greatly contributed to charity, to the various funds, he was devout and a follower of the Rymanower Hassidic rabbi. He had three son-in-laws who stemmed from distinguished families and were well versed in the study of the torah: Leibush Halpern, Shlomo Gimpel Wasserstrum and Moshe Rothenberg.

[Page 209]

Leibish Halpern

Leibish Halpern was a religious scholar and also a descendant of a rabbinical family, notably the Lemberger rabbi. In my memory, I still remember Leibish as an old man who came to the minha and maariv services. He always managed to study before and after services. We found the hair from his balding beard in the various religious texts. He never wasted time. At home, he studied the talmud and every few years he finished the complete cycle of the talmud and threw a party to celebrate the occasion. His oldest son, Hertz Halpern was also a scholar. His other sons, Yona and Yehoshua were no longer scholars but involved in the management of the business. Hertz's children were also busy working and discarded studies. His grandchildren however that managed to escape Hitler's furnace and found refuge in the USA or Israel have inherited the intellectual ability to continue the religious scholarly tradition of the family.

[Page 210]

Shlomo Gimpel Wasserstrum

Shlomo Gimpel Wasserstrum was a small man, a religious scholar and the poorest among the son-in-laws of Wolf Rapport. He rented an apartment from Mendel Schroit. His business consisted of purchasing wholesale butter that the farmers brought to the market. His brother-in-law, Leibish Halpern and his son Hertz were also involved in the same business. Shlomo Gimpel was not a rich person. He had four sons and four daughters: Shimshon, Hershel, Meir. Yossef, Bashe, Freide,Feige and Hinde. He has many grandchildren and great grandchildren that survived the war and are in the USA. All his children were married except for Yossef who was a few years older than I was. He was always dressed immaculate with a pressed collar and a tie. He spoke fluent Polish and had the head of an attorney. People were not impressed by his Polish but by his being the son of Shlomo Gimpel. He had a fine home. Shlomo Gimpel was a reserved person by nature, never attracted attention but was very knowledgeable in Jewish religious scholarship and when there was a need for a quorum at the religious court in Korczyn, he was asked to participate. He never boasted or showed his knowledge that was immense, especially in the talmud. He had an excellent memory and when his grandson came on Shabbath to review the studies of the week, the grandfather pointed out many explanations to his grandson without consulting a reference book. He knew entire pages of talmud by heart. He loved the life of the scholar and was respected for it by the town. May his memory be blessed.

[Page 211]

Moshe Rothenberg

Moshe Rothenberg, the third son-in-law, was one of the richest people in Korczyn. He stemmed from a distinguished family and was a very successful businessman. He dealt in cloth and owned a dye workshop. Yona, the son of Leibish, worked in the dye place. Moshe had six sons and three daughters, quite a large family to support. They dressed well and in stylish fashion. When the daughters married, the family had enough males to have a quorum for services. Indeed when the family arrived to shul they were visible. Moshe was a distinguished looking man, his sons were handsome and his daughters beauties. One of the latter married Avrum Neuman from a nearby township. He was well educated in talmud and also knew how to conduct services. He cantorial abilities were fully exposed on Sabbath and holidays when he led the services. The couple complemented each other, he by his singing and she by her beauty. She really picked a winner although in those days the parents had more to say in these matters than the couple. One of Moshe's sons, Leibish was an excellent scholar in religious matters. From this large family, only Israel Rothenberg survived and lives in Israel and two grandchildren, Yankel and Moshe Frei in London. The latter were the children of Shaul Frei, a son-in-law of Moshe Rothenberg

[Page 212]

Naftali Hertz Halpern
by Aron Atlas Bear, Jerusalem. Grandson of Naphtali Halpern.

All the people that knew him loved Naftali. He was an easy going and understanding in the relations between people and between man and his creator. He was a devout follower of the commandments. He completed the study cycle of the talmud six times. He was devoted to the study of the torah, to good deeds and most important to charity. Such was Naftali Hertz Halpern the son of Arieh Leibish Halpern who was the son-in-law of the well known

Zeev Rapport, the Korczyner golden dynasty. He died a natural death and the entire town followed the funeral cortege. His oldest daughter Tova Yochewed, my mother, was raised in the orthodox tradition. She was a real woman of valor and strictly observed the Jews laws. She married to the hamlet of Jashlusk where she was well known and shared the fate of the Jewish community. These were the last two Jewish generations in Korczyn and we must draw inspiration from them and continue Jewish life in spite of the fact that the candle of Korczyn was extinguished. Now, we must rekindle another light, not by writing an article or placing a memorial tablet in memory of the Jewish community of Korczyn but by drawing conclusions as to what happened. True, a Yizkor book was written to memorialize the souls of the kehilla but that is hardly enough. We must take stock as to why we remained alive and for what purpose. We will then conclude that the best way to ensure their memory is to continue in the ways of the Korczyner Jews. We must teach our children to love the torah and study it. We must stress the importance of Judaism so that they will remain faithful Jews and fill the displaced ranks of religious Jews that were killed by the German murderers, this would be the real memorial.

May he be blessed and sanctified; God will avenge the spilled blood and take revenge for the misdeeds.

[Page 213-215]

Naphtali Raab
recorded by Mordechai Schiff and written by Moshe Zucker

Naftali was a very rich man. He gave charity lavishly and secretly. He studied the torah but was essentially known for his charity. He dealt in linens and nobody came close to him in this field. Naphtali was the biggest merchant and owned a large house that faced the market. The tall build ing contained five apartments. One for himself, two for his sons ,Avraham and Eliezar, and two for his daughters with their husbands, Eliyahu Kaufman and Haim Dym nicknamed the spodick. He always wore the hat called a spodick, summer and winter. Naftali had another daughter married to Zishe Beck and they lived in Lemberg. He and his sons conducted the business. The son-in-laws had other business. The Raab store was a beehive of activity, postal parcels arrived and were dispatched to all corners of the world. The demand for linens was big and the area could not satisfy the demand in spite of the attempt of the Polish farmers to meet the demands. The Raab family had contacts with factories in Bohemia and received merchandise that was then stamped with the Raab name. Of course the factories produced fine linens that matched the Korczyn production. Otherwise the Raab family would have lost their well-established reputation. in this line of business. Nobody was able to outsell the Raab family. They had salesman that traveled and sold their merchandise throughout the region. One of the salesmen was Nuta Joskale who peddled the merchandise in Hungary. He loaded a coach of merchandise and left Korczyn after Pessah and returned two weeks before the next Pessah.

When he returned to Korczyn, he met Naphtali and settled accounts. He then started to prepare for the holiday. The salesman was always short but Naphtali did not terminate his employment, he merely added everything to his bill and he continued to represent the Raab firm. Suddenly, one year he returned practically on the eve of the holiday and informed Naftali that he was bankrupt and has no ability to pay. Needless to say that Nuta did not bake matzot or made other preparations for the holiday. Monday, the eve of the holiday, Nuta went to the first minyan or service and stood behind the oven in order not to be seen. As if per chance, Naftali also went to the first minyan and saw his salesman but played stupid. When the torah was read, Naftali was the reader, he called Nuta to the bima and read for him the section. Following the blessing, Naftali gave him a hearty welcome. Later in the day, he sent him the usual annual Pessah gift that consisted of a liter of Hungarian wine, a liter of chicken fat and six matzot. During Hol Hamoed Pessah, Naftali sent for Nuta to come to the house in order to settle the accounts. Nuta came and told hiss boss that he has money. Never mind said to him Naftali. You will continue to represent us and your debt will be inscribed in the account.

When the rabbi of Dzikow visited Korczyn, he stayed at the house of Naftali. The latter was a hassid of his. The whole town was in motion and many people came to ask for the rabbi's divine intercession. When Naftali became ill and later died, the entire town was greatly worried. Many people prayed for his recovery and special prayers were recited for him. His death was a sad event in the town and the Raab family lost their shining star. The entire family perished with the exception of some grandchildren who live in New York, Israel and Antwerp.

[Page 216-218]

Mendel Schroit

Mendel was a rich man that dealt in linens. His store and his flat above it were situated at the entrance to the market, on the left side of the church. The farmers from the area obtained all their metals from his store. He also provided them with their specific iron needs. Mendel was very busy all week, especially on market day. He employed Moshe Axelrad, Yehuda Hersh Axelrad's son, as a laborer who cut steel pipes and bore holes in them according to specifications. The noise, hammering and banging was heard in the distance. The store business was no longer conducted by Mendel but by his wife Haya since he was already an old man. He was known as a charitable man but his wife was a miser. Local beggars knew to avoid her and to approach only him.

At the annual Purim party, Mendel sat at the head of the table covered with a white tablecloth and silver candelabras. Under the tablecloth were laid out half and whole silver guldens in two separate piles. Mendel reached under the cloth and took some coins and handed them to the needy. Nobody knew the extent of the gift except for the giver and the receiver. He distributed according to the needs as he saw them. Charity was important but modesty was even more important. This is the way he distributed the Purim gifts as I saw it. I do not know how he distributed charity throughout the year. Mendel also loved to grant anonymous charity so that the receiver did not know the source of the charity, this of course prevented embarrassment to both sides.Mendel opened the doors to his house each Sabbath afternoon for the traditional third meal or Shalosh Seudot to which he invited the neighbors and town residents. Following the meal and the blessings, the participants prayed maariv and terminated the Shabbath services.

Mendel was not a scholar but envied educated people. He was an orphan and had to support himself. That did not allow time for education, He chose a scholar for a son in law, Shaul Reich who married his daughter Bashe Welcze. He also stressed education for his son Fishale or Fishel. Fishel was the son of Mendel and Haya Schroit. She was the second wife. The first one died and left Mendel with a daughter, Bashe. Fishel Schroit continued his studies, never entered the family business. Even after he married, his parents supported him.

According to my memory, Mendel also dealt in linens in his apartment above the metal shop. Supposedly, Yehuda Hersh Axelrad that lived near Mendel, in the courtyard, behind the metal shop, conducted the business. Yehuda was the one that handled the correspondence and shipments of merchandise for Mendel. Supposedly the profits of this business went to Mendel who gave it to charity without the knowledge of his wife.

So lived a person that hardly knew how to open a religious book. He envied scholarship and tried in his own way to partake in the commandments of the torah to give charity. In a place like Korczyn Jews complimented each other in their religious ethical sense by granting each other the needed support. Blessed be his memory

[Page 219-223]

Recollections......Dedicated to my father

I heard somewhere that my father was a follower of the Zanzer Rabbi, Rabbi Haim, while his younger brother was a follower of the Rymanower Rabbi. To date I do not know why they followed different rabbis.

I also heard that when my uncle received notice for the draft. He injured his eye and was rejected from military service. David was pleased since he did not want to serve three years in the Austrian Imperial Army. My father's younger brother Zalman left for the USA prior to the arrival of the military notice. The thought of appearing naked before gentile doctors repulsed him. After all he was not an animal in the market. Yet if he passed the medical examination, he would receive a uniform, a belt and a rifle with a bayonet. Then he would be told to fight a so-called enemy that he never met in his life and he might be killed. Who had time for such childish games. A Jew has to marry, raise a family and provide for them. The war games were more for young boys that played on the holiday of Lag Ba'omer [33 days in the count of the Omer when the plague stopped among the students of Rabbi Akkiba. Traditionally, young cheder boys play all kind of war games on that day] and not for grown men.

Fantasy of heroism left the Jews a long time ago. Jews lived with miracles and accepted the lot that was assigned to them and did not interfere with matters of state. Tradition and history taught the Jews to stay away from political matters and the Jews of Korczyn were no exception to the rule. This was the reason why my father and my uncles avoided the draft.

My father was the oldest son and expected the military notice. He visited the Zanzer rabbi and asked for advice. The latter told him to play sick and attract attention. He returned home and went to bed. The doctor was called and medications were prescribed. The medical visits continued and so did the prescriptions. Finally, the notice for the medical examination arrived. My father ignored it. The medical commission sent the doctor to inquire and he reported that my father was sick and testified to it. My father was rejected for military service. But there was an informer in town who also happened to be in competition with my father. He reported the entire event to the authorities that started to investigate the matter. The denunciation resulted in a great deal of trouble for all concerned parties. The Jewish community of Korczyn excommunicated the informer. A black candle was lit for him and no Jew related to him, he was branded for life in Korczyn. The investigation was hushed up and my father never became a soldier.

In view of these events, my uncles decided to follow different routes of escape from the draft. Besides the fear of non- kosher food, there was also the great fear of coming in contact with pork that is strictly forbidden in the torah. The Jew was also fearful of the commandment thou shall not kill, yet he was trained to become a possible killer. Young Jewish men were taken away from the marriage canopy to the army training bases and had to play soldier for three years. Many of them survived on black bread and sweetened black coffee, not a suitable diet for a field soldier. The soldiers were weakened physically but strengthened emotionally in their religious belief. Of course, Jewish soldiers that attended Shabbath services were always invited to Jewish homes for a warm meal. As a matter of fact, the shamash in each shul saw to it that each soldier should have place to eat since this was his only kosher meal in many days if not weeks. The feelings of the young pious soldiers at such tables can only be surmised. Their reflections took them back home to their family and to the warmth of their surroundings that they missed badly.

The main objection to military service were the concepts developed through the ages such as who needs military service, is the living space so small that one has to fight for every inch. The Austrian Emperor treated the Jews better than the Russian Czar. Still the two capitals Vienna and St.Petersburg were constantly on the verge of war due to territorial claims. The interested parties always excited their supporters to action. Entire armies at the ready for war and the Jews on both sides must support their empire. They were told to kill other Jews simply be cause they were on the other side of the border. This certainly did not make sense to the Jew. Fathers and sons that never met each other, never looked at each other, would at a moment's notice go into action that will result in the killing and wounding of many people on both sides of the war in the name of patriotism. This was not in the Yiddish tradition. Even the simplest gentile on the other side was not a personal enemy. He had no reason to harm me. Yet two armies dressed in different uniforms were told in no uncertain terms that the other side will destroy them at the first opportunity unless they are defeated first. Frequently, Jewish soldiers attacked other Jewish soldiers and only in death did they discover that they were Jews when they uttered the words of Shema Israel. The most that could be done was to bury the soldiers and recite the kaddish for them. Perhaps it could have been avoided had the soldiers known in advance but the chances were slim. A confusion of borders that constantly changed resulted in constant conflicts. Land changed hands at all times and nothing was permanent for only the Messiah could bring permanency. Thus, our forefathers reached the conclusion that the best thing was to stay away from all military fights

When I studied with Zalkale, the cheder teacher, he always mentioned that he was my brother's Leibish friend. This was the story. My father was previously married and had nine children. His wife and all the children died. The last one was Leibish who died at the age of 28. He was a talented man, a good student and a capable artist. His design of the sign east was framed under a window in our house in his honor. When my father married for the second time, he was already an older man while my mother was still a young girl. She gave him four sons, the oldest was Shlomo who was aged 6 when my father died. The youngest was Shia who was one year old. Haim Hersh was the second son and I was the third. He died on the third day of Hol Hamoed Sukkoth.

I also heard that when the old rabbi of Korczyn, Rabbi Shmuel Aron died. My father sided with the Zanzer faction that supported Mendel Rubin as his successor. Mendel Rubin lost the battle and from what I understood there were some physical contacts between the parties. All of this was of course forgotten with time. Rabbi Mendel left Korczyn following his defeat and settled in Palestine where he headed the Rabbi Meir Baal Haness Kollel or study center. Years later, Rabbi Mendel visited Korczyn to see his mother. He wore a floral colored overcoat with a large band or gartel that gave him the appearance of the mystical east and endowed him with a great deal of reverence. Shabbath, the rabbi received the sixth aliyah that was usually reserved for the presiding rabbi.

Elderly Jews called my father Yidale Lembik and not Schnek that was his official name. I do not know which was the correct name. My father's brothers and all their descendants carried the name of Schnek. But I also know that my father had a cousin in Dembitz whose family name was Lembik. Thus, I revealed to you readers the past that was never recorded and presently everybody knows it.

[Page 224-227]

My mother, Reisel, Yiddel's daughter

Reisel give me a drink.

The cheder for youngsters in Korczyn was in our street opposite my mother's home. The street was quiet without traffic so the children played safely in the street. The only traffic was when the neighbors brought a load of wood from the market for the residents. After the cheder was the house of Itzhak Treitik with a fenced garden. The entrance was in the next street. Then there was the cowshed of Yossel Shmaya where he kept his horse and bogey. On my mother's side of the street was the house of Steltzer and his garden. That was the extent of the street.

Yossel took his horse and bogey out in the morning after he prayed the morning prayers and returned home late in the evening. Thus, the children played during the cheder brakes. This cheder was for children aged three to six or seven. They studied the alphabet, reading and the torah. Children of different backgrounds and ages mingled in the study groups under different teachers. At the age of four, the children started to study a full day. Mothers packed a lunch for their children and some even brought warm food for the toddlers.

As time passed, they managed to organize their food schedule in accordance with their needs. The teacher observed each student and decided who needed special attention. Every child in Korczyn attended cheder. Two teachers were in the cheder. A long bench divided the room with seats on both sides. Each section had a long table as well as small tables surrounded with benches. The teachers sat next to the big tables where the instruction was done. The children reviewed their material at the small tables.

Gedalia Hopmeister, his real name was Davidowitz, had students from the wealthier homes and Baruch melamed, do not know his last name, had the poorer students. There was no competition between them and each taught according to his plan.

During the summer, the children also studied although a shorter period of time. They studied, ate and played in the street. It never dawned upon them to go home and take refreshments following the dry sandwiches or fruits that they ate during the study period. The cheder had a barrel of water with an attached cup for the use of the children to quench their thirst. Each day, water was added to the barrel from the well. But the barrel was exposed to the sun and the copper cup was already green and unappetizing. The water did not taste fresh and children preferred not to drink from the cup even when they were thirsty. They discovered a watering hole across the street, at my mother's house. The barrel stood in the shade and was filled each day with fresh water from the well behind the house. The cheder children came constantly and begged for a drink of water. The small children with their shirts hanging out of their pants, wearing the talit katan or fringes, peyot on the side of their head and a black kippa on top of it. Reisel, my mother, served personally all the water requests.

The entrance door was always open and some children even came with their noses running. My mother would take her apron and wipe the face clean and provided the youngster with a drink of water. Of course, the children never said thank you since this was not part of the lexicon of the cheder. Thus my mother was very busy tending to the thirst of the children, She never minded it and was rather pleased since she performed a good deed for the students who studied torah. [I would like to add that I was never known by my real name but always refereed as Moshe the son of Reisel, the daughter of Yidel]

[Page 228-233]

Mordechai Hersh Balczanker

My maternal grandfather was called Mordechai Hersh Baleczanker. As long as I remember, my grandparents lived in the village of Waltaszow near Rymanow. Prior to this place they lived in the village of Baleczanka,in the area of Rymanow and this was the reason for the family name. I do not know where their children, Reisel, my mother, Mendel, Lea, and Tzivia were born, whether in the first or second village. Perhaps he changed the place of residence out of necessity for the draft or for the granting of names. Or perhaps he was already married and had a family.

I had the opportunity to meet my grandfather when I visited the village of Waltaszow and later in Rymanow, following the death of my grandmother. He was a simple and honest man. I heard that in the village where he used to buy eggs, animal skins, the Greek Orthodox population considered him somewhat of a saint. There was never a doubt about. Once he made a mistake and returned to the place with a pack of merchandise on his back to make good an unintentional error.

During these days, the apartment of my grandfather was rented to a Greek Orthodox. The flat consisted of one room that had two beds, a bench and a few chairs, a clothing closet and a cupboard for laundry. He kept there the talit, the tefilin, a siddur, a psalm book, high holiday prayer books, torah books with their commentaries, mishnayot with commentaries and Hebrew word books. The same room served as a kitchen where simple meals were prepared, halot were baked for Shabbath and holidays and bread was baked for the entire week.

Lea, the second daughter, a hunchback, was still at home. When a grandchild arrived unexpectedly, room was made. Grandfather always accepted visitors, grandmother expressed some resentment but accepted the fact. The taste of the black bread from the flour that was ground locally is still in my mouth.

When the Rabbi of Rymanow, Rabbi Yossef, married his grandchild to the Hassidic court of Rizin , the entire area talked for two weeks prior to the event and one week after the wedding. I was fascinated by the stories and decided to invite myself to the wedding. The distance was about 20 minutes by horse and buggy but I did not have the money so I had to walk the distance. I don't remember whether I received a lift along the road or walked the full distance. I do remember that I wore my black hat but left the boots home in order to save them. I was a bootless member of the wedding. Of course, my grandmother asked the usual question, why did you come. I did not want to tell her that I wanted to attend the wedding. I attended the affair but did not see the canupial ceremony. More important people than myself also missed the event. For the entire market area was packed with guests that celebrated the wedding. Including the present author.

I managed to assemble some facts about my grandfather based on bits and pieces of information that I collected from various sources. Prior or after his wedding, probably after, my grandfather was supposed to report for the draft. He played stupid and decided to move to another village or possibly more than one. He figured that the draft would forget about him if he moved about and changed his name. For everybody knew him in Waltaszow even the authorities. Finally he assumed the name of Zucker that was the maiden name of his wife. His own original name disappeared from all records. When I met him he was already past military age and I am certain that he would have made a poor soldier. For he was a gentle person that would have never mastered the martial arts.

The state lost nothing by the fact that he traded eggs or skins with the Greek Orthodox population. He provided an income for his family. He was not a rich person but made a living and did not need the support of family or strangers. My grandmother never complained, never egged him on but managed with the available means to run the house.

My grand parents had four children, Reisel, my mother, Lea, Mendel and Tzivia. All the children grew up, married and left except for Lea, who was a hunchback. She was the last to leave the home and married well. When my father died, my mother was left with four children. My grandfather took the youngest Shia who was one year old to his place and Lea practically became his mother.

When Shia was about four or five he used to go with my grandfather to the shul in Rymanow. Shia carried his talit bag and siddur on shabbat. Once he showed off by carrying the items on his pinky. The finger twisted and became lame. The doctors tried to restore the finger but the pinky on the right hand remained lame for the rest of his life. At the age of five or six, Shia returned to Korczyn and started to study at the cheder of the Jasznitzer melamed or teacher. The teacher stressed the written letters and Shia developed a beautiful script in spite of the lame finger. He and his wife were the only victims of Hitler amongst the brothers. His two daughters managed to escape in time, one to Israel and the other one to England. I would like to point out that two of his grandchildren, Mendel's children, were also saved and live in Israel. I sidetracked a bit from the main theme and am certain that my grandfather will forgive me. Now let us return to the main theme.

Grandmother died and grandfather moved to Rymanow where there was a large Jewish population. He rented a room with a bed and a small kitchenette to prepare his simple meals. The entire week he dealt with skins of animals that he sold at the market. On Saturday, he was a regular participant at the table of the Rabbi Yossef. Here he felt like a member of the family and not a guest.

My mother was a widow for 13 years. The children grew up, married and left the home. She then married Mordechai Elias from Rymanow. He was a well to do person and distributed charity. My grandfather rarely visited the home of his daughter for he did not want to take advantage of the situation. When I was still an apprentice, I used to come for the holidays of Passover and Sukkot and saw the lonely life of my grandfather and it affected me. I promised myself that when I will finish my stage and work, I will never forget my grandfather. The latter however did not wait for that day, he passed away before my graduation. This indeed was a great blow for me. He was a saintly soul. He refused to accept charity and lived a simple and honest life. He never accepted things from his children. His mishnayot book printed in 1888 in Warsaw was given to me by my brother, Haim Hersh Schnek.

According to the records, my last name should be Schnek like my brothers in the USA, Haim and Shlomo, and the cousins, children of uncle David and

Zalman. The circumstances were such that I could not change the passport. The Austrian Empire did not recognize Jewish religious weddings and the children were registered under the mother's maiden name. Thus, I had the opportunity to record the life of my grandfather in the Korczyner yizkor book. Besides, the description showed another corner of the Jewish world and the daily struggles. This explanation I owed my landesman who may say that Mordechai Ballaczanker was a nice Jew but did he belong in our memorial book. Their complaints are justified. I urged and pushed the people to record the events but few participated. So we included everybody in order to have minyan or a quorum of ten so to speak.

[Page 234-237]

Yekutiel Kamelhar

The black Itzhak, as I remember, was a tall skinny Jew whose beard was already gray. The nickname he received due to his pitch-black beard still showed traces of the original color. He was a salesman of linens. I do not know whether he represented companies or himself. Life was difficult for he left after Passover and returned home for the High holidays, and left after Sukkoth and returned prior to Passover. This was the life style of a salesman whose clients were scattered over a large area. It was not an easy job but one made a decent salary. When his daughter Hanna grew up, he arranged for a nice marriage. She married Yekutiel Kamelhar, a scholar from Stanislaw. When I was a boy of 10 or 12, Yekutiel Kamelhar was no longer in Korczyn. He wrote a book and the Rabbi of Dzikow made some critical comments about it. The author ignored the criticisms although he was a Dzikower Hassid and visited the court from time to time. The critique hurt but the author refused to budge. According to Zalke the melamed or teacher, Yekutiel named the book, the good announcer, and the content was dedicated to the Hassidic court of Rezhin until the Rabbi of Rymanow, Rabbi Yossef. The Rabbi of Dzikow felt that Yekutiel should devote himself to more serious writing and gave an example of another brilliant writer. Yekutiel had full satisfaction several years later when the other writer left for Vienna and started to study. He shaved his peyot and beard, dressed modern and concentrated in general non-religious studies. Yekutiel's position was totally vindicated. The other writer was pushed into areas that merely distanced him from traditional life.

Yekutiel never abandoned his traditional life style. He studied and researched ways to strengthen the traditional life style that was being attacked from many directions. He tried to attract young forces to strengthen the struggle. Yekutiel never abandoned his way of life. He continued the traditional ways that dealt with the study of the torah. He studied torah with the young men of Korczyn as long as he resided in town. But he was not satisfied and left town.

I finished my apprenticeship and became a painter, survived WWI and came to America where I struggled to make a living and forgot about Yekutiel Kamelhar. It was only after WWII, when the Korczyner Landsmen started to meet in the Korczyner-Reisher synagogue, did I discover that Yekutiel Kamelhar was the Rabbi of the shul. I wanted to meet him but this was only possible on Shabbat or Holidays, for on weekdays I worked and I lived too far away in Brooklyn to travel. The president of the shul was Moshe Horowitz who used to build floors. He was not a scholar but observed Shabbath and Holidays, prayed daily and observed kashruth. He lived next to the shul and eventually became the president of the congregation. He was a nice person but was never able to judge people, especially scholars. Later I met Moshe Horowitz and asked him about the rabbi and he told me that he was fired. The rabbi interfered in the running of the shul, namely tried to prevent the decoration of the shul during the three-week morning period. Of course he was dismissed. He later left for Israel and shortly thereafter died there. I later discovered that prior to and during WWI, he was the head of the Stanislawer Yeshiva . He also headed the Yeshiva in Krakow and possibly Reishe. He refused to compromise and paid dearly for his conduct. It was a pity that in his old age he had to start to wander from place to place.

[Page 238-240]

Haim Dym

Haim Dym, the son in law of Naphtali Raab, was extremely orthodox, almost fanatical in his belief. The various sociological strata wore the same clothing on weekdays. The coachmen, the porter and the well to do wore the same clothing but the wealthier people replaced their clothing more often. Haim Dym was the exception. He carried a Hasidic hat or Kolpack, nicknamed spodik everyday of the week. There was one other person in Korczyn namely Itzikel Den, who was the son in law of the late Rabbi of Korczyn, Shmuel Aron Rubin. He also carried a spodik. He was a member of the Belzer Rabbi's family and Haim Dym was a Belzer Hassid. The Hassidim of Belz were known as the most pious Hassidim. The Kolpacks were their trademark and even though some of their Hassidim did not wear these hats, their piety was visible. They avoided looking at their wives, and certainly at strange women. As soon as a women approached, they lowered their eyes in order not to have contact with her.

Haim Dym was called spodik as a sign of his piety. He was also a religious scholar and a man of charity. He gave charity and collected charity from others. He used to make the rounds with the melamed or teacher Moshe Mechale. When they entered a home and they met a woman who insisted on giving a donation directly to them, Moshe Mechale would point to his stick that had a small receptacle attached to it. He would ask the lady to insert the coin into the container and then retrieve it. Thus direct contact was avoided. Haim Dym visited sick people and whenever they needed financial help he extended. He refused to participate in community life. He conducted himself with the utmost piety and hoped that others would imitate him. When many people left the main shul following WWI to join small groups, he remained attached to the main shul. He insisted on the unity of the Jewish community. He never read a newspaper but was always involved in the study of torah. His wife Roisale conducted the wholesale linen business, the experience she acquired from her father Naphtali Raab. Haim Dym knew nothing about the business. All the purchased items were sent from the warehouse under their apartment. Here they kept the merchandise and from here everything was sent and received. Roisale still managed to find time to cook soup for the sick and to bring it to them at home.

Haim Dym's children, especially the sons, were raised in a very pious tradition. They never cut their peyot nor did they curl them. His son David met me some years after I left Korczyn and criticized me for shortening my peyot. I had empathy for him that he expressed such pain on seeing me in this light. I never found out what happens to peyot that kept growing, do they reach the floor or do they stop growing at a certain stage? I never saw someone with peyot to the floor, so there must be a secret. This was the pious life of the Dym family. May their memory be blessed.

[Page 241-244]

My teachers

Gedalia was my first cheder teacher. He was nicknamed Hopmesiter but his real name was Davidowitz. He once dressed up as policeman for Purim and introduced himself as Hopmeister instead of Hauptmesiter and made merry in Jewish homes during the Purim meal. The nickname stuck long after the event and practically nobody knew his real name in Korczyn. Gedalia was a tall man with a dark blond beard and long peyot. He aspired to be a teacher of the higher grades but taught children the alphabet, reading, and writing. He had a nice script and corresponded with merchants in a Yiddish-German style of writing called Deutschemerish. In his school we always started the alphabet, reading Hebrew and the Torah. He always started with the section of Veikra regardless of the actual week section. When Veikra was finished. The children started to study the regular weekly section and before long the children advanced to the next cheder teacher.

It was known that Gedalia knew the books of the prophets and the scribes better than some of the talmudic scholars for they did not delve into these writings except where it concerned prayers, psalms, the story of Job or the book of Ester. The latter writings took up some interest since they pertained to particular events in Jewish history such as Purim.

Besides the books of the prophets of Samuel A and Samuel B, the cheder did not teach Jewish history. This concept was handed down from generation to generation. Only a few scholars dealt in the area, the rest stayed away from the field. The book called Shulchan Aruch or Set Table was widely accepted as the final authority on Jewish behavior. The great achievement of a Jewish student was to know a page of the Talmud with the commentaries. The sharp students who continued their intellectual pursuits of course came in contact with Jewish history, the prophets, and scribes, since they delved into talmudic commentaries that were based on these sources. However the great majority of students did not come into contact with Jewish history except through the stories of the torah.

Gedalia was an exceptional teacher who had a large background of Jewish information, but there was no demand for it, and he decided to become an elementary teacher. He was an excellent raconteur and every evening prior to the minha and maariv services, he told stories about the deeds of pious rabbis and the audience adored it. I never missed his stories; they were fascinating. The other people also enjoyed the stories, and his abilities to portray the events was fascinating. He was able to write letters to the German merchants in a mixture of Yiddish and German. This was quite an asset and many respectable merchants used this type of letter to deal with their German counterparts. Some young students established contact with German firms and received samples for sale. Sometimes, this was the beginning of a long commercial relationship. Gedalia apparently also started, in a similar fashion, to deal with Vienna. During the High Holiday season when the cheder was closed, or when he could arrange with Baruch the melamed to cover his class, he would travel to Vienna; he bought merchandise that he sold in Korczyn.

The merchandise consisted of used and out of fashion items, such as men's or women's clothing, shirts of the nobility with collars, tuxedos, pants, vests, high formal hats, all kinds of shoes and buttons. All of this merchandise was displayed on Wednesday in the market area. Men, women, Jews and Gentiles crowded around the display and selected the items that they liked. They haggled about the price but the items were sold. Jewish women showed their artistry by converting some of these items into excellent clothing items without a trace of the original style. Large items were reduced to smaller sizes. A large tuxedo became a pair of slacks for children, a German shirt was converted to a Jewish shirt by removing the collar and the cuffs. Shoes and boots were grounded into the Korczyner mud and they immediately lost their big city color. The soles of course were excellent. It did not take too much time for Gedalia to unload the merchandise. Farmers would buy the formal hats or some Jews would buy them for Purim. I do not know how much Gedalia made on these trips to Vienna His wife Perl Yente also dealt with colored and white linens at the Krosno market on Monday and at the Korczyner market on Friday. Nobody knew the financial situation of the family until his brother in law, Mordechai Rossdeutscher, returned from the USA and informed everybody that he will be the teacher of the cheder and Gedalia would be leaving for the States.

Apparently Gedalia was not making a living, for people with an income do not leave their place of residence. Gedalia left for the States and WWI started;

that prevented him from bringing the rest of the family to the States. Only with the end of the war was the family reunited in the States where Gedalia had already three sons, Leibish, Ben Zion and Hersch Davidowitz. Perl Yente Davidowitz had two sisters in the USA; Esther and Serl Rossdeutscher, both were married. Yente Perl and her four sons and one daughter had to wait until after WWI to be reunited with their family. When I visited the family in 1921 in the States, all the members were there and lived on Houston St. in New York City. I met Gedalia but he lacked the warmth of Korczyn. New York had changed him. He owned a store of clothing materials and remained independent to his last day. Something had changed inside that was difficult to describe. He was no longer the person of stories and fables although his clothing did not change radically. He still wore a beard and peyot, a velvet hat, a white shirt without a tie and a coat with straight pockets instead of the Hassidic coat or bekeshe with side pockets. Gedalia made some compromise with the new environment although it was not drastic. He also told the author that when he appeared in Federal court for his citizenship and the judge asked him how long he was in the USA, he answered by stretching himself out to his full length and said so long. The judge smiled and granted him citizenship. When will we have similar judges throughout the world that do not search all the details but accept face value statements.

[Page 245-248]

Moshe Mechale- My Torah and Rashi teacher

Moshe Mechale was an average size Jew with a slight pot belly, a short beard and took his profession very seriously. He was a happy go lucky fellow and lived in an apartment that consisted of one narrow but long room that contained the classroom. When I was one of his students, his wife Neche Dworah was away. She often left him and then returned home. They had two married daughters and a son named Haim who was my age. The son and the youngest daughter Zissel traveled with the mother. The mother usually went to the village and bought eggs that were later resold at the market. This provided her with an income. She left her husband often and then returned. After each reunion it was assumed that this was the end of the separation. Then the screams and shouts reappeared and everybody knew that she would disappear again for some time. Their son Haim tried to keep them together and in their later years they patched up their differences and lived together in her flat that she purchased from her savings. Moshe Mechale's food consisted of a fried potato and sometimes he even had some herring, bread and chicory coffee. During the summer, he loved fruits and sour milk. He was busy in his kitchen preparing his few items. The fire was kept constant in order to prepare his simple meals.

His oldest daughter Hinde, married to Israel Yaacov Soffer, occasionally brought him cooked meals in a pot with a cover. These meals radically altered his diet. He never asked her for the meals and never received a thank you. She came and left quietly. I do not know where he ate on Shabbat and holidays but he did not seem disturbed about it. He washed his hands and made the appropriate blessing prior to eating and then thanked the Lord for providing him with the food. Besides teaching, Moshe also held other non-paying honorary functions in Korczyn. Friday night after the services at the shul, he assigned the poor people to various homes for the Shabbath meal. He decided where one should go and used his judgment in assigning people. No one invited a guest without consulting Moshe and he was constantly reminded to provide a guest for the table since that was a great honor for the family, and the wife would treat him with special deference. He was also the treasurer of the special fund that the kehilla would raise frequently to provide the poor non-resident beggars with some financial contribution and sent them on their way. Moshe Mechale managed the fund and provided them with some contribution. He even visited nearby towns when the Korczyn kehilla collection was too small. This was done to provide the local poor people with the necessary assistance to subsist. There were no announcements about the distribution that Moshe Mechale gave but those that needed help knew about it. Moshe decided whether to give 20, 30, 40 or 50 pennies according to the appearance of the beggar. The better the appearance the larger the sum. He tore a page from his notebook and wrote in pencil that he moistened with his tongue, this amount is to be given to so and so, and told the receiver of the note where to collect the amount. It never happened that someone tried to erase and increase the amount.

Moshe Mechale was also the master of ceremonies at the poor weddings. I remember such a wedding when Moshe Mechale and Zalke the melamed told each other off in a joyous manner and befitting a wedding. Everything was spontaneous and with decorum befitting the religious atmosphere of the wedding. Today it would be called a show, then it was provided by two gifted people who did it to entertain the guests and to provide joy to the festivity. Moshe Mechale's main attraction was his role as the Purim Rabbi of Korczyn. Every Shabbath before Purim, Moshe Mechale dressed specially for the occasion and the entire township treated him with respect. On the top of his shtreimel or special Hassidic hat, he had a small pyramid, and a blue or red velvet coat or bekeshe, sometimes another color. [He never wore a black silk coat or bekeshe like the other Hassidic Jews in town]. He tied his coat with a white towel instead of the usual band or gartel and this gave him special attention. He stood next to the local rabbi during the service until the reading of the torah. Then he tapped on the table for silence and delivered a special Purim sermon.

The sermon was very erudite and scholarly, of course Haman received his due in the sermon. His sermon was a masterpiece of story telling that included all the Purim characters and events and showed his great knowledge and ability. Each year there was a different sermon built around a different topic. He was the only one that delivered sermons. The local rabbi never gave sermons. He took his position seriously and even the rabbi respected him for the job. He of course received the sixth alyah to the torah that was always reserved for the presiding rabbi of the congregation. Moshe Mechale was not a show off but took his religion seriously. He prayed quietly and concentrated in his prayers so as to be united with the Master. His talith covered his head and only his face would be seen.

[Page 249-250]

My first Talmud teacher- David Stretner [Shtern]

He was a son in law of Mendel Hotz, the binder. He came from a small city in Eastern Galicia called Stretin. He started the tractates of Baba Kama and Baba Matziyah that are the first pages that students studied in the Talmud. He also taught us to write and perform additions, subtractions, multiplications and divisions. I suspect that he taught everything he knew. His mathematics was very useful since I used them in keeping records for my mother. I inscribed all the debts that were accumulated by the local women during the week. So and so bought a quarter or a half kilo of flour to make noodles or kreplach or other dishes for the home. All accounts were settled at the end of the week and then started again at the beginning of the new week. Even women that had the money would ask for credit and then pay it at the end of the week. One such a person was Freide Ita Weisman, wife of Mendel Weisman. She accumulated bills the entire week and I settled all the accounts on Thursday or Friday. There were other households that also settled their accounts in this manner. All these accounts and the halot and the bread accounts barely amounted to a guilden.

David Stretner was an excellent reader of the torah and occasionally he read the torah on Shabbath. He knew the section of the week by heart and once started he could finish the entire section. Usually Zalke read the torah on Shabbath. David had a beautiful script and adjusted the letters to the space. He could write the Song of Songs scroll on a postcard. Once he set himself to a task, he finished it. His wife was also a very busy person. Both worked and managed to scrape a living. They rented a flat from Godale that consisted of one room that had a kitchen and a cheder room. They had one three year old son, I think his name was Abraham. I played with him for I liked to play with smaller children than myself. In wintertime, David collected from us two pennies to fill the kerosene lamp that stood on the table. We all made paper lanterns that would light the way home during the darkness. Of course, the night increased a sense of insecurity that David's lanterns erased.

Once my mother came to David with a demand. She received five guildens from her brother in law in the States, David Schenk, and wanted to send him a thank you note. She gave him a postcard and left. He wrote a beautiful letter as though she had dictated to him the letter. I was amazed how one could read the mind of another person without talking to them. That was David

Stretner. What happened to him and his family, the same thing that happened to every Jew in Korczyn.

[Page 251-259]

Zalke Melamed

My second talmud teacher was Zalke Melamed, his family name was Melamed. Zalke did not bother with mathematics, writing, or other peripheral subjects. He concentrated on the gemarah or talmud; even the section of the week of the torah was merely reviewed but not studied in depth. Besides many of the students already studied the torah section by themselves and were adept at reading it with the musical annotations. We were already about 10 or 11 years old and had already acquired a slight background. Only prior to the holiday of Shavuoth, did Zalke concentrate on the Hymn of Aldamous that is read on this holiday, its meaning and the particular intonation used in reading it. On the eve of Tisha b'Av [nine days in Av, the day of the destruction of the Temple] he shed many tears in teaching us the meaning of Job that is read on this day. Prior to the holiday of Sukkoth, we dealt with the Hymn Song of Songs and of course the scroll of Esther prior to the holiday of Purim. He had a fine cantorial voice that I still remember. He also had the ability to create for us students the images of the section of the week. I still remember the section of the week that dealt with the death of Rachel, and when Yaacov buried her along the road to Bethlehem. The great commentator of the torah, Rashi, mentions that when the Jews were exiled to Babylon they passed Rachel's grave and shed many tears. A voice was heard saying that the children of Israel will return to Israel. Zalke had the ability to create for us a tableau of the entire scene and enraptured us. Another instance was the section of the week of Haazinu, where Moses took the earth and the sky as witnesses to the effect that, if the Jews observed the commandments, the land will grant them sustenance, but if they did not obey the reverse will happen. We felt that we witnessed the entire scene, so creative was Zalke.

During the summer months, we concentrated on the study of the Saying of the Sages that was read on Shabbaths during the summer, and Bless my Soul that was read in the winter on Shabbaths in the winter. These teachings strengthened our moral fibers and penetrated our subconscious. He was an excellent teacher and a fine pedagogue. He tried to provide answers to questions and did the best he could with difficult questions. He took time, especially with the teaching of the Talmud, where apparent conflicts were resolved with the help of looking at the commentaries and their interpretations of the differences. He continued to search for the answer until he was satisfied that we students understood the problems and the possible answers. He encouraged students to think and ask questions that were then answered. Questions that were not resolved completely, he recorded them and the possible answers in the Talmud book on the margins. I was impressed with the serious approach to study that Zalke used. He awakened in me a great desire to learn and I began to think of studying for the rabbinate. I knew that he was not the greatest scholar in Korczyn but he was the best teacher.

To make ends meet, Zalke also sold prayerbooks, fringes and small talits. He sometimes displayed his wares in the shul prior to the services and before the cheder started. I was a regular customer of his since I wanted to own the Talmud books that I studied with him. I also loved bible story books in Hebrew rather than Yiddish, that was primarily directed to the womenfolk. I liked to read the stories of the famous and pious rabbis. I had no money to buy these items and refused to ask my mother for help. I worked and created toys for the customers, flags for Simhat Torah, dreidels for Hanukkah, masks for Purim and painted homes prior to Passover. All these activities provided me with some pennies and enabled me to purchase some of my spiritual needs. Zalke never encouraged me to purchase unless I asked for his advice. Although I was a star pupil, he treated me with respect and tact. There was another bright student in the class, Haim Hersch Weisman, Mendel Weisman's son. He had an exceptional mind that absorbed instantly the studies. He never asked questions. I shall later discuss my friends. Shabbath and Holidays, Zalke read the torah; on occasion David Stretiner read the torah. The latter was the better reader but Zalke had seniority and read with greater feeling. There were also many other aspirants to read the torah or conduct the services in the shul of Korczyn.

His apartment consisted of a kitchen and a room. The kitchen also contained the classroom and the family lived in the room. The kitchen was 8.5 feet wide and 13 feet long. Along the left side of the wall was the entrance door to the kitchen and straight through the kitchen was a door that led to the family room that was locked from the inside. The lock consisted of a single chain, there was no need for locks in Korczyn. The kitchen had two windows and the family room also had windows along the same wall. Near the right side of the kitchen wall, there was a bed-bench that served in the day as a seating place for the students. Alongside this bench there was a long narrow table where there was plenty of room for the large talmudic books. Along the left side of the table there was another bench, the length of the table. At the head of the table, facing the entrance sat Zalke the teacher. I do not remember the chair but am certain that it was not a modern stool but rather an old fashioned piece of furniture that aged with the occupants. Opposite Zalke's chair, at the end of the table, there was a rickety seat for one or two students in case of need. Zalke had about 10-11 students, five sat on one side of the table and five sat on the other side. The seats were comfortable and there was no crowding. The average age of the students was 10-13 years of age.

Behind Zalke was the kitchen that took up a quarter of the kitchen space. Here was a big oven that warmed Zalke's back and the entire room. The stove heated the entire apartment in the winter when cooking was done or when baking was done on Friday. The warmth spread through the entire flat. In the summer, the cooking was done with pieces of wood and the fumes went directly up the chimney. Zalke's breakfast consisted of bread and butter and chicory coffee that he ate in front of the students. Lunch and supper he ate alone for most of the students went home to eat. The study day consisted of 12 hours with two breaks for lunch and supper [between the evening services] in the winter and lunch in the summer. Where the stove in the kitchen ended, there was a door that led to the family room that was similar in size to the total kitchen space. There were two beds along the wall and a dresser that separated them and in the corner next to the door there was a clothing closet. I do not recall whether there was a chair in the room. Now that I described the interior of the teacher's place, I would like to describe the external side of the family.

Zalke had two children when I was a student there. Frumet, the oldest daughter, she was my age, and Ben Zion. I later discovered that he had subsequently another three children, Beile, Mechtsche, and Braindel. Thus the apartment had ample room for the large family. WWI destroyed the place and I do not know where the family moved to in Korczyn. Why do I present so many details in these pages? So that you readers would get the feel of life in Korczyn. Most of the families in the township had one room apartments where the family and frequently two generations lived. The winds of change started with WWI when people started to request to live in their own apartments. This was very difficult and required a long process of digestion. But the process started and there was no stopping it. Families that used to live in one room started to break up. As a matter of fact, the entire township was considered one family but no more. The transition was extremely painful as the example illustrates.

Zalke had a sister, Miriam Sara, I do not know whether she was a full sister. She left Korczyn as a girl and lived in Silesia, Germany, where she married. She visited Korczyn from time to time. The visits were painful for Zalke, since she dressed in the German style. When she left town, Zalke felt again at ease. Prior to WWI, Miriam Sara became ill and asked her brother to send Frumet to help her with the household. The brother was not too keen on the idea but consented, since it was for medical reasons and to maintain the family. Frumet prepared everything and decided with the advice of so called experts to wear a small hat so that her aunt would not be ashamed of her. How women in Korczyn knew the dress styles in the world I do not know, but apparently they have an instinct for these things. Zalke objected to the hat and fights ensued in the house until a compromise was reached. Frumet will wear the hat from the Krosno railway station. Frumet left and a few weeks passed. Zalke was fearful and wrote a letter to his daughter. The latter replied that the aunt was still sick and she was needed to run the household. Zalke wrote and Frumet replied but she remained in Germany. Zalke's mind constructed all kinds of devilish plans as to what may possibly happen to his daughter in Germany. Apparently, Zalke was afraid of German civilization even before Hitler. To move one inch away from Judaism was a terrible sin for Zalke. He finally dictated a sharp letter to his daughter urging her to return home. Refusal would be considered abandoning the faith. The students overheard the expressions as they were written. He was so fearful of loosing his children to the modern way of life that he even refused to give them a chance.

Zalke's son Ben Zion once dressed up and went to shul with a stiff collar. People reported it to his father. Zalke grabbed his son and tore the collar and the shirt from his son's back. Luckily, Toibe Melamed intervened and stopped the fight. Ben Zion lost his appetite for modernity. Somewhat later Zalke mellowed a bit with time, and allowed his children to wear stiff collars. We must complete the picture of the Melamed family. Toibe Melamed cooked, baked and took care of the household, but also dealt in linens. She displayed her linens at the Friday market in Korczyn. She sold a variety of plain and colorful linens that peasant woman bought. Her stand consisted of two boxes and a board. She would also travel to the market in Kros on Monday. I do not know how much of an income she made from her sales at the markets. I do not remember where she kept her merchandise in her apartment. For Zalke also had a large basket with books, fringes and storybooks. Where they kept all these items was a secret to me. Apparently there was room for everything. I still can not perceive how crowded conditions were in the shtetl. Yet these conditions did not prevent the Jews from living a fuller spiritual life than the Germans. The Jews lived in terribly crowded conditions and maintained their human dignity.

[Page 260-262]

Reuven Yossef

My third and last Talmud teacher was Reuven Yossef. He was a scholar and attracted all the students that intended to continue with their studies. I was about 12 or 13 years of age but did not like his style of teaching. He was dry, without inspiration and answered my questions without hesitation. His erudition was immense and questions did not phase him. He left me dry and I lost interest in studies. Perhaps, he thought it advisable for me to quit studying and earn a living. For he certainly did not make a living with all his knowledge that was immense. His wife had to sell linens at the markets to support the family, as did other wives of teachers. Even his only daughter he married to a forest attendant that had a steady income. His son Pinnie, my age, was not encouraged to study. True, he was a slow learner but had the father wanted, he would have pushed him to greater efforts. Apparently, his teaching career left him cold, for he constantly chewed his cigarette holder and chain-smoked nervously. His constant smoking affected his husky voice. I remained with him two seasons and then started to study by myself in the shul with other youngsters.

In this cheder, I came in contact with the opposite sex. The teacher had a daughter whose name I no longer remember. She was about 17-18, ready for marriage. She kept to herself, distant from the students that were much younger than her. During Hanukkah time, when the teacher was at shul for services or on some errand, the students used to play cards. Then the daughter would join the game and help me win the pot. I always suspected that she considered me an orphan and decided to help me. I never considered myself a helpless orphan but if she insisted to help I accepted it. She seemed to like me and the same goes for me. As a matter of fact, when she was later married to Reuven [do not remember his last name] I felt a bit down although I wished them happiness. This reminds me that I played cards during the permitted time following Hanukah and made between 10-12 guilden that was a considerable amount of money. The games were mostly held in our place and involved lots of noise but we were accustomed since I always worked on scenery, dreidels, masks and flags. My mother tolerated the noise and my conduct. She treated me as an adult. One thing I must stress that we paid serious attention to all things Jewish. But where are today all the serious Jewish leaders of Korczyn that led the Jewish community? Hitler killed them all.

[Page 263-267]

Hersch Yaacov Rossenhendler

He was a very well to do person, a merchant, a scholarly Jew. He also conducted occasionally the second half of the Shabbath service. He was a Dzikower Hassid and loved tunes that accompanied the prayers. Whenever he was at the Dzikower court for Shabbath or Holidays, he always picked up tunes that he sung at the shul in Korczyn. The tunes spread throughout the township and became very popular. Jews then used his tunes at their Shabbath tables. His new tunes were the latest hits in town for there was no real contact with the outside world. Only Hassidim and merchants that traveled out of Korczyn brought back news from other places, even if the items were outdated. The township accepted the items as the latest events and they made the rounds of the town. It did not matter that these events occurred last year. They heard the bible stories that occurred so many centuries ago and yet seemed so real to the average Jew. There were no newspapers and even if someone read one, he did it in great secret since it was considered improper to read papers. Thus, it took months for news items to reach Korczyn. Pogrom news or anti Jewish regulations traveled much faster but general items took a long time to reach Korczyn. Besides, people had patience and plenty of time, no great rush.

By the time the news item reached Korczyn, the event itself could have consumed or run its course. Still, the township discussed and interpreted the event and the implications. There were people in Korczyn that were very adept at connecting the events to the biblical scene and interpreting to present-day life. All of these discussions continued until more information arrived and strengthened or weakened the positions of the debaters. Some of the discussions transformed themselves into stories that assumed a life of their own. Hersch had no talent for stories but his mission was to bring tunes to Korczyn and this he fulfilled. He connected Korczyn to the cantorial Jewish world. He had a metal store in the Market Square that was three meters wide and very deep that led to his apartment that consisted of two or three rooms. Behind his flat was a piece of property. When I grew up, I was in steady contact with the shop since I was involved in many carpentry projects. I received boards from our neighbor Esther who received them from the yeast dealer. I made all kinds of wooden boxes and bought nails and tools from Hersch. From him I also received some practical coaching for my projects.

As I was getting older and saw the hardships at home. I realized that it was very difficult for my mother to buy boots for me. I therefore decided to use sparingly the boots, especially during the summer. Indeed, it was a real pleasure to run barefoot without the boots that felt tight or loose. Boots were made for the rich children that were sickly. I felt very strong and healthy and compared myself to a gypsy. We saw barefoot Gypsies one winter and my brother and I decided to imitate. My brother came down with a serious cold that affected him for the rest of his life while I hardly felt it. To walk in the summer rain barefoot was a real pleasure and I hardly used the boots. One day, I walked into the shul barefoot and I saw the look on Hersch Rossenhendler's face. It was the look of pity but in a paternal way. Since then I always came to shul with boots regardless of the weather. But generally, I preferred to walk barefoot to save the expense of wear and tear.

I was once invited to perform a Purim presentation at the house of Hersh Rossenhedler. My friends from cheder, Haim Hersch Weissman and Haim Fishel helped me with the presentation. We split the money gift three ways. Each participant then gave his share to a poor person in Korczyn. In order not be accused of using the money for myself, I decided that Shimon would be the cashier. But Hersh Rossenhendler insisted that I take the money gift for the Purim presentation. I took the money and gave it to my friend Shimon who was a nephew of Hersh. Shimon then divided it three ways. I am certain to this day, that Hersh was certain that I took the money since I was the poorest of the group. I was 13 or 14 years of age but set in my ways and decided to give charity to needier people than myself. Besides, I also enjoyed the adventure of performing.

I met again Hersh when I was 18-19 years of age. I was an apprentice painter in Reishe or Rzeszow. I dreamt of becoming a famous painter but had to accept daily reality that is to earn my daily bread. I used to travel to Korczyn for Passover and Succoth. I felt drawn to this place in spite of the fact that my mother no longer lived in Korczyn but married to Rymanow. During these travels I met again Hersh and talked to him. I wanted to continue to study religious texts and also to learn painting. I realized that I could not pursue both paths. Yet, I did not want to abandon Jewish studies or the Jewish way of life. For I was still deeply religious, wore my peyot although trimmed or curled. Later I removed them but let them grow when I traveled to

Korczyn. I gave the appearance of a Yeshiva student and was treated as such by the people that knew me even though I was no longer a student. While traveling with Hersh and involved in my own dreams, Hersh Rossenhendler suddenly asked me how I was doing. Of course, I did not describe the slave condition of an apprentice. But I did tell him that when I would finish my studies, I would receive a salary of 18 guilden a week. I did not describe the hardships that were still ahead. He then told me that if he were my age, he too would study a trade. I was surprised to hear these words. Perhaps he wanted to support me or perhaps this was a true sentiment. The fact that he made such statement in 1911 or 1912 was indeed a comforting thing to do. May his memory be blessed.

[Page 268-271]

Mendel Weissman

Mendel Weissman

I remember Mendel Weissman a long time ago. His daughter Esther was already married. He was a well to do person. He had a moderate beard and curled peyot that did not sway when he walked. I am certain that he followed the rules regarding the peyot. He dressed in the acceptable manner of Korczyn, a black velvet hat and a coat or bekeshe with straight side pockets on weekdays. The clothing was very clean and very presentable. A religious radiance shone from the man that distinguished him from other people. Mendel worked in a distillery until he married Frieda Ita. He was an excellent worker and was an expert in the field and as such was hired by one of the princes that had a liquor license to supervise his distillery. He came in contact with many officials, princes and workers due to his work in the distillery. He spoke Polish better than most Jews of Korczyn. Following his marriage, he settled in Korczyn and slowly abandoned the distillery business. Due to his excellent contacts with the various princes, he started to buy and sell wooded areas or forests. In the winter he checked his forests and hired the peasants who were unemployed as lumberjacks. They thinned the woods, cut the trees and cut them to various sizes for heating purposes to the various people. He hired haulers to deliver the requested wood. He knew how to organize his work.

I still remember to this day how Mendel dressed prior to his winter trips to his forests. He wore a big fur coat over his regular coat with the side pockets; the fur had a large sable collar that could cover the ears, several scarves around his neck; the sleeves ended in sable fur and were wide to enable the opposite hand to find shelter from the cold weather. He hired a peasant coach filled with straw and hay on all sides so that the cold weather was minimized. In addition the coach had many blankets to wrap the passengers during the trip. Thus started Mendel his winter trips that lasted sometimes weeks. But he always returned home for Shabbath and left with end of Shabbath. I do not remember that he ever missed a Shabbath at home. He also had a custom to bring fish for Shabbath for his poor neighbors. This was very difficult in the winter months when the rivers were frozen. Yet Mendel's workers cracked the ice and caught fish that he brought home and gave them to his neighbors. The latter cleaned, divided the portions, salted and peppered the fish. It was Mendel's task to sweeten and cook the fish and his wife baked and cooked the Shabbath meals.

Mendel had a good voice and occasionally led the mussaf or second half of the Shabbath service in the Korczyn shul. He knew enough Hebrew to understand the meaning of the prayers as did many other Jews of the township. He was not extreme in his religious conceptions, nor was he affected by modern trends in spite of his many contacts with the outside business world. Mendel was for many years a member of the kehilla leadership, and when Shulem Akselrad, the head of the kehilla died, Mendel Weissman was appointed head of the kehilla, and led it until WWI. During the war, he and his family left for Budapest and following the war returned to the city of Tarnow, Galicia. Prior to the war, Mendel received a license to sell tobacco, cigarettes and snuff. Reisel, his third daughter ran the shop until she married.[His oldest daughter Esther and Haya were already married and his oldest son Meir was in Switzerland]. Then Neche, the fourth daughter took over the business and she was assisted occasionally by her brothers Haim Hersh, my friend from cheder, Shulem, Wolf and Chaskel. Mendel was never seen in the store. He observed it in the morning on his way to the shul for the morning services.

He also unlocked the heavy lock and opened the heavy portals that led to the store. Now you saw the black and yellow arrows that symbolized the cigarette stores in the Austrian Empire. Of course, the Imperial eagle was another state sign that appeared on governmental institutions. The children opened the glass door somewhat later when they came to open the store for business. Once, early in a winter morning, on his way to shul for morning services, Mendel saw the lady water carrier of Korczyn on the ground frozen. She was a Christian women and laid motionless next to the cigarette store. He put down his talit and phylacteries on the snow and started to administer first aid to the woman. Yendzej Ganet passed by with his sled and Mendel stopped him. Both men lifted the drunken women onto the sled and took her to Joel Ettinger's saloon opposite the kehilla. Here she was placed on a bench and given a few shots of vodka. Slowly she regained consciousness. The story was told later by the sled driver to Shulem Weissman who repeated it to me. He also added that such Jews are no longer to be found. Of course, he was unaware that to save a human being, the talit and the phylacteries play a second role.

[Page 272]

Benyamin Rubin

Eliezar Rubin was a respected Jew in Korczyn, he was familiar with Jewish texts and was considered well to do in Korczyn. He had three sons; Benyamin, Mendel and Mechel. The first two always lived in Korczyn and Mechel lived in Kros. He was the son-in -law of Naphtali Rap. Apparently both families were of similar statue otherwise they would not have married their children. Mechel had a wholesale flour store in Kros and was a respectable member of the Jewish community. Mendel, the middle son, had a house in Korczyn towards the end of the market in the direction of the shul street. He dealt in linens. In contrast to his brothers that were dark, Mendel was blond-red leaning to the color red. He was also smaller in statue than his brothers. He had a long beard and dressed neatly; that gave him respectability. The most colorful of the brothers was Benyamin who was the tallest. He had a small beard for his size body. He devoted his life to Korczyn. This is where he was born and this is where he died.

Benyamin was poorer than his brothers. He dealt in apples. He visited the orchards with the first sign of spring and purchased the future harvest of apples. If his guess was correct he made money otherwise he lost. When the apples ripened, Benyamin hired a guard to watch the apples so that nobody picked them before he organized the picking crews. He spent many a sleepless night until the harvest was in. During the Austrian Imperial days, the harvesting and selling of apples proceeded smoothly since Benyamin had good connections and made some money to support his family. Benyamin also sold small onions that were seeded in the ground and grew in size. He always had many bags of large and small onions ready for the onion merchants. He of course always expected to get a higher price while the buyers always offered smaller bids. Finally compromises were reached and he made some money. He was not the most successful businessman, for his oldest son on reaching maturity left for Germany. He also wanted to avoid the draft. That was not the most respectable achievement for a Jewish religious youngster. The second son, Hersh, also left for Germany once he reached maturity..

Benyamin's apartment was located in the public bathhouse passage where the beginners cheder was located. It contained a kitchen and a large room where Benyamin, his wife Miriam and seven children [four girls and three sons] lived. To reach the apartment, one had to follow a long corridor from the passage where on the right side lived the old cantor Wolf, on the left side lived Feiwish, in the middle there were some rooms, following to the left was Benyamin's flat. All the entrances to the rooms were from the long corridor to the other side where Yona Peltz had his home near the small river I remember that the corridor was dark. After the cantor's flat, lived his son in law Yaacov Itzhak, in a flat that was long and narrow with a window that hardly provided light or air for the family of three children; two sons and a daughter. During WWI, the Russian and Austrian jockeyed for military positions in Korczyn. The Russians left a live shell in his flat. On entering the place, Yaacov pulled the cord from the shell and it exploded. He was blinded, crippled and shortly died in terrible pains. This was WWI, of course no comparison to what happened during WWII. Benyamin was an institution in Korczyn. He had children in Germany, Switzerland and a son Luzer in the USA. He himself never left the township. His children supported him in his old age until the Germans killed him. He contributed a great deal to the community. He had a nice and powerful voice that carried throughout the shul when he conducted services. He usually conducted the third meal services at the shul. He placed his hand to the right cheek and would sing various hymns appropriate to the third meal. Some of them invoked a mystical fervor that implied a departure of the sanctity of the Shabbath and the imminent arrival of daily reality especially for people that struggled to meet ends. Most of these participants were people that barely made it. The more affluent members of the community did not attend the shul third meals. They remained at home where they partook of the third meal with their neighbors and ended the Shabbath with prayers and the lighting of candles. The rabbi of Korczyn did likewise. I am certain that there were other singers at the shul meals but I do not remember them. The outstanding man at these meals was Benyamin Rubin. When an injustice took place, the voice of Benyamin was heard but nothing vengeful. He was always the secretary of the Hevra Kadisha or the burial society of Korczyn. He was already 80 years old when the Germans killed him, his daughter Tzivia, her husband Matitiyahu Gleicher and their children Naphtali, Toibe Ita, and Hersh with their families. Frieda Haya remained alive in Switzerland, Zelde in Israel and Luzer in the USA. The children of Benyamin that remained alive should memorialize their families and the six million Jews. Nobody remained alive from the brothers of Benyamin Rubin. Respect their memory.

[Page 276-281]

David Ringelheim

I remember Wolf Grin slightly as if in a dream. He had a son Shia Leib that owned a grocery. Wolf's son in law was David Ringelheim who dealt in cement and whitewash. Peasants and Jewish women used to buy pieces of chalk and place them in barrels to which water was added. The mixture cooked and boiled until a white stew appeared. Then more water was added and whitewash was the product. It was then used to paint the stove and the walls. A coloring was added to the whitewash to satisfy the taste of the ladies. This whitewash was the best protection for the homes and walls of Korczyn whether they were wood or brick. Only one, or possibly two, homes were painted by professional painters from Kros. The rest of the flats used whitewash to the best of my information. Some places had a small frame with the word east or praise the lord on the wall and that was the extent of the home decorations. A picture of Moses Montefiore or the Gaon of Wilno was not to be found in Korczyn. Statues were of course forbidden. Still every Jewish woman knew instinctually how to beautify her poverty and to decorate the place so that it was a nice place. Of course, the people lived with great expectations and hopes. They anticipated the arrival of the messiah. The Jew always attached himself to mankind or rather to the deliverance of mankind. There is no better material then the suppressed Jewish masses. But this is the lot in a world of sinners; the good is destroyed and the bad survives. This reminded me of the following situation. I was away for the first time from home. It was wintertime and I was an apprentice in Reishe or Rzeszow. Friday night and Saturday afternoon after mealtime, I visited the rabbi's house, rabbi Eleazar, to listen to his words of wisdom and to keep in contact with my past scholarship. I considered my present situation a mere corridor to get to a higher stage of painting, perhaps a higher artistic stage. I always dreamt of bringing together my widowed mother and my brothers Haim Hersh who was a carpenter apprentice in Linsk, and Shia who worked in a store in Krakow. This was my dream to unite the family. I therefore applied myself very hard in my studies. My mother struggled for thirteen years and I wanted to make her life a bit more meaningful. Thus I promised to come home for Passover from Reishe.

I was attached to Korczyn and was unable to break the spell of the place. For 16 years I lived here and dreamt many dreams and planned many plans that failed. I ascribed all the failures to the fact that I was an orphan, nice rationalization. Full of winter hopes for the visit home for Passover, I attended a Purim party at the home of Rabbi Eliezer where I met David Ringelheim who was a Hassid of the rabbi, I was very pleased to meet him and asked him whether he saw my mother. He inquired whether I would be going to Rymanow for Passover. The inquiry struck me very funny until I realized that my mother married to Rymanow. I burst out of the room and wept beyond control. My own mother did not bother to notify me of her intentions. All my plans were destroyed. Finally, I stopped crying and took control of myself. I do not recall whether I returned to the party or went home. My situation as an apprentice was far from satisfactory but I tried to make the best of it. According to my contract that I wrote in Yiddish, I was supposed to receive a certificate after one year's apprentice in accordance with the Austrian law. For there were apprenticeships that lasted three years. My teacher, Leizer Garfunkel, was paid 100 guilden. My mother took a loan by mortgaging the inherited flat left by my father. It was a difficult experience for me to be away from home. But the fact that I was going to be home for Passover made the time pass faster. The present news struck a deep blow. For all my plans were ruined. I did not want to stay with the owners for Passover for this would have lowered my standing in their eyes and they would have taken pith on the orphan. This situation I had to avoid if I wanted to retain my dignity as an apprentice. My mother certainly did not help the situation by keeping it a secret. I do not know how my brothers discovered the news since we never talked about it. Still I decided to leave the family and went to Korczyn for Passover. I visited the neighbors, Hersh and Liebe Katz and decided to stay with them. I did not have too much money since my tips did not amount to much. I offered the Katz family two guilden and they accepted. Thus I was left with two guilden in my pocket.

In Korczyn, I discovered that my mother stopped eating in order to economize and reduce her debts. As active as she was when the children were home she now became apathetic and tried to cut corners. The neighbors saw the situation and began to pressure her to remarry. They found for her a nice well to do elderly widower, Mordechai Elias from Rymanow. She was never a strong character and the pressure was great. Besides, she felt that she should marry and help her situation. How my mother discovered that I was in Korczyn, I do not know for there were no telegrams or correspondence. Yet, the first or second day of Hol Hamoed Passover, I received an invitation to visit her and my brothers in Rymanow. I visited my mother and met my brothers and my stepfather and his entire family that consisted of grandchildren and great grandchildren. They all treated my mother as a real mother. Later I met Israel Shalom Nochmales who I describe later in the book and he told me that Mordechai gave lots of charity. This impressed me and I respected him for it. We children never took advantage of his financial situation and he treated as very well when we came for Passover or Sukkoth. When I was already in the USA, in the thirties, my mother passed away. Mordechai passed away a few years later, killed by a horse and buggy out of control. He was almost ninety when he passed away. His goodness and his helpfulness to the needy must be officially recorded. I also want to take this opportunity to thank David Ringelheim for the news that he brought me that day in Reishe and I was too selfish to accept it. The fact remained that Mordechai was a decent human being. Wolf Ringelheim, David's son that now lives in the USA, would certainly have more to say on his family.

[Page 282-283]

Leib Wolf Freund

Many people frequently ask whether the old way of life was not better than the present one with all the modern conveniences and the need for them. As a matter of fact many people would not do without these conveniences and getting them forces them to chase them. In short there is no end to the rat race.

I knew Leib Wolf from childhood. We were neighbors; his parents Yankel and Yahet lived in a flat owned by Sender Fessel. That house was attached to our flat. A long narrow shed separated the two apartments. Leib Wolf was the youngest of the couple's children. They had three daughters; Pearl Yente married to Gedalia Dawidowitz, Esther and Seril also married. Leib Wolf's older brother, Matityahu was also married. Only Leib remained at home and read storybooks. His appearance was not impressive, he had long curled peyot, dreamy eyes, no interest in reality. He only dealt with angels, paradise and hell. He was familiar with all the heavenly paths and was very fearful of transgressing or committing a sin. When his uncle Yoel Freund lost his vision, Leib read daily to him the psalms and he repeated. This situation added to his absent- mindedness. When I left Korczyn in 1908, Leib was still single and at home. Twelve years later, 1920, I had to leave Poland illegally. I crossed the border to Czechoslovakia and reached the border town of Mesze Labretz. I discovered that Leib lived here and was married with five children. He had three sons and two daughters. He also had his own house and a milking cow. I visited him and saw the same absent-minded person. He was the Hebrew teacher of the area. I did not see his students or his family. But his wife, like other women in these places, helped support the family. Following the war, I met one of the Leib Wolf's sons in the USA. He was clean shaven and dressed modern. I asked myself whether this was a descendent of Leib Wolf and the answer was affirmative. These members of the family of Leib Wolf perished: Leib Wolf, his wife Sheindel the daughter of Moshe, their children; Yachet, Yaacov and Sarah. Mordechai Tzvi and Moshe survived the war and are in the USA.

[Page 284-285]

Shmuel Aron Kokoshke

I do not know the origin of the nickname Kokoshke. He was also called Shmuel Aron the son of Bine. His actual family name was Teller. When I was no longer in Korczyn, I heard that the writer Yossef Weber explained the origin of the nickname. I am certain that he knew what he was talking about. At the time, Shmuel Aron was already married and had a family to support. In this Yizkor book there is a reference to Shmuel Aron as the fish dealer. Although Yossef Weber changed the story a bit, still Shmuel Aron emerged as a saintly figure that avoided fights. The author created the story and altered some scenes so that people would not recognize the true characters. Of course, the newspaper item arrived in town and the people figured out who was who in the story. True, the author created a beautiful story but some people felt ill at ease with their roles. The jokers of the town had a field day with the portrayal of his wife and she took it out on her husband. She called him the Pisher by substituting the p for an f; in Yiddish it is the same letter but the p is with a dot and the f is without one. This was her revenge on the author who did a beautiful job of describing her as a true woman of valor fighting to sustain her family as other Jewish woman did at the time. She complained that she was villified in the story that showed her limited ability to understand her role in the story. Yet she felt that she was mistreated when in reality she was portrayed as she was. Shmuel Aron Kokoshke, a nickname of praise, his wife and all the children perished in the Shoa. May they find rest in the heavens. Honor their memory.

[Page 286-290]

Shmayahu

Shmayahu was an institution in Korczyn. He and his four sons dealt with horses. Shmayahu was an old widower and lived with his daughter Dworah whose husband was in the USA. She and her children; Avraham, Berl and Charna waited for her husband to send her tickets to join him. Shmayahu's youngest son, Chaim also lived in the flat. He already owned a coach that transported people from Korczyn to Kros and back. He kept his coach and horse neat. His coach lacked springs but was kept in excellent condition. The number of seats was limited and handlebars assisted people to mount and descend from the coach. The oldest son Itzik transported merchandise from the Krosno railway station to Korczyn and back. He also transported large loads to other places in the area. He was a responsible person and people trusted him with their merchandise. His coach was large and needed a team of two horses. He also occasionally used a porter for the heavy loads. Itzik was considered a well do to person, he had a nice seat in the shul, his shtreimel or hat and coat were clean and he was familiar with the prayers, much more so than his brothers. Next to his house, he had a stable for the coach and the horses as well as a fenced drive in.

Shmayahu's second son, Yossel also dealt with transporting goods to and from Kros. But he only had one horse and handled smaller loads. Frequently he also transported passengers. Occasionally he went to Rymanow and elsewhere with passengers. The ride was not comfortable since he pushed in as many passengers as the coach would be able to hold. The people sat where they found places. Yossel saw to it that the coach was packed solid. He himself was well built and his horse was massive. On occasion, the passengers pushed the coach, especially uphill, for there was a mountain before Krosno. Yossel's clothing did not reveal wealth. On the contrary, his clothing was old and worn but clean. He had his own home and provided for his family. Moshe, the third son of Shmayahu, had a simple coach. He only transported passengers to Kros and back. His coach was primitive and his horse was weak. He barely managed to get the people to their destination. He had a small house with a thatched roof and managed to scrape a living. I remember that Shmayahu always used to clean Moshe's horse in the market since he neglected to do it. The other brothers always kept their horses in excellent condition.

One day, Dworah received her tickets for America and she left Korczyn. Chaim soon married and took over Dworah's place that consisted of a kitchen and large room. Shmayahu remained with the young couple. Several years later, Dworah brought her father to the USA. But he was too old to work and there were no horse businesses in the area so Shmayahu was bored. He went from house to house to visit people from Korczyn but they worked or were busy. He entered many homes without a mezuzah on the door. This was a sacrilege to him. He was not a scholar but knew the Jewish customs of Korczyn. Except for prayers in the shul, he had no other things to do. He felt a stranger in a strange land. Everything was not kosher, even the sidewalks were treif or non-kosher. Finally, his daughter sent him back to Korczyn after two years in the USA. I remember when he returned to Korczyn and brought suspenders that Shlomo sent for his brother. Suspenders were the in things in those days. Shmayahu was not pleased with Shlomo's behavior in the USA since he lapsed in his religious practices. He accepted the need for change of clothing but saw no reason for lapse in Jewish practice. Finally, Shmayahu returned to Korczyn and lived with his son Chaim and occasionally received some money from his daughter Dworah, so that he should not fall a burden to his family. He made himself useful by tending to the horses of his sons. He had a feeling where he was needed and appeared. He was very familiar with horses and even wild horses were no match for him. He knew how to handle them. When I left for the USA, he was already 75, totally gray but carried himself well and his simple clothing gave him statue. Honor his memory.

[Page 291-293]

Avraham, the slow one.

Each township in Eastern Europe had rich, poor, intelligent, slow and a few mentally retarded people. All these elements made up the community or kehilla. The latter functioned as a unit in good, happy, and sad times. It absorbed the stress and pressures of the outside and inside and frequently acted as a big family. We could not measure all townships by the same yardstick as we could not measure two people except twins for their outer and inner similarities. Even the income structure of the townships could not be compared since the level of living and management was different. A family with a certain income could live well and even give charity while another family barely scrapped the week with the same sum. Thus, there developed differences within each community. But there was one characteristic that was common to all townships. They took care of the slow, the mentally retarded and even the insane. The atmosphere of these townships was conducive to restrain these people from overactive actions and there were always people that provided and helped them with their problems and needs. There were few old maids or bachelors that remained single due their mental status. The matchmakers already worked out all the patterns so that these people could lead a family life. Of course, there were exceptions or extreme cases that were beyond help. Still these couples functioned although very few produced offspring. Apparently, nature has a way to protect itself. Of course, there were always elements that tried to play with these unfortunate people, notably children. The townships had their hands full in keeping these people calm so as not to provoke them and cause outbursts of anger or pain that could be harmful to all parties concerned. The townships handled as best they could these situations for there were no psychological or psychiatric services to give advice. Still, the townships did a remarkable job in controlling these people. Even the police rarely intervened in these cases.

The marriage of two mentally retarded or slightly insane people was a mitzva for it helped two lost souls. The entire community was usually involved, especially the well to do. They took care to provide the couple with a place and implements to start house. They would also provide some income so that the couple could exist. These people were usually the guests at the wedding and they danced the first mitzvah dance to set off the festivities of the wedding. As a matter of fact, most regular weddings were not better organized or prepared than the special weddings. One such wedding involved the cantor's son Avraham, also called Avraham the stupid one. He was meek and good-natured but slow. He was getting older and still a bachelor. They matched him up with an elder girl that was a hunchback. I think my mother was the matchmaker for she was a sister to my mother and lived with my grandparents in a village near Rymanow. Lea listened to my mother and other people and accepted the marriage. Avraham did some postal errands for the Raab family business. He carried parcels from and to the post office. Perhaps he also did errands for other people in town so that he could earn a few pennies and provide for the home. Avraham and Lea lived together until the Germans took them away with the entire community. Avraham certainly did no harm to the Germans, he had a right to live, certainly more so than the German killers. Avraham's stupidity affected no one but the German wisdom destroyed the world.

[Page 294-296]

The Wife of the Kehilla Leader and Neche the Fool.

Our community leader Shulem Akselrad married late in life with a girl from Stryj. He was already a grandfather and his grandchildren were already elder children. His two sons, David and Simon lived in Korczyn and had children. Only the youngest son, Bended lived at home. He was about twenty years of age. Shulem led a nice life without a wife for many years. Suddenly, he married a relatively young girl from the big city that did not wear a wig and spoke mainly Polish. There was no outcry but a married woman with her own hair in Korczyn was not Jewish. The fact that she spoke Polish added insult to injury. Few Jews understood or conversed in the language in Korczyn including Shulem himself. But nobody wanted to start with the kehilla leader that had excellent relations with the local administration. Mrs. Akselrad had no friends in Korczyn and did not attempt to make ones. The Jewish women in town avoided her for fear of being pointed out as having lapsed in their Jewish behavior. The younger set dared not look in her direction. She only related to Bendet Akselrad who was older than his stepmother. He made peace with his father's decision. He accepted her language and her dress for he himself lived in Budapest with his regiment and was thus more familiar with the ways of the world.

She was not an ugly woman but the fact that she had no dowry indicated that she had no resources and was forced to marry an elder person, especially a community leader. In the summer evenings, one could see Bendet and his stepmother promenading from their home to the market, on to the shul and until the house of Godal where the Jewish homes ended. No other unmarried couple in Korczyn dared to promenade in such fashion but nobody wanted to start trouble for Shulem Akselrad was a powerful men with good connections. His wife had a strictly kosher home, dairy and meat were separate. No rumors to the contrary were ever circulated in town. Shulem prayed each day, whether he came each day to shul nobody knew. Even very religious Jews would on occasion miss services for various reasons. But on Shabbath and the holidays he always came with his full traditional garb, a streimel, a silk bekeshe and a gartel that sparkled with cleanliness. He also wore a stiff collar and a tie since he married. The township forgave him these indulgences.

I discovered more about the conduct of the wife of the community leader from our neighbor, Neche the fool. Neche married a vagabond in order not to remain an old maid. She lived with her sister and mother, both widows. The husband disappeared after the wedding and she remained a married woman without a husband. She shore her hair and carried a hat; that was the extent of her marriage. Her husband was never seen again. This Neche went occasionally to see the wife of the community leader. I do not know what she did there. She could not clean or scrub the floors but obviously there was some relationship between them. Neche did not speak Polish, so apparently, the conversation must have been in Yiddish. Once I overheard Neche tell her mother that the wife of the kehilla leader dressed immodestly in her house. Neche could not understand such behavior. Let all the characters that I mentioned here rest eternally in heaven.

[Page 297-301]

Ber Fishel

Ber Fishel was younger than myself by three or four years. We did not study together in the cheder. As a matter of fact, we were never friends in Korczyn. Only in 1914 when WWI started, we found ourselves in the same military company and became friends that lasted for a long time. As a matter of fact, we continued our friendship through correspondence when I left for America. The friendship ceased when I was forced to stop it for personal reasons that I am sure he shared with me until his dying day.

When I met Ber, he was already set in his ways and knew what he wanted while I was still in the clouds so to speak. I had no definite position and was ideologically unattached. Still our friendship developed and we understood each other. He was the first open Zionist in Korczyn and this took a certain amount of bravery in those days while I remained attached to my Yeshiva outlook in spite of the fact that I no longer practiced it since I left Korczyn. We always discussed items and he was interested in everything, a pity that he disappeared so young.

I am certain that his disappointed love life had something to do with it but this is an old story. I do not know who broke the relationship; whether Neche, his girl friend, by going to Palestine or Ber by marrying a girl from Krakow. I am certain that the separation was a real tragedy for the couple. I listened to both sides but was helpless in the matter. I am not certain whether they could have patched up their differences and lived happily after. The fact remained that the separation was bitter for both parties and affected them for they had read enough romantic novels where things end differently. I personally preferred a relationship that developed after the marriage ceremony but this was my personal view. The fact remained that I was their friend and saw them suffer.

Ber helped me a great deal with general knowledge to which I had no access. He knew well Hebrew literature, read German literature and was familiar with Yiddish literary life. On occasion he used to write for Hebrew or Yiddish publications. He had something to say and said it orally and in writing. The fact that he came from Korczyn presented problems since one had to be careful about the written material. Where he received his knowledge in the religious township of Korczyn was a real question that he never answered. But I felt that he traveled far away from the religious environment that he lived in. His discussions showed me that I still had lots to learn even in Jewish knowledge. He never embarrassed me but pushed me to advance myself in general knowledge. Finally, after seven months of active duty in the Imperial Austrian Army, I received liberty and went to Budapest.

The city was cosmopolitan and offered many opportunities. I tried to acquire what I lacked spiritually. I concentrated on the German language that I lacked. I purchased grammar books and dictionaries to improve my German.

I wrote letters to Ber in German and he corrected them. He did not receive liberty and had to stay at the base. I also wrote to several female friends in German. They never corrected me even if I made serious errors and I know that I made them. I also visited the Weissman family in the city. Here I met Neche and her brother that lived with the family. As I visited the family, I also became involved in the romantic relationship between Ber and Neche and even heard some of the fantasies. He in his military uniform dreamt of sweeping his beloved damsel off the ground and she saw her lover on a white horse. The fantasies reached the skies and then crashed at the wall of reality. They drifted apart before they even lived together. This served me a lesson not to involve myself romantically and led me to concentrate in other intellectual spheres and failures. There is no set road for every person. Ber and Neche exhausted themselves spiritually in the affair and suffered greatly. All their dreams and hopes vanished as the clouds. One has to have luck for such romance to fulfill itself. Obviously it was not in their cards. I am amazed that I was the so-called expert that listened to both parties and was supposed to render decisions or comfort to the parties. Still I tried to use my common sense and did the best that I was able to do. Dear Ber, I knew how much you suffered. You were a Zionist and did not see the creation of the State of Israel. Neche left you and went to your dreamland where she married and had son that would carry on her memory. Honor to both of you.

[Page 302-309]

Haim Wolf [Koref]

Haim Wolf was not my friend but the friend of my brother Shlomo. He was about two and a half or three years older than myself. He was no scholar but studied the talmud for two seasons. Thus he was familiar with the religious needs of the Jewish community, whether it pertained to the section of the week, or a holiday or what specific holidays required. Haim became closer following my creation of the sign Shaviti that was attached to the stand used by the leader of the service in the shul. He played with letters and tried to arrange them in artistic forms. His first expressions in Jewish artistry consisted of drawing a menorah, a crown, a star of David and other Jewish symbols. He had ability and was quite capable and could have drawn the same sign that made me a bit famous in Korczyn. However I beat him to it and this established me as the religious artist of the township that was entrusted with the flags for Simhat Torah, dreidels for Hannukah and presentations for Purim. All these activities enabled me to buy a talmud, a book, or a story book about a saint.

Haim Wolf was an only child. His father, Yankel was a tailor that sewed jackets and pants for the peasants and sold them at the fair. He managed to build a brick building in the market. The ground floor had a cigarette and a grocery store and the family lived upstairs in a large apartment. The tailor was known as a miser. He never borrowed or loaned. He was a quiet withdrawn person. He hardly received an aliyah to the torah on Shabbath or Holidays. Perhaps he resented it but never showed it. He dressed clean, his clothing without patches or repairs, although his bekeshe was very old. His father implanted the need for cleanliness in the son. Haim wore a hat, an overcoat that was very old but clean and spotless. His boots always had a shine in spite of the mud in Korczyn that destroyed shoes. He once explained to me his theory of walking that consisted of stepping lightly on the ground without pressing the entire body to the ground. When entering mud, the lightness prevented the foot from sinking and splashing the mud all over. He showed me his manner of walking and I agreed with him. I left home at the age of 16 to learn a trade but decided to return for Passover and Sukkoth to Korczyn. I was drawn to the township where I spent so many hours in the shul between the minha and maariv service and the days spent studying the Talmud. Haim was already then my best friend.

He assumed my artistic duties in the township and asked many questions regarding painting that I could not answer since I did not know the answers. He once asked me to sketch for him a woman dressed in a formal dress that was ordered from him. I draw the picture but it lacked the necessary proportions. Still, Haim told me that he corrected the picture. All these things he did for free but once he was married he started to charge for the various artistic activities and developed certain ideas that provided him with an income. He designed and built a walled fence around the Jewish cemetery and surmounted the wall with broken glass so that nobody could climb over the fence and vandalize the cemetery. Even the Germans did not touch the cemetery and it remained protected to this day. Thus the name of Haim Wolf has been memorialized. He did not make money on this project but saw to it that all his helpers were paid. He did not want to be accused of making money. The cemetery also contained the tombs of Jews from nearby villages and even from the city of Kros that died 60-70 years ago.

Each year, the tombstone chiseler came to Korczyn to inscribe the new tombstones. Haim slowly learned the trade and started to take orders from people as to what they wanted to inscribe on the tombstone and what designs they wanted. He than created models into which he poured the liquid cement and polished them. Then he lettered the tombs. He also fixed the old tombstones, especially the lettering and earned some money. People that came later to the USA told me that he had good taste. He also undertook and built facilities for the shul. The shul's outhouse consisted of three flimsy walls attached to the outer wall of the shul. The walls consisted of attached planks. A passerby could not see the entrance but there was one. Inside there was a long board with 7-8 holes for people to squat but children and even adults stood on the board and tended to their needs. As a result, the areas of the holes were infested with urine and many people preferred not to use the toilet. Nobody cared for the place and nobody was interested in cleaning the area. People urinated all along the walls rather than use the outhouse.

Haim built nice facilities opposite the shul next to Mechale, the baker's house. The place was clean and Haim even cemented passage way from the shul to the outhouse so that people could reach the facilities in the winter. Only Haim could think of all of these jobs as part of his cleanliness. He also designed the Eliyahu chair for the shul that was used in the ceremony of circumcision of newborn babies. The carpenter built the chair, the painter painted it and Haim presented it to the shul as a gift. Indeed it was religious symbol and a true gift to the community for generations to come for the chair is used only when needed. Thus, Haim tried to erase his reputation as a miser by giving such a nice gift to the shul. It was not my intention to delve into the relationship between the community leadership and Haim, Yaacov and preceding generations of Korefs. Suffice it to say that news reached me that the leadership of the kehilla asked 1000 guilden of Haim Wolf for the burial of his father in 1920. Haim tried to reduce the price but the chevrah kadisha or burial society refused to budge. He refused to pay and the corpse remained in his house for three days. When people asked him what he intended to do, he replied that his father was sewing clothing. The kehilla had to bury him after three days for free since this was the law.

The leadership of the community and Haim Wolf started a war of words and innuendoes. Haim used every occasion to criticize indirectly the leaders and they had to take it without being able to reply in kind. Each Saturday after the first part of the service and prior to the reading of the torah, the shamash announced the local announcements and sometimes the rabbi would give a sermon. One Shabbath, there were no announcements and no sermon, Haim Wolf mounted the bimah or reading platform and banged on the table to indicate that he had something to say to the congregation. The leader of the kehilla, Eliyahu Kaufman, called out the line to take out the torah. In effect, he blocked Haim from talking. The latter lost control of himself and hit Eliyahu in the face. We can skip the events that followed the incident. The heavenly court will settle that matter and it is not for us to judge the case. Following the event, Haim became the so called rabbi of some unwanted youngsters who sat with him after the prayers and he explained to them some lines of the section of the week. This gave him an opportunity to continue his criticisms directed at certain people. Most of the participants at his lectures sided with him and became his supporters. In Korczyn both camps coexisted and continued to live sided by side, never reverting to the shedding of blood. True, Haim raised a hand against another Jew but we can understand the pain inflicted on the son at the burial of his father who was a hard working person and lived from the sweat of his brow.

I still remember that Haim once told me prior to WWI that if he were a writer like Mendele Mocher Sfarim he would create more piety in the township of Korczyn. I knew that he was not a reader of books but under the influence of Haim Levy Tzeiger he was familiar with the famous Jewish author who enabled him to fantasize. He was no reader but he grasped concepts and observed events that he sketched. In his older years he became the rabbi of some youngsters and helped them with their study. I would like to end the Wolf story by stating that since the community had to bury his father without payment, they buried his father next to the fence; not the most respectable place in a Jewish cemetery. Haim built a mausoleum around the tombstone as was the custom for holy men or famous rabbis. The town jesters claimed that he did it so that his father would not escape.

[Page 309-310]

Yesterday, today and tomorrow

The Jewish immigrants to the USA lived in their own communities that reflected the area they came from be it Litvaks, Galitzianers, Hungarians, Roumanians, Polish, Ukrainian etc. About 40 years ago these separations slowly melted down and real integration started, except for the German Jewish population. They came earlier and were wealthier and looked down on all other Jewish immigrants. Still, the Jewish melting pot absorbed them eventually and their institutions. The various groups brought with them the various antagonisms to each other from the old country. A Litvak looked down on a Galitzianer and vice-versa, a marriage between two people from these groups was considered a mixed marriage among Jews in those days. In reality, there were hardly any differences between the groups, they were all poor immigrants. Still Litvaks never missed an opportunity to attack Galitzianers and claim superiority. The Galitzianers of course ignored these remarks.

Eventually, all these differences disappeared and today there is hardly a memory of them. Most children and grandchildren today hardly know where their parents were born, there are of course some exceptions. The latter were due to the fact that their parents dragged the children to the meetings of the Landsmanschaft. Thus, they acquired some basic facts about their parents and knew that they came from places where people lived. They also heard that there were families that still remained there. The children became aware of Jewish civilization and continuity. Their parents transplanted some of the values to the new country. These values and the opportunities of the new place enabled the parents to endure the hardships of the beginning. The foundation was there and it took some time for it to begin to blossom again. Thus, the need to survive the difficult period; this was the raison d'être for the Landsmanshaften, to help each other overcome these difficulties.

[Page 311-312]

The Korczyner-Reisher Synagogue

About 80-90 years ago Korczyner and Reisher Landsmen met and established a synagogue; no date was recorded. Korczyn was a small town with about 200 families and Reishe or Rzeszow had about 10,000 Jews. The two towns were a distance from each other in Galicia. Why did they create a single shul? None of the present leaders of the congregation could provide a sensible answer. The fact remained that the congregation was worth about $90,000. The Korczyner Landsmen took a mortgage of about $35,000 for the shul on Willet St. yet, today, the Korczyner - Reisher Landsmanschaft contributed $200 to the Korczyner Yizkor book and they also give twice yearly checks for the Korczyner Relief Society in the amount of $50. That was the extent of the assistance rendered by the Korczyner-Reisher Synagogue to the cultural and historical activities of Korczyner people. We were of the opinion that it could have provided greater help. The same could be said of the cemetery that was shared by the two towns. No records were kept as to the composition of the graves and their origins. The present leadership no longer knows the origin or composition of the people that were buried at the cemetery. Here in the USA the Korczyner and Reisher joined a union that build a synagogue for their members that lived mainly on the Lower East Side in New York. Those that passed away were also assured of burial places that were purchased for all the members of the shul.

[Page 312-313]

Who came once to the USA

Prior to WWI, most Jewish immigrants from the Austrian Empire were men who avoided the draft of the Austrian Imperial Army. They did not want to eat treif and to play soldier. Furthermore, the burden of the draft fell on the poor elements of Jewish society whose parents could not help them dodge the draft. The Russian Jews left for similar reasons as well as for the terrible anti-Jewish persecutions and the great poverty. Thus, the main motive for many Austrian Jews was military rather than economic. Economically, they managed somehow to exist, especially in Korczyn where their spirituality was fulfilled. The fear of losing the Jewish religious spirit prevented many people from going to the States. Thus the Landsmanshaften were created to morally and religiously support the members. They adapted to the customs and ways of modern America. They organized shtibelech or small shuls in storefronts where the people of the same village or area in the old country prayed. Here they found some solace in each other's arms. Of course, if the membership was large, a synagogue was built. These activities required money for the places had to be maintained and the new poor immigrants paid for it. There was also a need for torah readers and leaders of services. In the old country this was no problem for there was a large reservoir of experienced people but in the USA there was a serious shortage. Some people were still a bit familiar with the daily prayers and perhaps Shabbath prayers but to conduct holiday services was another problem. Improvisations and arrangements had to be made.

Jewish scholars did not leave Europe unless they were forced to. These people attracted followers as soon as they reached the USA shores. The Jewish immigrants were hungry for the home tunes and melodies of the old country. Synagogues, shuls and study centers evolved from the yearning for the ways of the old home. Of course these institutions assumed an American approach. People dressed modern during the week and on Shabbath and Holidays they wore top hats or hard hats that added a certain festivity to the day. People participated in the prayers and partook in the various religious activities as they used to do in the old country. Instead of selecting a head of the community that was very influential and well connected, here in the USA an elected president of the congregation was usually a person that made it in the new country, not necessarily a scholar. The congregation also elected other officers such as a vice-president, gabbai or manager of the services and shamash. Most of the people thus elected were not scholars or pious, but rather people that wanted to be involved in the congregation. A katzav [butcher in Yiddish] from Korczyn became a butcher in the USA. The landsmanschaften were the breeding ground for many congregations and relief institutions. They also attracted with time people from nearby places that were few in numbers. Thus the landsmanshaften became in themselves small melting pots and helped in the overall melting pot of the Jewish population. Each group contributed some characteristics into the general common unity of American Jewry.

[Page 314-316]

Yankel Guzik

Yankel Guzik came to the USA about 100 years ago and suffered all the humiliations of the immigrant. He worked as a tailor in a shop. The hours were long but Shabbath and Holidays he did not work. He considered himself a Korczyner landsman and together with the Reisher Landsmen created the combined synagogue. He also continued his activities on behalf of the Korczyner poor people in the old country. Their needs were numerous; poor people, sick people, old maids, orphans etc. Yankel collected money from the Korczyner in the USA and helped the Jewish people in Korczyn. He became an institution and nobody refused him assistance. Everybody answered his call for help. When he had time, he would visit the Landsmen at their homes and collect in person their donations. He soon attracted Raphael Meisner to help him with his work. The latter also worked in the garment industry that attracted many Jewish immigrants. Together they made the rounds among the Korczyner some of them had already left the lower east side for better living places. Some of these people also made large contributions to the fund such as Jetre, Pasternak and Goldstein. They appreciated the work being done by the collectors.

I remember when Yankel Guzik came to Korczyn about 1904-5; he was already an old and sick man. He took the advice of his doctors and went to the Karlsbad spa in Czechoslovakia. On the way he stopped in Korczyn. He no longer had family in the shtetl but had strong feelings for it. He came with my cousin Dora Birman who was married to Max Birman. Max and Yankel Guzik's son were business partners. Yankel Guzik and Dora Birman traveled to Europe and back together but had different destinations.. Even here in Europe they met. I remember that Yankel made a very poor impression on Korczyn. His appearance was ghostly in spite of his excellent dress that consisted of a suit made to order, a stiff collar, a black tie and a small hard hat. He was dressed in the latest American fashion but his health appearance made a poor impression. Apparently clothing could not hide the ravages of time even in the USA. At the time, it was decided with the advice of Yankel that Dora Birman would take my older brother Shlomo, aged 14, to the USA. His brother Haim Hersh and myself would follow after WWI. Thus events tend to be connected to each other whether we acknowledged them or not. Yankel died in the USA but all efforts to locate the date of death proved fruitless. The date deserved to be printed here. Sorry that such important element of information was omitted. Many important elements of information would be omitted since the facts are missing. In conclusion I can merely state that when I arrived in the States, Yankel was already dead for many years but left the charity work in the capable hands of Raphael Meisner.

[Page 317-322]

Raphael Meisner and Eliyahu Katz

Yankel Guzik died prior to WWI and Raphael Meisner became the help institution for Korczyn in the USA. If we listed all the charitable deeds we would need an entire book. We limit ourselves to a few instances to show the wide variety of activities that he performed. Prior to Passover, he provided the poor people of Korczyn with financial assistance for the holiday. He also helped marry the poor spinsters in Korczyn. Poor people visited him and never left the place without some contribution. Following WWI, three quarters of Korczyn was destroyed including the study center, the shul and the public bathhouse. It was Raphael Meisner that helped to rebuild these places. The walled fence around the cemetery that stands to today was built with the money that Raphael Meisner and Eliyahu Katz collected in the States. Both were workers in the garment industry but gave of themselves in their help to the needs of Korczyn.

I remember that both used to visit me at home to collect the dues. These visits occurred during the slack season in the garment industry when the workers had some time off. Then they visited the Landsmen and collected the dues. They had a list of people and received nice contributions. Nobody refused these collectors for everybody appreciated their work. When the wealthy donors passed away, the collectors continued to visit the homes of the children and received donations. The latter were smaller than their parents used to give as they were no longer attached to Korczyn as their parents. Still the collectors visited every Landsmen to collect dues.

Eliyahu Katz

With the end of WWII, we realized the extent of work done by Meisner and Katz. All the survivors managed to find the address of Meisner and pleaded for help. His house became the center for the Jewish refugees from Korczyn. Unfortunately, most of the well to do donors were no longer alive. Still the team continued to wake the conscience of the former Korczyner for assistance and managed to help those that needed. During those days, I read in the newspaper the survival story of one of Haim Dym's children that survived the war and reached Belgium. I was so moved by the news item that I volunteered to drive the team to visit the landsmen. Only then did I realize the amount of work involved and I felt good that I contributed to the effort. I also helped the team to save their energies for they traveled by bus, subway and trams. They tried to introduce a modern collection system but it did not succeed. The personal touch continued and raised some money. At the time Raphael Meisner was already in his eighties and Elihau Katz was in his nineties. Both felt like fathers to the rescued Jews of Korczyn. Meisner's house was the planning center for help for the immigrants. His wife and children were involved in all the activities in spite of the fact that the children were raised in the States. In the days following WWII, we received the first tragic reports about the survivors and met to discuss ways and means to help the survivors. The meeting place was of course the home of Raphael Meisner. Mrs. Meisner tended to the home but contributed immensely with suggestions and comments that proved essential in providing help to the survivors. As a matter of fact, the entire family was involved in the project of helping the survivors. The most important element was the fact that all survivors had an address in the USA where they could get an update on the Korczyners that survived the war. Some of these people were lone survivors without an address and frequently with little hope. Their inquiries were always answered and gave some hope.

We called a big emergency meeting in the Reisher-Korczyner synagogue where Raphael was the main speaker. There were no other people to assume leadership roles in helping the Korczyner survivors. Everything depended on Raphael Meisner. The big donors did not attend the meeting. One had to visit them personally to get donations. The number of big donors declined with time, the next generation was not that interested. At one of the meetings of the Korczyner society, Raphael decided to nominate me to be the president of the Korczyner Relief Society. I was in for a shock. I was never involved in community affairs and suddenly to handle a society was more than I bargained for. But I took the job and organized meetings and 1 learned the mechanics of running meetings. I was also the secretary of the Jewish Ethical society so that I had some experience. At the meetings I never spoke since I let Raphael handle all the discussions. By nature I am shy and not a fluent orator and that inhibited me from talking. Suddenly, both figures, Meisner and Katz, passed away in rapid succession and I remained with the Korczyner society. I expected that people would step forth to assume the leadership but nobody did. Everybody was pleased with the situation and I continued. Perhaps someday someone would take over but in the meantime I continued. I am presiding the society for 18 years and see no replacement. I am very thankful that Meisner and Katz selected Haim Davidowitz as my secretary. He was very experienced and stood by my side all these years.

[Page 323-325]

Korczyner Landsmen in the USA

The destiny of the Jewish people apparently intended for the Jews to be scattered all over the world so that there could be traces everywhere of the Jewish shtetls. In spite of Hitler's plans to eradicate all Jewish traces in Europe, he failed since everywhere there were a few roots that reminded the world of the shtetl and the Jews. 70-80 years ago, some young Jews from Korczyn came here to avoid the draft. Those that had parents with connections and means or had disabilities remained at home. Some also came to the States to earn a few dollars and intended to return home to Korczyn. Most of them remained in the States and adjusted their religious life style to the country. They never separated themselves from Korczyn and always gave a hand to those that collected monies for Korczyn like Meisner and Katz. Following WWI the contributions increased as the needs increased with the destruction of the study center and the bathhouse. The local Jewish kehilla had no money for reconstruction. Only the USA could support the community. So the kehilla leadership turned to the two Jewish collectors to raise the necessary funds and the Korczyner replied in the affirmative and according to their abilities.

Between those landsman that succeeded in the USA there were some that knew personally Meisner and Katz from the old country and tried to get some attention but they always gave donations. Some old Korczyner died but their relatives or family members were asked to contribute and they did. We can conclude that these two people had a very good response in their collections for Korczyn. As soon as the slack season started in the garment industry, they planned their campaign of visits to the landsman and even figured out the amount to request. They visited every landsman and with the money helped rebuild the institutions of Korczyn and at the same time also helped the individual needs of the Jewish community in Korczyn; such as financial help for Passover for the poor people. There were also personal appeals for help that were answered. Their crowning task was the financing of a walled fence around the cemetery in Korczyn. Haim Wolf Koref conceived the plan and Meisner and Katz paid for it. The cemetery remained intact to today due to its glass topping. The Korczyner kehilla could have never financed such project.

Following the destruction of WWII, the Korczyner Jewish survivors discovered the address of the American help institution named Raphel Meisner. A steady stream of letters and inquiries reached the address. That address passed from hand to hand amongst the Korczyner survivors. Meisner tried to help and provided as much as possible for their needs. Meanwhile, the big donors had passed away. The medium donors continued their donations and even increased them. At the time, the Korczyner Relief Society was formed to handle the needs of the survivors. The organization continued with the activities to the present. I remember the times prior to Passover when the Meisner home became the planning center for sending care packages to all the

Korczyner Jewish survivors. The planning of the content of the packages was a big logistical problem. The entire Meisner family was involved in the project, especially the children that were raised in the USA. Mrs. Meisner cleaned the kitchen but gave us great insight into the needs of people prior to holidays. Her suggestions were always appreciated. Finally, the packages were ready to be shipped to all the Korczyner Jewish survivors.

[Page 326-328]

The Meisner Family

In 1904-5, my brother Shlomo and Leibish Dawidowitz were boarders at the Meisner home. Immigrants preferred to stay with people that they knew from the old country. The rent was smaller and they felt at home away from home. The landlord gave advice and food and also provided a familiar atmosphere. This enabled the immigrant to look for a job and to save some money when he started working.. In those days families were large but there was always room for borders. The landlady frequently acted as the mother for the new immigrants and helped them with advice and information. They considered it a mitzvah. The borders were usually from the same shtetl or were family members. My brother remained with the Meisner for some time and then left due to his peddling business that forced him to frequently change his flat. Eventually, he married and had a family. For 44-45 years, he never saw the Meisner family. The latter left the Lower East Side and moved to Brooklyn where they purchased a house. In the new house, they raised and married their children. Here they also saw their first grandchildren.

In 1948, Shlomo and I went to the Meisners about relief activities. When Mrs. Meisner saw my brother, she went to the kitchen drawer and took a small pair of scissors and handed them to Shlomo. This belonged to you. She kept the item for forty years. This was Mrs. Beile Meisner. She kept an insignificant item for 40 years for somebody who was a boarder for a short period of time. We can thus understand the character of these people and their devotion to helping those that needed help and were less fortunate than themselves.

Respect the memory of Raphel and Beila Meisner.

Mr. and Mrs. Meisner

[Page 329-331]

Raphael's daughter Sara

The picture would be incomplete without a description of the Meisner household that was the center of information and help for the Korczyner Jews from before WWI to the total destruction of the community during WWII. Sara played an important role in these activities based on first hand experience. In those days the relief activities assumed different shapes due to the scattering of the survivors. Basically, the pattern of collecting donations did not change as far as I can tell, although I joined these efforts towards the tail end of the operations. Still I received a basic idea of relief activities. Mr. Meisner remained an outsider in America in spite of his many years in the States. He barely spoke English. At work and in the neighborhood he spoke Yiddish; in the shul he went to he spoke Yiddish. Thus there was no need to learn English or become Americanized. He had some minor contacts with the outside world so to speak, at the post office in sending packages, or at the bank for money transactions. This was where Sara came into the picture. She was born in Korczyn but came to the USA as a toddler with her mother. She was raised in the States and became the porter of the packages to the post office as well as other relief duties that involved English. She handled the mailing lists with all the camp addressees and kept track of the survivors throughout the world.

The Meisner home was always a beehive of activity. There were always problems somewhere in the world that affected Korczyner survivors and they turned for help to the Meisners. Raphael Meisner was already too old to handle the burden, so it fell on Sara's shoulders. She accepted the task in spite of the fact that she had her own family to care for. Her family lived together with her parents until her parents passed away. The two families were the center of all the relief activities of the Korczyner Jews. Sara's sister and brothers married and moved to their own homes. But Sarah continued with her relief activities as though driven by a religious fervor.

Sara Meisner with her family.

[Page 331]

Sam Meisner, Raphael's son

With the passing of Raphael Meisner in 1953, his son Sam, born and raised in the USA, assumed the position of treasurer of the society. This was part of the tradition at home of helping Korczyner Jews. The position involved many financial headaches with deposits and withdrawals but Sam attended to the job. Sam was the second child of the Meisners and was a lawyer by profession. He took on the job as part of his father's tradition. Many Korczyner landsman only heard of the name Meisner. My name and Haim's, the secretary, were unknown. We were newcomers and used the magical name of Meisner to establish contacts. Until today, the family name rings a bell for Korczyner and opens purses for contributions. Thus a second generation of descendants of Korczyn continued in the tradition of their parents and gave charity for the needy of Korczyn.

Everybody has his privacy and his family, but we were all raised with some overall values that tied us to some similar roots in the past. We continued with the chain of the past into the future. Future generations that dig for information about their past will be able to find some information about their origins of their ancestry. No stranger will be able to give them these facts. We followed the tradition of the past that recorded history. We tried to follow the same pattern by describing the kehilla of Korczyn as the people lived it. We did the best that we knew in recording the history of the shtetl. We described the events in good spirit and in spirit of individual respect that could serve as a model to future generations.

[Page 333-338]

Meir, the son of Nahum Kirschner

Meir was a tailor prior to being bar-mitzvahed. His father Nahum Kirschner was a water porter and his mother sold milk. She milked cows at certain farms and sold the milk and butter that she made to Jewish customers. She also sold head kerchiefs to the wives of farmers at the Korczyner market on Fridays and at the Krosner market on Mondays. All these activities enabled the family to get by without charity handouts. Nahum was not educated but wanted a better life for his children. His older son, Mordechai Leib, he placed as an apprentice with a tailor who was not very successful, and his younger son he placed with Moshe Schneider for four years without pay. This indeed was lucky for Moshe was considered an excellent tailor that sewed clothing for the gentry and the local well to do. He was always busy and had four to five helpers and one or two apprentices that sewed buttons, stitched materials, delivered ready merchandise, handled packages and helped the landlady with various chores. Even without experience, an apprentice was very handy in such a busy place. As soon as the apprentice learned some trade skills, he was no longer available for household duties but had to help in the shop and a new apprentice was hired.

It was customary for an apprentice to eat at home the first year and with the master the next three years. The faster the apprentice learned the trade the more useful he became to the master. The food at the master's house was usually better than at home. Besides, he acquired a trade that would sustain him. The apprentice rarely received a tip for his slaving. Sometimes the owner or the parents would toss a few pennies to the apprentice. The workers ate with the master. The landlady was busy preparing food for her family and the shop workers. Meir finished his apprenticeship very well. He soon found a job in a bigger city but nothing to brag about. He earned a salary that enabled him to eat, pay for his lodging and purchase some clothing. He visited on Passover and Sukkot dressed in modern style, collar and tie. He considered himself important and his parents were very pleased. He soon had to report for the draft and decided to leave for the States where his older brother worked. He joined his brother who was not very successful in the USA. Meir was an experienced tailor and had immediately many job opportunities in the garment industry for his skills were in demand.

The garment unions enabled their workers to obtain wages that allowed them to live in modest comfort. Some of the workers became independent and succeeded in creating big operations where the materials went in and the final products emerged. The American manufacturers competed well with their European counterparts and insured that their workers should share in the benefits. Meir tried several times to become independent but failed. He was always accepted back in the shops where his reputation was excellent. He married and led a quiet life. He was not knowledgeable; perhaps he remembered some Hebrew letters that his Yashnitzer teacher taught him, or some written letters that was the custom of this teacher to teach. He taught the students the Latin alphabet and some mathematics. Some of the older students enjoyed this information. Whether Meir remembered any of this information I am doubtful. He knew that his possibilities were limited and therefore was not interested in scholarship but in reality; and that meant a trade. Thus he was not interested in Judaic studies but did learn to pray and to handle a Yiddish newspaper. In the USA he read the Yiddish paper 'The Forwards' that became his university. Meir like many other immigrants read these papers that provided them with background information and rounded out the education that they never acquired. Many of them never mastered the ability to write legible letters, but their general knowledge did increase. Here in the USA, those that had natural abilities managed to compete successfully with those that were privileged in the old country. The States were an equalizer of sorts; here all the privileges of Korczyn did not help but the individual had to prove himself. Everyone had to make a path for himself and Meir knew the road. He had no children but had a nice income. He bought a house in Boro Park and his door was always open. The place had three flats that Meir rented to poor people without profit.

The grounds looked very impressive. He helped his parents, brothers and sisters in Korczyn. We must compliment his wife that handled the financial accounts and the correspondence. She influenced Meir to help the needy people, especially of Korczyn. They donated large amounts to the various appeals of the Korczyner society. After WWII, they continued to give large donations in spite of the fact that they helped some of their family members that survived the war. When Meir started to be sick, I was embarrassed to travel and ask for donations. They called us and insisted that we accept the donations. When Meir passed away, his sick wife continued to send checks to the Korczyner Relief Society. As a matter of fact, we even stopped calling her to remind her of the appeals but the contributions kept arriving.

We had many Meirs in the USA. They continued the religious life of the shtetl and contributed greatly to help other Jews. They observed Shabbath and Holidays, prayed daily, and belonged to shuls where they listened to lectures and studied mishnayot. Pity that I did not have the chance to encounter many Meirs but I would like to take this opportunity to memorialize all those that were not mentioned by name in the book. Please excuse us for the omissions that may never be rectified.

[Page 339]

Hannah Malka the Glazier

I do not know the background of Hannah Malka or how she became a glazier. But she installed windows in Jewish homes in Korczyn She was an old lady as I remember her. She did not carry a case of glass on her back as was the custom amongst glaziers in those days.

She knew the dimensions of the windows in Korczyn and precut the panes at home. She then carried them to the house for installation. Occasionally, she used her diamond cutter to adjust the panes so that they fitted perfectly. Then she nailed them into the frame and glued them. Apparently her husband was in the business, and when he died she continued the trade and made a few pennies. She never left Korczyn proper. The peasants bought glass panes from her on market days. They knew where she lived and they gave the dimensions and she cut it for them. She also provided them with some small nails and glue so that they installed at home. I do not know how much she earned but she maintained herself. The fact that such a trade should fall into the hands of a woman was rare in those days.

[Page 340-345]

The old and new study center

During the Russia-Japanese war of 1904, all the moves and battles were discussed and interpreted in the study center when the Jews came to pray the evening services. Prior to the afternoon service or minha or during the break between the minha and maariv service and after the services, congregates formed circles to discuss the world events. Merchants that returned from the big cities reported the latest war stories and shared them with the local congregants as though the material was fresh; in reality some of these items were already old news. The Port Arthur battles and the fights between the Japanese and the Russians became first hand information for the local population. The storytellers had a field day and added their fantasies to the news. It was a pleasure to hear how the Japanese inflicted defeats to the Russians who were hated by the Jews. The Jews disliked the Russian Czars for the cruel treatment that they received at their hands. Some Jews discovered lines in the scriptures that explained the entire situation and all of this was a mere foreplay before the arrival of the Messiah.

Some of the more pragmatic thinkers searched for more precise clues and interpretations and found them in abundance. They also concluded that that the deliverance was at hand. Some of them were local people, others were wanderers that traveled from place to place and preached the same stories. Jews associated the Russian Empire with Amalek and, as the latter suffered a defeat, so will the Russian Czars for the wrongs that they did to the Jews. Moshe Mechale the teacher was a specialist in strategic military moves and related them to various lines in the Bible. How he could interpret military moves without ever having left Korczyn was never answered. But he was the military expert and developed the various military theories and interpretations of the various moves to the people, who did not have the slightest knowledge of where the places were or what importance they possessed. He enraptured us with his stories and interpretations. To this day it is a mystery to me where he received all his information. Gedalia Hopmeister, the cheder teacher, was also considered a military expert. He knew his Bible and all the military battles in it, and nobody could match him in the area. He was also an excellent raconteur and always had some new stories about this or that Rabbi or Holy man. I was always one of his listeners.

Korczyn kept itself spiritually busy by tending to the various needs that uplifted the spirit. Even the poor people were treated with respect and dignity. In those days, Shulem Akselrad decided that the old study center must be replaced with a new building. He was the only one that wore a collar with a tie. The rest of his clothing was in the Korczyner style. This man decided to replace the study center of Korczyn. A place that every inch was holy for present and previous generations. The old benches, tables, book closets, the holy ark that were sanctified by hundreds of pious people were to be replaced. The people were not in the mood for such a radical move; even the rabbi was not enthused with the idea. But nobody wanted to start a fight with the kehilla leader. The wooden beams in the walls were already moldy, the shingle roof let the raindrops enter, and the tables and benches gave way. But when did the rabbi had time to look at these things? He only knew that the Jews needed an income and for this he prayed daily and with great fervor on the High Holidays. On Simhat Torah he danced and managed to infuse into the old study center some joy that carried the participants with it. Who needed a new shul in these days; on the contrary the old place fitted more the invocations of the congregates and their needs. Besides, a new shul would detract from concentrating, and frivolous thoughts could enter the mind. Shulem knew how the community felt and beforehand obtained a building certificate to the effect that the old study center was not safe and endangered the congregates. With such paper nobody argued.

I do not remember what happened to the wood from the old shul, the beams, the roof beams, roof planks and the shingles. There was enough wood to heat the homes of the poor for several winters. But the poor people were afraid to use materials from the shul for fear of sacrilege. Probably, everything was burned near the cemetery as old books and pages are buried at the cemetery. Had personal use been made, the news would have reached everybody in Korczyn. The old study center was dismantled and the new one built in its place. During the construction of the study center, Jews prayed at the Rabbi's house and at other places throughout Korczyn. We already mentioned that the real unfinished synagogue of Korczyn had about twenty people during services, winter or summer. The walls consisted of bricks without plaster, the roof was not finished and during the rains the worshippers avoided the wet spots. The community could not finish the construction of the synagogue and it stood there for years. We should go into greater detail about the synagogue but presently we will leave the topic. The worshippers, especially the leader of the services and the readers of the torah deserved a special mention and perhaps we will mention them later.

The builders designated the holy place by stretching ropes along the earmarked walls. Rows of bricks were added to each layer and the structure rose taller with each passing day. The window panels and door frames were fortified. The new windows were three times larger than the old ones. The semicircle shaped windows with the Star of David and the multicolored glass gave the place the feeling of sanctity. The light entered mainly from the East and the West. The East Side had the Holy Arc and the praying lectern that reduced the window space. But all the walls had ample window space that provided light. Along the northern side was the women's section that was separated from the men's section by a wall that contained small windows through which one could hear the prayers. At the southern end there was an entrance hall where the heating stove and the water barrel stood. When the study center was reopened, everybody received their old seats next to new tables. Chandeliers were suspended from the ceilings as befitted a new holy place. I do not remember whether there were festivities prior to the opening of the new shul. The old holy arc was used in the new place. During the construction it was kept in a safe place together with other religious artifacts. The community accepted the new shul but with hesitation. Was it needed at the time, would the prayers be conducive, would it bring harmony etc. These were the questions in the minds of the people of Korczyn. The community and the Rabbi slowly moved into the spirit of the new shul. Everything was done here as it was done in the old place. Still, it was beautiful while the old one had layers of chalk that were painted for generations prior to the Passover holidays.

The service leaders wrapped in their talit knew how to infuse joy in the service of Shabbath and to arouse the congregation to join in the services. The weekly services were conducted by everyone that had Yahrtzeit or memorial service for a member of the family that passed away. Some people also liked to conduct services and nobody minded. Some people conducted evening services such as Shilem the baker or Motie Grin. The good service leaders on Shabbath were Zalke Melamed, Shulem Shochet, Hersh Yaacov Rossendler, Eliezar Raab and the very good cantor Avraham Neuman, son in law of Moshe Rothenberg. Of course these were my favorites as opposed to other people that had their own. Whenever Eliazar Rab traveled to the Rabbi of Zhikow, we knew that he would return with a new melody that would soon be the hit of the shul. The tune would make the rounds of the community and became part of the town until Eliezar Raab would bring something new and again the process repeated itself. These cantors infused joy and rapture into the congregants that stimulated their piety through the musical experience. Thus the Jew was elevated to higher spheres during the services, although at home the reality was far from joyous. Slowly but surely the community accepted the new shul.

[Page 346-348]

The Holy Ark

About two weeks after Shavout, two Jewish workers from outside started to build a new holy arc. The work was done in the synagogue and services were held while the work was in progress. The working noise stopped when the services reached certain portions of the service. From wood planks and pellets they shaped the new arc according to their plan. They were skilled wood craftsmen that worked steady and long hours. Their work took them to the High Holidays. They wanted to produce an arc that befitted a new holy place. Decorating artists that carved ornaments into the wood soon joined them. The shaped animals and symbols on the arc gave it beauty. One of these carvers was a real artist and created a masterpiece with singular taste and harmony. Suddenly the main artist disappeared and several weeks later another wood specialist appeared. This one created the illusion of a fine artist, tall, blond, elegantly dressed, mustached and perfumed. In reality he barely handled simple decorations that ordinary cabinetmakers created. He worked for a while and disappeared. A few other wood artists added bits and pieces to the arc. One saw the difference between the various styles of decoration. Between all the decorators of the arc there was not a single Jew; Gentiles did all the work. The Jewish part consisted in placing the torahs in the arc.

Nobody interfered with the two Jewish arc builders. The community accepted their plans without comment. They signed a contract and were paid a fixed sum for completing the job. They worked very hard and did a competent job. Two lions holding the Ten Commandments towered the arc. The more exposed parts of the arc showed the fine carved creations of the wood carver while the hidden places showed simple and standard work. Those in the know stated that the arc compared favorably with other arcs in the area. The new arc curtain and the Torah coats that were sewn by the women for months were now fully displayed. The Torahs found their new permanent home. The entire community celebrated the event with songs and dances. The lectern and the torah reading table were also finished by the same two Jewish cabinetmakers that built the arc. They were from the city of Treve near Lesko, and lived at the home of our neighbor Liebe, the wife of Hersh Katz, during their stay in Korczyn. She was an excellent cook and I observed them from they moment they arrived to their departure. My brother Hersh Haim's decision to become a cabinetmaker was probably influenced by the proximity of these craftsman. My own decision to become a painter and a writer was also influenced by them as well as other events. True, I did not reach great heights in either field but I am pleased with my achievements.

With end of the Jewish holidays and the festivities, the fall weather set in. Life resumed the usual routine. The cold winds and snowstorms started to sweep across the country but the Jews did not miss the daily morning or evening services. Young men and elder people came to the synagogue during the day or after services to study. The new synagogue became the resting-place for many scholars who spent their time studying the torah by the candle lights. The winter was soon over and Purim approached with its special joy and mud in the streets. But Passover was not too far behind with the summer in the background. All creatures of nature would be able to soak in the rays of the sun without limitations. A pity that mankind could not share the wealth of nature in a similar manner.

[Page 349-353]

The painting of the study center

One nice day after Passover, a strange looking Jew appeared in the shul. His hat was well creased, his jacket and pants indicated untidiness and his crooked shoes had covered many muddy streets. A well-worn shirt with a tie gave a clue of modernity and a scissors cut beard without peyot. This indeed was an interesting person in Korczyn. Prior to the minha service, the stranger looked at the ceiling of the synagogue and said that the place deserved to be painted. The crowd immediately surmised that he was connected to the trade. Some people even knew that Eliezar Raab saw his work in the synagogue of the Dzikower Rabbi and recommended the man. He had two conditions; he required food and plenty of vodka while working. It soon appeared that he had another weakness namely he tended to disappear after working for a while at a place. He called himself Yakub. He started many jobs, left them in the middle, took on new jobs, then returned to finish his first job. Yakub imposed very heavy demands but the community was willing to meet the demands. The community leaders assigned eating days to the painter and messengers brought him the food. The main problem was to keep him in high spirit by a constant supply of vodka. This job was entrusted to Haim Broder; his family name was Denn and it originated from the city of Brody. Haim was a simple Jew, not a scholar or rich person. He knew his prayers, the section of the torah for the week and the psalms as most of the Jews of Korczyn. He was a quiet person as opposed to his wife who was a woman of valor. The family bought and sold wheat but never made it big, and Haim could not support such a project from his pocket. Still he accepted the job of supervising the painting of the shul and apparently received the consent of his wife. He devoted himself wholeheartedly to the task except for Monday and Friday when he was busy at the Krosner and Korczyner markets. The rest of the time he left the business to his wife and supervised Yakub or more precise saw to it that his throat was wet and amused him when he was depressed. He fulfilled both tasks.

Yakub assembled a tall ladder of about 20 feet. He purchased paints and other items of necessity in the local stores and collected various pots and old containers. With the help of ropes and burnt coals he designed the outlay of his plan. He started with the bulkhead, then with the corners and back to the center. He created sections that he filled with painted creations in a free style. He never created two similar designs even if it meant simple ornamentation. He worked alone and very rapidly. He maneuvered the big ladder with ease from place to place. He had many fantasies and was familiar with the bible that inspired him to recreate the scenes on the ceiling. The spirit fired his imagination and the colors and the scenes enlivened the dull ceiling background of the holy place that consisted of chalk mixed with some blue. The colors were mixed with water and proved lasting as long as the building was kept dry. Many public buildings and homes in Galicia were painted in a similar fashion and lasted for many years if not decades. Of course, repainting a shul was a big financial outlay and few communities had the necessary resources.

Yacub's wanderings enriched many small town shuls with nice artistic works and gave the worshippers a taste of art. Without him, many of the communities would have simply painted their shuls. Apparently, Yacub had talent and under ordinary circumstances could have developed into an outstanding artist. Yacub worked for a while in Korczyn and one day disappeared and took on another job in another community. He remained there for a while and then returned to Korczyn to finish the job. His disappearance or reappearance surprised no one. It was accepted as a matter of fact. Haim of course felt bad about the situation but he did everything he could to keep him painting. Nobody criticized him for the painter's disappearance. People accepted it as a way of life. No fights erupted over the event. No accusations or acrimonious debates occurred. People respected each other and were concerned with their daily needs. Crime for pleasure was unheard of even amongst the so-called lower elements of Jewish society. It was only the master race that developed the policy of mass murder of innocent people.

Haim provided the expensive tastes of Yacub in the following manner. Each day, Haim walked around in the shul with a box and collected contributions for the painting of the synagogue. People contributed very generously. I frequently witnessed the collection since I was already a barmitzvah boy and studied in the synagogue. Yacub inspired me and I waited each day to see the advancement he made in his painting. One day he told me, you see this point on the ceiling, and tomorrow I will paint four angels there and you will die. The next day I looked all over but did not see the angels. Perhaps he took pity on me. He had a ringing voice that was melodious when he sang and induced me to fantasize. He was very moody and if things did not go his way or he felt slighted, he would kick the paints or the containers and the worshippers would be frightened. Nobody dared to talk to Yacub when he was in such mood. People had patience and understanding for the artist. We have but praise for the artist.

[Page 354-355]

Created by me for your Admiration

With the departure of Yacub, I had ample time on my hands and was still impressed with his work. He inspired me to contribute something to the shul. I decided to embellish the lectern that was used by the leader of the service. The present lectern had no decorations, the carpenters just finished it. I took the exact measures and bought the finest drawing paper and the necessary paints and proceeded. I had no experience in the field. I began to look for symbols that could be placed on the lectern. I consulted the Wilno printed talmud that had on the first page two interwoven columns of symbols. I also checked the High Holiday prayer books for inspiration. Indeed, many symbols appeared, notably a crown supported by two lions. The problem was space and proportion. How could I enter all the items into a limited space. I concentrated and tried many solutions. I also feared competition and it drove me to devote myself completely to the job. Finally, I finished the drawing. Now I started the coloring patterns. I lacked experience in the area but continued my work while experimenting with various methods. I had to match the colors, the lions had to be yellowish, the crown gold while the leaves green. All the work was done behind a curtain. The artistic work done, I took it to the shul, removed the glass from the lectern, inserted the sign and returned the glass. I now admired my work, the colors, the written words, torah crown, (know where you stand) and the words created by me for your admiration. The work of art was signed Moshe the son of Yehuda Halevi.

[Page 356-358]

Purim gifts

In the old country, the custom of sending gifts to each other on Purim was celebrated. Even the poor people sent gifts. Thus, the stigma of receiving gifts was erased and it was considered a mitzvah to give. With the approach of Purim, Shlomo the son of Reisel, the oldest of her four orphans, began to plan the sending of gifts. His best friend was David Dym, the son of Haim Dym, they went to the same cheder and played together. Shlomo had the idea of building a wooden box and presenting it as a gift to David for Purim. Such a gift was usually placed on a plate surrounded with candy, raisins and hamman tash or cookies. The plate was wrapped with a clean towel and sent with a younger brother to the party. The wooden box was my brother's first primitive project in the field of carpentry. Later he created beautiful art objects of wood with simple tools, a pocketknife, small saws, a hammer, pliers, and small nails. Shlomo, then about ten or eleven years old, decided to celebrate the mitzvah of giving and made the box that he sent to David with his younger brother Moshe.

David's parents were in the textile business and Roizale Dym, mother of David, sent material for four pair of slacks for Shlomo. Obviously, the gift was meant for all the children of the house. In normal circumstances, Shlomo's mother would never accept charity gifts but on Purim it was different. To return a Purim gift was considered in bad taste and even sinful. In ancient days in Palestine, the Jews set aside portions of agricultural produce for the poor people and in the Diaspora the tradition of sending gifts to the poor people continued without lowering their self-esteem. The next Purim, Shlomo sent his friend David a miniature wood sled that fitted a small doll. The muddy streets no longer enabled the sled to glide but the symbolic effect was there. He again received for himself and his brothers' material for pants. The third Purim, Shlomo was already twelve and left home. His brother Moshe decided to send David a nice gift. He received material for three pair of pants. The next year, Moshe decided not to send a gift to David since he was not his friend. He feared that it would be construed as charity rather than a Purim gift. Thus, he decided to stop sending gifts to David. The sending of Purim gifts enabled people to help needy people that otherwise would not accept help. Self-esteem was very important in the shtetls and even the granting of charity involved tact and the right approach. An entire system of values and traditions developed on the manner of giving Purim gifts without insulting the givers or the recipients.

[Page 359-360]

Bread on Bread or the third Shabbath meal

When my mother bought occasionally a herring and sliced it into seven or eight pieces, the house took on a festive mood. With a slice of herring one could finish two slices of bread and satisfy the hunger. Besides, herring was not bought each day, for it was an expensive item. A herring could serve as the basis for several meals for the family and even a snack for our neighbor Esther. A herring was sliced, onions were sliced and added, vinegar and sugar were also added. Thus a dish was created for the family of five and some was left for the next day. My mother knew how to keep the children in line with her five or six special dishes that she prepared for the family. Her ability to provide food for the family could be a topic for another chapter.

On an occasional Saturday afternoon, prior to the third meal of the Shabbat, my mother allowed us to go to Moshe Sroka, a nickname, to purchase on loan a piece of herring for a penny. The herring was eaten with bread and chewed as though it was a lump of sugar. The mixture of bread and herring produced a delicious sensation in the mouth. One Saturday, I asked my mother for permission to get a piece of herring. It so happened that there was no jam, honey or sour milk to spread on the bread. I had the idea that a piece of herring would moisten the bread. Apparently, my mother did not have the money and refused to consent to the purchase. She insisted that I control my appetite. I could have gone to Sroka and purchased the piece of herring. My mother would have had to pay for it. But we were raised to tell the truth and I was not going to cross her. Perhaps she figured that everybody should get a piece of herring and this would entail costs that she could not afford. Anyway, I realized that I would not taste salty matter in my mouth on this Saturday. I could not extend the story too long for the time for the third meal would pass with the appearance of the three stars ending Saturday. So I decided to take a piece of the rim of the bread and chew it together with a soft piece of the bread. I thus created the illusion of eating herring. I accomplished two things, I ate the third meal and created the taste of herring.

[Page 361-365]

Ethical personalities

I remember the terrible poverty of the shtetls and wonder how people lived under such conditions. How did they manage to maintain their high morality throughout the areas. For Jews lived in the most isolated places and sometimes were single families amongst large populations. Yet the number of murder crimes were abysmally low, except for the libel murders that turned out to be false accusations created for demagogic needs. Our neighbors on the other hand committed many murders particularly against the Jewish population and gave various religious or political justifications for these deeds. The aim of course was to erase the Jewish community. Some Jews lapsed and converted to the dominant religion that accepted them and publicized their names if they gained fame. However, the main Jewish body, it could not absorb and digest. The simple Jew remained attached to his beliefs. Who inspired him to adhere to tradition and customs regardless of the sacrifice of personal privileges. He suffered hunger, deprivation and ridicule but persisted in reciting the psalms, reciting the blessings, keeping Kasher and observing Shabbath and Holidays. All the sufferings and the promise of a better future did not induce the Jew to convert to the dominant religion.

The average Jew was not versed in the metaphysical complexities of religions but was raised on the simplicity that one must serve God directly without intermediaries. The Jew was raised with the knowledge that he was responsible for his acts and nobody could obliterate them for him. No indulgences could clean his deeds. Nobody could assume his deeds but himself. He must keep his slate clean if he wants a stake in paradise. The well to do man was respected to the extent that he gave charity and worked for the community. The poor honest and God fearing man was also respected in the shtetl. The rabbi of the community was the highest moral personality. He kept an eye on all the human dealings in the community and had the backing of the Jewish population. He tried to be fair in the arguments or disputes between the members of the kehilla and attempted to lead the community in a righteous path. Disputes occurred and they assumed a religious tone but there were no murders. The disputes were settled through negotiations, discussions and persuasions. Even the simple village Jew saw that justice was done even if the sides were not evenly matched. Every Jew was part of the community that was supported by the torah. The latter was not the exclusive domain of a privileged caste but belonged to every Jew. He could study it whenever he had the time. The aspiration of the Jew was to study the torah in order to improve his spirituality.

In all the towns, the rabbis adjudicated disputes, fights and arguments. They also answered the religious inquiries regarding the rules of Kashrut. Most of the rabbis were highly moral people that set examples in their conduct and created the necessary atmosphere for their spiritual leadership. Even the loudest people would lower their speech when talking to the rabbi who represented the community and not necessarily his own interest. When conflicts arose between poor and rich or whether this institution should receive help, the rabbi influenced public opinion to make the right decision. His influence in social life was very important as well as his abilities to bring the various factions together. He of course knew what was going on in the city and attempted to prevent problems. We had rabbis that were highly moral leaders and influenced a small group of people while others influenced masses beyond the borders. A Gaon of Wilno, a Baal Shem Tov, a Hafetz Haim influenced every Jewish community. Every Jew that looked for the truth could find an ethical personality that would serve him as a guide in his trip through life.

The prophet Elijah was a host to the poorest and humblest Jewish homes located in the most distant places. His moral integrity served as a basis for the Jewish communities throughout the world. Our leaders were morally inspired by generations of spiritual leaders that influenced them. Even the few well to do Jews in history submitted themselves to the rule of the torah or its representatives. We have to remember that Jewish history remembers the spiritual leaders rather than the wealthy merchants. Jews organized themselves wherever they lived. The small communities maintained their religious life while the big communities tried to spread their influence into many areas of Jewish life. The torah was the glue that bound the Jews until the Germans killed them in the name of progress that was baseless and devoid of human values. How could progress be based on killing innocent people and could this nation claim any moral leadership. The obvious answer is in the negative. The Jews proved that in spite of their slaughter their values were correct while the values of their neighbors were based on false premises. Nobody can forgive a person for what he did to other innocent people. One can not ask for forgiveness and enjoy all the comforts of life. The outside appearance is not important what is essential is the inner feeling and if that is not clean than there is no value. Man must rise above the animal.

And now we must find a key that would open the door to our own continuation as a people after the horrible destruction. We must revert to the past and draw from the moral sources our renewed inspirations to serve as a beacon of light for the world. Just as in the past we were not impressed by the wealth and power of the noble but lived a righteous life, so must we now stop looking over the fence and concentrate on our own spiritual values.

[Page 366-372]

Delayed the reading of the torah

A person today has no conception of what life was in a small shtetl years ago. Everything was encased in an order, rich and poor had to function within the prescribed system. There were gradations in income; some worked on the spot while others had to travel to markets in villages and towns to make ends meet. The common denominator of Jewish life stressed simplicity of life. The reason was twofold; one, most Jews were poor and could not afford things and second, wealth was considered a means to perform good deeds. To collect money for the sake of collecting was not the right thing to do. To collect for a sick person, for an old maid about to be married, for an orphan, were the accepted things and Jews gave from their meager incomes. Of course they saved for Saturday and Holidays. The entire week the family ate dry foods, poor in nutrition but the Saturday and Holiday meals were richer in content and included fatty substances that the body needed. Few people could afford to eat meat during the week. The Jewish mother was called on to devise all kinds of dairy dishes that she varied daily in order not to be repetitive. She used carrots, garlic, onions and other ingredients to alter the tastes of the foods. Borscht soup or other liquid meals were spiced and salted and served once a day for the children. Herring was sliced into eight parts and served once in a blue moon. We could write volumes on how our mothers coped with the meager resources to provide food for their families and clothing on their backs. Clothing items were patched, fixed and handed down from one to the other. The cost of the education of the boys was a heavy burden for most of the families. Yet, no one was in despair; there was self-confidence. This was felt in all the shtetls throughout Eastern Europe in spite of the abysmal poverty that prevailed throughout the countries. I shall now describe community life.

During my days, Korczyn had a population of about 300 families. There was a Rabbi, a religious judge or dayan, two shamashim, two slaughterers, a cantor, a study center and a synagogue, a bathhouse divided into a steam room and warm bath room for people that could not take the steam. Woman also used the latter. The facilities had mikvot attached to them, the steam room mikva received cold water from a spring and the second mikva received preheated water. The Jews prayed the entire week in the study center where services were held throughout the day. Few people missed services, except for those that were ill. The study center was packed in the evening for services. Saturdays and holidays there were services in the synagogue and in the study center. There were no other service facilities during my time. The study center was big enough to accommodate all congregants of Korczyn but the synagogue could not be left without services. It was empty the entire week but services were held on Saturday and holidays even during the coldest days of the winter. Usually a synagogue was not heated. The unfinished synagogue of Korczyn provided no shelter against the weather elements; as a matter of fact, it was as cold inside as outside the synagogue. On cold Saturdays, one saw the steam from the mouths of the worshipers as they prayed for it was bitter cold. But they never missed the services at the synagogue, on occasion they would pop into the study center to warm up and return to the synagogue.

Amongst the worshippers at the synagogue, there was Moshe Kirschner who conducted the services and was also the reader of the torah. He took his job seriously and did the best he could for there were no experienced readers in this congregation. He lacked proficiency in the reading of the services and in reading the torah but did the best he could do. He worked very hard to prepare himself for the tasks. He was an exception in the family of brothers and uncles that stressed the need to improve himself spiritually. On Rosh Hashana and Yom Kippur, the old cantor with a raspy voice conducted the second half of the services as well as the Kol Nidrei service. As far as I remember, the cantor only performed these services in Korczyn. He used to conduct services in the study center when he was younger. The services in the synagogues were fast and simple. As a matter of fact, the synagogue finished the service when the study center was at the half way mark of the services. No cantorial singing was part of the synagogue service. Most of the people were simple people that came to pray and went home. No snobs or well-connected people were found here. But these people maintained the synagogue by conducting services there, without them the place would have been deserted the entire year.

The synagogue was never finished; the walls were not cemented, the construction beams were exposed as were the beams that held the roof shingles. The roof had holes and when it rained on Saturdays one had to choose a dry place to avoid the puddles. The synagogue had no wooden floor. Nobody knew how long it had remained in this unfinished condition. But rumors had it that the dead people congregated there at midnight during the weekdays and that children and adults better avoid the place. For if one is near the place, he may be called up to the torah and the party must go. At the end of the reading, the visitor must leave the reading platform by going backwards. Otherwise he remained there permanently. People told stories about people or their souls being stuck in the synagogue for generations. The place was immense and unfinished and lent itself to many legends. Anyway, during the daytime it was safe for the dead people, and the souls apparently played games only at night. The same entrance that led to the synagogue also led to the study center. Students closed their talmud books prior to midnight in order to leave the study center before the night activities started.

Besides ghosts, the people had real income problems. There was competition and rivalries but it rarely emerged to the surface and certainly not in the study center or in the synagogue. Here the people prayed for divine intervention on their behalf. But on occasion grievances flared up and they hit the stunned congregation. I remember a case when a person went up to the reading platform and informed the congregation that he wanted to delay the reading of the torah. Pandemonium broke loose, everybody wanted to know what was the problem but that could not be discussed since it was Saturday. Negotiators and intermediaries went back and forth between the parties and tried to solve the problem temporarily until after Saturday. Committees were formed, messengers went and came, the protagonists softened their stands. True, both sides had apparently legitimate grievances but the study center on Saturday was not the place to solve them. Finally, both parties consented that the issue would be resolved during the week and the reading of the torah proceeded. The scene did not last too long but one saw the recourse that a party had against a wrong done by someone else, be it a mighty or rich person. Compromise and mediation solved the problem. These cases were limited but they occurred. Most of the fights were solved before they erupted.

It was difficult to conceive such scene in the Christian church where a simple person stopped a service to express a grievance against someone in the community and the members proceed to solve the problem. In democratic countries such events take place daily. We the worshippers did not see in the dispute as an insult to the worship place, on the contrary we felt all responsible for what happened and wanted to contribute to solve the problem and when it was resolved we felt spiritually richer. The community did the right thing. These feelings bound us in the Diaspora and gave us the strength to withstand all the pressures and deprivations. That Saturday, the service was finished rapidly and we rushed home pleased that a wrong was corrected.

[Page 373-375]

Desecration of the eastern wall

The eastern wall in the study center belonged to the well-established people in the township. They comprised the richest element and consisted of an innkeeper, a merchant, and even a watchmaker. There were no small merchants or peddlers along the eastern wall. Well educated or respected Jews could aspire to the wall. On occasion it happened that someone who could barely read the prayers managed to procure a seat along the wall. Such person usually contributed large amounts of charity or was very active in community life or both. Even a scholar was not automatically granted a seat along the wall but had to pay for it. Nobody could just take a place along the eastern wall without the approval of the community leadership. Of course through inheritance one could obtain the seat of one's parents, regardless of the feeling of the leadership. The event involved Benyamin the son of Chaim who inherited a seat amongst the well to do along the eastern wall. There were many contenders who were better qualified but he inherited the seat.

Benyamin lost his business, sold everything in Korczyn and looked for a customer to buy his seat in the study center. He offered the place to all the well-qualified people but they refused to purchase or lacked the money to acquire the seat. He decided to sell the seat on the block. Nathan Nute, the butcher, bought the seat. He was neither a scholar nor a respected individual in Korczyn. He sold and bought animals as well as meat. He hardly made a living from the business. His sons lived in Germany and married out of the faith. They supported him and he led a nice and comfortable life.

Nathan was always neatly dressed and clean but this did not deserve a seat along the eastern wall. For the occasion he acquired a new bekeshe and a shtreimel. He also shaped his beard and curled his peyot to gain respectability. He slid into the seat so as not to attract attention. He never occupied the full seat. He took care not to crease his new clothing that fitted him well. He was quiet pleased with himself in the new seat. He even studied a bit the section of the week and on occasion made a small comment. Moshe Zak was his new neighbor in the study center. He also was not from the elite of the town and felt that Nathan dragged him down socially. He was angry that occasionally turned to a boiling point. What was the sense of seating along the wall if everybody can sit there; but he managed to control himself. One Saturday, he no longer contained himself and went over to Naphtali the dumb one and told him to take his seat along the wall. At last Moshe had some satisfaction. What happened later between the neighbors in the study center only God knows. We must mention that when the Nazis kicked Nathan's sons out of Germany, their wives joined them and they all came to Korczyn where they shared the fate of the Jewish community. Poles killed some members of the family. The local killers were never brought to justice. Thus both sides cooperated to eliminate Jewish presence in Korczyn.

[Page 376-379]

A Jewish letter carrier by Mordechai Schiff from Jerusalem

Zalman Leib Den was the Jewish letter carrier of Korczyn. His appearance was similar to all other Jews of the place. During the weekdays he wore a bekeshe and a black velvet hat. He had a beard and peyot. On Saturdays and holidays he wore a silk capote or light coat and a shtreimel. He dressed like all other Jews and there was no official sign on him. Saturday night and sometimes Sunday morning he delivered special deliveries. The mailman had one problem, he could not read Latin letters. So Zalman asked the postmaster of the area to read the names and he jotted them down in Hebrew letters. Everybody received the mail and the system functioned very well. As long as Zalman was the postmaster, he was the bridge between Korczyn and the rest of the world. He took the letters to mail and distributed the mail that he received. He knew everybody in Korczyn and even those that left the township. He was the one that bridged members of the family that were separated by great distances. He also knew what was cooking in many families since he made the daily rounds of the township. Sometimes he knew the contents of the letters without opening them.

Sometimes women could read in his face the contents of their letters prior to reading them. Zalman was also a host to many people that had no place to sleep. He knew what took place in Korczyn and therefore knew the needy as well as the homeless that he met on the streets. They all had a place at his home. He retired because he no longer could carry the mail. The job was transferred to his son Elimelech who read the Latin script. But he was not lucky; the government soon took away his job. The position that his father held for a lifetime, the son kept for a short period of time. The job was given to a gentile who made his appearance in Korczyn. He was a tall man with a hat that had a shiny visor and above it was the Austrian Eagle. He had a big bag that hung on his shoulder that contained the mail. He took out letters and started asking people where the parties lived. He could not figure out the names and the addresses and exactly where the people lived. He was totally confused. It took him quite a while to figure out where the people lived. For Korczyn had no official street names and numbers. So and so lived near the synagogue, the bathhouse, etc. Even the stores had no signs or names. There may have been one or two signs but they were not important since no one paid attention. Everybody knew where everybody was and where to buy what was needed.

The same applied to people that had no stores or permanent addresses or special trades. But everybody knew Itzik, Yossele, Moshe, Haim Shmay's, Haim Hersh Mayer's, Reisel Yidale's, Feige Haya's, Shmerl balegole etc. People did not use last names that were imposed by the Christian world on them, they managed to live with their own names. Korczyn was the Yiddish name for Korczyna, the removal of the letter a gave it a kosher stamp of approval. Krosno was called Kros by the Jews, Sanok was Sunik and Rzeszow was Reishe. These names functioned amongst the Jews. The moment something was sent outside to an official institution, then the name and address and official town name had to be used. The township of Korczyn was mapped out so that a Jew could find with ease his direction. There was a market and Jews lived along three sides of it. Their flats and stores were located here. Some homes were further out but they belonged to the front properties of the market. Along the left side stretched the road to the synagogue, the study center and further on that was densely populated by Jews. Behind the study center there was already a small street where the bathhouse and the beginning cheder were located. The street led back to the market and was inhabited by Jews. Jews also inhabited the right side of the market to the mill. There were also some Jewish families in the Targowicze area market for animals that was also along the right side of the market. There were about 200 Jewish families and the mailman had his hands full. Frequently, he resorted to Jewish help to untangle addresses. But this was our destiny.

[Page 380-382]

A Punishment

Yosef the butcher was the poorest amongst his colleagues in the township. The poverty perhaps drove him to accuse the shochet of being too harsh with his slaughtered animals or the rabbi that sometimes declared his meat to be not kosher that resulted in a great loss. A story was told that once the butcher, rather a small person in comparison with the other butchers, met the shochet, who was exceptionally big. One was going from Kros to Korczyn and the other one in the opposite direction. Shalom the shochet slapped the butcher so hard that he had to hide his swollen face for a long time. That was meant as a warning not to spread insinuation as to his piety or honesty. The butcher had another disastrous encounter with the kehilla's religious leadership. Following the slaughtering of an animal, he went to ask the local rabbi whether the meat was kosher since there were some disturbing signs. The rabbi ruled that the meat was not kosher. The butcher then went to the dayan, religious judge, who ruled that the meat was kosher. Of course the butcher did not inform the latter that there was already a ruling. This created a scandal. For it was accepted traditionally that once an opinion was asked the parties had to abide by it. The rabbi and the dayan were furious but neither could ignore his ruling. There were no other scholars in the field in Korczyn to help resolve the dilemma. The town was in turmoil for the religious leaders lost face. The meat in question could not be sold as kosher.

The rabbi's son Asher came to visit his father. He was also rabbi but in another town. The congregants noted that the dayan Mates and the rabbi's son were involved in halachic discussion regarding the meat decision. Each side used precedents to strengthen their ruling. No decision was reached. The Jews in town did not want to enter a religious battle between two religious authorities, but they felt that the prestige of the Jewish community was at stake. Pressure was applied and both sides apologized to the community and slowly ended the dispute. Their wrath they turned to the butcher who involved them in the scheme. Most people finally forgot about the story when Yosef the butcher appeared one Saturday at the study center with a hat instead of a shtreimel. The congregants knew immediately that this was his punishment. For every married man in Korczyn wore a shtreimel on Shabbath and the butcher also wore it up this Saturday. Everybody saw it but nobody pointed. The community understood that this was the punishment meted out by the religious leaders to the butcher for his dealings. The next Saturday he also appeared with the hat. Obviously, this was the punishment and it affected the butcher to the extent that he soon he left Korczyn for the States.

In the USA he opened a kosher butcher store and brought his entire family to the country. Later he closed the store and became a religious supervisor. His beard he never trimmed and the peyot he rolled behind his ears so as not attract too much attention. A long coat and velvet black hat he wore. On

Saturday he wore his shtreimel. Here in the States he lived in peace with the religious leadership.

[Page 383-386]

A tragically comical story as told by Mechel Horowitz Petach Tikva, Israel

Berl Schmier, the son in law of Israel Pinzeles, was very involved in community affairs. He sold textiles but had ample time for social activities and gained entrance to many homes and was well versed in the social life of the city. He also performed various sensitive errands as a result of which he earned some zlotys. In Poland there was a law that each merchant, tradesman or artisan must obtain a yearly permit without which he could not operate. To obtain the permit, one had to file a statement describing the nature of the business establishment and the activity intended to be performed in the place. Then, one obtained the permit from the tax department that enabled the business to continue. At the end of each year, Jewish businessman petitioned the tax office for a reduction of taxes based on poor sales. The businessman filed a petition listing his income and his expenses. He tried to draw a black picture so that the official would consent to lower taxes. One of the receivers of these requests was an Armenian gentile with a beard and piercing eyes that seemed to ex-ray the individual facing him. Everybody tried to avoid him. He spoke fluent Yiddish and this seemed to frighten the Jews in Korczyn that were used to the services of translators that gave them time to think of the answers. This time they were interviewed in their language and he considered everybody a cheat and increased taxes where he could. Jewish merchants preferred to avoid him and would send their papers or requests to the tax department with Berl Schmier and paid him a half a zloty for the service. He was familiar with the official and seemed to get along with him. Berl became a sort of a semi official handler of tax papers.

Once, a merchant of Korczyn applied for a loan of 200 zlotys to the bank Zaliczkowa in Kros. He listed his wealth, his business activities, the possibilities of business expansion and the need for the loan. Berl handled all these papers. It also happened that another party by the same name applied to the tax department for a reduction of taxes. He of course blackened the picture to the state, listing every item that would help his case, a large family, a sick wife, poor sales, poor location of the store, etc. There were course specialists in writing these requests in order to get the reduction. The inspector received many such requests and sometimes did reduce the tax payments. It depended on the official and the one in Korczyn was not favorably disposed to Jewish requests. Thus Jews looked to somebody that could influence the decisions. Jews were always accustomed to pray for miracles, for interventions, for help. Most of the time they prayed to God to help them with their problems but they also prayed for good middlemen to help them with their earthly problems. However, the devil intervened and Berl delivered the letters to the wrong places for the envelopes merely listed the name of the sender and both names were similar. The bank received the application for tax reduction and the tax office received the application for a loan. Of course the bank refused the loan and the tax office increased the tax assessment.

The news reached the study center between the minha and maariv services. It became the topic of the evening and of course Berl was ridiculed. He explained the reason for the confusion but the listeners were not impressed. They had a good laugh at the expense of Berl, although they sympathized with the two merchants. The story broke the monotony of the winter months and became the topic of conversation for some time.

[Page 387-391]

American bluffers

In 1903 my cousin Dora Birman visited Korczyn. She visited some of the more famous doctors in Europe that suggested a stay at the spa of Karlsbad. Following the treatments, she visited her father's birthplace. Her father already lived in the States as did her own family. My mother received her cousin and cleaned the place in order not to be embarrassed. She prepared a fine meal, although cooking was not her forte. The cousin received a straw sack with fresh straw that would serve her as a sleeping place. There were no hotels in Korczyn. The straw sacks were usually filled once a year with fresh straw prior to Passover. But with the arrival of such an important guest, the straw sacks were replenished with new straw, clean sheets were spread and bed blankets dusted. Even the table was covered with a brand new tablecloth as though it was a holiday in the middle of the week. The floor was washed instead of the usual sweeping with a broom. Only before Passover did we clean so extensively. Nobody washed floors every week. Only aristocratic homes indulged in such activities. The rest of the people could not afford it and the places were very crowded.

Our small place had four children and our mother. Friends and visitors always came and went. Beggars entered the house hoping, and usually getting, a coin donation or a piece of bread or a plate of soup if the food was ready. Sometimes it was a plate of potato soup, or a bean and noodle soup or other cooked dishes. The beggar usually had the choice, money or food. Our subtenant Ester also competed with us by giving money donations to beggars. Please excuse me for digressing from the topic. My mother had even prepared a pillow gift with geese feathers that she plucked herself as well as dried mushrooms that I have never seen in the States. How she knew that these items were non existent in the States, I do not know. Anyway, everything was prepared with tender care for the guest. The latter took Israel's coach at the railway station in Kros and within a half-hour was at our home. She complained that the ride was too rough. Young people walked from Korczyn to Kros in about 45 minutes; the coach took less although the actual road was longer. The coach was also pleasant and everybody had a seat. Furthermore, the coach had shock absorbers to smooth the ride, the seats were upholstered, the legs of the passengers were covered with blankets to protect them from dust or rain. The road was paved with stones that eliminated the monotonous sliding of the coach. The ride was pleasant and reminded one of the carousel rides in the circus. The wheels were delicate and rimmed with rubber. Only the hoofs of the horses made that familiar and repetitious noise. Yet the guest complained about the terrible ride.

I asked her how the rides were in the States and she said that all roads in the USA were smooth like our wooden floor. I accepted that the USA builds homes, provided jobs, supplied food, beverages and clothing. But I found it difficult to believe that the roads were like our floor. This seemed to bother me for years. Even when I visited the big cities in Galicia or the city of Budapest seventeen years later, I noticed that certain roads were evenly paved but certainly not like our floor. The massive urban transportation only strengthened my thesis that the comparison was a bit far fetched. At the time, I met another cousin from the USA, Luis Schnek, who traveled to the spa of Karlsbad in Czechoslovakia. Actually, I met both cousins at the spa of Teplitz Scheinow. Louis was but skin and bones. He owned a haberdashery store that he estimated to be worth about 30,000 dollars. He considered himself an average businessman. I was astounded; in Korczyn a merchant with a store of 1000 dollars was considered a wealthy person and certainly acted the part. People treated him with deference and here Luis stated that he is not a rich person. I could not make sense of these discussions. Furthermore, he complained that the mattress of the spa was terrible. This reminded me of the complaints of my cousin about her bed in our house, on her previous trip. I examined the mattress and concluded that the Emperor could sleep on it. But Luis insisted that the bed was terrible and in the USA they have better beds. He brought the latest news about my brother and described the USA for me. Of course, there were many exaggerations as I found out later. I arrived in the USA in 1921, and the next day, my cousin Luis took me to the barbershop and had the barber remove the mustache and all other unnecessary hair without even asking me. We then walked for a while and he suggested that I always look ahead and never back. Only later did I understand the meaning of the sentence.

[Page 392-393]

Did you already pray Minha
By Moshe Zucker

One evening we were at the Meisner home and discussed ways of helping the Korczyner survivors throughout the world. At the meeting were Raphael Meisner, Eliyahu Wolf, Haim Dawidowitz and myself. We also mentioned the departed Korczyner and their contributions for the various relief actions including the Passover gifts for the poor in Korczyn prior to WWII. If all these donors would still be alive we would not have money problems in helping the Hitler survivors. They felt more attached to Korczyn than their children who also give to our relief fund but smaller amounts, for they never experienced first hand the poverty of Korczyn. We had to remind them and remind them again about the need to help. From the recent arrivals to the States we could not expect help since they still struggled to establish themselves, but we maintained contact with them and hoped that they would help us in the future.. Haim the secretary mentioned frequently the cases of people that suddenly made it and started to help the society.

Meisner and Wolf were still the main door bell ringers and collectors, and I facilitated their task by chauffeuring them about to save their energies. But time did not stand still. Their constant personal appearances emphasized the need for help. At the meeting we also discussed ways and means of helping survivors with urgent problems. Our agenda was lengthy and we discussed the various items and were engrossed in the discussions when I suddenly asked the other members whether they prayed minha, they answered in the negative and we stood up as one and prayed. The scene reminded me of troops responding to the visit of an officer. With such spiritual soldiers God could truly boast. Honor their memory.

[Page 394-396]

To Tashlich
By Moshe Zucker

When Meisner and Wolf passed away, we asked ourselves who would now visit the Korczyner landsmen to collect their dues. Haim had the list of all members and their previous donations. Some sent automatically their dues while others had to be visited in person. The system was difficult to change for the people were accustomed to it. Mendel Rubin, thegrand son of the Korczyner rabbi, and I organized the visits. I could not bring myself to visit people that I never met. Besides, my beardless and peyotless appearance did not inspire confidence to give. Mendel's appearance on the other hand was fit for the job. He dressed and looked as though he left Korczyn yesterday and certainly made a better impression for collecting charity than myself. Still we managed to collect some donations. We concentrated on Brooklyn for this was where I lived and I only had a limited time. We could not reach those that lived in far away areas. This job was left to Haim who bombarded them with letters and reminders. How the old collectors managed to visit everybody every year we can not answer. Apparently they were young in spirit and were steeped in the tradition of working for other poor people.

The work of anonymous charity can not be measured in money terms or any other terms. Even the promise of heavenly rewards can not be measured. Most of us like to be rewarded immediately even if it is only with some honor. But Meisner and Wolf did not care for honors. They devoted themselves to the task of helping their landsmen be it in Korczyn or the USA. They worked ceaselessly to awaken in us the need to help and this was their precious contribution. They created all the contacts with the Korczyner Jews throughout the world and enabled us to stay in contact to this day. They formed the basis for the entire help activity prior, during and after WWI and WWII. Many people knew the name Meisner for this was the first address that the survivors of Korczyn wrote to but this is another chapter.

Here I would like to mention Mendele, who although well connected in Korczyn, here in the States he worked for a living. True he never made it big but was pleased with his life. He was the first stop on our planned visits in Brooklyn. He lived near Prospect Park in Brooklyn. We passed the park and I asked whether he visited the place and he answered spontaneously that he visited the place to cast his sins or Tashlich. It appeared that many areas in Brooklyn have no access to water bodies where religious Jews could cast their sins on Rosh Hashana. So they assemble right after the holiday and travel to the park to perform the service. Thus, Jews solved their religious problems in the States.

[Page 397-400]

The Eruvin or enclosure in Korczyn.

The story was told by Shmuel Leib Kaufman, Ramle, Israel and edited by Moshe Zucker

All communities that contained very religious Jews had a special problem on Shabbath or Holidays since they were not permitted to carry items. They could not even carry a prayer book or a talit to shul. Only if a wire that symbolically demarcated the area as one domain fenced in the shtetl, were they permitted to carry prayer books and prayer shawls. Women could wear their kerchiefs to shul, the tcholent could be picked up from the bakery, and food could be sent to the shul for the third meal. Of course, there was always the possibility that someone forgot an item in one's pocket and carried it on Shabbath. True, an unintentional sin but still a sin for the very observant. When a place had no enclosure, the children were the main porters on Shabbath. They became quite knowledgeable in the area and knew all the ins and outs. The non-Jewish neighbors were not enthused about this Jewish custom of symbolically enclosing them in their areas and sometimes tore the wires. The custom was easily practiced in ancient Palestine but in the shtetl it frequently presented problems. The youngsters were aware of these problems and frequently tried to avoid them. Still Jews tried to observe the custom in spite of the objections of the local non-Jewish population that frequently created wedges that prevented the running of the wires.

Korczyn had a special problem with the enclosure for the church stood in the midst of the Jewish population and the enclosure wire had to run through the church property. Three sides of the Market Square were inhabited by Jews; along the fourth side was the church along the road to Kros. The church protruded between Haim Horowitz's and Mendel Schroit's houses. The entrance to the church was from the Market Square. The bishop of Lemberg was a native of Korczyna and he built a beautiful church fit for a large city. The location of the church prevented continuous running wire for the Jews in Korczyn. The Jews tried to enclose the area. According to one version, Avraham Haim Horowitz paid a Polish farmer to stretch the wire across the church property to the house of Mendel Schroit. Whether this was strictly kosher from a halacha point is doubtful but we would accept it for the purpose of the story. Someone noticed a strange wire on the church property soon cut the wire. Perhaps the same fellow that installed it. Another version stated that the wire was stretched from Horowitz's house to a point that nearly bordered the church property and then continued to Schroit's house. This wire was cut during a procession from the church to the cemetery when the crucifix entangled itself in the wire. Thus Korczyn had no enclosure. The Jewish community filled a petition to the court but lost the case.

Shmuel Leib Kaufman

Zishe Beck, the son in law of Nafthali Raab, petitioned the Austrian crown for a wire permit but the appeal was rejected. The Jewish community leaders tried to appeal to a higher judicial instance according to Shmuel Leib Kaufman. He stated that the community wrote a letter to the son of the famous Dzikower Rabbi, Nafthali Haim, who was in Palestine. He suggested that some important leaders of the community should travel to the grave of the famous rabbi Mendele of Rymanow and recite particular psalms. They were to abstain from chit chatting on their way back and merely discuss spiritual matters until they reached the office of the kehilla of Korczyn. There they were to recite a particular line of the torah. The messengers abided by all the requests until they reached the office. Then they had to decide who would be the spokesman and recite the line. Since they considered such discussion mundane, they started to murmur and point fingers until all three lost courage and headed home without reporting to the community leaders. None of these leaders lived longer than the year in question. Apparently, the heavenly verdict was quite severe and unintended. My father told the story to me every year when we read the particular line of the torah. He also believed that had we followed the instructions to the letter, Korczyn would have had an enclosure.

[Page 401-407]

Haim Dawidowitz
By Moshe Zucker

Who amongst Korczyner did not know Haim, whether he received or gave to the Korczyner Relief Society. His address was known amongst all the landsmen. His entire family was from Korczyn and everybody knew them and he reminded people of the fact. His devotion to charity, especially to the charity of Korczyner was indeed a mitzvah. It was difficult to give an overall picture of Haim Dawidowitz's activities on behalf of the Korczyner for the aims changed with the times. Haim became secretary of the Korczyner Relief Society in 1946. The society tried to help every survivor in every way but we lacked experience for we did not know what the survivors really needed. Our funds were also limited since we depended mostly on small contributions. We had to balance our expenses with our income. Gone were also the big givers of early Korczyn that contributed to Meisner's appeals. We reorganized the entire collection system and established some definite guidelines. We could devote some pages to describe the activities of Haim who did a real big job in establishing an accounting system to help run the organization but we lack the energy and the will power. He had great experience in financial matters and was involved in many societies. All this knowledge he placed at our disposal. Perhaps someone could have done a better job but nobody stepped forth. He collected all the addresses and letters and established a filing system of Korczyners. He also began to add new members and placed them on the mailing system, as he did in the other societies, where he also organized the book system. He also began to look for Korczyner that could help the organization as well as those that still needed help. He decided who would get what, a very difficult decision by any standard. Most of the members of the society were not involved in these decisions.

Some of the needy people had perhaps complaints or expected more than they received but our funds were limited. We lacked the great orator to awaken the conscience of the Korczyners to do more but also the survivors kept to themselves their experiences and did not share them with the rest of us. Perhaps their material would have acted as a stimulus for contributions, but this was not the case. They kept their past to themselves or shared with their friends. The society never received this material. As a matter of fact, we did not even know whether all the people that claimed to be from Korczyn were really from the hamlet or nearby places. Few of the survivors participated in the activities of the society thus we had no way of knowing the real situation. Still Haim made decisions as best as he could and based on the evidence at his disposal. His letters of hope and encouragement reached everybody. Perhaps the donations were limited but this was all that we could send. He never ignored people and answered all the mail. He found people of Korczyn and established contact with them. He corresponded with all landsmen

Following WWII, the emergency meetings of the Korczyner landsmanshaft were well attended. Different people attended different meetings. As time passed less and fewer people attended the meetings and the collection declined. Haim called and wrote letters asking for donations. Things reached such situation that we sent 60-80 invitations to a meeting and five or six people showed. We tried all kinds of devices but no response. We decided to follow the other societies who also ceased their meetings and decided to invest all our energies in creating a yizkor book of Korczyn. Haim immediately sent out letters informing all the members that the society is preparing to publish a book People were invited to sent materials or to write items for the book and some responses were very impressive. We accepted all the materials. Some of course did not bother to write; this was their loss. Nobody could claim that they did not know about the yizkor book. We advertised it and send everybody reminders.

Now I shall return to Haim. I saw that the interest in the yizkor book was small, very few members placed orders. Haim on the other hand continued with his relief activities year after year without ever complaining. He sent packages or cash prior to Passover and Rosh Hashana to all the needy of Korczyn. The yizkor book with all the publicity netted a quarter of the expenses that were paid for the book. I must confess that I never took an interest in the financial aspects of the society until the yizkor book expenses appeared. Suddenly, things did not add up. I could not explain things nor did I understand many activities. I asked Haim for an updated list of the membership and also explanations as to the nature of the givers. It soon transpired that many recipients were not from Korczyn but needed help and Haim gave them. This was reckless especially since it involved public money. Of course, we were also at fault for not taking an interest in the activities of the society and letting Haim make all the decisions. I as president must also share the blame for not being more involved in the activities of the financial aspects of the Korczyner Relief society. True, he did not squander the money or use it for personal use, still public money must be accounted for. I therefore decided that in the future, I will be more involved in the activities and take a greater interest in the running of the society. We must also thank Haim for his hard work in the organization and urge him to cooperate with other members so as to produce the best results in the future.

Haim Dawidowitz and his wife

[Page 408-413]

The study center

By Michael Horowitz

Michael Horowitz

Our study center was the most precious building, and with the completion of the new entrance, it accommodated all the men of Korczyn as well as guests. From the ceiling were suspended six big lamps and 12 chandeliers that used candles. The latter were greatly used in the shul. When someone had a yahrtzeit or Memorial Day for a departed member of the family, he donated candles to be lit in the shul. Someone made a promise, candles were given and lit even during the weekdays. Of course, Shabbath and Holidays, the place was ablaze in candle lights as well as lights from the oil lamps. The scent from the burning materials created a special effect that mixed with the pious feeling of the place. The smoke of the pipes and cigarettes added to the general atmosphere that swept into the vacuum of the building. The children frequently picked up the cigarette butts and lit them with the burning candles. These were their first experiences with cigarettes that resulted in coughing and choking until they got the hang of it. The youngsters tried to imitate the adults. Sometimes the teachers spotted the smokers and administered instant punishments as well as moral lectures but the teachers could not see everything.

In spite of the darkened ceiling, we could still see the beautiful work that Yakub did 34 years ago. The community could not afford to hire an artist to repaint the study center and just to paint the shul was a pity. So layers of dust accumulated but the signs of the zodiac and other creations were still visible. Nobody wanted to obliterate this beauty with paint, nor could it be washed since water would have dissolved the paintings. Thus the shul aged with the ceiling and the paintings. At the door of the study center, on the right and next to the first window, stood Simha [Diller] shamash with his stand of goodies. On the windowsill he displayed some chocolate bars, apples, candy, and a box of cookies. On a bench nearby he had baskets of apples, various sizes and colors. He sold them without a scale. He had golden delicious, green, and small apples. He also had a basket with fruits that were already touched and sold them for pennies. On Saturday, Simha gave his merchandise on credit. He had tags with the names of his clients and tags with the numbers 5, 10, and 15 pennies. Following a transaction, he would join the price tag with the name tag and present it for payment during the week. The accounting system worked very well. On the entrance door to the study center, Simha wrote with chalk each Friday, the time for lighting candles and the end of the Shabbath. On the other door, there was an announcement to the public that the cost of using the steam bath will hence be 20 pennies and 5 additional pennies for small brooms. A tub of water will cost 30 pennies. The public is asked to visit the bathhouse after 2 PM. The statement was signed and sealed with the seal of the kehilla.

Moshe Dawid Fesel sat close by Simha shamash. He was a jovial man and liked to pock the ears of the youngsters and when he managed to hit one, he exploded with joy. The youngsters accepted these pranks. To the left of the door was the stove built from bricks. The corners were bolted with irons. A specialist built the stove. The side door to the stove was wide enough to admit logs, especially in the winter when the stove burned all the time. Above the stove, there was a window with iron bars where people used to put their wet towels from the mikve. Behind the stove, stood crazy Meir. He hardly left the position. Occasionally, he would shout an expression and then bite his fingers. Along the stove usually sat several property owners such as Eliezar Raab, Hersh Holoshitz, Benyamin Rubin, Israel Blank, Yehiel Weinberg, Menashe Hofstater and Hersh Katz. Next was a table with candle drippings. A lamp stood in a pot of sand on the table. The Jews read a holy book or recited psalms or repeated the good deeds performed by well known rabbis such as the Rabbi Mendale, Rabbi Hersh and Rabbi Yossele from Rymanow.

Following the services, people headed home unless news items reached the shul. Then the worshippers discussed the items from all points of view. News was scarce and it barely reached Korczyn. Prior to WWI and especially after it, new winds began to reach the township. Zionism reached the Jewish masses. The youngsters espoused the idea and it gained many adherents. The old generation was fearful of the new development and feared for their families. The young generation openly challenged the older generation and its ways of thinking. Neither party wanted to understand the other one. Both fought for Jewish survival but with different approaches and different philosophies. Local and national elections became battlegrounds of ideologies. No longer was the public pacified with a few statements. The people wanted to know and asked questions that had to be answered. The business as usual approach came to an end. Answers had to be provided. The same changes also appeared in Korczyn.

Still some of the old ways remained. Shlomo Yossef the matchmaker from Dukla appeared in shul with his umbrella. Shlom Binem Zucker whispered in his ear that he needed a husband for his daughter. The matchmaker presented his clients, this one was a jewel, educated and fine looking, etc. He collected all the requests, sorted them and filed them in his particular filing system in order to prevent a mix up of possible matches. One had to remember the social hierarchy in each place when dealing with matchmaking.

Following the services, Jews sat along long tables and studied Gemarrah with commentaries, mishnayot, Shulhan Arouch, the section of the week with Rashi commentaries; the children reviewed the material they had studied during the day. The elder fellows sat at their own tables. When the lights did not reach people, they bought candles for five pennies and read by them. The shul was busy until midnight. Then the night watchman announced the hour and people headed home. The streets were deserted and restful.

אויפן בילד : מעכעל האראָוויץ, זיין
מוטער און שוועסטער וועלכע זיינען
אומגעבראַכט געוואָרן דורך די דייטשן
אין יאָר 1942 אין קאָרטשין.

בילד פֿון : מרדכי
האראָוויץ, מעכעלס
ברודער, אומגעקו־
מען אין אוישוויץ.

Mechel Horowitz, his mother and sisters that were killed by the Germans in 1942 in Korczyn

Mordechai Horowitz, brother of Mechel Horowitz, was killed in Aushwitz

[Page 414-417]

On the eve of the Heshvan Yarid in Kros
By Mechel Horowitz

Sunday morning at about 5 AM when the grocery men, butchers, village peddlers, fur dealers, egg dealers and skin merchants rushed to the shul, they found Simha the shamash sweeping the floor and arranging the place. He stood there and sprinkled the floor with water. He was angry since he did not sleep well. Besides being shamash he was also a baker and worked all night preparing pastries and cookies for the Krosner market. He was also angry at Binem Alster and Haim Halpern who did not yet pay him his monthly salary and he was angry at Avraham the cantor who helped him sweep the shul. The latter only worked with one hand since he took a fall while going to the schochet with a chicken. He slipped on the ice and broke his right hand. He only swept with his left arm. The family took him to Stepke the famous expert but he remained disabled. Many people prayed silently and alone since they were in a rush.

Simha donned his talit and phylacteries and started to conduct the service. He led a very fast pace and some of the worshippers urged a slower pace, notably Benyamin Rubin, Israel Blank, and Hersh Haim Rothenberg. Simha pointed out that he must prepare for the fair in Kros and merchants have lots of preparations.

The people heading to the fair finished the service, and without breakfast headed to the market to see their coachman that would carry the merchandise. Now they waited for the drivers to finish their Sunday service at the church. Finally the coachmen appeared, most of them were familiar with each other and the merchandise for most of them used the same coachmen. Still most merchants preferred to arrange things beforehand and finalize items with a shot at the inn. Monday morning, the coaches were already loaded and ready to go. The merchants squeezed themselves into the available slots and the trip started. When the coaches reached the mountain before Kros, all people left the coaches for the horses barely ascended the mountain. They then rejoined their seats on the other side of the mountain and soon reached the city. Shmuel Aron Teller carried not only baked goods for the market but also kosher butters and cheese for his very religious customers in Kros.

The Sunday prior to the fair, all the merchants assembled everything that went to the market. The textile merchants took all their wares, the haberdashers crated all their goods: shirts, underwear, children shoes, gloves, meters, glasses, multi color hair ribbons, and sewing kits. Clothing merchants took their thick coats with quilted linings, breeches, and winter coats. Nahum Kirschner and his son in law took crates of winter and summer scarves and shawls. Mechel Kirchner sold fur hats with earflaps that he sewed himself. The grocery people fixed their stands so that the roofs remained in place and protected them against the rain or snow in the winter and the sun in the summer. The skin merchants portrayed their wares that were in bags. Shmuel Lipales, Moshe Lutman's brother, also sold leather leggings, wax and cattle skins. The baker Shilem Weinstein with his breads, halot, rolls, and bagels also traveled to the fair. The butchers hired drivers to drive the purchased animals back to Korczyn. Most of the inhabitants of the hamlet placed great faith in the fair. They hoped that it would provide them with a nice income that would take care of their taxes, rents, food, clothing, wood for the winter, schooling expenses and other necessities. Sunday evening approached, the skies darkened suddenly, the fear of rain or snow immediately affected the mood of the local Jews. Still most of them went to the evening services.

[Page 418-420]

This is the gate to the heavens and the righteous will enter it

By Mechel Horowitz

In the twenties of the century, Zionism penetrated the Jewish youth that started to read a newspaper or a book. Some even started to write and understand Jewish history. These sparks began to affect the pacified ranks of the Jews of Korczyn. They still went to shul twice a day but sparks of revolt began to circulate against the established order in the study center. This place kept the Jewish community together. Prior to WWI, the synagogue was part of the establishment but since then the place was empty all week, and only a few people prayed there on Saturdays and Holidays. Thus the study center was the center of the Jewish community and here everything was institutionalized. Seats went from father to son, call ups to the torah were influenced by charity donations. There was a strict social hierarchy that ruled within the study center. Things were accepted until new winds started to sweep the area including Korczyn. People began to notice these discriminations and resented them. They disliked the transfer of power from father to son if the latter did not possess the qualities or knowledge of his father. Furthermore, there were artisans that were more familiar with Jewish studies than some of the well to do merchants or their sons, yet were never called up to the torah. People became aware of their status and resented mistreatment.

Suddenly, there was a request for a new shul under the name of Yad Haritzim. Such shuls existed in large cities prior to WWI. These shuls grouped religious artisans that conducted their services. There were even shuls of tailors, shoemakers and even porters, if their numbers were significant. The Korczyner artisans demanded a place to conduct their services where they could feel at home. They even had service leaders and readers of the torah. The kehilla leadership was not enthused about the idea but did not want to create antagonisms and decided to grant the group the room that Simha used as an utility room. The group obtained the necessary permit, painted the interior and the entrance and began to conduct services. For the High holidays, they hired an out of town cantor. This was a novelty since Korczyn always had ample service leaders but they concentrated in the study center. Thus, the township had a bit of competition between the study center and the new shul.

The two shuls functioned simultaneously until someone complained to the authorities and they closed the Yad Haritzim shul. Supposedly, the books of the shul were not in order. Negotiations and examinations started until matters were corrected. The fight lasted due to the third meal expenses of herring. Finally, the examiners were satisfied with the explanations and the shul reopened for services. Here was placed the seat of Eliyahu that Haim Wolf designed and a wood artist carved. The worshippers took great pride in the artistic seat. The shul was kept clean and orderly. Once Haim Wolf Koreff decided to write in beautiful letters above the entrance to the shul, the following quotation: This is the gate to the heavens and the righteous will enter it. The quotation irritated some of the leaders of the community but they decided not to make an issue. This was the first time that an inscription was placed above an entrance to a synagogue and not the main shul.

[Page 421-426]

The Zionist Organization in Korczyn

By Mechel Horowitz

In 1920 following WWI, the Zionist organization in Korczyn resumed its activities that were suspended during the war. The organizers were Ber Fischel, Matityahu Katz and Wolf Gleicher. The office was reopened and a Hebrew school was established. The youth actively helped these efforts, amongst them Asher Schiff, Wolf Kalb, Dawid Margolies, Wolf Ringelheim and Shlomo Yossef Akselrad. The first meeting took place at Shmayahu's place with the straw roof and the small windows at the level of the ground. Most religious parents objected to their children attending the Hebrew school. Attendance was low but the students soon gained proficiency in reading and writing Hebrew and learned Hebrew songs that made the rounds of the township and gained many sympathizers for the school. I remember that the local Zionist society invited the famous Zionist lecturer from Warsaw, Dr. Milikowski, to speak for the members. The Belzer Hassidim in town, with the help of the rabbi, prevented the speaker from addressing the audience in the study center. Dr. Milikowski tried to speak to the audience following the evening services but the noise and the ensuing fights disrupted the lecture. The lecturer left the study center and said the disruptions merely strengthened the cause of Zionism and indeed it did with time.

Ber Fischel and Matityahu Katz frequently lectured to the members of the Zionist society and developed a variety of cultural activities for the Jewish youth. The Russia-Polish war of 1920 brought an end to all Zionist activities since many young Jews fled to Germany, Holland and other places. The activities resumed in 1926 when room was rented from Mindel Rothenberg; the room was below the mayor's office. The entrance was through a hall that led to a small room where Yankel Roizner, nicknamed Smont, once lived. The room was long and dark; there was but one window and hardly any light. The members brought pieces of furniture and the room took on the appearance of a meeting place. Ber Fishel brought a replica statue of Dr. Herzl and others brought pictures to decorate the walls. Meetings and lectures were held each night and the participation grew. The lectures dealt with various topics on Zionism, especially Herzl's writings. The youth was encouraged to attend the meetings. Saturday afternoon, lectures and discussions took place. Matityahu Katz with his bekeshe and shtreimel never missed an event nor did Pinhas Wertheim. Wolf Gleicher lectured on a variety of topics. Women participated in the discussions. The attendance grew and new quarters were rented from Fishel Schroit. The first floor became the center of activities as well as the school. The school attracted many girls in spite of the opposition of the rabbi. He preached on Saturdays to the worshippers against sending children to the Zionist school.

Ber organized various youth entertainment programs that attracted many local as well as Krosner youth. The program was very successful and attracted a great deal of attention. Ber even wrote a play entitled "Home" that received a glowing report from Nahum Sokolw's [word famous Zionist leader] daughter. The play was staged in the new hall of Fishel Schroit. All the preparations and materials were assembled and created locally. We built a stage, I created the decorations, Ber was the choreographer and director. The play was a big hit. We decided to create a theater circle in Korczyn with the following actors: Ephraim Weinstein, Mendel Halpern, Naphtali Erreich, Wolf Fessel and Moshe Boim. Girls also joined the circle, including Chaya Weinstein, my two sisters, Fradel and Tzipra Yente Horowitz, Bashe Halpern and others whose names I no longer remember. I later directed the theater group that staged many plays. The benefits went to the Keren Hayesod for Palestine.

The same evening that the play entitled "Home" was staged, religious fanatics broke into the Zionist clubhouse, removed the bookcases and set them on fire. Over 150 Yiddish and Polish books were torched. The vandalism was discovered on Sunday and passions ran high. Everybody knew who participated in the act. Dr. Moshe Rubenfeld, the local medical doctor and a native of nearby Kros, called the police. Examinations and investigations began as to the torchers. There were arrests and mothers pleaded with the police to release their sons that were innocent. None of the culprits confessed and all arrested were released. The event reached the major Yiddish newspapers in Warsaw, Haint and Moment, and the Polish newspapers, Nowi Dzienik and Chwila. Books came from all the major Polish cities such as Warsaw, Reishe, Tarnow. Private libraries sent many books, notably the library of Zamir. It sent several hundred books including the works of Peretz, Shalom Aleichem, Shulem Ash and others. The library greatly expanded. The religious element however pressured the owner of the club house, Mendel Schroit to cancel the lease. We moved to the Polish mayor's office and rented a hall there for a year. We then met in Wolf Kirschner's flat but this was no solution. Finally, my mother built a permanent clubhouse that served us many years.

The membership of the Zionist movement steadily grew and the Hebrew school grew in numbers and stature. Korczyn assumed an important place in all regional Zionist conferences. Thanks to Ber Fischel and the Zionist youth movement, our hamlet achieved acclaim. Suddenly in 1928 Ber Fischel died after a long illness. This was a real blow to the movement. We enlarged his picture and placed in the club house as an inspiration to the members. With his death, Matityahu Katz and Pinhas Wirtheim assumed the leadership of the Zionist movement, and from 1932 until 1939 I was the local leader of the Karen Kayemt l'Israel . In 1938, there were elections for the community leadership. Two factions were contesting the elections, the Zionists and the others. We the Zionists had no money for the campaign so Haim Wolf Koreff suggested that we stage a Purim a play entitled "Yossef Shpiel". Tickets would be sold and the money would cover the election campaign. The local Zionist clubhouse adopted his suggestion and preparations began for the play.

Mendale Katz, Avraham Mordechai Katz's son, owned the script. He leased the text for 5 zlotys. The costumes and the renting of the municipal hall were an expensive proposition but we undertook the project. Haim Wolf provided the melodies. The roles were assigned according to the abilities. Mendel Halpern was Yaacov, Mendel Weinstein was Yossef, Yossef's brothers were Wolf Fessel, Leibush Kuflick, Naphtali and Hersh Erreich, Moshe Gutwein, Shlomo Horowitz, Ephraim Weinstein and Moshe Boim. Yossef Diller and Yehoshu Ringelheim were the leading statesmen. All the tickets were sold and the hall was packed. The walls were decorated and the police maintained order. Guests from Kros arrived as well as some Christian guests. Mendel Weinstein as Yossef was a great success and used his soprano voice very effectively. His separation from his father was well staged. An accordion provided the musical background. The sight of religious Jews with beards who came to see the play was very impressive. The show was very successful and it played in Szedlitz and in Stryzow, nearby towns. The income covered the election campaign and the rest went to the Keren Kayemet L'Israel fund. The memory of the energetic youth that worked so feverishly to stage the production and to be involved in the life of the Jewish community was very painful. Gone were the youth and all the dreams of Korczyn.

[Page 427-429]

Home and environment
By Shalom Weissman, Jerusalem

שלום וייסמאַן

Picture of Shalom Weissman

The basic education of a child began at home where he absorbed the basic approach to life from his parents. Here the child saw some order and learned the problem solving approaches of life. He saw the broom placed in a particular place and the table set in a particular fashion.. Every child learned that a certain order must be followed, whether they liked it or not. The same applied to the outside world. The child that acquired decision-making abilities at home applied the same techniques on the outside. Of course, adjustments had to be made depending on the individual and the environment. The basic pattern of behavior that we acquired as children remained with us for the rest of our lives. The individual child would of course bend slightly to absorb different pressures in order to survive. The child acquired the ability to handle problems and would resort to them whenever they confronted him in later life. Many psychological theories have been written on ways to change the individual patterns of behavior, but they all admitted that the task was very difficult if not impossible. Behavior patterns that were acquired in youth were impossible to erase; perhaps they could be modified. We adhere to these patterns even if we have to pay a price for them.

When I was a young child barely reaching the table, my father took me and my younger brother Wolf to shul. It was a weekday, no prayers or celebrations, but a serious event was about to take place. I do not remember the names of the parties and perhaps it is better this way. But the story was very interesting. One party claimed that he loaned the other party money. The latter denied the claim and added that even if he borrowed money he repaid it along time ago. It was decided that the accused party would swear before the torah in public that he was innocent. An announcement was posted at the shul to the effect that so and so would swear before the torah that he was innocent. The event would take place on such day and hour. Many people decided to witness the event. For a Jew to swear before the torah was something unheard off. A black covered bed was brought to the shul, candles were lit throughout, the menorah before the lectern was lit. The impression was that of Yom Kippur eve or a funeral Everybody feared the unknown. Someone read the lines of the torah that stated the consequences that the Jews would face if they disregarded the commandments.

I do not remember whether the oath was given before an opened torah or before the opened holy arc or perhaps the party regretted the whole incident and canceled the oath. Sixty years have passed since the event and many items I have forgotten. I remember to this day my father's words on the way home. Do not swear even if it is true. His moral advice remained with me to this day and I have avoid swearing even in non-religious matters. How lightly people swear about themselves, their wife or children, is always very puzzling.

I have always tried to avoid swearing and so far have been successful with my father's advice except in one instance when I arrived to Palestine. The English officials insisted that I swear allegiance upon entering the country. I swore in order to gain admittance but it bothered my conscience. I was brought up in a very religious environment that I do not necessarily follow all the precepts but my father's moral teachings I tried to follow to the best of my ability. The home and the environment shape the individual and give him the tools to face the future.

[Page 430-431]

Another Reminiscence
By Shalom Weissman, Jerusalem

I remember that following the dancing of Simhat Torah in the shul, a Torah was brought home and people were called up to it. At one point, the children were called up, a talit was spread over us, the older members recited a special blessing and then we recited the blessing prior to the reading of the Torah. On this holiday, everybody was called to the Torah. The mysterious feeling under the talit remained with me to today, but at the time I wanted to experience the feeling by myself and not with a group of youngsters. Still the feeling of participation in the general joy was good and remained with me into adulthood. The holiday atmosphere affected us all in different ways. The custom of reading the Torah on Simhat Torah in our house lasted until WWI. My father, the head of the kehilla, wanted to be called to the Torah when the new cycle of reading started. This was traditionally reserved for the rabbi of the town. So a compromise was arranged, my father and some followers took a Torah home, he received the section he wanted, all the people were called up and then they finished the service. Drinks were served as well as pastries and cooked items that my mother prepared.

The snacks and dishes varied with each holiday and to this day the taste of the Simhat Torah refreshments remained in my mouth. Our neighbors used to come to our house for the reading of the Torah on Simhat Torah and following the service we all wished ourselves that we should celebrate the holiday next year in the same manner. The reading and the service were conducted in the kitchen that was large and accommodated the crowd. Following the service, my elder sister Reizel, brought a silver tray with goodies and placed it on the table. She made several trips until the table was set. I decided to help my sister and pulled the tray from her hands. I lost control and the tray fell on the table. All the drinks and snacks spilled. I was then merely eight years old. The participants and my father did not loose their cool. Another tablecloth was brought and spread. More snacks and drinks were brought and amidst the celebration and the joy my misdeed was forgotten. But the misdeed remained inscribed in my memory and always floated to the surface with the approach of the holiday. The incident also served as a tableau of painting of the entire Simhat Torah scene in our house.

[Page 432-435]

You should buy another laundry basin

By Zev Weissman, Jerusalem

זאב ווייסמאַן

Zev Weissman

When I compared the relationship between the general population in Korczyn and us, I am astounded. The great social distances between the general population were alarming. A simple peasant bowed and removed his hat before anybody with authority. He whispered the usual greeting and tried to reduce himself to nothingness. The receiving party looked at the peasant with the lowest of contempt as though he was from another planet. The peasant was considered the lowest element in society. The officials lorded over him and never let him forget that he was a peasant. The Polish language was shaped in such a manner as to introduce social variation within the language itself. Even a simple policeman felt his superiority over the next in line and expected respect from him. Within the Jewish population, especially in the small towns, there were no such distances between rich and poor, the rabbi and the artisan. The community respected the elderly, the scholars and the deserving. Money was respected but within limits. Even the poor beggars had self-respect and were treated with respect. The rich person was expected to give charity regardless how he felt about it. The well to do felt that their possessions were temporary and they were mere guardians. They expected to be judged as to how well they used the resources. This was the conception of the Jew in the small town until Hitler arrived and destroyed him.

I am reminded of an event that happened in our house. Women spent a great deal of time with laundry. There were tablecloths, towels, bed sheets, pillowcases and shirts that had to be cleaned for Shabbath. I still remember the large basin with hot water to which detergents were added and then the dirty laundry. Individual items were then pulled and soaped on a board by hand. The item was then squeezed and twisted to remove the water content and placed on the side. When the laundry was soaped, it was returned to the basin. Hot water was poured over the laundry and individual items started to be pulled and twisted until the water content was removed. Then the item was hung to dry. The process took quite some time and sometimes the process had to be repeated if the laundry was not clean. In the summer, the last step in the laundry process was done at the river where the clean running water did the job. Still the laundry had to be hung to dry.

A still better method that appeared at the time consisted of using copper basins. They were filled with water, detergent, laundry and allowed to boil. The heat dissolved all grease spots and then the regular process was followed as described above. The basin was suspended under a tripod, a fire was started under the basin and the laundry boiled for some time. These basins were rather expensive and only the well to do could afford them. People borrowed our basin from my mother. Once a neighbor came to borrow the basin but my mother needed it for her own laundry and told her so. The neighbor stated that Freide Ita Weissman should buy another basin in order to be able to loan it to the people that needed it. My mother ordered another one in Krosno. The new one was made in the same manner as the old one so that there would be no difference between one and the other. The neighbor did not force her to do it but she had a legitimate complaint according to my mother.

[Page 436-438]

Moshe- you can carry already
By Moshe Zucker

Freida Ita Weissman , the wife of the kehilla leader, was a religious woman and well versed in religious customs. She always tried to fulfill them. In the morning when she got up and washed her fingernails and attended to her needs, she immediately tended to her prayers that she knew by heart. She then tended to household chores of baking, cooking and cleaning. Prayers that she knew by heart were recited while performing these duties. Others were recited when she had the available time. She changed often the order of prayers in order to fit her schedule. Still she fulfilled all the mitzvot that applied to her. She lived a religious life and was philosophically religious in her dealings with life. She absorbed a great deal from her father, the teacher, who explained everything to his students. She listened and recorded it. Her knowledge was broad and well based. She was an only daughter and her father taught her various commentaries in his spare time that helped to explain difficult points in religious texts. The material was familiar to scholars but rarely did a woman receive such information or education. She was raised as a son that he did not have.

Freida Ita continued to study and observe strictly the laws With age her piety intensified. She prayed three times a day, recited the psalms, read commentaries, glanced at the local news and prepared food for her household. Her schedule was full. She was sorry to see changes in her own family and in other people but allowed for compromises. She adhered rigidly to all commandments but always excused others if they did not comply entirely with the commandments. She refused to accept total rejection but accepted partial compliance. I visited the family in Budapest during WWI. I frequently visited them Saturday afternoon after lunch. I lived a distance from them. The distance exceeded the one permitted to walk on Shabbath. During one of these visits, I arrived at their house while they still ate. I pulled out a kerchief to blow my nose when Mrs. Weissman was aghast and said Moshe you are carrying. She of course implied that I carried a kerchief on Shabbath. This act seemed to have devastated her and I invented a silly excuse to the effect that the kerchief was tied around my neck. It was a lie but it calmed her. I felt terrible about lying and having to watch myself over things that I no longer observed. I felt ill at ease.

The next Saturday, I walked along the Tabac Street where the Weissmans lived. Jewish refugees from Galicia that fled the war torn areas inhabited this area. I observed our landsmen in their Saturday best. They did not forget to take with them their praying shawls and phylacteries. The area was full of small shuls where Jews prayed the way they did at home. The Jews wore shtreimels and overcoats and from the windows we heard the traditional Jewish songs of the Shabbath mealtime. The war or the fact that everything was left behind at home in the war area did not sadden the festivity of the day. It was one thing to see a Jew with a nice shtreimel and clean silk bekeshe or coat. The Christian neighbors could tolerate this exotic costume. It was however different when someone wore a shtreimel that had holes in it, the kippa could be seen from under the shtreimel and the well-worn bekeshe that had seen better times. Such scene did not bring respect to the Jew. With age the silk bekeshes shredded and holes emerged that exposed other clothing items. A particular problem was the sleeves that were frequently used as kerchiefs and through wear and tear showed the effects. Even when one had a kerchief tied around the neck, it took effort to loosen and used it. It was simpler to wipe with the sleeves or the ends of the bekeshe True, I did not personally see these instances but I saw some of the shtreimels and bekeshes and they were a disgrace. Total disrespect for the religion.

I thus entered the Weissmans' house and told them a story that happened. Whereupon Freida Ita turned to me and said: Moshe you are allowed to carry. Today, forty-three years later, the customs of old Korczyn seem to be so morally high as opposed to our neighbors who resorted to violence to today.

[Page 439]

Bashe Motik'sBy Mordechai Schiff, Jerusalem

In Korczyn there was a Bashe Motik's who was a busybody. Where there was trouble there she appeared and helped. She had a feeling for trouble spots and appeared uninvited. She was not a rich person but with her limited resources managed to assist people in need. She did not ask for a thank you. She assisted people as a way of religious life. She did not anticipate rewards except the reward of the heavenly master. She was always busy helping people and did not rest until she helped in some way. She did her work secretly but the deeds were known in Korczyn. For example, Aron Gutwein stated at her graveside that she once saved him from financial ruin by loaning him fifty kroners. Korcyn had many such women. Respect her memory.

[Page 440]

[Page 441]

Dedicated to
An Eternal Tombstone
For an Eternal Memorial
For the saints of Korczyn
Killed by the Germans
On the 29th day of the month of Av in the year Tashab [1942] in Korczyn,Transported and murdered in other placesMurdered in German concentration camps
The saints of nearby villages
Kombornia, Ikrzenia, Krosczenko, Adzikson, Toraszowka
The saints of
Lodz, Kielce, Radom, Krakow and other cities that were in Korczyn during these tragic days
Moshe Zucker
Itzhak Englard-Wasserschtrum

[Page 442]

[Page 443]

מצבת זכרון במרתף השואה בהר־ציון בירושלים

אן אָנדענק־מצבה אויפן הר־ציון אין ירושלים

The memorial that was erected in the cellar of the Holocaust Memorial at Mount Zion in Jerusalem. The memorial is dedicated to the Jews of Krosno and Korczyn that were killed by the Germans the 25th of Av in the year Tashab

[Page 444]

[Page 445]

Israel Platner
Remember

Oh! God Remember
Our Saints from Everywhere
And the Jews from Korczyn,
Murdered by the Germans and Ukrainians
Together with the Jews from the nearby town of Kros,
They were hanged, burned and shot at
They are scattered over fields, woods, mountains and valleys
They were never buried properly.
We cleanse them with our warm tears,
The spiritual heroes
Our pure saints
Remember them God!
The Jewish daughters
And the Jewish sons,
The holy martyrs
Of Kros and Korczyn
Toronto, October 1967
[William Leibner freely translated the poem]

[Page 446]

[Page 447-456]

List of victims

AlsterBinem, wife Feige, children Deworah, Pearl and Yehudith

AmsterDavid, wife-Charna- and children

Apel--Yaacov Dan, wife- Reitze, son-Shmuel Aron

AxelradItzhak, wife-Cila and child

Axelrad -Shimshon

Beer--Yosef, wifeMalka +daughter Gele

Beer--Haim, wife Nehe+-4 children.

Bezenschtock, Avraham, wife-Ethel +- children: Simha, David, Miriam

Blank, Aron, wife-Lea - children: Miriam and Rivka

Bleichfeld, Avraham yehoshua

Boim--Moshe

Bruder--Hersh Leib, wife-Czarne +- 2 children

Cohen--Haim, wife - Roize +-child

Den--Beer, wife -Hava, children: Yudel, Leizer, Tziporah, Golde and child

Den--Israel Itzhak, wife -Haitshe +-children: Shmuel, Rivkah

Diller--Simha+-children: Yankel, Freidel+husband., Malka +-husband

Dorschewitz--Liebe

Dorschewitz--Hinde

Dym--Arie, wife+-child .

Eichhorn--Rikel +-husband +-2 daughters

Eichhorn--Shimon +-wife+-2children

Eichhorn--Yankel +-wife+-3 children

Eichhorn--Zishe, wife- Esther+-children Berish, Rivkah, Hannah

Eisen--Aron, wife-Esther Moshe Shabtai +-Zishe

Engelhard--Moshe, wife-Rachel+-daughter Hene

Engelhard--Bashe

Engelhard--Dworah

Englard--Feiga

Epstein--Moshe, wife - Hodes +8 children

Erreich--Shmuel, wife - Hannah + children: Matityahu, Naphtali, Reisel

Erreich--Beer, wife +-child

Erreich--Pessel+-child. Hersh, Sarah, dau+-husb

Ettinger--Leibe

Ettinger--Hannah

Feigenbaum--Avraham, wife-Haya +- 4 children

Feit--Leizer, wife -Lea

Fenner--Itzhak, wife -Miriam +-child

Ferber--Shimon, wife -Liebe +- 2 children

Ferber--Yosef, wife-Beile +- 2children

Fessek--Moshe David +-children: Benyamin, Sender, Yehoshua, Shmuel Mehel

Fessel Feige +-children: Sender, Mindel, Esther, Haya Ite, Breindel

Fessel--Elimelech, daughter Rikel with husband and child, Bertshe

Fessel--Eliyahu

Fessel--Heitche
Fessel--Rachel
Fessel--Eliezar Lippe Lea
Fessel--Avraham, wife - Lea
Fessel--Haim David, wife- Lea +children: Wolf, Beile, Sarah
Fessel--Beerish, wife-Hannah Tzirel+- children: Sarah, Godel
Firsichbaum--Shlomo +-wife
Frei-- Shaul, wife -Haya+- children Avraham, Bashe, Feige
Freifeld--Rachel+- daughters: Hannah, Rivkah, Feige
Freifeld--Yacov+-wife +- son +-daug
Frenkel--Sender, wife -Rivkah
Freund--Hersh+-children: Shmuel, Yahet*
Freund--Wolf, wife Haya +- 3 children*
Geler--Yanka (worked in the drug store.)
Gleicher--Wolf, wife - Lea +-child Mindel Sender
Green-- Zishe, wife-Feige +- child
Green--Yeshua Leib, wife - Rachel +- children Pessil +-husband, Mindel
Green--Eliyahu, wife- Beila +-2 children
Gutwein--Sarah
Gutwein--Haim, wife -Esther +- 4 children
Gutwein--Yudel, wife -Malka +-children: Moshe, Nissa, Tzirel, Mindel
Halperin Mend +-wife +-child
Halpern--Hersh +-wife +- child
Halpern--Lea
Halpern--Bashe
Halpern--Gittel
Halpern--Mendel
Halpern--Haim, wife - Nehema +-children Hersh, Aron Rachel
Halpern--Mendel, wife- Fradel
Halpern--Yona, wife-Breindel + son Wolf, daughter: Miriam+-husb
Holoschitz--Yehudith
Holoschitz--Beile +-Yosef +-children Yehudit, Devorah
Horowitz--Bendet, wife -Rachel+-Berta, daughter
Horowitz--Hava nee Kalb, wife of Moshe, children: Shimshon, Moshe
Horowitz--Itzhak, wife - Reisel
Horowitz-- Naphtali, wife -Rachel + daughter Hannah
Horowitz--Sarah, son Mordecai, his wife Reisel +-child,
Horowitz--Yehezkel, Shlomo, son, Mechel and wife
Infeld--Leibish +- wife
Infeld--Naphtali,
Infeld--Matityahu, wife-Tzeril+-4 children
Infeld--Hersh+-wife+-child
Infeld--Yantshe, wife - Tzirel+- 4 children
Kalb--Rehel
Kamelhor--Yekutiel
Kandel---Mendel, wife - Hinde
Kanner-- Avraham Itzhak, wife - Lea

Katz-- Hannah Rikel
Katz-Gleicher-- Matityahu, wife -Tzivia+-child.Yehoshua, Nissan, AVRAHAM
Kaufman--Meir, wife - Tziporah + son Israel, + daughter Bashe, daughter
Kaufman--Hanah
Kirmer-- Sarah
Kirschner--Nahum, wife-Lea
Kirschner--Benyamin+- wife +- 2 children
Kirschner--Wolf, wife-Rivkah+-David Leib, son
Kirschner--Moshe, wife-Ita+-children: Avraham, Esther
Kirshner--Yahet
Kizelstein--Moshe +-wife+- 2 children
Koref--Haim Wolf, wife -Nehe +- children: Yankel, Gutshe
Kratzer--Pessah, wife - Miriam +- 2 children
Kresh--Malka
Kuplik--Yehoshua, wife -Hene+- children Meir, Shmuel, Malka
Landau--Mordecai, wife-Pearl+-child
Langer--Henie, the daughter of Itzhak Beer
Leichtag--Moshe, wife- Hannah +- 4 children
Leiner--Mordechai and wife +-children
Lerman--Moshe, wife -Haya+- 2 children
Lerner--Yehoshua, wife -Esther+- 4 children
Levi Mendel, wife Hannah+- 4 children
Levi--Yaacov +-wife
Lewitman--Yehezkel +-wife
Lewitman--Moshe, wife-Feiga Fessel+-children- Mordechai, Benie
Lewitman--Shmuel
Lieber--Wolf, wife - Hannah+-2 children
Maltz--Yaacov Shaul, wife -Taube+-child ren: Mehel, Itzhak, Yosef, Haya, Sheindel
Margolis--Israel, wife - Haya Liebe +-children: Mehel, Moshe Yaacov, Ethel
Margolis--Yeshayahu, wife-Reisel +-children: Hersh, Nehe, Pearl
Margolis--Bunem, wife Beile Hendel +-children: Gittel, Avraham, Yehoshua
Meisner--Shmuel Hirsh, wife -Sarah +-child
Melamed Zalke, wife-Taube+- Braindel, dau
Melamed--Beile +-child
Mendel, wife-Rivka (Mordechai Rossdeutchers son-in-law)
Pasterna--Tuvia, wife -Matel+-children Eliezer, Bracha, Taube, Hannah+-husb
Penner--Itzhak, wife -Miriam+- child
Pineles-- Zissel, wife-Hene, daughter
Pinter--Avraham, wife -Blime +- child
Pinzel--Naphtali
Podolanski--Shmuel Aaron, wife-Hava +-children: Roize, Motel
Push--Motel +-wife+- 4 children
Raab--Moshe Shmuel+-wife
Raab--Naphtali
Raab--Shabtai+-wife +-children: Naphtali, Shmuel, Yona
Rahwal--Raphael, wife - Tzipe +- 2children
Rathaus--Moshe, wife -Ronie +- children: Sarah+-husband, Hene+-husband

Reich--Nachmen Leibish, wife -Rechele +-children: Yossef, Ritze
Rek--Naphtali, wife -Haya +- 4 children
Ringelheim--Eidel+ children: .Moshe Yehoshua, Avraham, Lea Haya, Mindel, Feige
Ritter--Leibish, wife -Beile +-children: Mindel, Mendel
Rosenhandler--Itche, wife-Nissel +-children: Wolf, Leibele
Rosenhandler Motel +-wife
Rosenman--Mendel, wife-Freide +- Lea,
Rossdeitcher--Mordecai, wife-Braindel
Rothenberg--Shimon Wolf, wife - Ethel
Rothenberg--Leibish+-child.Yankel, Pessil
Rothenberg--Hersh Haim, wife - Feige +-children: Yantze, Aron, Leibish, Motel, Lea
Rothenberg--Aron
Rubin--Oscar +-wife +- child
Rubin--Benyamin, wife -Tile
Rubin--Eliazer Shifra +-8 children
Rubin-- Samuel +-wife
Rubin--Yehoshua, wife - Shprintza +- 2 children
Rubin--Eliyahu, rabbi, wife -Malka +- 6 children
Rubin--Rivka
Schechter--Meir, wife-Rywka+-children: Yehezkel, Freidel, Malka
Scheiner--Asher +-wife +-child
Scheiner--Haim Israel+-children: Pinhas, Avraham+-wife
Schenker--Moshe Hersh, wife-Rahel +-children: .Haim, Aron, Menashe, Esther, Hannah
Schiff Pearl + daughter, Yocheved
Schiff--Yaacov Pinhas, wife and daughter Nechema
Schiff--Sheindel
Schiff Getzel, wife- Sarah, + children: Bashe Miriam Wolf
Schimmel Moshe, wife-Hinde
Schlanger Kalman, wife -Rivkah
Schmier--Berl, wife-Golde + daughter Beile
Schperber Kalman +-wife
Schpitz--Nahum, wife -Fradel
Schprung--Avraham +-wife+-child
Schprung--Yankel, wife-Hannah + son Yosef
Schreiber--David, wife-Sima +- 2 children
Schrott--Mendel
Schwerd--Eliyahu, wife-Lea +- 3 children
Teller-- Shmuel Aaaron, wife -Hene +-children: Lieber, Yankel, Mendel+-2daughters
Tuchman--Mordecai, wife-Ethel +- child
Tzwik--Nathan, wife - Sarah
Weber--Yosef +-wife .
Weber--Aron, wife-Dinah
Weinig--Naphtali, wife - Treine+- children: Wolf, Leib, Avraham
Weinstein--Rachel Leah+- children: Ephraim+-wife, Mendel, Haya
Weissman-- Moshe, wife - Hannah +-Simha, son
Weissman--Yehiel, wife - Lea +- children: Reisel, Yente
Wekselbaum--Shlomo +-wife

Whitman--Moshe, wife-Frimet
Wilner-- Moshe+-children: Aidel+-husband -Feibish, Frumet
Wohlmut--Yehoshua Heshel, wife - Pertshe +- 4 children
Zilberberg--Yosef, wife -Hendel
Zilberberg-- Itzhak, wife -Esther + son Avraham,
Zilberberg-- Avraham

* Note:
The following names were taken word for word from the victims listed in the Korczyna Yizkor
book but nevertheless are in error in the original print. Hersh and Leib Wolf Freund were
brothers of my Great grandmother Esther Wasserberg née Freund.
FREUND Hersh+children: Shmuel, Yahet KorczynaFREUND Wolf, wife Haya + 3 children
Korczyna
This is incorrect. Haya was Hersh's daughter His wife Roiza died before the Holocaust. They
are all in the picture on page 480 in the Korczyna YB dedicated by Hersh's surviving son, my
cousin Benzion a"h. Leib Wolf's wife name was Scheindel Josefowicz. His three children that
were killed were Surah, Yaakov, and Yachet (after the same paternal grandmother as Hersh's
daughter.) Leib Wolf's children used their mother maiden name Josewicz (Josefovitz) of his two
sons that survived the war, (page 283 Korczyna YB) Max (Mordechai Tzvi) died about two
years ago and Martin (Moshe) is still living in Queens. He's about 94. There is a picture of Leib
Wolf and his family in Jack Joseph's book "An unbelievable thing". Jack Joseph is a nephew of
Scheindel Josephowicz. Last I asked he was still around at age 84.
Dovid Shatz

[Page 454-455]

List of Korczyner Jews that were murdered by the Germans in other cities and Jewsfrom other areas that were murdered in Korczyn during the month of Av in the year Tashab

City of Krosno. Korczyner Jews murdered in Krosno

Akselrad, Bendet and his wife Tzila
Akselrad, Shmuel and his wife
Akselrad, Meshulem
Diller, Yossef and his wife and children
Ettinger, Moshe and his wife and children
Hoizner, Yudel and his wife Beile nee Platner
Horowitz, Ben Zion and his wife Sarah
Horowitz, Moshe, the son of Ben Zion
Kriger, Baruch and his wife Sarah
Kriger, Elimelech son of Baruch
Kriger, Hersh son of Baruch
Kriger, Braindel daughter of Baruch
Krieger, Shifra daughter of Baruch
Kriger, Yaacov son of Baruch
Platner, Mordechai and his wife Hanah
Platner, Dobtche, daughter of Mordechai
Privirt, Benyamin and his wife and children
Scheiner, Naphtali
Tischler, Yossef and his wife Rachel
Tischler, Dov
Tischler, Tziporah
Tischler, Yehiel Aron
Tischler, Sarah
Tischler, Elimelech
Weinber, Itzik and his wife
Weinberg, Mendel
Weinberg, Nissan
Weinberg, Sima Beile

Krosner families murdered in Korczyn

Lambig, Eliazar
Lambig, Dawid
Lambig, Lea
Lambig, Haim
Lam, Malka
Lam, Rachel Lam, Franko Mahler, Eliazar
Mahler, Haya Rivka wife Eliezar
Mahler, Hersh
Mahler, Wolf
Mahler, Raphael
Mahler, Moshe
Mahler, Sarah
Mahler, ;Hersh
Mahler, Yanka

[Page 456]

Korczyner Jews murdered in other places

Englard, Wolf and wife and children
Holloshitz, Shmuel Aron and wife
Holloshitz, Mordechai and family
Holloshitz, Moshe and family
Holloshitz, Ethel, her husband and children
Holloshitz, Esther, her husband and family
Holloshitz, Sarah and husband
Willner, Shmuel and wife and children
Willner, Shimon and wife and children
Willner Avraham and wife and children
Fischler, Eli and wife and children
Kaufman, Avraham and wife and children
Kaufman, Yaacov
Kaufman, Sime wife of Yaacov

Strassberg, Zishe and wife and children

Jews from Ikrzenia

Fennig, Eli
Fennig, Manes
Fennig, Hesse
Fennig, Vite

Jews from Kombornia
The Feit family, individual names unknown

Jews from Krosczienko
The Shtern family, individual names unknown

Jews from Adzikon and Toraszowka,
names unknown
May God avenge the victims

[Page 457]

In memory to the saints
The hundreds of Jews from various townsFrom Krakow, Radom, Kielce, Lodz and other placesThat the Germans sent to Korczyn and murdered them with the Korczyner Jews in the month of Av in the year Tashab

[Page 458]

Eternal memorial page in memory of my dear parentsShimshon the son of Itzhak Englard, my fatherFeige the daughter of Shlomo Gimpel, Englard, my motherBashe Enlard and her husband Tzvi Haim, my sister and brother in lawFrimet, their three year old daughterZev Englard, his wife and three children, my brotherDworah Englard, my sister

The Germans murdered all in the month of Av Tashab. Itzhak Englard

אחותי   אמי

דבורה ענגלאַרד הי״ד   פייגא ענגלאַרד הי״ד

Picture on the right of Feige Englard and left of Dworah England
The Germans in Av of Tashab murdered them. Itzhak Englard-Wasserstrum

[Page 460]

Eternal memorial page in eternal memory.To our parents and sisters that were murdered by the Germans in 1944 in AuschwitzOur father, Israel the son of Haim Englard, died in Lodz in Heshvan, TartzahOur mother, Sara Hadas Englard, murdered in Auschwitz in 1944Our three sisters; Dworah Hendel, Yochewed Miriam and Tziporah MindelThe Germans murdered them in 1944 in AuschwitzHaim Englard and Rachel Englard-Wasserstrum, New York

[Page 461]

Eternal memorial page in eternal memory.My uncle Moshe Englard, his wife Rachel and their daughter HeneThe Germans murdered all in Av, Tashab, Korczyn. Itzhak Englard

[Page 462]

Eternal memorial page for the victims by relativesYossef Shaul Frei shHaya Frei, wife of Yossef, shTheir three children: Avraham, Bashe and Feige FreiThe Germans murdered all in Av, Tashab, Korczyn. Itzhak Englard-Wasserstrum

[Page 463]

Eternal memorial page for the victims by relativesArieh Leib Rothenberg shYaacov Rothenberg, son of Arieh shPesil Rothenberg, daugh of Arieh sh The Germans murdered all in Av, Tashab, Korczyn. Itzhak Englard

[Page 464]

Eternal memorial page for a close friendThe Saint Yossef Reich sh Died in the death camp of Plaszow at the hands of the Germans, Itzhak Englard

[Page 465]

Eternal memorial page for my closest and dearest friendThe Saint Yossef Weber and his wife shThe Germans killed them in the month of Elul Tashab. Itzhak Englard

[Page 466]

מצבת־עד

לזכרם של הקדושים

אשתי : אסתּר הי״ד

בּני : בּעריש, וּבנותי : רבקה וחנה הי״ד

זושא אייכהאָרן
ירושלים

Eternal memorial page in memory of my familyPicture of the family. My wife Esther Eichorn shMy son Berish Eichorn, my daughters; Rivka and Hannah Eichorn, sh Zishe Eichorn, Jerusalem

[Page 467]

Eternal memory To my brother Yehoshua Zucker and his wife shKilled in 1942 in Czechoslovakia. Moshe Zucker New York

[Page 468]

Eternal memorial for my family that perished My father, Berish Dov the son of Lea and Eliezar Lipa FesselMy mother, Alte Chana Tzirel the daughter of Ethel and Shimon Z. RothenbergMy sister, Sarah, dau of Berish shMy sister, Feige Rachel dau of Berish shMy brother, Gadel Asher son of Berish shMy grandfather, Shimon Wolf the son of Hanna and Leibish Rothenberg shMy grandmother, Ethel the daughter of Gadel Asher and Sarah GutweinMy grandfather, Eliezar Lipa, the son of Naphtali PesselUncle, Moshe the son of Lea and Eliezar Lipa FesselUncle, Eliyahu the son of Lea and Eliezar Lipa Fessel and his wifeUncle, Naphtali the son of Lea and Eliezar Lipa FesselAunt, Tzirel the dau of Lea and Eliezar Lipa FesselAunt, Rachel the dau of Lea and Eliezar Lipa FesselThe husband of Rachel, Berish the son of Elimelech FesselAunt, Hannah the dau of Lea and Eliezar Lipa FesselAunt, Haitche the dau of Lea and Eliezar Lipa FesselRachel Freifeld and her daughtersThe daughter of Hannah and Leibish RothenbergHersh Haim and the entire family, son of Hannah and Leibish RothenbergYehuda Gutwein and his entire family, son of Gadel Asher and Sara GutweinThe entire family of Gutwein Aron and Yantche InfeldThe entire family of Elimelech Fessel the son of Naphtali Fessel Hersh Tzvi Fessel and his wife the son of Naphtali FesselEternal Rest. May God avenge themYaacov Itzhak Fessel, Stockholm Sweden

דוב בעריש פעסעל הי"ד   חנה אלטע צירל הי"ד

בן ר' אליעזר ליפא ז"ל   בת ר' שמעון זאב ראטענבערג הי"ד

In memory of my dear parents

Picture on the right of Dov Berish Fessel sh, the son Eliezer Lipa
Picture on the left of Hannah Alte Tzirel, daughter. of Shimon Zev Rothenberg sh Yaacov Itzhak Fessel, Stockholm Sweden

[Page 470]

Eternal memorial to parents and family. The Germans murdered them.My father, Eliezer the son of Naphtali Yossef Raab shMy mother, Haya the daug. of Moshe Shmuel shMy brother, Moshe Shmuel and his wife Sara shMy sister Freida Sarah Rivka and her husband Sender Frenkel shMy sister Matil and her husband Yaacov Werner with their children sh Naphtali Werner and Shprintze Werner and their daughter. Gnendil Werner shHene Feige Werner and her husb. Herz Engel and their childrenLemil, Eliezar and Yeshayahu Engel shMy sister, Bluma and her husband Itzhak Hebenschrit and their childrenPerl, Rachel and Leah Hebenschrit shMy sister, Feige and her husband Mordechai Yossef Taube and their childrenMoshe, Ben Tzion and Bluma Taube shDwoshe Rubin, New York

[Page 471]

In memory of the victims

471   קאָרטשינער יזכּור־בּוך

לזכרם של הקדושים
הי״ד

רבקה פרענקעל ר׳ סענדער׳ס פרוי, הי״ד	ר׳ סענדער פרענקעל הי״ד

רבקה ר׳ אריה דים׳ס פרוי הי״ד	הדס ר׳ משה עפשטיין׳ס פרוי, הי״ד	משה שמואל ראב הי״ד

Pictures, top page, Sender Frenkel sh and his wife Rivka [nee Rubin] Frenkel Bottom page, Moshe Shmuel Raab sh, center, Hadas Epstein sh wife of Moshe Epstein and Rivka Dym sh wife of Arie Dym.

[Page 472]

Eternal memorial to my parents, brothers and sisters.They were muredered by the Germans in Av of Tashab [12th of August, 1942] in Korczyn.My father,   Dawid RingelheimMy mother,   EidelMy brothers; Moshe, Yehoshua, Avraham RingelheimMy sisters; Lea, Haya, Esther, Feige and MindelWolf Ringelheim, New York

[Page 473]

לזכרם של הורי אחי ואחיותי הקדושים

הי"ד

ר' דוד רינגעלהיים ז"ל, זיין פרוי און קינדער

וואלף רינגעלהיים

Picture of Dawid Ringelheim and his family Wolf Ringelheim, New York

[Page 474]

Eternal memorial My father,   Yehoshua KuflickMy mother, Hene KuflickMy brothers, Meir and Shmuel KuflickMy sister,   Malka KuflickSimha Kuflick, New York

[Page 475]

מצבת־עד

לזכרם של נשמות הקדושים

אחי   אמי   אבי
צבי הירש הי"ד   נחמה הי"ד   חיים האלפערן הי"ד

אחותי   אחי
רחל הי"ד   אהרן הי"ד

לייביש אטלאס־האלפערן
ניו־יארק

Eternal memorial

Pictures, top right, my father, Haim Halpern My mother, Nehema Halpern My brother, Tzvi Hersh Halpern Bottom right, My brother, Aron Halpern My sister, Rachel Halpern Leibish Atlas-Halpern, New York

[Page 476]

Eternal MemorialMy father, Mordechai PlatnerMy mother, Hannah PlatnerMy sister Beile Platner and her husband Yudel HoiznerMy sister Dobtche PlatnerMy brother Yossef PlatnerIsrael Platner, Toronto Canada

[Page 477]

מצבת־עד

צום אייביקן אָנדענק

פֿון אונזערע עלטערן, ברידער און שוועסטער
וואָס זיינען דערמאָרדעט געוואָרן, דורך די דייטשן ימ״ש,
כ״ט אב, תש״ב, אין קאָרטשין

מוטער	פֿאָטער
רחל שענקער הי״ד	משה צבי שענקער הי״ד

שוועסטער		ברידער
אסתר		מרדכי
חנה מלכה		חיים זאב
		אהרן
		מנשה

אונזער ברודער אהרן
הי״ד

ד׳ ינקום דמם

יוסף און פנחס שענקער
טאָראָנטאָ, קאַנאַדא

Eternal Memorial To our parents, brothers and sisters. They were muredered by the Germans in Av of Tashab [12th of August 1942] in Korczyn. My father, Moshe Tzvi Schenker My mother, Rachel Schenker My brothers; Mordechai, Haim Zev, Aron, Menashe Schenker Picture of Aron Schenker on the page My sisters; Esther and Hannah Malka Schenker Yossef and Pinhas Schenker, Toronto Canada

[Page 478]

Eternal MemorialThe Germans killed themMy father, Shimon Beer from JaszlisekMy mother Taube Yochewed BeerMy sisters; Miriasm and Malka BeerMay God avenge their deathAron Atlas, Jerusalem

[Page 479]

לזכרם של הקדושים

יצחק אקסעלראד מיט זיין פרוי
און זיין שוועסטער הינדע הי"ד

ר' שמשון אקסעלראד און זיין
טאכטער הינדע הי"ד

In memory to the victims

Picture on the right, Shimon Akselrad and his daughter Hinde Akselrad Picture on the left, Itzhak Akselrad and His wife and sister Hinde Akselrad

לזכרם של הקדושים

ר' הירש פריינד, זיין פרוי
זיין זון שמואל, און טעכטער חיה און יאכעט
ה"י ד

בן ציון פריינד
ניו־יארק

In memory to the victims Picture of Hersh Freund His wife, his son Shmuel and his daughters Haya and Yahet Freund Ben Zion Freund, New York

לזכרם של נשמות הקדושים

ר' שמואל אהרן טעללער
הי"ד

ר' שמחה דיללער (שמש)
הי"ד

נתן צוויק
הי"ד

אברהם פייגענבוים
הי"ד

In memory to the victim

**Pictures, top right, Simha Diller, shamash Top left, Shmuel Aron Teller
Bottom right, Avraham Feigenbaum Bottom left, Nathasn Zwick**

[Page 482]

לזכרם של נשמות הקדושים

אברהם שפרונג
הי״ד

אברהם פריי
הי״ד

יעקב (יאנקעל) פרייפעלד
הי״ד

מאטל פוש
הי״ד

In memory to the victims

Pictures, top right, Avraham Frei Top left, Avraham Schprung Bottom right, Motel Push Bottom left, Yaacov [Yankel] Freifeld

[Page 483]

לזכרם של הקדושים

הירש מרגליות הי"ד
בן ישעיהו מרגליות הי"ד

יעקב (יאַנקעל) דילער
הי"ד

דוד שרייבער הי"ד
(משולם ווינשטיינ'ס איידעם)

הירש לייב ברודע
הי"ד

In memory to the victims

Top right, Yaacov [Yankel] Diller Top left, Hersh Margolies, son of Yehoshua Margolies Bottom right, Hersh Leib Brode Bottom left, Dawid Shreiber, Meshulem Weinstein's son in law

[Page 484]

לזכרם של הנשמות הקדושות

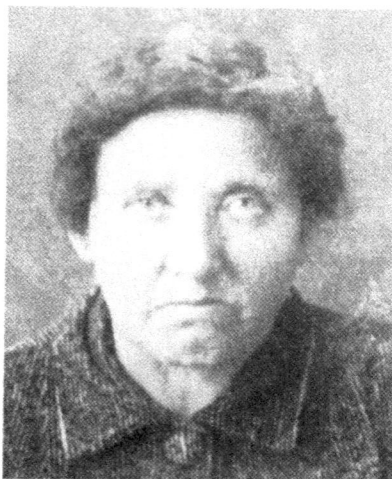

מרים קויפמאן
הי״ד

חנה האָראָװיץ (איר טאָכטער)   רחל (ראָכטשע) האָראָװיץ
הי״ד   הי״ד

In memory to the victims

Pictures, top Miriam Kaufman Bottom right, Rachel [Rechtche] Horowitz
Bottom left, Hannah Horowitz daughter of Rachel Horowitz

[Page 485]

לזכרם של הנשמות הקדושות

רחל פרייפעלד
ה י " ד

און אירע 2 טעכטער

חנה רבקה
ה י " ז

פייגע
ה י " ד

און אסתר קירשנער-זילבערבערג
ה י " ד

In memory to the victims

Top left, Rachel Freifeld and her daughters Bottom right, Feige Freifeld
Bottom center, Esther nee Freifeld Kirzner-Zilberberg Bottom left, Hannah Rivka Freifeld

[Page 486]

לזכרם של הנשמות הקדושות

טשארנע פייט־אמסטער
ה י״ ד

חנה פאסטערנאק
ה י״ ד

הענדל גלייכער־זילבערבערג
ה י״ ד

איידל ווילנער־שעכטער
ה י״ ד

In memory to the victims

Top right, Hannah Pasternak Top left, Tcharne Feit-Amster Bottom right, Eidel Willner-Schechter

Bottom left, Jendel Gleicher-Zilberberg

[Page 487]

Eternal memmorial for the Kaufman familyMy brother, Meir the son of Haim Eliyahu, killed in KorczynMy brother Avraham the son of Haim Eliyahu, killed in Antwerp BelgiumMy sister, Feige the dau of Haim Eliyahu, killed in PrzenyslMy sister, Gittel the dau of Haim Eliyahu, killed in Antwerp, BelgiumMy sister, Braindel the dau of Haim Eliyahu, killed in LembergMy sister, Roize the dau of Haim Eliyahu, killed in KrosnoMy sister, Golde the dau of Haim Eliyahu, killed in LembergThe Germans during WWII killed them allShmuel Arie Kaufman, Israel

[Page 488]

Eternal memorial for my parents and familyMy father, Menahem Mendel the son of Avraham WeissmanMy mother Freide Ita WeissmanMy sister Esther Weissman and her husband Haim Dawid Zwiebel and theirchildren; Hersh Pinhas, Tirzah, Nehe, Rivka Zwiebel shMy sister Haya Weissman and her husbandhAIM Reuven Rubin and theirChildren Rivka and her husband Hersh, Golda, and Malka Rubin Haim Hersh Weissman and his wife Sara and their childrenMeir Weissman and his wife YehuditReisel Weissman and her husband Itzhak Kanarek Niha Weissman-Rand diedShulem Weissman, Jerusalem

[Page 489]

An eternal memorial to my parentsMy father, Shmuel the son of AvrahamMy mother, Golde the daughter of TzviSarah Dawidowitz, New York

An eternal memorial to my parentsMy father, Betzalel the son of Moshe ZilbermanMy mother, Sarah Taube the daug. of Yehiel ZilbermanMy sisters; Rivka and Hannah Malka ZilbermanMeir Zilberman, New York

An eternal memorial to my parentsMy father, Zelig the son of Avraham Langer My mother, Freidel the dau of Avraham Haya Langer New York

An eternal memorial to my parentsMy father, Dawid the son of Meshulem AkselradMy mother, HawaMy brother, Gedalia the son of DawidYaacov Aleksander, Israel

[Page 490]

אַ מצבה לזכרון

פאַר די קדושים פון איסקזשיניא

ווֹעלכע די דייטשן ימש״ו, האָבן דערמאָרדעט אין קאָרטשין, אב, תש״ב

מאנעם פעניג הי״ד
פון איסקזשיניא

אליהו פעניג הי״ד
פון איסקזשיניא

וויטע פעניג הי״ד
פון איסקזשיניא

העסע פעניג הי״ד
פון איסקזשיניא

In memory to the victims of IkrzeniaThey were murdered by the Germans in Korczyn in Av of Tashab

Top right, Eliyahu Fennig Top left, Manes Fennig Bottom right, Hesse Fennig Bottom left, Vite Fennig In memory to the victims Pictures, top right, Simha Diller, shamash Top left, Shmuel Aron Teller Bottom right, Avraham Feigenbaum Bottom left, Nathasn Zwick

[Page 491]

אַ מצבה לזכרון
פֿאַר די קדושים

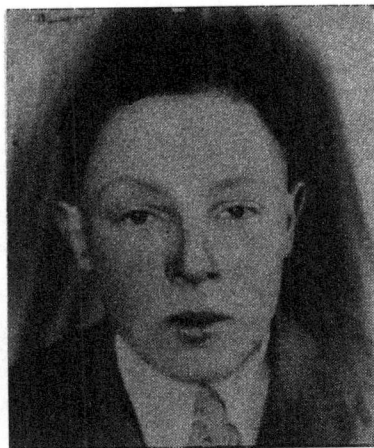

אברהם פֿײַט הי״ד
פֿון קאָמבאַרניאַ

יוסף שטערן הי״ד
פֿון קאָרשטשענקאַ

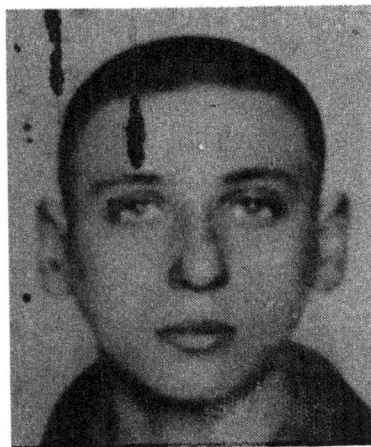

מרדכי האָראָוויץ הי״ד
(שטאָט אומבאַקאַנט)

אליהו האָראָוויץ הי״ד
(שטאָט אומבאַקאַנט)

זיי אַלע זיינען דערמאָרדעט געוואָרן אין קאַרטשין, אב תש״ב,
דורך די דייטשן ימח שמם וזכרם

In memory to the victims

Top right, Yossef Shtern from Krosczenko Top left, Avraham Feit from
Kombornia Bottom right, Eliyahu Horowitz, birth place unknown Bottom left, Mordechai
Horowitz, birth place unknown They were all killed in Korczyn in Av of Tashab

[Page 492]

אַ מצבה לזכרון
פאר די קדושים

ליבע פרידמאַן הי"ד
פון זאַסטאָוו נעבן קראָקאַוו

הירש דוד פרידמאַן הי"ד
פון קראָקאַוו

פּאָולאַ גוטרייך
(שטאָט אומבאַקאַנט)

די דייטשן ימש"ו האָבן זיי דערמאָרדעט אין קאָרטשין
אב, תש"ב

In memory to the victims

Top right, Hersh Dawid Friedman from Krakow Top left, Liebe Friedeman from Zastow near Krakow Bottom, Paula Gutreich, birth place unknown They were all killed in Korczyn in Av of Tashab

[Page 493]

An eternal memorial to our parentsThe Germans killed themOur father, Yaacov thye son of Aron AderOur mother, Esther the daug. of Mechel AderOur brother, Itche Ader and his wife and childrenOur brother, Benyamin Ader and his wife and daughterOur sister, Roize Ader and her husband Meshel and their son and daug.Our sister, Haya Ader and her husband and daughterOur sister Perl AderOur sister Sara AderYossel Ader and Malka [nee Ader] Tenzer, New York

[Page 494]

[Page 495]

An Explanation

The pictures of the victims on pages 481-492 we received from Zishe Eichorn.

Hundreds of Jews from near and far received shelter in Korczyn. The reasons were varied, some thought a small place would offer protection from the Germans and the Germans brought some there. About two weeks before the liquidation of the Jewish community, the Judenrat ordered all Jews to bring identification photos. These photos remained in the office of the Jewish community after the destruction of the community. The Polish authorities removed hundreds of pictures from the office of the community and they found their way into private hands. Some of the landsmen managed to obtain some of these photos and a few sent them to us. We memorialized for eternity those pictures that we received. May the few pictures symbolize the entire Jewish community of Korczyn and other places that were killed in the month of Av in the year of Tashab.

May God avenge their deaths.

List of names that appear in the Korczyn Yizkor book and their occupations.
The "sh" notation indicates that they were killed during the Shoah

Akselrad, Meshulem very well do in Korczyn
Atlas Aron, grandson of Hirsh Halpern
Atlas, Leibish survived war
Baletschanker Mordechai Hersh
Bau Rikel nee Eichorn + husband and 2 children. sh
Beck Zishe
Ber Fishel Haim
Bezenshtock Simha supplied merchandise from Tarnow sh
Bezenshtock, Avraham sh
Bezenshtock, Dawid son oof Avra sh
Bezenshtock, Ethel wife of Avra.   sh
Bezenshtock, Miriam, daugh of Avra. sh
Bezenshtock, Simha, son oof Avra sh
Blank Aaron owner of tavern, died in Russia
Blank Lea wife of Aaron, sh
Blank Meir son of Aaron, survived in Russia
Blank Miriam dau. of Aaron, sh
Blank Rivka dau. of Aaron, sh
Brener, Israel lived in Domaradz
Kirschner David Leib shot by polish policeman. Son of Wolf sh
Dawidowicz Moshe
Den Haim as Haimel Broider, influential individual
Denn Itsche
Denn, Leizer sh
Dorschowitz Israel Meir
Dym Arie, single, disappeared in Russia
Dym Haim
Dym Naphtali, family survived in Russia
Dym, Chaim
Dym, linen production
Eichorn Berish son of Zishe, d. in Russia
Eichorn Braindel wife of Chaim, d.
Eichorn Chaim d
Eichorn Esther, wife of Zishe + Rivka aged 18 and Hanah aged 16, sh
Eichorn Esther, wife of Zishe sh
Eichorn Hanah daugh. of Zishe sh
Eichorn Jacob + wife + 3 children, sh
Eichorn Rivka daugh. of Zishe sh Eichorn Simon +wife +2 child. sh

Eichorn Zishe son Chaim, survived in Russia
Eichorn, Blima dau of Chaim sh
Eidel, the daughter of Moshe Willner
Epstein, Moshe shot by the Gestapo sh
Erreich, Ber member of the Judenrat, sh
Erreich, Hanah Pessel nee Eichorn, wife of Shmuel + 3 child. sh
Erreich, Shmuel sh
Fessel Itzhak
Fessel Moshe Dawid, sh
Firsichbaum Shlomo + wife shot
Frei Shaul, services were held in his home
Freund Leib Wolf
Gadli, my Hebrew teacher
Geller Yanka sh
Gleiche Avramtsche r, son of Mendel Gleicher. Lived in Krosno. Killed in Dinow
Gleicher, Wolf restaurant owner
Gleicher Mendel very well do do people in Korczyn
Gleicher Yudel. son of Avra. Gleicher. Lived in Krosno. Killed in Dinow
Grin Eli, member of the Judenrat, sh
Grin Zishe, single, disappeared in Russia
Gutwein Godele, owned house
Gutwein Sarah charity
Guzik Wolf Yankel
Halpern Mendel, the son of Yona, judenrat police sh
Halpern Naphtali Hirtz
Halpern, Chaim
Halpern. Herz owned house
Halpern-Leibish
Hannah Malka, the glazier
Holloshicz, Jehudith, shot by the Gestapo
Holloshitz, Yosef owned vinegar factory
Horowitz Michael
Horowitz Naphtali
Horowitz Shlomo family survived in Russia
Horowitz, Shlomo member of the Judenrat, sh
Infeld Naphtali member of the Judenrat, sh
Infeld, Yantsche
Ita Kirschner wife of Moshe Kirschner sh
Kamelhar Yekutiel
Kanner Itzhak
Kanner, Avraham Itzhak, nicknamed Peitash
Katz Eli Wolf
Kaufman Shmuel Leib
Kaufman, Haim Eliyahu owned soda factory
Kawalek, mother and son sh
Kirschner Meir Nachum
Kirschner Michael owner of house

Kirschner Naphtali, the son of Moshe, judenrat police sur.
Kirschner Wolf and his 12 year old son, apple dealer shoah
Kokolin Percze nee Katz, aunt of Zishe Eichorn sh
Kokoshka Shmuel Aron
Korb Mrs., the wife of Yossef Korb and infant, shot by the Gestapo
Korb, Yossef
Koref, Haim Wolf, cigarretee store owner
Koref Yantsche single, disappeared in Russia
Koref.Chaim Wolf sh
Kratzer, Pessah Haim Halpern's son in law sh
Krawtchik [Schiff] Bashe
Leichtog Chana and children. Wife of sochet sh Leichtog Moshe the shochet sh
Levy Yaacov, pharmacist sh.
Lewitman Moshe sh
Lewitman Moshe the son, lived in Germany sh
Lewitman Yehezkel assistant head the Judenrat.sh
Lezer Aisik, family survived in Russia
Lezer Avraham, family survived in Russia
Lezer, linen production
Maltz Yossef, shot by the Gestapo
Margolies Bunem, owned metal store
Margolies Israel supplied merchandise from Krakow sh
Mechale Moshe
Mechel Kirchner died
Meisner Raphael
Meisner Sam
Melamed Zalke
Mendel Halpern, , the son of Hertz, member of the Judenrat, sh
Holoshitz. Mendel survived war
Shroit, Mendel
Mendel Weinstein, single, disappeared in Russia
Mener, Fishel
Kirschner Moshe, ritual slaughterer sh
Rothenberg Moshe
Moshe Willner's son –in-law, husband of Eidel shot by the Gestapo sh
Pinter Yehezkel family survived in Russia
Pinter, linen production
Pinzel, Naphtali, the dumb one, shot by the Gestapo
Platner Israel
Platner Israel
Podlanski, Sima sur
Raab Eliezar services were held in his home
Raab, Naphtali and his descendants called Raabes, very well do do people in Korczyn
Raab, Shabtai sh
Raab Avraham,
Raab Elieazar, brother of Elieazar
Rapport Wolf

Rapport, Wele, very well do people in Korczyn
Reck Naphtali
Reich Avraham Yossel
Reich Nachman Leibish -Belzer hassid, d
Reich Shaul
Reich Yossele sh
Reich, Bashe Welke
Reich, linen production
Reich, Shaul
Reuven Yossef
Ringelheim Dawid
Ringelheim.Avraham
Ringelheim.Yehoshua
Ritter, Leibish
Rosenman Mendel, single, disappeared in Russia
Rossenhendler Hersh Yankel
Rosshendler Itsche, owner of metal store, nicknamed Broider
Rosshendler Motel sh
Rosshendler, Motel sh
Rosshendler, Hersh Yaacov
Rosshendler, Itsche sh
Rothenberg, Moshe very well do do people in Korczyn
Rothenberg. Moshe
Rubin, Mendel. very well do do people in Korczyn
Rubin Benyamin
Rubin Eli Rabbi of Korczyn sh
Rubin Eliezar who moved into the apartement of his brother, Mendel
Rubin Eliyahu -rabbi
Rubin linen production
Rubin Mendel, family survived in Russia
Rubin Mordechai Eliezar- rabbi
Rubin Shmuel Aaron-rabbi
Rubin, Oscar a grand son of of Benyamin Rubin. head the Judenrat.sh
Rubin, Shmuel-rabbi
Schiff Mordechai - Bashe Motik's
Schiff Getzil
Schiff Jochewed
Schiff Yochewed sh
Schiff, Leibele, haulage company sh
Schprung Yankel
Schroit, Mendel very well do do people in Korczyn, d
Shmayahu
Shprung, Yankel sh
Rubin Simha the son of Mendel Rubin
Stretiner Dawid
Tulipan Bluma, nee Eichorn wife of Ephraim +3 child. sh
Tulipan Ephraim sh

Tzeiger Haim Levi, scholar
Wasserstrom Itzhak Englard
Wasserstrom Shlomo Gimpel
Weber Yossef
Weber Rothenberg Yossef
Weber. linen production
Weber. Yossef member of the Judenrat, sh
Weissberger Karol, manager at Weglowka sh
Weissman Mendel
Weissman Shulem
Weissman Zeev
Willner Feibush, son of Moshe Willner, shot by the Gestapo sh
Willner, linen production
Willner, Moshe
Kirschner, Wolf shot by polish policeman. Son of Mechel sh
Zucker- Haim
Zucker Moshe

Table of Contents of the Original Yizkor Book

Introduction to the Appendices

This appendix has been added at the time of the publication of the translation of the Yizkor Book by the Yizkor-Books-In-Print Project. It contains new material that was not a part of the original Yizkor Book, however it was felt that this material would be of interest to anyone reading the this book.

The next section is a list of Jewish names from residents of Korczyna obtained from Yad Vashem Archives, the Meyer Denn files from Korczyna and other private research and letters and documents.

The following sections are all provided by Rabbi Edward Boraz, who led a group of Dartmouth College students on a mission to restore the cemetery in Koroczyna in the summer of 2012. First there is a description of the trip along with images showing the work they accomplished; following is a list of the headstones photographed during that work by the Dartmouth students and Rabbi Edward Boraz. Then we present two sermons delivered by Rabbi Edward Boraz which concern Korczyna.

APPENDIX – Material not in the original Yizkor Book

Last Name	First name	Maiden Name	Birth Date	Birth Place	Residence	Occupation	Father	Mother	Gender	Spouse	Other	Source

List of Jewish Names in Korczyna, near Krosno, Galicia

The Source indicated the origin of the information:

YA   Yad Vashem Archives

D   DennFiles from Korczyna

P   Private research, Letters and Documents

APPENDIX – Material not in the original Yizkor Book

Last Name	First name	Maiden Name	Birth Date	Birth Place	Residence	Occupation	Father	Mother	Gender	Spouse	Other	Source
ADER	Esther				Korczyna	midwife			F			D
AKSELRAD	Yossef Ben			Korczyna	Korczyna				M			P
AKSELRAD	Ides			Korczyna	Korczyna				F	Yossef Ben		P
AKSELRAD	Dwora			Korczyna	Korczyna		Yossef Ben	Ides	F			P
AKSELRAD	Shimshon		b.1834	Korczyna	Korczyna		Yossef Ben	Ides	M			YI
AKSELRAD	Malka	Leibner	b.1818	Dukla	Korczyna		Dawid Leib		F	Shimshon		P
AKSELRAD	Meshulem		b 1843	Korczyna	Korczyna	Head Kehi	Yossef Ben	Ides	M			YI
AKSELRAD	Rachel				Korczyna				F	Meshulem		P
AKSELRAD	Dawid		b.1862		Korczyna		Meshulem	Rachel	M			P
AKSELRAD	Hawa	Hirsh							F	Dawid		P
AKSELRAD	Chana Sar		b.1889	Korczyna	Korczyna		Dawid	Hawa	F			P
AKSELRAD	Gedalya			Korczyna	Korczyna		Dawid	Hawa	M			P
AKSELRAD	Israel		b1892	Korczyna	Korczyna		Dawid	Hawa	M			P
AKSELRAD	Susia/Reisel		d.1946	Ukraine	USSR				F	Yaakov		P
AKSELRAD	Mina	Sher	b.1927	Ukraine	Israel		Yaakov	Susia/Reise	F	Yaakov		P
AKSELRAD	Yehuda		b.1895	Korczyna	USA		Dawid	Hawa	M			P
AKSELRAD	Yossef Ben		1893	Korczyna	Korczyna		Dawid	Hawa	M			P
AKSELRAD	Malka Leja		b1897	Korczyna	Korczyna		Dawid	Hawa	F			P
AKSELRAD	Ides		b1870	Korczyna	Korczyna		Meshulem	Rachel	F			P
AKSELRAD	Shimson		b.1872	Korczyna	Korczyna		Meshulem	Rachel	M			YI
AKSELRAD	Haya-Asna	Drimer			Korczyna				F	Shimson		P
AKSELRAD	Shlomo Yos		b.1898	Korczyna	Israel		Shimson	Haya-Asna	M			P
AKSELRAD	unk		b.1830	Korczyna	Korczyna		Yossef Ben	Ides	M			P
AKSELRAD	unk			Korczyna	Korczyna				F	Shlomo Yos		P
AKSELRAD	unk			Korczyna	Korczyna		Shlomo Yos	unk	F			P
AKSELRAD	Cila	Rath		Korczyna	Korczyna	2nd marriage			F	Shlomo Yos		P
AKSELRAD	Itzhak		B.1908	Korczyna	Korczyna		Shimson	Haya-Asna	M			YI
AKSELRAD	Cila	Fish	b. 1908	Korczyna	Israel				F	Itzhak		YI
AKSELRAD	Meshulam		b.1939	Korczyna	Israel		Itzhak	Cila	M			P
AKSELRAD	Rachel	Brant		Rumania	Israel				F	Meshulam		P
AKSELRAD	Hinde	Shimel		Korczyna	Korczyna		Shimson	Haya-Asna	F			P
AKSELRAD	Bila			Korczyna		2nd wife of			F	Meshulam		P
AKSELRAD	Frida		b.1876	Korczyna	Sanok		Meshulam	Bila	F	Dawid Isr		P
AKSELRAD	Bendet		b.1886	Korczyna	Krosno		Meshulem	Bila	M			YI
AKSELRAD	Cile	Freifeld		Domaradz	Krosno				F	Bendet		YI
AKSELRAD	Shmuel		1909	Krosno	Krosno		Bendet	Cile	M			YA
AKSELRAD	Klara	Rosenberg		Dembice	Krosno				F	Shmuel		P
AKSELRAD	Erenka		1935	Krosno	Krosno		Shmuel	Klara	F			YA
AKSELRAD	Shalom		1911	Korczyna	Krosno	Beamter	Bendet	Cile	M			JU
AKSELRAD	Awraham		1922	Korczyna	Krosno		Bendet	Cile	M			P
AKSELRAD	Yehuda		1924	Korczyna	Krosno		Bendet	Cile	M			P
AKSELRAD	Lewi		1930	Krosno	Krosno		Bendet	Cile	M			JU
AKSELRAD	Chana	Bentcher	B.1872	Stryi	Korczyna	3rd wife of			F	Meshulam		P
AKSELRAD	Wolf-Zeew		b.1905	Brno	Israel		Meshulam	Chana	M			YI
AKSELRAD	Yehudit	Hyman		Frankfurt	Israel		Shimon	Unk	F	Wolf-Zeew		P
AKSELRAD	Baruch		b.1943	Israel	Israel		Wolf-Zeew	Yehudit	M			P
AKSELRAD	Dwora				Brno		Meshulam	Chana	F			P
AKSELRAD	Moshe								M			P
AKSELRAD	Cypre								F	Moshe		P
AKSELRAD	Lipe			Korczyna	Krosno				M			P
AKSELRAD	Hinde Git	Akselrad		Korczyna	Krosno		Lipe	Rachel	F	Alexander		P
AKSELRAD	Hershel			Korczyna	Krosno		Lipe	Rachel	M			P
AKSELRAD	Ciwia Lea	Kalb							F	Hershel		P
AKSELRAD	Ides			Korczyna	Krosno		Lipe	Rachel	F			P
AKSELRAD	Yossef Bendet		b.1888	Korczyna	Krosno		Lipe	Rachel	M			P
AKSELRAD	Chana	Hausner	b.1890	Korczyna	Krosno				F	Yossef Bendet		P
AKSELRAD	Lipe		b. 1908	Korczyna	Krosno		Yossef Bendet	Chana	M			P
AKSELRAD	Mechel			Korczyna	Krosno		Yossef Bendet	Chana	M			P
AKSELRAD	Moshe Liebe			Korczyna	Krosno		Yossef Bendet	Chana	M			P
AKSELRAD	Dora			Korczyna	Krosno		Yossef Bendet	Chana	F			P
AKSELRAD	Sara Reila			Korczyna	Krosno		Yossef Bendet	Chana	F			P
AKSELRAD	Esther Lea			Korczyna	Krosno		Yossef Bendet	Chana	F			P

APPENDIX – Material not in the original Yizkor Book

Last Name	First name	Maiden Name	Birth Date	Birth Place	Residence	Occupation	Father	Mother	Gender	Spouse	Other	Source
AKSELRAD	Frimet			Korczyna	Krosno		Yossef Bendet	Chana	F			P
AKSELRAD	Gittel			Korczyna	Krosno		Yossef Bendet	Chana	F			P
AKSELRAD	Itche/Itzhak		b.1930	Korczyna	Krosno		Yossef Bendet	Chana	M			P
ALSTER	Binem				Korczyna				M			YI
ALSTER	Feige				Korczyna				F	Binem		YI
ALSTER	Pearl				Korczyna		Binem	Feige	F			YI
ALSTER	Deworah				Korczyna		Binem	Feige	F			YI
ALSTER	Yehudit				Korczyna		Binem	Feige	F			YI
ALTHOLTZ	fam				Korczyna							P
AMSTEL	Chaim				Korczyna				M			P
AMSTEL	fam				Korczyna							P
AMSTER	Dawid				Korczyna				M			YI
AMSTER	Czarne				Korczyna				F	Dawid		YI
APFEL	Yaacov			Debica	Korczyna		Hersh		M			YA
APFEL	Reitze				Korczyna				F	Yaacov		YI
APFEL	Shmuel Aron				Korczyna		Yaacov	Reitze	M			YI
ATLAS HALPERN	Haim				Korczyna				M			YI
ATLAS HALPERN	Necheme				Korczyna				F	Haim		YI
ATLAS HALPERN	Leibish				Korczyna		Haim	Necheme	M			YI
ATLAS HALPERN	Tzvi Hersh				Korczyna		Haim	Necheme	M			YI
ATLAS HALPERN	Aron				Korczyna		Haim	Necheme	M			YI
ATLAS HALPERN	Miriam				Korczyna		Haim	Necheme	F			YI
ATLASS	Shimon Ber				Korczyna				M			YI
ATLASS	Aron				Korczyna				M			YI
ATLASS	Toibe Yochewed				Korczyna				F	Aron		YI
ATLASS	Miriam				Korczyna		Shimon		F			YI
ATLASS	Malka				Korczyna		Shimon		F			YI
BALETCHANKER	Mordechai Hersh				Korczyna				M			YI
BALETCHANKER	Haya Roize	Zucker			Korczyna				F	Mordechai		YI
BALETCHANKER	Lea				Korczyna		Mordechai	Haya	F			YI
BALETCHANKER	Mendel				Korczyna		Mordechai	Haya	M			YI
BALETCHANKER	Reisel				Korczyna		Mordechai	Haya	F			YI
BALETCHANKER	Tzivia				Korczyna		Mordechai	Haya	F			YI
BARUCH	unk				Korczyna	teacher			M			YI
BARUCH	Rikel	Eichorn			Korczyna				F			YI
BAU	unk				Korczyna				M	unk		YI
BAUM	Adolph				Korczyna				M			YA
BAUM	Moses				Korczyna		Adolph		M			YA
BAUMGARTEN	Natan				Korczyna				M			P
BAUMGARTEN	Schaja			Korczyna	Korczyna				M			P
BAUMGARTEN	Hindza	Hirsh		Korczyna	Korczyna				F	Schaja		P
BAUMGARTEN	Hersh		b.1912	Korczyna	Korczyna		Schaja	Hindza	M			P
BAUMHOL	fam				Korczyna							P
BECK	Zishe				Korczyna				M			YI
BECKHARDT	Ted				Korczyna				M			P
BEER	Esther	Leibner		Korczyna	Zmigrod		Shragai F	Sheindel	F	Wolf		P
BEER	Wolf			Korczyna	Korczyna				M			P
BEER	Yossef				Korczyna				M	Yossef		YI
BEER	Malka				Korczyna				F			YI
BEER	Fishel Ch.				Korczyna				M			YI
BEER	Moshe				Korczyna				M			YI
BEER	Haim				Korczyna				M	Haim		YI
BEER	Neche				Korczyna				F			YI
BEER	Yossef				Korczyna				M	Yossef		P

APPENDIX – Material not in the original Yizkor Book

Last Name	First name	Maiden Name	Birth Date	Birth Place	Residence	Occupation	Father	Mother	Gender	Spouse	Other	Source
BEER	Malka				Korczyna				F			P
BEER	Gele				Korczyna		Yossef	Malka	F			P
BEER	Fishel				Korczyna				M			P
BEER	Moshe				Korczyna				M			P
BEER	Haim				Korczyna				M			YI
BEER	Neche				Korczyna				F	Haim		YI
BEER	Ita				Korczyna		Haim	Neche	F			YI
BEIN	fam				Korczyna							P
BERGER	Jakub			Korczyna	krosno	tailor			M			D
BERGER	Reisel	Rieger					Leizer		F	Jakub		D
BERGER	Salomon		b 28/10/1918				Jakub	Reisel	M			D
BEZENSHTOCK	Avraham				Korczyna				M	Avraham		YI
BEZENSHTOCK	Ethel				Korczyna				F			YI
BEZENSHTOCK	Simha				Korczyna	haulage	Avraham	Ethel	M			YI
BEZENSHTOCK	Dawid				Korczyna		Avraham	Ethel				YI
BEZENSHTOCK	Miriam				Korczyna		Avraham	Ethel				YI
BIGAJER	Hersh				Korczyna				M			P
BIRMAN	Max				Korczyna				M			YI
BIRMAN	Dora				Korczyna				F	Max		YI
BLACK	Itzhak				Korczyna							YI
BLANK	Aron				Korczyna	tavern			M			YI
BLANK	Lea				Korczyna				M	Aron		YI
BLANK	Meir				Korczyna		Aron	Aron	M			YI
BLANK	Miriam				Korczyna		Aron	Aron	F			YI
BLANK	Rivka				Korczyna		Aron	Aron	F			YI
BLEICHFELD	Avraham Y				Korczyna				M			YI
BLIK	Pinhas				Korczyna				M			P
BOBKER	fam				Korczyna							P
BOIM	Moshe				Korczyna				M			YI
BREITOWICZ	Mechel			Korczyna	Krosno				M			P
BREITOWICZ	Liebe			Korczyna	Krosno				F			P
BRENER	Haya			Korczyna	Korczyna				F			YA
BRENNER	Israel			Domradz	Korczyna				M			YI
BROIDE	Hersh				Korczyna				M	Hersh		P
BROIDE	Czarne				Korczyna				F			P
BRUDER	Hersh Leib				Korczyna				M			YI
BRUDER	Tzarne				Korczyna				F	Hersh	2 child.	YI
COHEN	Haim				Korczyna				M			YI
COHEN	Roize				Korczyna				F	Haim		YI
DAN	Yaacov				Korczyna				M			YI
DAN	unk.				Korczyna				F	Yaacov		YI
DAN	Shmuel Aron				Korczyna		Yaacov	unk.	M			YI
DAWID	Mechel				Korczyna				M			P
DAWIDOWITZ	Gedalia				Korczyna	teacher			M			YI
DAWIDOWITZ	Pearl Yente	Freund			Korczyna				F	Gedalia		YI
DAWIDOWITZ	Hersh				Korczyna		Gedalia	Pearl	M			YI
DAWIDOWITZ	Ben Zion				Korczyna		Gedalia	Pearl	M			YI
DAWIDOWITZ	Moshe				Korczyna		Gedalia	Pearl	M			YI
DAWIDOWITZ	Leibish				Korczyna		Gedalia	Pearl	M			YI
DAWIDOWITZ	Haim				Korczyna				M			YI
DAWIDOWITZ	Avraham				Korczyna				M			YI
DAWIDOWITZ	unk				Korczyna				F	Avraham		YI
DAWIDOWITZ	Shmuel				Korczyna		Avraham	unk	M			YI

APPENDIX – Material not in the original Yizkor Book

Last Name	First name	Maiden Name	Birth Date	Birth Place	Residence	Occupation	Father	Mother	Gender	Spouse	Other	Source
DAWIDOWITZ	Golde				Korczyna				F	Shmuel		YI
DAWIDOWITZ	Sarah				Korczyna		Shmuel	Golde	F			YI
DENN	Chaim			Korczyna	Korczyna				M			D
DENN	Ryfka	Feurlich		Korczyna	Korczyna				F	Chaim		D
DENN	Salomon			Korczyna	Korczyna				M			D
DENN	Malka			Korczyna	Korczyna				F	Salomon		D
DENN	Moses			Korczyna	Korczyna		Salomon	Malka	M			D
DENN	Ber				Korczyna				M			YI
DENN	Haitsche				Korczyna				F	Ber		YI
DENN	Golde				Korczyna		Ber	Haitsche	F			YI
DENN	Yudel				Korczyna		Ber	Haitsche	M			YI
DENN	Leizer				Korczyna		Ber	Haitsche	M			YI
DENN	Tziporah				Korczyna		Ber	Haitsche	F			YI
DENN	Yudel				Korczyna		Ber	Haitsche	M			YI
DENN	Itsche				Korczyna							YI
DENN	Leizer				Korczyna							YI
DENN	Zalman			Korczyna	Korczyna	mailman			M			YI
DENN	Malka			Korczyna	Korczyna				F	Zalman		D
DENN	Esther			Korczyna	Korczyna		Zalman	Malka	F			D
DENN	Hene			Korczyna	Korczyna		Zalman	Malka	F			D
DENN	Liebe		b 19/9/1901	Korczyna	Korczyna			Hene	F			D
DENN	Elimelech				Korczyna		Zalman	Malka	M			D
DENN	Machla			Korczyna	Korczyna		Elimelech		F			D
DENN	Chaya Pearl		22/4/1905	Korczyna	Korczyna		Elimelech		F			D
DENN	Chaskel			Korczyna	Korczyna		Elimelech		M			D
DENN	Yaacov				Korczyna				M			YI
DENN	unk				Korczyna				F	Yaacov	children	YI
DENN	Ber				Korczyna				M	Ber		YI
DENN	Golde				Korczyna		Ber	Haitsche	F			YI
DENN	Yuda I.				Korczyna	m.Ja 1907	Leib	Malka	M	Yuda		YI
DENN	Suza	Dershowicz Suza				Korczyna		Lezer	Chana	F			D
DENN	Chaim				Korczyna	b.Ma1911	Israel	Chaje	M			D
DENN	Shulem W				Korczyna	b.Ju 1915	Israel	Chaje	M			D
DENN	Israel Shim			Korczyna	Korczyna				M			D
DENN	Beile	Tanc		Korczyna	Korczyna		Dawid	Lea	F	Israel Shim		D
DENN	Chaim			Korczyna	Korczyna		Israel Shim	Beile	M			D
DENN	Zussel	Kalb		Korczyna	Korczyna				F	Chaim		D
DENN	Mechel			Korczyna	Korczyna		Chaim	Zussel	M			D
DENN	Israel Itzhak				Korczyna		Chaim	Zussel	M			YI
DENN	Chaya	Mendelowitz		Korczyna	Korczyna				F	Israel Itzhak		D
DENN	Yosef Yehu			Korczyna	Korczyna		Chaim	Zussel	M			D
DENN	Ruchel			Korczyna	Korczyna		Chaim	Zussel	F			D
DENN	Gele			Korczyna	Korczyna			Ruchel	F			D
DENN	Chawa			Korczyna	Korczyna			Ruchel	F			D
DENN	Salomon Itz			Korczyna	Korczyna			Ruchel	M			D
DERSHOWITZ	Leser				Korczyna				M	Leser		YI
DERSHOWITZ	Chana L.	Gutwein			Korczyna				F			D
DERSHOWITZ	Suza				Korczyna	b.1885	Leser	Chana	F			YI
DERSHOWITZ	Shulem				Korczyna	shochet			M			D
DERSHOWITZ	Israel Meir				Korczyna				M			YI
DERSHOWITZ	Hinda		1917	Korczyna	Korczyna				F			YA
DERSHOWITZ	Liba		1915	Korczyna	Korczyna				F			YA
DEUTSCH	fam				Korczyna							P
DEUTSCH	Markus											P
DILLER	Simha				Korczyna	shamash			M			YI
DILLER	Freidel				Korczyna				F	Simha		YI
DILLER	unk				Korczyna				M			YI
DILLER	Malka				Korczyna		Simha	Freidel	F	unk		YI
DILLER	Yankel				Korczyna		Simha	Freidel	M			YI
DILLER	Yossef				Korczyna		Simha	Freidel	M			YI
DILLER	unk			Korczyna	Krosno				F	Yossef	children	YI
DYM	Haim				Korczyna	textile			M			YI
DYM	Roizele				Korczyna				F	Haim		YI
DYM	David				Korczyna		Haim	Roizele	M			YI
DYM	Arie				Korczyna				M			YI

APPENDIX – Material not in the original Yizkor Book

Last Name	First name	Maiden Name	Birth Date	Birth Place	Residence	Occupation	Father	Mother	Gender	Spouse	Other	Source
DYM	Rivkah				Korczyna				F	Arie	children	YI
DYM	Naftali				Korczyna				M		the family	YI
DYM	unk				Korczyna				F		children	YI
DYM	Shyja			Korczyna	Krosno				M			D
EDER	Aron				Korczyna				M			P
EICHORN	Chaim				Korczyna				M			YI
EICHORN	Braindel				Korczyna				M	Chaim		YI
EICHORN	Zishe				Korczyna		Chaim	Braindel	M		Russia	YI
EICHORN	Esther				Korczyna				M			YI
EICHORN	Berish				Korczyna		Zishe	Esther	M		Russia	YI
EICHORN	Rivka				Korczyna		Zishe	Esther	S			YI
EICHORN	Hannah				Korczyna		Zishe	Esther	S			YI
EICHORN	Blima				Korczyna		Chaim					YI
EICHORN	Jakob				Korczyna				M			YI
EICHORN	unk				Korczyna				F	Jakob	children	YI
EICHORN	Simon				Korczyna				M		the family	YI
EICHORN	unk				Korczyna				F	Simon	2 child	YI
EICHORN	unk				Korczyna				M			YI
EICHORN	Rikel				Korczyna				F	unk	children	YI
EISEN	Aaron		1888	Korczyna	Korczyna		Szmuel		M			YA
EISEN	Ester		1888	Korczyna	Korczyna				F	Aaron		YA
EISEN	Moshe		1915	Korczyna	Korczyna		Aaron	Ester	M			YA
EISEN	Reisel				Korczyna				F	Moshe		YA
EISEN	Shapsi		1921	Korczyna	Korczyna		Aaron	Ester	M			YA
EISEN	Zishe		1928	Korczyna	Korczyna		Aaron	Ester	M			YA
EISEN	Shmuel				Korczyna				M			YA
EISEN	Yaacov				Korczyna		Aron	Esther	M			YI
EISENBERG	T								M			P
EISENBERG	Rickel	Akselrad		Korczyna	Krosno				F	T		P
EISENBERG	Isidore				Korczyna	USA			M			K.C.
EISENBERG	Osias				Korczyna	USA			M			K.C
EISENBERG	Rachel				Korczyna	USA			F			K.C
EISENBERG	Rikel								M			P
EISENBERG	T								F			P
EISENSTEIN	Batia	Akselrad	b.1932	Krosno	Krosno		Bendet	Cile	F			P
ELIAS	Mordechai				Korczyna				M			P
ELLOWICZ	fam				Korczyna							P
ENGEL	Herz				Korczyna				M			YI
ENGEL	Hene Feige	Werner			Korczyna				F			YI
ENGEL	Lemil				Korczyna		Herz	Hene Feige	M			YI
ENGEL	Elieazar				Korczyna		Herz	Hene Feige	M			YI
ENGEL	Yeshayahu				Korczyna		Herz	Hene Feige	M			YI
ENGELHARDT	Itzhak				Korczyna				M			YI
ENGELHARDT	Moshe				Korczyna		Itzhak		M			YI
ENGELHARDT	Rachel				Korczyna				F	Moshe	child	YI
ENGELHARDT	Hene				Korczyna		Moshe	Rachel	F			YI
ENGELHARDT	Shimshon				Korczyna		Itzhak		M			YI
ENGELHARDT	Feige	Gimpel			Korczyna				F	Shimshon		YI
ENGELHARDT	Dworah				Korczyna		Shimshon	Feige	F			YI
ENGELHARDT	Bashe				Korczyna		Shimshon	Feige	F	Tzvi		YI
ENGELHARDT	Tzvi				Korczyna				M			YI
ENGELHARDT	Frimet				Korczyna		Tzvi	Bashe	F			YI
ENGLARD	Haim				Korczyna				M			YI
ENGLARD	unk				Korczyna				F	Haim		YI
ENGLARD	Israel				Korczyna		Haim	unk	M			YI
ENGLARD	Sarah Hadas				Korczyna		Haim	unk	F	Israel		YI
ENGLARD	Dworah Hendel				Korczyna		Israel	Sarah	F			YI
ENGLARD	Yochewed Miriam				Korczyna		Israel	Sarah	F			YI
ENGLARD	Tziporah Mindel				Korczyna		Israel	Sarah	F			YI
ENGLARD	Haim				Korczyna		Israel	Sarah	M			YI

APPENDIX – Material not in the original Yizkor Book

Last Name	First name	Maiden Name	Birth Date	Birth Place	Residence	Occupation	Father	Mother	Gender	Spouse	Other	Source
ENGLAND	Rachel	Wasser strum				Korczyna		Israel	Sarah	F		YI
EPSTEIN	Moshe				Korczyna	dayan			M			YI
EPSTEIN	Hadas				Korczyna				F	Moshe	8 child	YI
ERREICH	Ber				Korczyna	judenrat			M			YI
ERREICH	unk				Korczyna				F	Ber		YI
ERREICH	Avraham				Korczyna				M			YI
ERREICH	Shmuel				Korczyna		Avraham		M		child	YI
ERREICH	Hannah	Fessel			Korczyna				F	Avraham		YI
ERREICH	Matityahu				Korczyna		Shmuel	Hannah	M			YI
ERREICH	Naphtali				Korczyna		Shmuel	Hannah	M			YI
ERREICH	Reisel				Korczyna		Shmuel	Hannah	F			YI
ERREICH	Hersh				Korczyna		Shmuel	Hannah	M			YI
ERREICH	Hannah Pessel	Eichorn			Korczyna				M	Shmuel	the family	YI
ERREICH	Hersh				Korczyna			Hannah	M			YI
ERREICH	Sarah				Korczyna			Hannah	F			YI
ERREICH	Chana			Korczyna	Korczyna		Chaim		F			YA
ERREICH	Rose		1910	Korczyna	Korczyna		Jakob		F			YA
ERREICH	Samuel			Zmigrod Nowy	Korczyna		Abraham		M			YA
ETTINGER	Leib			Korczyna	Korczyna		Chaim		M			YA
ETTINGER	Yoel				Korczyna	innkeeper			M			YI
ETTINGER	Leibish				Korczyna		Haim		M			YI
ETTINGER	Hannah				Korczyna				F			YI
ETTINGER	Moshe				Korczyna				M			YI
ETTINGER	unk				Korczyna				F	Moshe	children	YI
FABIAN	Benyamin				Korczyna				M			P
FEIGENBAUM	Moshe				Korczyna				M			YI
FEIGENBAUM	Haya				Korczyna				F	Moshe		YI
FEIGENBAUM	Avraham			Jodlowa	Korczyna		Moshe	Haya	M			YI
FEIT	Avraham			Kombrnia	Korczyna				M			YI
FEIT	Leizer				Korczyna				M			YI
FEIT	Lea				Korczyna				F	Leizer		YI
FENNER	Itzhak				Korczyna				M			YI
FENNER	Miriam	Ettinger			Korczyna				F	Itzhak	child	YI
FENNING	Eli			Ikrzenai	Korczyna				M			YI
FENNING	Hesse			Ikrzenai	Korczyna				F			YI
FENNING	Manes			Ikrzenai	Korczyna				M			YI
FENNING	Vite			Ikrzenai	Korczyna				F			YI
FERBER	Yossef				Korczyna				M			YI
FERBER	Beile				Korczyna				F	Yossef		YI
FERBER	Dawid				Korczyna				M			YI
FERBER	Shimon				Korczyna				M			YI
FERBER	Liebe				Korczyna				F	Shimon		YI
FERBER	Shimon				Korczyna				M			YI
FERBER	Liebe				Korczyna				F	Shimon		YI
FERBER	Yossef				Korczyna				M			YI
FERBER	Beile				Korczyna				F	Yossef		YI
FESSEL	Shmuel m				Korczyna		Moshe		M			YI
FESSEL	Moshe				Korczyna		Moshe		M			YI
FESSEL	Benyamin				Korczyna		Moshe		M			YI
FESSEL	Sender				Korczyna		Moshe		M			YI
FESSEL	Rachel			Korczyna	Krosno				F	Lipe		P
FESSEL	Alexander								M			P
FESSEL	Hinda Gitt	Akselrad		Korczyna	Korczyna		Lipa	Rachel	F			P
FESSEL	Alexander								F			P
FESSEL	Shmuel Mehel				Korczyna		Moshe		M			YI
FESSEL	Naphtali				Korczyna				M			YI
FESSEL	Elimelech				Korczyna		Naphtali		M			YI
FESSEL	Rachel				Korczyna		Elimelech		F	husband		YI
FESSEL	Tzvi				Korczyna		Elimelech	Rachel	M			YI
FESSEL	unk				Korczyna				F	Tzvi		YI

APPENDIX – Material not in the original Yizkor Book

Last Name	First name	Maiden Name	Birth Date	Birth Place	Residence	Occupation	Father	Mother	Gender	Spouse	Other	Source
FESSEL	Elieazar Lipa				Korczyna	cantor	Naphtali		M			YI
FESSEL	Lea				Korczyna				F	Elieazar		YI
FESSEL	Berish Dow				Korczyna		Elieazar	Lea	M			YI
FESSEL	Hannah Tzirel				Korczyna				F	Berish		YI
FESSEL	Gedalia Asher				Korczyna		Berish	Hannah	M			YI
FESSEL	Sarah				Korczyna		Berish	Hannah	F			YI
FESSEL	Feige Rachel				Korczyna		Berish	Hannah	F			YI
FESSEL	Yaacov Itzhak				Korczyna		Berish	Hannah	M			YI
FESSEL	Moshe Dawid				Korczyna		Elieazar	Lea	M			YI
FESSEL	Eliyahu				Korczyna		Elieazar	Lea	M			YI
FESSEL	Naphtali				Korczyna		Elieazar	Lea	M			YI
FESSEL	Tzirel				Korczyna		Elieazar	Lea	F			YI
FESSEL	Rachel				Korczyna		Elieazar	Lea	F			YI
FESSEL	Hannah				Korczyna		Elieazar	Lea	F			YI
FESSEL	Haitsche				Korczyna		Elieazar	Lea	F			YI
FESSEL	Feige				Korczyna				F			YI
FESSEL	Esther				Korczyna			Feige	F			YI
FESSEL	Mindel				Korczyna			Feige	F			YI
FESSEL	Haya Ita				Korczyna			Feige	F			YI
FESSEL	Breindel				Korczyna			Feige	F			YI
FESSEL	Sender				Korczyna			Feige	M			YI
FESSEL	Haim Dawid				Korczyna				M			YI
FESSEL	Lea				Korczyna				F	Haim		YI
FESSEL	Sarah				Korczyna		Haim	Lea	F			YI
FESSEL	Wolf				Korczyna		Haim	Lea	M			YI
FESSEL	Beile				Korczyna		Haim	Lea	F			YI
FESSEL	Avraham				Korczyna				M			YI
FESSEL	Lea				Korczyna				F	Avraham		YI
FESSEL	Benjamin			Korczyna	Korczyna				M			YA
FESSEL	Michael			Korczyna	Korczyna		Dawid		M			YA
FEURLICH	Meilech			Korczyna	Korczyna				M			D
FEURLICH	Cyppe Ides			Korczyna	Korczyna				f	Meilech		D
FEURLICH	Ryfka			Korczyna	Korczyna		Meilech	Cyppe Ides	M			D
FEURLICH	Jehuda		B.30/4/1905	Korczyna	Korczyna			Ryfka	M			D
FINDLING	Selig			Korczyna	Krosno				M			P
FINDLING	Sheindel	Breitowicz		Korczyna	Krosno				F			P
FINKELSTEIN	Ira				Korczyna				M			YI
FINKELSTEIN	Solek				Korczyna				M			YI
FINKELSTEIN	Shlomo				Korczyna				M			YI
FINKELSTEIN	unk				Korczyna				F	Shlomo		YI
FISCHEL	Ber				Korczyna	activist			M			YI
FISCHLER	Eli				Korczyna				M			YI
FISCHLER	unk				Korczyna				F	Eli		YI
FLAPPAN	Leizer			Korczyna	Krosno				M			D
FLAPPAN	Rachel	Kalb		Korczyna	Krosno		Shmuel	Chaya	F	Leizer		D
FLAPPAN	Fradela		b3/4/1907	Korczyna	Krosno				F			D
FLAPPAN	Chaya Rivk		b24/2/1909	Korczyna	Krosno		Leizer	Rachel	F			D
FLAPPAN	Malka		b 25/3/1911	Korczyna	Krosno		Leizer	Rachel	F			D
FORGEL	fam				Korczyna							P
FREI	Shaul				Korczyna	cantor	Leizer	Rachel	M			YI
FREI	Haya	Rothenberg			Korczyna				F	Shaul		YI
FREI	Bashe				Korczyna		Shaul	Haya	F			YI
FREI	Feige				Korczyna		Shaul	Haya	F			YI
FREI	Avraham				Korczyna		Shaul	Haya	M			YI
FREIFELD	Hindzia			Korczyna	Korczyna				F			YA
FREIFELD	Lajbek			Korczyna	Korczyna		Jakob		M			YA
FREIFELD	Jakob			Domaradz	Korczyna		Leib		M			YA
FREIFELD	Renia			Korczyna	Korczyna		Jakob		F			YA
FREIFELD	Siolek			Korczyna	Korczyna		Jakob		M			YA
FREIFELD	Janciu			Domaradz	Korczyna		Leib		F			YA

APPENDIX – Material not in the original Yizkor Book

Last Name	First name	Maiden Name	Birth Date	Birth Place	Residence	Occupation	Father	Mother	Gender	Spouse	Other	Source
FREIFELD	Shaul			Korczyna	Korczyna		Jakob		M			YA
FREIFELD	Yaacov				Korczyna				M			YI
FREIFELD	Leib				Korczyna		Yaacov		M			YI
FREIFELD	Rachel				Korczyna				F			YI
FREIFELD	Hannah Riwka				Korczyna			Rachel	F			YI
FREIFELD	Feige				Korczyna			Rachel	F			YI
FRENKEL	Sender				Korczyna				M			YI
FRENKEL	Rivkah	Raab			Korczyna				F	Sender		YI
FREUND	**Wolf**				Korczyna				M			YI
FREUND	**Sheindel**				Korczyna				F	Wolf		YI
FREUND	Leib Wolf				Korczyna		Yaacov	Haya	M			YI
FREUND	Sheindel				Korczyna				F	Leib		YI
FREUND	**Mordechai Tzwi**				Korczyna		Leib	Sheindel	M			YI
FREUND	**Moshe**	Josephowicz			Korczyna		Leib	Sheindel	M			YI
FREUND	Sarah				Korczyna		Leib	Sheindel	F			YI
FREUND	Yaacov				Korczyna		Leib	Sheindel				YI
FREUND	Yahet				Korczyna				F	Yaacov		YI
FREUND	**Esther**				Korczyna		Yaacov	Yahet	F			YI
FREUND	Seril				Korczyna		Yaacov	Yahet	F			YI
FREUND	Pearl Yente				Korczyna		Yaacov	Yahet	F			YI
FREUND	Matityahu				Korczyna		Yaacov	Yahet	M			YI
FREUND	Hersh				Korczyna				M			YI
FREUND	Yahet				Korczyna		Hersh		F			YI
FREUND	haya				Korczyna		Hersh		F			YI
FREUND	Shmuel				Korczyna		Hersh		M			YI
FREUND	Ben Zion				Korczyna		Hersh		M			YI
FRIES	Leib				Korczyna				M			P
FRISCH	Yehiel			Korczyna	Korczyna				M			D
FRISCH	Rachel	Mendelowitz		Korczyna	Korczyna				F	Yehiel		D
FRISCH	Simche	Mendelowitz		Korczyna	Korczyna		Yehiel	Rachel	F			D
GADLI	unk				Korczyna	teacher			M			YI
GELB	Aron			Korczyna	Korczyna				M			D
GELB	Malie	Kalb		Korczyna	Krosno				F	Aron		D
GELB	Mala			Korczyna	Korczyna		Aron	Malie	F			D
GELLER	Yanka				Korczyna	technician			F			YI
GETZEL	Haya Liebe				Korczyna				F			YI
GETZEL	Basha				Korczyna			Haya	F			YI
GIMPEL	Zelma Shul	Schlanger		Cologne	Israel		David Isr	Rachel	F			P
GLEICHER	Mendel				Korczyna				M			YI
GLEICHER	Avramtsche				Korczyna		Mendel		M			YI
GLEICHER	Beile				Korczyna				F	Avramtsche		YI
GLEICHER	Yudel				Korczyna		Avramtsche	Beile	M			YI
GLEICHER	Yudel				Korczyna		Avramtsche	Beile	M			YI
GLEICHER	Wolf				Korczyna	restaurant			M			YI
GLEICHER	Lea				Korczyna				F	Wolf		YI
GLEICHER	Mindel				Korczyna		Wolf	Lea	F			YI
GLEICHER	Sender				Korczyna		Wolf	Lea	M			YI
GLEICHER	Matityahu				Korczyna				M			YI
GLEICHER	Tzivia	Rubin			Korczyna				F	Matityahu		YI
GLEICHER	Hersh				Korczyna		Matityahu	Matityahu	M			YI
GLEICHER	Naphtali				Korczyna		Matityahu	Matityahu	M			YI
GLEICHER	Toibe				Korczyna		Matityahu	Matityahu	F			YI
GLEICHER	Hendel	Zilberberg			Korczyna				F			YI
GLEICHER	Leah			Korczyna	Korczyna		Sender		F			YA
GOLDBERGER	fam				Korczyna							P
GRAU	Mendel				Korczyna				M			P
GRIN	Eli				Korczyna	Judenrat			M			YI
GRIN	Motie				Korczyna				M			YI
GRIN	Elimelech				Korczyna				M			YI

APPENDIX – Material not in the original Yizkor Book

Last Name	First name	Maiden Name	Birth Date	Birth Place	Residence	Occupation	Father	Mother	Gender	Spouse	Other	Source
GRIN	Beila				Korczyna		Elimelech		F			YI
GRIN	Eliyahu				Korczyna				M	Eliyahu		YI
GRIN	Eli				Korczyna	Judenrat			M			YI
GRIN	Motie				Korczyna				M			YI
GRIN	Zishe		1912	Korczyna	Korczyna		Yehoshua		M			YA
GRIN	Feige				Korczyna				F	Zishe		YI
GRIN	Rachel		1885	Dynow	Korczyna		Elimelech		F			YA
GRIN	Beila				Korczyna		Elimelech		F			YI
GRIN	Eliyahu				Korczyna				M			YI
GRIN	Beile				Korczyna				F	Eliyahu		YI
GRIN	Yehshua Leib				Korczyna				M			YI
GRIN	Rachel				Korczyna				F	Yehshua		YI
GRIN	Pessie				Korczyna		Yehshua	Rachel	F	husband		YI
GRIN	Mindel		1920	Korczyna	Korczyna		Yehshua	Rachel	F			YA
GRIN	Wolf				Korczyna				M			YI
GRIN	Shia Leib					Korczyna		Wolf		M		YI
GRIN	Rachel				Korczyna		Elimelech		F			YI
GRIN	Elimelech				Korczyna				M			YA
GRIN	Beila		1912	Dukla	Korczyna		Elimelech		F			YA
GRIN	Yehoshua				Korczyna				M			YA
GRUNSPAN	fam				Korczyna							P
GUTERBAUM	Bluma				Korczyna				F			P
GUTMAN	Moshe Y				Korczyna		Yehuda		M			YA
GUTMAN	Moshe			Korczyna	Korczyna		Yehuda		M			YA
GUTREICH	Paula				Korczyna				F			YI
GUTWEIN	Lea				Korczyna				F			YI
GUTWEIN	Yochewet				Korczyna		Haim	Esther	F			P
GUTWEIN	Meir				Korczyna				M			P
GUTWEIN	Pearl				Korczyna				F			P
GUTWEIN	Rachel				Korczyna				F			YI
GUTWEIN	Yossef				Korczyna				M			YI
GUTWEIN	Benyamin				Korczyna				M			YI
GUTWEIN	Godele Asher				Korczyna	prop.owner			M			YI
GUTWEIN	Sarah				Korczyna				F	Godele		YI
GUTWEIN	Yudel				Korczyna			Sarah	M			YI
GUTWEIN	Malka				Korczyna				F	Yudel		YI
GUTWEIN	Mindel				Korczyna			Sarah	F			YI
GUTWEIN	Moshe				Korczyna			Sarah	M			YI
GUTWEIN	Nissan				Korczyna			Sarah	M			YI
GUTWEIN	Tzirel				Korczyna			Sarah	F			YI
GUTWEIN	Sime				Korczyna			Sarah	F			YI
GUTWEIN	Sarah	Katz			Korczyna				F	Chaim		YI
GUTWEIN	Lea				Korczyna				F	Elieazar		YI
GUTWEIN	Yaacov Itzhak				Korczyna				M			YI
GUTWEIN	Haim				Korczyna		Yaacov		M			YI
GUTWEIN	Esther				Korczyna				F	Haim		YI
GUTWEIN	Cirel			Korczyna	Korczyna		Yehuda		F			YA
GUTWEIN	Nissan			Korczyna	Korczyna		Yehuda		M			YA
GUTWEIN	Sima			Korczyna	Korczyna		Yehuda		F			YA
GUTWEIN	Yehuda		1884	Korczyna	Korczyna				M			YA
GUZIK	Wolf Yankel				Korczyna				M			YI
HAK	Mose				Korczyna				M			P
HALPERIN	Mendel		1890	Korczyna	Korczyna				M			YA
HALPERN	Yona				Korczyna				M			YI
HALPERN	Breindel				Korczyna				M			YI
HALPERN	Mendel				Korczyna	Judenrat	Yona		M			YI
HALPERN	Fradel				Korczyna				F	Mendel		YI
HALPERN	Wolf				Korczyna		Yona		M			YI
HALPERN	Miriam				Korczyna		Yona		F			YI
HALPERN	Lea				Korczyna				F			YI
HALPERN	Chaim				Korczyna	well to do			M			YI
HALPERN	Necheme				Korczyna				F	Chaim		YI
HALPERN	Aron				Korczyna		Chaim	Necheme	M			YI

APPENDIX – Material not in the original Yizkor Book

Last Name	First name	Maiden Name	Birth Date	Birth Place	Residence	Occupation	Father	Mother	Gender	Spouse	Other	Source
HALPERN	Hersh				Korczyna		Chaim	Necheme	M			YI
HALPERN	unk				Korczyna				F	Hersh		YI
HALPERN	Rachel				Korczyna		Chaim	Necheme	F			YI
HALPERN	Hertz				Korczyna	prop.owner			M			YI
HALPERN	Leibish				Korczyna				M			YI
HALPERN	Naphtali Hertz				Korczyna		Leibish		M			YI
HALPERN	Tova Yochewed				Korczyna		Leibish		F			YI
HALPERN	Yehoshua				Korczyna		Leibish		M			YI
HALPERN	Bashe				Korczyna				F			YI
HALPERN	Gittel				Korczyna				F			YI
HALPERN	Mendel				Korczyna				M			YI
HALPERN	Freidel			Korczyna	Korczyna		Jakob		F			YA
HALPRIN	Freidel		1914	Korczyna	Korczyna				F			YA
HANNAH	Malka				Korczyna	glazier			M			YI
HAUSNER	Chaim			Korczyna	Korczyna				M			P
HAUSNER	Chana			Korczyna	Korczyna				F	Chaim		P
HAUSNER	Itche /Itzhak			Korczyna	Korczyna		Chaim	Chana	M			P
HAUSNER	Wolf			Korczyna	Korczyna		Chaim	Chana	M			P
HAUSNER	Eidel			Korczyna	Korczyna		Chaim	Chana	F			P
HAUSNER	Rebecca			Korczyna	Korczyna		Chaim	Chana	F			P
HEBENSTREIT	Itzhak				Korczyna				M			YI
HEBENSTREIT	Bluma	Raab			Korczyna				F	Itzhak		YI
HEBENSTREIT	Rachel				Korczyna		Itzhak	Bluma	F			YI
HEBENSTREIT	Lea				Korczyna		Itzhak	Bluma	F			YI
HELLOSCHICZ	Hersh				Korczyna				M			YI
HELLOSCHICZ	Yossef				Korczyna	vinegar			M			YI
HELLOSCHICZ	Beile				Korczyna				F	Yossef		YI
HELLOSCHICZ	Jehudith				Korczyna		Yossef	Beile	F			YI
HELLOSCHICZ	Dworah		1925	Korczyna	Korczyna		Yossef	Beile	F			YA
HELLOSCHICZ	unk				Korczyna				M			YI
HELLOSCHICZ	Esther				Korczyna				F	unk		YI
HELLOSCHICZ	unk				Korczyna				M			YI
HELLOSCHICZ	Ethel				Korczyna				F	unk		YI
HELLOSCHICZ	Mordechai				Korczyna				M			YI
HELLOSCHICZ	Mendel				Korczyna				M			YI
HELLOSCHICZ	Moshe				Korczyna				M			YI
HELLOSCHICZ	Sarah				Korczyna				F			YI
HELLOSCHICZ	Shmuel Aron				Korczyna				M			YI
HOLLOSCHITZ	Beila		1890	Niebylic	Korczyna		Jehuda		F			YA
HOLLOSCHITZ	Yosef		1887	Korczyna	Korczyna		Hersh		M			YA
HOLOSZIC	Ides			Korczyna	Korczyna		Tzwi		F			YA
HOROWITZ	Sarah				Korczyna				F			YI
HOROWITZ	Mordechai				Korczyna			Sarah	M			YI
HOROWITZ	unk				Korczyna				F	Mordechai		YI
HOROWITZ	Benedet				Korczyna				M			YI
HOROWITZ	Rachel				Korczyna				F			YI
HOROWITZ	Berta				Korczyna		Benedet	Benedet	F			YI
HOROWITZ	Itzhak				Korczyna				M			YI
HOROWITZ	Reisel				Korczyna				F	Itzhak		YI
HOROWITZ	Yehezkel				Korczyna				M			YI
HOROWITZ	Michael				Korczyna		Yehezkel		M			YI
HOROWITZ	Shlomo				Korczyna		Yehezkel		M			YI
HOROWITZ	Mechel				Korczyna		Yehezkel		M			YI
HOROWITZ	unk				Korczyna				F	Mechel	Russia	YI
HOROWITZ	Fradel				Korczyna				F			YI
HOROWITZ	Mordechai				Korczyna				M			YI
HOROWITZ	Tzipe Yente				Korczyna				F			YI
HOROWITZ	Moshe				Korczyna				M			YI
HOROWITZ	Shimshon				Korczyna		Moshe		M			YI
HOROWITZ	Naphtali				Korczyna				M			YI
HOROWITZ	Rachel				Korczyna				F	Naphtali		YI
HOROWITZ	Hannah				Korczyna		Naphtali	Rachel	F			YI
HOROWITZ	Shlomo				Korczyna				M		Russia	YI
HOROWITZ	Ben Zion				Korczyna				M		Krosno	YI
HOROWITZ	Sarah				Korczyna				F		Krosno	YI

APPENDIX – Material not in the original Yizkor Book

Last Name	First name	Maiden Name	Birth Date	Birth Place	Residence	Occupation	Father	Mother	Gender	Spouse	Other	Source
HOROWITZ	Moshe				Korczyna		Ben Zion	Sarah	M		Krosno	YI
HOROWITZ	Mordechai				Korczyna				M			YI
HOROWITZ	Eliyahu				Korczyna				M			YI
HOROWITZ	Hawa	Kalb			Korczyna				F			YI
HOROWITZ	Shimon				Korczyna			Hawa	M			YI
HOROWITZ	Moshe				Korczyna			Hawa	M			YA
HOROWITZ	Sara		1872	Korczyna	Korczyna				F			YA
HOROWITZ	Shmelke			Korczyna	Korczyna				M			D
HOROWITZ	Asher			Korczyna	Korczyna				M			D
HOROWITZ	Hennie	Kobulaner		Korczyna	Korczyna				F	Asher		D
HOROWITZ	Benzion			Korczyna	Korczyna		Asher	Hennie	M			D
HOROWITZ	Sara			Korczyna	Korczyna				F	Benzion		D
HOSTATER	Menashe				Korczyna				M			YI
HOTZ	Mendel				Korczyna	binder			M			YI
INFELD	Leibish				Korczyna				M			YI
INFELD	unk				Korczyna				F	Leibish		YI
INFELD	Matityahu				Korczyna				M			YI
INFELD	Tzeril				Korczyna				F	Matityahu		YI
INFELD	Naphtali				Korczyna	judenrat			M			YI
INFELD	Hersh				Korczyna				M			YI
INFELD	unk				Korczyna				F	Hersh		YI
INFELD	Yantsche			Korczyna	Korczyna				M			YI
INFELD	Tzirel			Korczyna	Korczyna				F	Yantsche		YI
JOSKALA	Nute			Korczyna	Korczyna				M			YI
KALB	Chaim			Dukla	Korczyna				M			D
KALB	Ester	Judkowicz		Korczyna	Korczyna				F	Chaim		D
KALB	Leizer				Korczyna		Chaim	Ester	M			D
KALB	Chawa			Korczyna	Korczyna				F	Leizer		D
KALB	Simon			Korczyna	Korczyna				M			D
KALB	Leie		m.Ju 1927	Korczyna	Korczyna				F	Simon		D
KALB	Mania			Korczyna	Korczyna		Simon	Leie	F			D
KALB	Chana	Horowitz	m.Ju 1927	Korczyna	Korczyna				F			D
KALB	Samson		b10/10/1928	Korczyna	Korczyna		Leib	Chana	M			D
KALB	Pinkas M		b2/4/1931	Korczyna	Korczyna		Leib	Chana	M			D
KALB	Rehel			Korczyna	Korczyna				F			YI
KALB	Dawid			Korczyna	Korczyna				M			D
KALB	Leja			Korczyna	Korczyna				F			D
KALB	Asher			Korczyna	Korczyna				M			YI
KALB	Moshe			Korczyna	Korczyna				M			YI
KALB	Yekutiel				Korczyna				M			YI
KALB	Yossef Itzh			Korczyna	Korczyna				M			D
KALB	Feige			Korczyna	Korczyna				F	Yossef Itzh		D
KALB	Shmuel Ber			Korczyna	Krosno		Yossef Itzh	Feige	M			D
KALB	Leibish		b27/8/1900	Korczyna	Korczyna		Shmuel Ber		M			D
KALB	Riwka Chaya			Korczyna	Korczyna		Israel	Frime	F	Leibish		D
KALB	Serl			Korczyna	Korczyna				M			D
KALB	Asher			Korczyna	Korczyna				M			D
KALB	Shulem			Korczyna	Korczyna				M			D
KAMELHAR	Hannah				Korczyna				F	Yekutiel		YI
KAMELHAR	Itzhak				Korczyna				M			YI
KANAREK	Reise;	Weissman			Korczyna				F	Itzhak		YI
KANAREK	Mendel				Korczyna				M			YI
KANDEL	Hinde				Korczyna				F	Mendel		YI
KANDEL	Avraham Itzhak				Korczyna				M			YI
KANNER	Lea				Korczyna				F	Avraham		YI
KANNER	Itzhak				Korczyna				M			YI
KANNER	Eli Wolf				Korczyna				M			YI
KATZ	Hersh				Korczyna				M			YI
KATZ	Liebe				Korczyna				F	Hersh		YI
KATZ	Hannah	Rikel			Korczyna				F			YI
KATZ	Matityahu				Korczyna	infkuential			M			YI

APPENDIX – Material not in the original Yizkor Book

Last Name	First name	Maiden Name	Birth Date	Birth Place	Residence	Occupation	Father	Mother	Gender	Spouse	Other	Source
KATZ-GLEICHER	Tzivia				Korczyna				F	Matityahu		YI
KATZ-GLEICHER	Avraham				Korczyna		Matityahu	Tzivia	M			YI
KATZ-GLEICHER	Nissan				Korczyna		Matityahu	Tzivia	M			YI
KATZ-GLEICHER	Yehoshua				Korczyna		Matityahu	Tzivia	M			YI
KATZ-GLEICHER	Samuel Leib				Korczyna				M			YI
KAUFMAN	Haim Eliyahu				Korczyna	soda			M			YI
KAUFMAN	Meir				Korczyna		Haim		M			YI
KAUFMAN	Tziporah				Korczyna				F	Meir		YI
KAUFMAN	Israel				Korczyna		Meir	Tziporah	M			YI
KAUFMAN	Bashe				Korczyna		Meir	Tziporah	F			YI
KAUFMAN	Feige				Korczyna		Meir	Tziporah	F			YI
KAUFMAN	Avraham				Korczyna		Haim		M			YI
KAUFMAN	Gittel				Korczyna		Haim		F			YI
KAUFMAN	Breindel				Korczyna		Haim		F			YI
KAUFMAN	Roize				Korczyna		Haim		F			YI
KAUFMAN	Golda				Korczyna		Haim		F			YI
KAUFMAN	Shmuel Arie				Korczyna		Haim		M			YI
KAUFMAN	Hannah				Korczyna				M			YI
KAUFMAN	Yaacov				Korczyna				M			YI
KAUFMAN	Sime				Korczyna				F	Yaacov		YI
KAUFMAN	Hannah				Korczyna				F			YI
KAUFMAN	Miriam				Korczyna				F			YI
KAUFMAN	Majer			Korczyna	Korczyna		Chaim		M			YA
KAUFMAN	Cypora			Bircza	Korczyna		Natan		F			YA
KAUFMAN	mother				Korczyna				F			YI
KAWALEK	Sarah				Korczyna				F			YI
KAZUCH	Mary				Korczyna				F			D
KIRMER	Mechel				Korczyna	influential			M			YI
KIRSCHNER	Lea				Korczyna				F	Mechel		YI
KIRSCHNER	Wolf				Korczyna	apples	Mechel	Lea	M			YI
KIRSCHNER	Rivkah				Korczyna				F	Wolf		YI
KIRSCHNER	Dawid				Korczyna		Wolf	Rivkah	M			YI
KIRSCHNER	Meir Nahum				Korczyna	scarves			M			YI
KIRSCHNER	Moshe				Korczyna	shochet			M			YI
KIRSCHNER	Ita				Korczyna				M	Moshe		YI
KIRSCHNER	Naphtali				Korczyna		Moshe	Ita	M			YI
KIRSCHNER	Avraham				Korczyna		Moshe	Ita	M			YI
KIRSCHNER	Esther				Korczyna		Moshe	Ita	F			YI
KIRSCHNER	Mordechai Leib				Korczyna				M			YI
KIRSCHNER	Yahet				Korczyna				F			YI
KIRSCHNER	Michael				Korczyna				M			YI
KIRSCHNER	Wolf				Korczyna		Michael		M			YI
KIRSCHNER	Dawid Leib				Korczyna		Wolf		M			YI
KIRSCHNER	Benyamin				Korczyna				M			YI
KIRSCHNER	unk				Korczyna				F	Benyamin		YI
KIRSCHNER	Nahum				Korczyna				M			YI
KIRSCHNER	Lea				Korczyna				F			YI
KIRSCHNER	Meir				Korczyna				M			YI
KIRSCHNER	Moshe				Korczyna				M			YI
KIZELSTEIN	unk				Korczyna				F	Moshe		YI
KIZELSTEIN	Pertsche	Katz			Korczyna				F			YI
KOKOLIN	Shmuel Aron				Korczyna				M			YI
KOKUSHKA	Roizy				Korczyna				F			YI
KORB	Beila				Korczyna			Roizy	F		m.Ja1914	YI
KORB	Yossef				Korczyna	metal			M			YI
KORB	Haim Wolf				Korczyna	cigarette			M			YI
KOREF	Neche				Korczyna				F	Haim		YI
KOREF	Yankel				Korczyna		Haim	Neche	M			YI
KOREF	Gutsche				Korczyna		Haim	Neche	F			YI
KOREF	Yantsche				Korczyna				S			YI
KOREF	Pessah				Korczyna				M			YI

APPENDIX – Material not in the original Yizkor Book

Last Name	First name	Maiden Name	Birth Date	Birth Place	Residence	Occupation	Father	Mother	Gender	Spouse	Other	Source
KOREF	Gesla			Korczyna	Korczyna	tailor			M			D
KOREF	Mozes			Korczyna	Korczyna		Gesla		M			D
KOREF	Beile			Korczyna	Korczyna			Roizy	F	Mozes		D
KRATZER	Miriam				Korczyna				F			YI
KRATZER	Bashe	Schiff			Korczyna				F			YI
KRAWCIK	Malka				Korczyna				F			YI
KRESH	Ber				Korczyna				M			YI
KRIGER	Hersh				Korczyna		Ber		M			YI
KRIGER	Braindel				Korczyna		Ber		F			YI
KRIGER	Elimelech				Korczyna		Ber		M			YI
KRIGER	Schifra				Korczyna		Ber		F			YI
KRIGER	Yaacov				Korczyna		Ber		M			YI
KRIGER	Baruch			Korczyna	Krosno				M			YI
KRIGER	Sarah			Korczyna	Krosno				F	Baruch		YI
KRIGER	Yehoshua				Korczyna				M			YI
KUPFER	Harry			Korczyna	Krosno				M			D
KUPFER	Hershel			Korczyna	Krosno				M			D
KUPFER	Mark			Korczyna	Krosno				M			D
KUPFER	Moniek			Korczyna	Krosno				M			D
KUPFER	Rozia			Korczyna	Krosno				F			D
KUPLIK	Hene				Korczyna				F			YI
KUPLIK	Malka				Korczyna		Yehoshua	Hene	F	Yehoshua		YI
KUPLIK	Meir				Korczyna		Yehoshua	Hene	M			YI
KUPLIK	Shmuel				Korczyna		Yehoshua	Hene	M			YI
KUPLIK	Leibush				Korczyna	active			M			YI
KUPLIK	Pesla				Korczyna				F			D
KUREF	Moses Y	Gebel			Korczyna			Pesla	M	Moses		D
KUREF	Beila	Korb			Korczyna				F			D
KUREF	Elieazar D				Korczyna				M	Elieazar		P
LAMBIG	Lea				Korczyna				F			P
LAMBIG	Haim				Korczyna		Elieazar	Lea	M			P
LAMBIG	Yehuda				Korczyna				M			P
LAMBIG	Franka				Korczyna				F			P
LAMM	Malka				Korczyna				F			P
LAMM	Rachel				Korczyna				F			P
LAMM	Mrs.	Akselrad		Korczyna	Korczyna		Yossef Ben	Ides	F	Elisha		P
LANDAU	Mordechai				Korczyna				M			YI
LANDAU	Pearl				Korczyna				F	Mordechai		YI
LANDAU	Avraham				Korczyna				M			YI
LANGER	Zelig				Korczyna		Avraham		M			YI
LANGER	Freidel				Korczyna				F	Zelig		YI
LANGER	Haya				Korczyna		Zelig	Freidel	F			YI
LANGER	Henie				Korczyna		Ber		F			YI
LANGER	Moshe				Korczyna				M	Moshe		P
LAUTMAN	Feige				Korczyna				F			P
LAUTMAN	Mordechai				Korczyna		Moshe	Feige	M			P
LAUTMAN	Benie				Korczyna		Moshe	Feige	M			P
LAUTMAN	Yehezkel				Korczyna	Judenrat			M			P
LAUTMAN	Yehiel				Korczyna				F			P
LAUTMAN	Karola	Akselrad	b.1903	Korczyna	Brno		Meshulam	Chana	F	Yonas		YI
LAUTMAN	Yonas				Brno				M			P
LAUTMAN	Anie		b.1932		Brno		Yonas	Karola	F			P
LEIBNER	Shragai Fei				Korczyna				M	Shragai Fei		P
LEIBNER	Sheindel	Gross			Korczyna				F			P
LEIBNER	Nute Nathan		b1844	Korczyna	Zmigrod		Shragai F	Sheindel	M			P
LEIBNER	Pearl Ruch	Tzimet	b.1851	Zmigrod	Zmigrod				F			P
LEIBNER	Rachel Y	b.1853		Korczyna	Korczyna		Shragai F	Sheindel	F	Yehiel		P

APPENDIX – Material not in the original Yizkor Book

Last Name	First name	Maiden Name	Birth Date	Birth Place	Residence	Occupation	Father	Mother	Gender	Spouse	Other	Source
LEIBNER	Yehiel Aro	Weinberg			Korczyna				M			P
LEIBNER	Ester				Korczyna		Shragai F	Sheindel	F	Wolf Ber		P
LEIBNER	Ephraim		b.1875	Korczyna	Israel		Yehiel	Rachel Y	M			P
LEIBNER	Gittel	Grau			Korczyna		wife#2		F	Shragai Fei		P
LEIBNER	Ephraim		b.1868		Korczyna		Nathan N	Pearl Ruch	M			P
LEIBNER	Sprince	Findling		Zmigrod	Zmigrod				F	Ephraim		P
LEIBNER	Pearl		b.1900	Zmigrod	USA		Ephraim	Sprince	F			P
LEIBNER	Sima			Zmigrod	Dukla		Ephraim	Sprince	F			P
LEIBNER	Serl			Zmigrod	Zmigrod		Ephraim	Sprince	F			P
LEIBNER	Yaakov		b.1905	Zmigrod	Krosno		Ephraim	Sprince	M			P
LEIBNER	Moshe			Zmigrod	Zmigrod		Ephraim	Sprince	M			P
LEIBNER	Shimshon			Zmigrod	Zmigrod		Ephraim	Sprince	M			P
LEIBNER	Reisel			Zmigrod	Zmigrod		Ephraim	Sprince	F			P
LEIBNER	Mania			Zmigrod	Zmigrod		Ephraim	Sprince	F			P
LEIBNER	Rachel Y	b.1853		Korczyna	Korczyna		Shragai F	Sheindel	F	Yehiel		P
LEIBNER	Ephraim		b.1875	Korczyna	Israel		Yehiel	Rachel Y	M			P
LEIBNER	Miriam	Lustgarten	b.1886	Korczyna	Israel				F	Ephraim		P
LEIBNER	Avaham M		b.1909	Korczyna	Berlin		Ephraim	Miriam	M			P
LEIBNER	Sheindel		b.1911	Tarnow	Berlin				F	Avaham M	P	P
LEIBNER	Feige		b.1938	Berlin	Berlin		Avaham M	Sheindel	F		P	P
LEIBNER	Tzvi		b.1912	Korczyna	Korczyna		Ephraim	Miriam	M			P
LEIBNER	Raisel		b.1915	Korczyna	Korczyna		Ephraim	Miriam	F	Gerhard		P
LEIBNER	Aron		b.1920	Korczyna	Korczyna		Ephraim	Miriam	M			P
LEIBNER	Itzhak Arie		b.1879	Korczyna	Korczyna		Yehiel	Rachel Y	M			P
LEIBNER	Chyfra	Katz		Korczyna	Korczyna				F	Itzhak Arie		P
LEIBNER	Nissim		b.1915	Korczyna	Korczyna		Itzhak Arie	Chyfra	F			P
LEIBNER	Fradel		b.1890	Korczyna	Korczyna		Yehiel	Rachel Y	F			P
LEIBNER	Chana Gitte	Grau		Korczyna	Korczyna	2nd wife	Mayer L.	Beile Ite	F	Shragai Feib		P
LEIBNER	Moshe				Korczyna	shochet			M			YI
LEICHTOG	Hannah				Korczyna				F	Moshe		YI
LEICHTOG	Dawid Leib				Korczyna				M			YI
LEINER	Mordechai				Korczyna				M			YI
LEINER	unk				Korczyna				F	Mordechai		YI
LEINER	Shulem L				Korczyna				M			D
LEIZER	Eisik				Korczyna				M			YI
LEIZER	Avraham				Korczyna				M			YI
LEIZER	Arie				Korczyna				M			YI
LEMBICK	Moshe				Korczyna				M			YI
LERMAN	Haya				Korczyna				F	Moshe		YI
LERMAN	Yehoshua				Korczyna				M			YI
LERNER	Esther				Korczyna				F	Yehoshua		YI
LERNER	Jakob			Brody	Korczyna				M			YA
LEWAJ	Regina			Stryj	Korczyna		Dawid		F			YA
LEWAJ	Mendel				Korczyna				M			YI
LEWI	Hannah				Korczyna				F	Mendel		YI
LEWI	Haim				Korczyna				M			YI
LEWI	Yaacov				Korczyna	pharmaci			M			YI
LEWI	Regina				Korczyna				F	Yaacov		YI
LEWI	Moshe				Korczyna				M			YI
LEWITMAN	Feige	Fessel			Korczyna				F	Moshe		YI
LEWITMAN	Yehezkel				Korczyna				M			YI
LEWITMAN	Benie				Korczyna		Yehezkel		M			YI
LEWITMAN	Mordechai				Korczyna		Yehezkel		M			YI
LEWITMAN	Shmuel				Korczyna		Yehezkel		M			YI
LEWITMAN	Wolf				Korczyna				M			YI
LIEBER	Hannah				Korczyna				F	Wolf		YI
LIEBER	Shmuel				Korczyna				M			YI
LIPOLES	Moshe				Korczyna				M			YI

APPENDIX – Material not in the original Yizkor Book

Last Name	First name	Maiden Name	Birth Date	Birth Place	Residence	Occupation	Father	Mother	Gender	Spouse	Other	Source
LOTROKOWSKI	Bella				Korczyna				F			D
LUTMAN	Elieazar				Korczyna				M			P
MAHLER	Haya R				Korczyna				F	Elieazar		P
MAHLER	Hersh				Korczyna		Elieazar	Haya	M			P
MAHLER	Wolf				Korczyna		Elieazar	Haya	M			P
MAHLER	Moshe				Korczyna		Elieazar	Haya	M			P
MAHLER	Sarah				Korczyna		Elieazar	Haya	F			P
MAHLER	Yanka				Korczyna		Elieazar	Haya	F			P
MAHLER	Raphael				Korczyna		Elieazar	Haya	M			P
MAHLER	Hanoch				Korczyna		Raphael		M			P
MAHLER	Eliyahu				Korczyna				M			YI
MAJEROWICZ	Leon			Korczyna	Korczyna				M			D
MAJERS	Leo			Korczyna	Korczyna				M			D
MALTZ	Abraham			Korczyna	Korczyna				M			D
MALTZ	Chaya			Korczyna	Korczyna				F	Abraham		D
MALTZ	Yaacov Shaul				Korczyna		Eliyahu		M			YI
MALTZ	Taube				Korczyna				F	Yaacov		YI
MALTZ	Itzhak				Korczyna		Yaacov	Taube	M			YI
MALTZ	Sheindel				Korczyna		Yaacov	Taube	F			YI
MALTZ	Yossef				Korczyna		Yaacov	Taube	M			YI
MALTZ	Mali				Korczyna		Yaacov	Taube	F			YI
MALTZ	Chaja			Korczyna	Korczyna		Jakob	Taube	F			YA
MALZ	Haya		1910	Korczyna	Korczyna		Jakob	Taube	F			YA
MALZ	Mali		1918	Korczyna	Korczyna		Jakob	Taube	F			YA
MALZ	Yosef		1912	Korczyna	Korczyna		Jakob	Taube	M			YA
MALZ	Michael		1888	Korczyna	Korczyna				M			YA
MALZ	Tauba		1882	Korczyna	Korczyna		Moshe		F			YA
MALZ	Towa		1881	Korczyna	Korczyna		Moshe		F			YA
MALZ	Jakob		1878	Nowy Sacz	Korczyna		Eliyahu		M			YI
MALZ	unk				Korczyna				M			YI
MANDEL	Rivkah				Korczyna				F			YI
MANDEL	Israel				Korczyna	hauler			M			YI
MARGOLIS	Haya				Korczyna				F	Israel		YI
MARGOLIS	Moshe				Korczyna		Israel	Haya	M			YI
MARGOLIS	Yaacov				Korczyna		Israel	Haya	M			YI
MARGOLIS	Mechel				Korczyna		Israel	Haya	M			YI
MARGOLIS	Ethel				Korczyna		Israel	Haya	F			YI
MARGOLIS	Yeshayahu				Korczyna				M			YI
MARGOLIS	Reisel				Korczyna				F	Yeshayahu		YI
MARGOLIS	Hersh				Korczyna		Yeshayahu	Reisel	M			YI
MARGOLIS	Neche				Korczyna		Yeshayahu	Reisel	F			YI
MARGOLIS	Pearl				Korczyna		Yeshayahu	Reisel	F			YI
MARGOLIS	Reisel				Korczyna				M			YI
MARGOLIS	Bunem				Korczyna	metal			F	Bunem		YI
MARGOLIS	Beile				Korczyna		Bunem	Beile	F			YI
MARGOLIS	Gittel				Korczyna		Bunem	Beile	M			YI
MARGOLIS	Avraham				Korczyna		Bunem	Beile	F			YI
MARGOLIS	Reisel				Korczyna				M	Israel		YI
MARGOLIS	Israel				Korczyna				F			YI
MARGOLIS	Liebe				Korczyna		Israel	Liebe	F			YI
MARGOLIS	Mebel				Korczyna		Israel	Liebe	M			YI
MARGOLIS	Moshe Yaakow				Korczyna		Israel	Liebe	F			YI
MARGOLIS	Ethel				Korczyna	activist			M			YI
MARGOLIS	Dawid				Korczyna	dayan			M			YI
MARGOLIS	unk				Korczyna				M			YI
MATES	Moshe				Korczyna	teacher			M			YI
MAZNY	Hyman			Korczyna	Korczyna				M			D
MECHALE	Neche Dworah				Korczyna				F			YI
MECHALE	Haim				Korczyna		Moshe	Neche	M			YI
MECHALE	Hinde				Korczyna		Moshe	Neche	F			YI

APPENDIX – Material not in the original Yizkor Book

Last Name	First name	Maiden Name	Birth Date	Birth Place	Residence	Occupation	Father	Mother	Gender	Spouse	Other	Source
MECHALE	Zissel				Korczyna		Moshe	Neche	F			YI
MECHALE	Shmuel Hirsh				Korczyna				M			YI
MEISNER	Sarah				Korczyna				F	Shmuel		YI
MEISNER	Raphael				Korczyna	charity			M			YI
MEISNER	Beile				Korczyna				F	Raphael		YI
MEISNER	Sam				Korczyna	charity			M			YI
MEISNER	Hersh			Korczyna	Korczyna				M			D
MELAMED	Ruchel	Denn		Korczyna	Korczyna		Chaim	Zussel	F			D
MELAMED	Zalke				Korczyna	teacher			M			YI
MELAMED	Israel Hersh			Korczyna	Korczyna	Heder teacher			M			D
MELAMED	Rachela				Korczyna	Korczyna			F	Israel Hersh		D
MELAMED	Chaim			Korczyna	Korczyna		Israel Hersh	Rachela	M			D
MELAMED	Sisla			Korczyna	Korczyna				F	Chaim		D
MELAMED	Hersh			Korczyna	Korczyna		Chaim	Sisla	M			D
MELAMED	Hersh			Korczyna	Korczyna				M			D
MELAMED	Ruchli			Korczyna	Korczyna				F	Hersh		D
MELAMED	Solomon			Korczyna	Korczyna		Hersh	Ruchli	M			D
MELAMED	Israel Hersh			Korczyna	Korczyna				M			D
MELAMED	Rachela			Korczyna	Korczyna		Chaim	Susla	F	Israel Hersh		D
MELAMED	Pinkas		27/1/1918	Korczyna	Korczyna		Israel Hersh	Rachela	D			D
MELAMED	Beile		b 3/4/1920	Korczyna	Korczyna		Israel Hersh	Rachela	F			D
MELAMED	Esther		b3/4/1920	Korczyna	Korczyna		Israel Hersh	Rachela	F			D
MELAMED	Dawid		b 9/1/1923	Korczyna	Korczyna		Israel Hersh	Rachela	M			D
MELAMED	Susla		b 21/1/1925	Korczyna	Korczyna		Israel Hersh	Rachela	F			D
MELAMED	Toibe				Korczyna				F	Zalke		YI
MELAMED	Braindel				Korczyna		Zalke	Toibe	F			YI
MELAMED	Beile				Korczyna		Zalke	Toibe	F	child		YI
MELAMED	**Ben Zion**				Korczyna		Zalke	Toibe	M			YI
MELAMED	**Frumet**				Korczyna		Zalke	Toibe	F			YI
MELAMED	**Mechel**				Korczyna		Zalke	Toibe	M			YI
MELAMED	Baruch				Korczyna				M			YI
MELAMED	Miriam Sara				Korczyna				F	Baruch		YI
MELAMED	unk				Korczyna				M			YI
MENDEL	Rivkah				Korczyna				F			YI
MENDEL	Chaje				Korczyna		Pinkas	Sarah	F			D
MENDELOWICZ	Fishel				Korczyna				M			YI
MENDELOWITZ	Jakob			Korczyna	Korczyna				M			D
MENDELOWITZ	Neche			Korczyna	Korczyna				F	Jakob		D
MENDELOWITZ	Abraham			Korczyna	Korczyna		Jakob	Neche	M			D
MENDELOWITZ	Pinkas			Korczyna	Korczyna				M			D
MENDELOWITZ	Ester			Korczyna	Korczyna				F	Pinkas		D
MENDELOWITZ	Chaye			Korczyna	Korczyna		Pinkas	Ester	M			D
MENDELOWITZ	Bashe		b 18/2/1901	Korczyna	Korczyna			Chaye	F			D
MENDELOWITZ	Baile		b 8/10/1904	Korczyna	Korczyna			Chaye	M			D
MENDELOWITZ	Awraham M		b 12/10/1906	Korczyna	Korczyna			Chaye	M			D
MENDELOWITZ	Bline		b 10/4/1909	Korczyna	Korczyna				M			D
MENDELOWITZ	Chaim			Korczyna	Korczyna				M			D
MENDELOWITZ	Shulem Wo		b 21/10/1915	Korczyna	Korczyna				M			D
MENER	Asher				Korczyna				M			D
MONCZNY	Hyem				Korczyna				M			D
NEIGER	Hene				Korczyna				F	Asher		D
NEIGER	Liebe				Korczyna	b.Se.1901	Asher	Ilena	F			D
NEIGER	Rita				Korczyna				F			P
NEUMAN	Rita				Korczyna				F			P
NEUMAN	Avraham				Korczyna	cantor			M			YI
NEUMAN	Dawid Isr			Sanok					M			P
NOYES	Sara	Akselrad	b1866	Korczyna	Sanok		Meshulem	Rachel	F	Dawid Isr		P

APPENDIX – Material not in the original Yizkor Book

Last Name	First name	Maiden Name	Birth Date	Birth Place	Residence	Occupation	Father	Mother	Gender	Spouse	Other	Source
NOYES	Yehuda		b 1893	Sanok			Dawid Isr	Sara	M			P
NOYES	Tzirel	Wolfman	b.1895		Sanok				F	Yehuda		P
NOYES	Israel		b1925		Sanok		Yehuda	Tzirel	M			P
NOYES	Sara		b.1929		Sanok		Yehuda	Tzirel	F			P
NOYES	Dawid Isr			Sanok	Sanok				M			P
NOYES	Meshulem		b..1910	Sanok	Israel		David Isr	Frida	M	Bronia		P
NOYES	Zalman				Korczyna				M			P
OLING	Samuel				Korczyna				M			P
OSTROW	Samuel				Korczyna				M			P
OSTROW	Shlomo				Korczyna				M			P
OSTROWIECKI	Chana	Akselrad	b.1942	Israel	Israel		Wolf-Zeew	Yehudit	F	Giora		P
OSTROWIECKI	Szlomo				Korczyna				M			D
PASTERNAK	Matel				Korczyna				F	Tuvia		YI
PASTERNAK	Bracha				Korczyna		Tuvia	Matel	F			YI
PASTERNAK	Elieazar				Korczyna		Tuvia	Matel	M			YI
PASTERNAK	Hannah				Korczyna		Tuvia	Matel	F	unk		YI
PASTERNAK	unk				Korczyna				M			YI
PASTERNAK	Taube				Korczyna		Tuvia	Matel	F			YI
PASTERNAK	Tille				Korczyna	socialite			F			YI
PASTERNAK	Yehezkel				Korczyna				M			YI
PASTERNAK	Yona				Korczyna				M			YI
PAWLOWICZ	Tuvia				Korczyna				M			YI
PELTZ	Itzhak				Korczyna				M			YI
PENNER	Miriam				Korczyna				F	Itzhak		YI
PENNER	Zissel				Korczyna				M			YI
PINELES	Henie				Korczyna				F	Zissel		YI
PINELES	Yeheskel				Korczyna				M			YI
PINTER	Yeheskel				Korczyna				M			YI
PINTER	Avraham				Korczyna	linen			M			YI
PINTER	Blime				Korczyna				F	Avraham		YI
PINTER	Naphtali				Korczyna				M			YI
PINTER	**Kalman**			Korczyna	USA				M			P
PINZEL	Israel				Korczyna				M			YI
PINZEL	Israel				Korczyna				M			YI
PLATNER	Mordechai				Korczyna				M			YI
PLATNER	Hannah				Korczyna				F	Mordechai		YI
PLATNER	Dobtsche				Korczyna		Mordechai	Hannah	F			YI
PLATNER	Beile				Korczyna		Mordechai	Hannah	F			YI
PLATNER	Israel				Korczyna				M			YI
PLATNER	Sima				Korczyna				F			YI
PODLANSKI	Shmuel Aron				Korczyna				M			YI
PODLANSKI	Hawa				Korczyna				F	Shmuel		YI
PODLANSKI	Motel				Korczyna		Shmuel	Hawa	M			YI
PODLANSKI	Roize				Korczyna		Shmuel	Hawa	F			YI
PODLANSKI	Benyamin				Korczyna				M			YI
PRIWIRT	unk				Korczyna				F	Benyamin		YI
PRIWIRT	Avraham				Korczyna				M			YI
PUSZ	Motel				Korczyna	teacher			M			YI
PUSZ	unk				Korczyna				F	Motel		YI
PUSZ	Naphtali Yossef				Korczyna	well to do			M			YI
RAAB	Avraham				Korczyna	well to do	Naphtali		M			YI
RAAB	Elieazar				Korczyna		Naphtali		M			YI
RAAB	Haya				Korczyna				F	Elieazar		YI
RAAB	Freide				Korczyna		Elieazar	Haya	F			YI
RAAB	Motel				Korczyna		Elieazar	Haya	M			YI
RAAB	Blume				Korczyna		Elieazar	Haya	F			YI

APPENDIX – Material not in the original Yizkor Book

Last Name	First name	Maiden Name	Birth Date	Birth Place	Residence	Occupation	Father	Mother	Gender	Spouse	Other	Source
RAAB	Feige				Korczyna		Elieazar	Haya	F			YI
RAAB	Dwosche				Korczyna		Elieazar	Haya	F			YI
RAAB	Sarah				Korczyna				F			YI
RAAB	Moshe Shnuek				Korczyna				M			YI
RAAB	Sarah				Korczyna				F	Moshe		YI
RAAB	Shabtai				Korczyna				M			YI
RAAB	unk				Korczyna				F	Shabtai		YI
RAAB	Yona				Korczyna		Shabtai	unk	M			YI
RAAB	Naphtali				Korczyna		Shabtai	unk	M			YI
RAAB	Shmuel				Korczyna		Shabtai	unk	M			YI
RAAB	Raphael				Korczyna				M			YI
RAAB	Mendel				Korczyna				M			D
RAHWAL	Tzipe				Korczyna				F	Raphael		YI
RAHWAL	Shmuel H				Korczyna	teacher			M			D
RAMRAS	Wolf				Korczyna	influential			M			YI
RAPAPORT	Pessel				Korczyna				F	Wolf		YI
RAPAPORT	Bashe				Korczyna		Wolf	Pessel	F			YI
RAPAPORT	Haya				Korczyna				F	Wolf	sec. Wife	YI
RAPAPORT	Fishel				Korczyna		Wolf	Haya	M			YI
RAPAPORT	Frumet				Korczyna		Wolf	Haya	F			YI
RAPAPORT	Mindel				Korczyna		Wolf	Haya	F			YI
RAPAPORT	Pessel				Korczyna		Wolf	Haya	F			YI
RAPAPORT	Moshe				Korczyna				M			YI
RATHAUS	Ronie				Korczyna				F	Moshe		YI
RATHAUS	Hene				Korczyna		Moshe	Ronie	F	husband		YI
RATHAUS	Sarah				Korczyna		Moshe	Ronie	F	husband		YI
RATHAUS	Beril			Korczyna	Korczyna		Hersh		M			YA
RECK	Betzalel Yaakow				Korczyna				M			YI
RECK	Hersh Elimelech				Korczyna	well to do			M			YI
RECK	Beril				Korczyna		Hersh		M			YI
RECK	Naphtali				Korczyna				M			YI
RECK	Haya				Korczyna				F			YI
RECK	Hencia			Korczyna	Korczyna		Moshe		F			YA
RECK	Avraham Yossel				Korczyna	linen			M			YI
REICH	Nachman Leibish				Korczyna				M			YI
REICH	Rechele				Korczyna				F	Nachman		YI
REICH	Ritze				Korczyna		Nachman	Rechele	F			YI
REICH	Yossef				Korczyna	well to do	Nachman	Rechele	M			YI
REICH	Saul				Korczyna				M			YI
REICH	Bashe Welke				Korczyna				F	Saul		YI
REICH	Yossef				Korczyna				M			YI
REUWEN	Dawid				Korczyna				M			YI
RINGELHEIM	Eidel				Korczyna				F	Dawid		YI
RINGELHEIM	Avraham				Korczyna		Dawid	Eidel	M			YI
RINGELHEIM	Yehoshua				Korczyna		Dawid	Eidel	M			YI
RINGELHEIM	Moshe				Korczyna		Dawid	Eidel	M			YI
RINGELHEIM	Wolf				Korczyna		Dawid	Eidel	M			YI
RINGELHEIM	Lea Haya				Korczyna		Dawid	Eidel	F			YI
RINGELHEIM	Mindel				Korczyna		Dawid	Eidel	F			YI
RINGELHEIM	Feige				Korczyna		Dawid	Eidel	F			YI
RINGELHEIM	Haya				Korczyna		Dawid	Eidel	F			YI
RINGELHEIM	Esther				Korczyna		Dawid	Eidel	F			YI
RINGELHEIM	Leibish				Korczyna				M			YI
RITTER	Beile				Korczyna				F			YI
RITTER	Mendel				Korczyna		Leibish	Beile	M			YI
RITTER	Mindel				Korczyna		Leibish	Beile	F			YI
RITTER	Yankel				Korczyna				M			YI
ROIZNER	Moshe				Korczyna				M			YI
ROSEMAN	Mendel				Korczyna				M			YI
ROSEMAN	Fieda				Korczyna				F	Mendel		YI

APPENDIX – Material not in the original Yizkor Book

Last Name	First name	Maiden Name	Birth Date	Birth Place	Residence	Occupation	Father	Mother	Gender	Spouse	Other	Source
ROSEMAN	Lea				Korczyna		Mendel	Fieda	F			YI
ROSEMAN	Fradel				Korczyna		Hersh		F			YA
ROSEMAN	Hersh Yaakow				Korczyna	cantor			M			YI
ROSENBERG	Rachel	Akselrad	b.1911	Korczyna	Krosno		Yossef Bendet	Chana	F	UNK		P
ROSENBERG	UNK			Korczyna	Krosno				M			P
ROSENBERG	Miriam						UNK	Rachel	M			P
ROSENBERG	Josef						UNK	Rachel	F			P
ROSENHANDLER	Itsche				Korczyna	metal			M			YI
ROSENHANDLER	Nissel				Korczyna				F	Itsche		YI
ROSENHANDLER	Leibele				Korczyna		Itsche	Nissel	M			YI
ROSENHANDLER	Wolf				Korczyna		Itsche	Nissel	M			YI
ROSENHANDLER	Motel				Korczyna		Itsche	Nissel	M			YI
ROSENHANDLER	unk				Korczyna				F	Motel		YI
ROSENHANDLER	Freide			Korczyna	Korczyna		Hersh		F			YA
ROSMAN	Mendel			Korczyna	Korczyna				M			YA
ROSMAN	annie				Korczyna	USA			F			K.C
ROSNER	Naftule				Korczyna	USA			M			K.C
ROSNER	Samuel				Korczyna	USA			M			K.C
ROSNER	Sara				Korczyna	USA			F			K.C
ROSNER	Mordechai				Korczyna	teacher			M			YI
ROSSDEUTCHER	Braindel				Korczyna				F	Mordechai		YI
ROSSDEUTCHER	Esther				Korczyna				F			YI
ROSSDEUTCHER	Serl				Korczyna				F			YI
ROSSDEUTCHER	Moshe				Korczyna				M			YI
ROSSMAN	Hersh Chaim,				Korczyna				M			YI
ROTH	Schiya			Korczyna	Korczyna				M			D
ROTH	Dobba	Kalb		Korczyna	Korczyna				F	Schiya		D
ROTH	Eisig		b 19/11/1931	Korczyna	Korczyna		Schiya	Dobba	M			D
ROTH	Mechel		b20/20/1940	Korczyna	Krosno		Schiya	Dobba	M			D
ROTH	Mechel			Korczyna	Korczyna				M			D
ROTH	Shprincze	Kalb		Korczyna	Korczyna		Samuel	Ester	F	Mechel		D
ROTH	Lea		b 22/4/1905	Korczyna	Korczyna		Mechel	Shprincze	F			D
ROTH	Ita		b 7/6/1912	Korczyna	Korczyna		Mechel	Shprincze	F			D
ROTHENBERG	Feige				Korczyna				F	Hersh		YI
ROTHENBERG	Aron				Korczyna		Hersh	Feige	M			YI
ROTHENBERG	Leibish				Korczyna		Hersh	Feige	M			YI
ROTHENBERG	Motel				Korczyna		Hersh	Feige	M			YI
ROTHENBERG	Lea				Korczyna		Hersh	Feige	F			YI
ROTHENBERG	Yantsche				Korczyna		Hersh	Feige	F			YI
ROTHENBERG	Arie Leib				Korczyna	influential			M			YI
ROTHENBERG	Pessil				Korczyna				F	Arie		YI
ROTHENBERG	Yankel				Korczyna		Arie	Pessil	F			YI
ROTHENBERG	Shimon Wolf				Korczyna	cantor			M			YI
ROTHENBERG	Etel				Korczyna				F	Shimon		YI
ROTHENBERG	Hannah Czarne				Korczyna		Shimon	Etel	F			YI
ROTHENBERG	Leibsh				Korczyna		Shimon	Etel	M			YI
ROTHENBERG	Yaacov				Korczyna		Leibsh		M			YI
ROTHENBERG	Peshe				Korczyna		Leibsh		F			YI
ROTHENBERG	Hannah				Korczyna				F	Leibsh		YI
ROTHENBERG	Moshe				Korczyna	well to do			M			YI
ROTHENBERG	Mindel				Korczyna				F			YI
ROTHENBERG	Rehel				Korczyna				F			YI
ROTHENBERG	Freida			Korczyna	Korczyna		Tzwi		F			YA
ROZENMAN	Moshe				Korczyna	doctor			M			YI
RUBENFELD	Eliyahu				Korczyna	Rabbi			M			YI
RUBIN	Malka				Korczyna				F	Eliyahu		YI
RUBIN	Shmuel A				Korczyna				M			YI
RUBIN	Mendel				Korczyna				M			YI
RUBIN	Mordechai E				Korczyna	Rabbi			M			YI

APPENDIX – Material not in the original Yizkor Book

Last Name	First name	Maiden Name	Birth Date	Birth Place	Residence	Occupation	Father	Mother	Gender	Spouse	Other	Source
RUBIN	Elieazar				Korczyna				M	Elieazar		YI
RUBIN	Schifra				Korczyna				F			YI
RUBIN	Benyamin				Korczyna		Elieazar	Schifra	M			YI
RUBIN	Mechel		Korczyna		Krosno		Elieazar	Schifra	M			YI
RUBIN	Pepi		Korczyna		Krosno				F	Mechel		P
RUBIN	Osias		Korczyna		Krosno		Mechel	Pepi	M			YI
RUBIN	Mendel				Korczyna		Elieazar	Schifra	M			YI
RUBIN	Shmuel				Korczyna	Rabbi			M			YI
RUBIN	Yochewed				Korczyna				F	Shmuel		D
RUBIN	Asher				Korczyna	Rabbi	Shmuel	Yochewed	M			D.
RUBIN	Benyamin				Korczyna				M			YI
RUBIN	Miriam				Korczyna				F	Benyamin		YI
RUBIN	Naphtali				Korczyna		Benuamin	Miriam	M			YI
RUBIN	Tzivia				Korczyna		Benuamin	Miriam	F			YI
RUBIN	Zelda				Korczyna		Benuamin	Miriam	F			YI
RUBIN	Luzer				Korczyna		Benuamin	Miriam	M			YI
RUBIN	Frieda				Korczyna		Benuamin	Miriam	F			YI
RUBIN	Hersh				Korczyna		Benuamin	Miriam	M			YI
RUBIN	Oscar				Korczyna	judenrat			M			YI
RUBIN	unk				Korczyna				F			YI
RUBIN	Benyamin				Korczyna				M			YI
RUBIN	Tilli				Korczyna				F	Benyamin		YI
RUBIN	Samuel				Korczyna				M			YI
RUBIN	unk				Korczyna				F	Samuel		YI
RUBIN	Yehoshua				Korczyna				M			YI
RUBIN	Shprintze				Korczyna				F	Yehoshua		YI
RUBIN	Haim R				Korczyna				M			YI
RUBIN	Haya	Weissman			Korczyna				F	Haim		YI
RUBIN	Rivkah				Korczyna		Haim	Haya	F			YI
RUBIN	Hadassah				Korczyna				F			P
RUBIN	Eliyahu				Korczyna	Rabbi			M			YI
RUBIN	Malka				Korczyna				F	Eliyahu		YI
RUBIN	Shmuel Aron				Korczyna				M		Israel	YI
RUBIN	Mendel				Korczyna				M		Russia	YI
RUBIN	Mordechai Eliezer				Korczyna	Rabbi			M			YI
RUBIN	Elieazar				Korczyna				M			YI
RUBIN	Schifra				Korczyna				F	Elieazar		YI
RUBIN	Pepi				Korczyna				F	Mechel	Krosno	YI
RUBIN	Osias				Korczyna		Mechel	Pepi	M		Krosno	YI
RUBIN	Shmuel Aron				Korczyna	Rabbi			M			YI
RUBIN	Benyamin				Korczyna				M			YI
RUBIN	Miriam				Korczyna				F	Benyamin		YI
RUBIN	Oscar				Korczyna	judenrat			M			YI
RUBIN	unk				Korczyna				F			YI
RUBIN	Benyamin				Korczyna				M			YI
RUBIN	Tilli				Korczyna				F	Benyamin		YI
RUBIN	Samuel				Korczyna				M			YI
RUBIN	unk				Korczyna				F	Samuel		YI
RUBIN	Yehoshua				Korczyna				M			YI
RUBIN	Shprintze				Korczyna				F	Yehoshua		YI
RUBIN	Haim Reuven				Korczyna				M			YI
RUBIN	Haya	Weissman			Korczyna				F	Haim		YI
RUBIN	Rivkah				Korczyna		Haim	Haya	F			YI
RUBIN	Rochel			Korczyna	Korczyna				F			YA
RUBIN	Moses				Korczyna	USA			M			K.C
SCHACKNER	Meir				Korczyna				M			YI
SCHECHTER	Riwka				Korczyna				F	Meir		YI
SCHECHTER	Freidel				Korczyna		Meir	Riwka	F			YI
SCHECHTER	Malka				Korczyna		Meir	Riwka	F			YI
SCHECHTER	Ester				Korczyna		Meir	Riwka	F			YI
SCHECHTER	Yehezkel				Korczyna		Meir	Riwka	M			YI
SCHECHTER	Dawid				Korczyna		Dawid		M			YA
SCHECHTER	Mechel				Korczyna		Meir	Riwka	M			YA
SCHECHTER	Michael		1905	Rzeszow	Korczyna		Dawid		M			YA
SCHECHTER	Asher				Korczyna				M	Asher		YI
SCHEINER	unk				Korczyna				F			YI
SCHEINER	Haim				Korczyna				M			YI
SCHEINER	Avraham				Korczyna		Haim		M			YI

APPENDIX – Material not in the original Yizkor Book

Last Name	First name	Maiden Name	Birth Date	Birth Place	Residence	Occupation	Father	Mother	Gender	Spouse	Other	Source
SCHEINER	unk				Korczyna				F	Avraham		YI
SCHEINER	Pinhas				Korczyna		Haim		M			YI
SCHEINER	Naphtali				Korczyna				M		Krosno	YI
SCHEINER	Moshe t				Korczyna			Moshe	M			YI
SCHENKER	Mordechai				Korczyna				M			YI
SCHENKER	Moshe Tzwi				Korczyna				M			YI
SCHENKER	Rachel				Korczyna			Moshe	F			YI
SCHENKER	Moshe Hersh				Korczyna				M			YI
SCHENKER	Mordechai				Korczyna				M			YI
SCHENKER	Haim Zeew				Korczyna		Mordechai		M			YI
SCHENKER	Aron				Korczyna		Mordechai		M			YI
SCHENKER	Menashe				Korczyna		Mordechai		M			YI
SCHENKER	Yossef				Korczyna		Mordechai		M			YI
SCHENKER	Pinhas				Korczyna		Mordechai		M			YI
SCHENKER	Hannah				Korczyna		Mordechai		F			YI
SCHENKER	Esther				Korczyna		Mordechai		F			YI
SCHENKER	Getzel				Korczyna				M			YI
SCHIFF	Sarah Bashe				Korczyna				F	Getzel		YI
SCHIFF	Miriam				Korczyna		Getzel	Sarah	F			YI
SCHIFF	Wolf				Korczyna		Getzel	Sarah	M			YI
SCHIFF	Sheindel				Korczyna				F			YI
SCHIFF	Pearl				Korczyna				F			YI
SCHIFF	Yochewed				Korczyna			Pearl	F			YI
SCHIFF	Mordechai			Korczyna	Korczyna				M			YI
SCHIFF	Perla	Gleicher		Korczyna	Korczyna				F	Mordechai		P
SCHIFF	Jachet Dressel			Korczyna	Korczyna		Mordechai	Perla	F			P
SCHIFF	Yaacov Pinhas				Korczyna	shochet			M			YI
SCHIFF	unk				Korczyna				F	Yaacov		YI
SCHIFF	Nechema				Korczyna		Yaacov	unk	F			YI
SCHIFF	Leibele				Korczyna	hauler			M			YI
SCHIFF	Asher				Korczyna	activist			M			YI
SCHIFF	Moshe				Korczyna				M			YI
SCHIMMEL	Hinde				Korczyna				F	Moshe		YI
SCHIMMEL	Kalman				Korczyna				M			YI
SCHLANGER	Rivkah				Korczyna				F	Kalman		YI
SCHLANGER	Berl				Korczyna				M			YI
SCHLANGER	Mordechai		0.1921	Rzeszow	Israel		David Isr	Rachel	M	Sara		P
SCHLANGER	Yossef				Korczyna	coachman			M			YI
SCHMIER	Golda				Korczyna				F	Berl		YI
SCHMIER	Beile				Korczyna		Berl	Golda	F			YI
SCHMIER	Arie				Korczyna				M			YI
SCHNECK	Zalman				Korczyna		Arie		M			YI
SCHNECK	Dawid				Korczyna		Arie		M			YI
SCHNECK	Yehuda				Korczyna		Arie		M			YI
SCHNECK	Reisel				Korczyna				F			YI
SCHNECK	Haim Hersh				Korczyna		Arie		M			YI
SCHNECK	Leibish				Korczyna		Arie		M			YI
SCHNECK	Shia				Korczyna		Arie		M			YI
SCHNECK	Shlomo				Korczyna		Arie		M			YI
SCHNECK	Moshe	Zucker			Korczyna		Arie		M			YI
SCHNECK	Moshe				Korczyna	tailor			M			
SCHNEIDER	Shulem				Korczyna	cantor			M			YI
SCHOCHET	Dawid				Korczyna				M			YI
SCHREIBER	Sima				Korczyna				F	Dawid		YI
SCHREIBER	Mendel				Korczyna	influential			M			YI
SCHROIT	unk				Korczyna				F	Mendel		YI
SCHROIT	Bashe Wieklke				Korczyna		Mendel	unk	F			YI
SCHROIT	Haya				Korczyna				F	Mendel	2marriag	YI
SCHROIT	Fishel				Korczyna		Mendel	Haya	M			YI
SCHROIT	Bertha				Korczyna	USA			F			K.C

APPENDIX – Material not in the original Yizkor Book

Last Name	First name	Maiden Name	Birth Date	Birth Place	Residence	Occupation	Father	Mother	Gender	Spouse	Other	Source
SCHUBIN	Wolf Leib											
SCHUSS	Eliyahu				Korczyna				M			YI
SCHWERD	Lea				Korczyna				F	Eliyahu		YI
SCHWERD	Rachel	Noyes	b.1895		Israel		David Isr	Frida	F	Wolf Matis		P
SHEINOWITZ	Malka		b.1910	Korczyna	Krosno		Yossef Bendet	Chana	F	UNK		P
SHEINOWITZ	UNK								M			P
SHEINOWITZ	Rachel	Akselrad	b.1911	Korczyna	Krosno		Yossef Bendet	Chana	F	UNK		P
SHEINOWITZ	Miriam	Sheinowitz					UNK	Rachel	F			P
SHEINOWITZ	Malka		b.1910	Korczyna	Krosno		Yossef Bendet	Chana	F	UNK		P
SHEINOWITZ	UNK	Akselrad							M			P
SHMAYAHU	Itzik				Korczyna	hauler	Yossef		M			YI
SHMAYAHU	Berl				Korczyna		Yossef		M			YI
SHMAYAHU	Chaim				Korczyna		Yossef		M			YI
SHMAYAHU	Dworah				Korczyna		Yossef		F			YI
SHMAYAHU	Moshe				Korczyna		Yossef		M			YI
SHMAYAHU				Kroscienko	Korczyna							YI
SHTERN	Avraham				Korczyna				M			YI
SILBERBERG	Israel Yaakow				Korczyna				M			YI
SOFER	Hinde	Mechale			Korczyna				F	Israel		YI
SOFER	Kalman				Korczyna				M	Kalman		YI
SPERBER	unk				Korczyna				F			YI
SPERBER	Kalman				Korczyna				M			YI
SPERBER	unk				Korczyna				F	Kalman		YI
SPERBER	Salmon				Korczyna				M			P
SPETT	Mayer				Korczyna				M			P
SPINDLER	Nahum				Korczyna				M			YI
SPINDLER	Elle			Korczyna	Korczyna				M			D
SPINDLER	Chaya			Korczyna	Korczyna				F	Elle		D
SPINDLER	Moses			Korczyna	Korczyna		Elle	Chaya	M			D
SPITZ	Fradel				Korczyna				F			YI
SPITZ	Yankel				Korczyna				M	Yankel		YA
SPRUNG	Hannah				Korczyna				F			YI
SPRUNG	Avraham				Korczyna		Yankel	Hannah	M			YA
SPRUNG	Yossef				Korczyna		Yankel	Hannah	M			YI
SPRUNG	Awraham		1905	Korczyna	Korczyna		Jakob		M			YA
SPRUNG	Wolf				Korczyna				M			YA
SPRUNG	Chaja		1918	Blazowa	Korczyna		Wolf		F			YA
SPRUNG	Hannah			Korczyna	Korczyna				F			YA
SPRUNG	Jakob		1880	Korczyna	Korczyna				M			YA
SPRUNG	Yosef		1903	Korczyna	Korczyna		Yosef		M			YA
SPRUNG			1940	Korczyna	Korczyna		Abraham		M			YA
SPRUNG	Zishe				Korczyna				M			YI
STARSBERG	unk				Korczyna				F	Zishe		YI
STARSBERG	Izaak				Korczyna				M			P
STAUB	unk				Korczyna				F			YI
STELTZER	fam				Korczyna							P
STERN	Dawid				Korczyna	teacher			M			YI
STRETINER	Chaskel		1921	Korczyna	Korczyna		Meir		M			YA
SZECHTER	Meir				Korczyna				M			YA
SZECHTER	Ester		1928	Korczyna	Korczyna		Meir		F			YA
SZECHTER	Fradl		1920	Korczyna	Korczyna		Meir		F			YA

APPENDIX – Material not in the original Yizkor Book

Last Name	First name	Maiden Name	Birth Date	Birth Place	Residence	Occupation	Father	Mother	Gender	Spouse	Other	Source
SZECHTER	Meir			Korczyna	Korczyna				M			YA
SZECHTER	Rywka			Korczyna	Korczyna		Szmuel		F			YA
SZECHTER	Mania				Korczyna				F			P
TABACZNIK	Irwing				Korczyna	USA			M			K.C
TABACZNIK	Mania				Korczyna				F			D
TANNER					Korczyna	USA			F			K.C
TANNER	Mordechai Yossef				Korczyna				M			YI
TAUBE	Feige	Raab			Korczyna				F	Mordechai		YI
TAUBE	Moshe				Korczyna		Mordechai	Feige	M			YI
TAUBE	Bluma				Korczyna		Mordechai	Feige	F			YI
TAUBE	Mendel				Korczyna				M			YI
TELLER	Shmuel Aron				Korczyna				M			YI
TELLER	Nene				Korczyna				F	Shmuel		YI
TELLER	Henech				Korczyna		Shmuel	Nene	M			YI
TELLER	Liebe				Korczyna		Shmuel	Nene	F			YI
TELLER	Yankel				Korczyna		Shmuel	Nene	M			YI
TELLER	Mendel				Korczyna		Shmuel	Nene	M			YI
TELLER	Yossef			Korczyna	Krosno				M			YI
TISHLER	Haya			Korczyna	Krosno				F	Yossef		YI
TISHLER	Elimelech			Korczyna	Krosno				M			YI
TISHLER	Sarah			Korczyna	Krosno				F			YI
TISHLER	Tziporah			Korczyna	Krosno				F			YI
TISHLER	Yehiel Aron			Korczyna	Krosno				M			YI
TISHLER	Avraham				Korczyna				M			P
TRAM	Itzhak				Korczyna				M			YI
TREITEK	Mordechai				Korczyna				M			YI
TUCHMAN	Ethel				Korczyna				F	Mordechai		YI
TUCHMAN	Ephraim				Korczyna				M			YI
TULIPAN	Bluma	Eichorn			Korczyna				F	Ephraim		YI
TULIPAN					Korczyna							P
TZEIGER	Haim Lewi				Korczyna	scholar			M			YI
TZWIEBEL	Haim Dawid				Korczyna				M			YI
TZWIEBEL	Esther	Weissman			Korczyna				F	Haim		YI
TZWIEBEL	Hersh Pinhas				Korczyna		Haim	Esther	M			YI
TZWIEBEL	Tirtze				Korczyna		Haim	Esther	F			YI
TZWIEBEL	Neche				Korczyna		Haim	Esther	F			YI
TZWIEBEL	Rivkah				Korczyna		Haim	Esther	F			YI
TZWIEBEL	Sarah				Korczyna				F			YI
TZWIK	Nathan				Korczyna				M			YI
TZWIK	Sarah				Korczyna				F	Nathan		YI
WACHTER	Irwing				Korczyna				M			P
WASSERBERG	**Menashe**				Korczyna				M			P
WASSERBERG	**Esther**	Freund			Korczyna				F			P
WASSERSTRUM	Shlomo Gimpel				Korczyna				M			YI
WASSERSTRUM	Frieda				Korczyna				F	Shlomo		YI
WASSERSTRUM	Bashe				Korczyna		Shlomo	Frieda	F			YI
WASSERSTRUM	Feige				Korczyna		Shlomo	Frieda	F			YI
WASSERSTRUM	Hershel				Korczyna		Shlomo	Frieda	M			YI
WASSERSTRUM	Hinda				Korczyna		Shlomo	Frieda	F			YI
WASSERSTRUM	Meir				Korczyna		Shlomo	Frieda	M			YI
WASSERSTRUM	Shimshon				Korczyna		Shlomo	Frieda	M			YI
WASSERSTRUM	Yossef				Korczyna		Shlomo	Frieda	M			YI
WASSERSTRUM	Itzhak	Englard			Korczyna				M			YI
WASSERSTRUM	Itzhak	Englard			Korczyna				M			YI

APPENDIX – Material not in the original Yizkor Book

Last Name	First name	Maiden Name	Birth Date	Birth Place	Residence	Occupation	Father	Mother	Gender	Spouse	Other	Source
WEBER	Yossef	Rothenberg			Korczyna				M			YI
WEBER	Aron				Korczyna	Brezower			M			YI
WEBER	Dinah				Korczyna				F	Aron		YI
WEBER	Yossef				Korczyna	writer			M			YI
WEBER	unk			Korczyna	Korczyna				F	Yossef		YI
WEBER	unk				Korczyna				F			YI
WEINBERG	Beile			Korczyna	Krosno				F			YI
WEINBERG	Itzik			Korczyna	Krosno				M			YI
WEINBERG	unk			Korczyna	Krosno				F	Itzik		YI
WEINBERG	Mendel			Korczyna	Krosno				M			YI
WEINBERG	Nissan			Korczyna	Krosno				M			YI
WEINBERG	Sime			Korczyna	Krosno				F			YI
WEINBERG	Yehiel				Korczyna				M			YI
WEINBERG	Wolf				Korczyna		Naphtali	Treine	M			YI
WEINIG	Naphtali				Korczyna				M			YI
WEINIG	Treine				Korczyna				F	Naphtali		YI
WEINIG	Wolf				Korczyna		Naphtali	Treine	M			YI
WEINSTEIN	Rachel				Korczyna	well to do			F			YI
WEINSTEIN	unk				Korczyna				F			YI
WEINSTEIN	Shulem				Korczyna	baker			M			YI
WEINSTEIN	Rachel Lea				Korczyna	well to do			F			YI
WEINSTEIN	Ephraim				Korczyna			Rachel	M			YI
WEINSTEIN	unk				Korczyna				F			YI
WEINSTEIN	Haya				Korczyna			Rachel	F			YI
WEINSTEIN	Mendel				Korczyna				M			YI
WEINSTEIN	Mendel				Korczyna				M			D
WEINSTEIN	Shulem				Korczyna	baker			M			YI
WEISS	Baruch				Korczyna	teacher			M			YI
WEISSBERGER	Karol				Korczyna	manager			M			YI
WEISSBERGER	Karol				Korczyna	manager			M			YI
WEISSMAN	Yehiel				Korczyna				M			YI
WEISSMAN	Lea				Korczyna				F	Yehiel		YI
WEISSMAN	Reisel				Korczyna		Yehiel	Lea	F			YI
WEISSMAN	Yente				Korczyna		Yehiel	Lea	F			YI
WEISSMAN	Mendel				Korczyna		Yehiel	Lea	M			YI
WEISSMAN	Frieda				Korczyna		Yehiel	Lea	F			YI
WEISSMAN	Esther				Korczyna		Yehiel	Lea	F			YI
WEISSMAN	Haya				Korczyna		Yehiel	Lea	F			YI
WEISSMAN	Haim Hersh				Korczyna		Yehiel	Lea	M			YI
WEISSMAN	Meir				Korczyna		Yehiel	Lea	M			YI
WEISSMAN	Shulem				Korczyna		Yehiel	Lea	M			YI
WEISSMAN	Wolf				Korczyna		Yehiel	Lea	M			YI
WEISSMAN	Chaskel				Korczyna		Yehiel	Lea	M			YI
WEISSMAN	Reisel				Korczyna		Yehiel	Lea	F			YI
WEISSMAN	Avraham				Korczyna				M			YI
WEISSMAN	Moshe			Korczyna	Korczyna				M			YA
WEISSMANN	unk				Korczyna				F			YI
WEKSELBAUM	Shlomo				Korczyna				M			YI
WEKSELBAUM	Hene F				Korczyna				F			YI
WELLER	Isaak			Ustrobny	Korczyna				M			D
WELLER	Feige			Korczyna	Korczyna				F	Isaak		D
WELLER	Josef		b 14/5/1929	Korczyna	Korczyna		Isaak	Feige	M			D
WERNER	Aron Yaakow				Korczyna				M			YI
WERNER	Matil	Raab			Korczyna				F	Aron		YI
WERNER	Naphtali				Korczyna		Aron	Matil	M			YI
WERNER	Shprintze				Korczyna				F	Naphtali		YI
WERNER	Genedil				Korczyna		Aron	Matil	F			YI
WERNER	Hene Feige				Korczyna				F			YI
WERTHEIM	Pinhas				Korczyna				M			YI
WERTHEIM	Pinhas				Korczyna				M			YI

APPENDIX – Material not in the original Yizkor Book

Last Name	First name	Maiden Name	Birth Date	Birth Place	Residence	Occupation	Father	Mother	Gender	Spouse	Other	Source
WHITMAN	Frimet				Korczyna		Moshe		F			YI
WHITMAN	Moshe				Korczyna				M			YI
WHITMAN	unk				Korczyna				F			YI
WILLNER	Lea	Leibner	b.1875	Korczyna	Korczyna		Yehiel	Rachel Y	F	Moses		P
WILLNER	Frimet		1873	Korczyna	Korczyna		Moshe		F			YA
WILNER	Moses			Korczyna	Korczyna				M			P
WILNER	Samuel Ch		b.1901	Korczyna	Korczyna		Moses	Lea	M			P
WILNER	Szymon		b.1902	Korczyna	Korczyna		Moses	Lea	M			P
WILNER	Itzhak Eisi		b.1904	Korczyna	Korczyna		Moses	Lea	M			P
WILNER	Abraham		b.1907	Korczyna	Korczyna		Moses	Lea	M			P
WILNER	Eidel		b.1909	Korczyna	Korczyna		Moses	Lea	F			P
WILNER	Frimet		b.1911	Korczyna	Korczyna		Moses	Lea	F			P
WILNER	Shyja Chaskel		b.1915	Korczyna	Korczyna		Moses	Lea	M			P
WILNER	unk				Korczyna				F	Avraham		YI
WITMAN	Moshe		1872	Korczyna	Korczyna		Chaim		M			YA
WITMAN	Pertsche				Korczyna				F			YI
WOHLMUT	Yehoshua				Korczyna				M			YI
WOHLMUT	Pertsche				Korczyna				F	Yehoshua		YI
WOLF					Korczyna	cantor			M			YI
WOLF	Haim				Korczyna			Yaacov	M			YI
WOLF					Korczyna	cantor			M			YI
WOLF	Yaacov				Korczyna	tailor			M			YI
WOLF	Haim				Korczyna			Yaacov	M			YI
YOSSEF	Pinhas				Korczyna		Reuven		M			YI
YOSSEF	Moshe				Korczyna				M			YI
ZAK	Moshe				Korczyna				M			YI
ZILBERBERG	Hendel				Korczyna				F			YI
ZILBERBERG	Itzhak				Korczyna				M			YI
ZILBERBERG	Esther				Korczyna				F	Itzhak		YI
ZILBERBERG	Avraham				Korczyna		Itzhak	Esther	M			YI
ZILBERBERG	Yossef				Korczyna				M			YI
ZILBERBERG	Hendel				Korczyna				F	Yossef		YI
ZILBERMAN	Hannah M				Korczyna		Moshe	Sara	F			YI
ZILBERMAN	Meir				Korczyna		Moshe	Sara	M			YI
ZILBERMAN	Moshe				Korczyna				M			YI
ZILBERMAN	Sara Toibe				Korczyna				F	Moshe		YI
ZILBERMAN	Betzalel				Korczyna		Moshe	Sara	M			YI
ZILBERMAN	Rivkah				Korczyna		Moshe	Sara	F			YI
ZILBERMAN	Hannah Malka				Korczyna		Moshe	Sara	F			YI
ZILBERMAN	Meir				Korczyna		Moshe	Sara	M			YI
ZISSEL	Peshe				Korczyna				F			YI
ZISSEL	Peshe				Korczyna				F			YI
ZUCKER	unk				Korczyna				F			YI
ZUCKER	Haim				Korczyna				M			YI
ZUCKER	Moshe				Korczyna				M			YI
ZUCKER	Shulem Bunem				Korczyna				M			YI
ZUCKER	Yehoshua				Korczyna				M			YI
ZUCKER	unk				Korczyna				F	Yehoshua		YI
ZWIRN	Solomon				Korczyna				M			YA
ZWIRN	Oscar		1898	Domaradz	Korczyna		Solomon		M	Solomon		YA
ZWIRN	Bronia				Korczyna		Oscar	Bronia	F			P
ZWIRN	Dawid				Korczyna		Oscar	Bronia				P
ZWIRN	Lazar				Korczyna		Oscar	Bronia	M			YA
ZWIRN	Shmuel				Korczyna		Oscar	Bronia	M			YA
ZWIRN	Lazar		1936	Dziedzina	Korczyna		Oscar	Bronia	M			YA

Project Preservation Work at the Korczyna Jewish Cemetery

In the summer of 2012 a group of students from Dartmouth College in Hanover, New Hampshire, USA traveled to Korczyna, Poland to restore the Jewish Cemetery. The group was led by Rabbi Edward Boraz from the Hillel foundation on the campus. The group consisted of Dartmouth College students, both Jewish and non-Jewish. They were joined by local students from the town and spent several days cleaning up head stones, resurrecting overturned headstones, photographing, translating and cataloging the headstones, and erecting a new gate for the cemetery.

View of the headstones in the Korczyna Jewish Cemetery

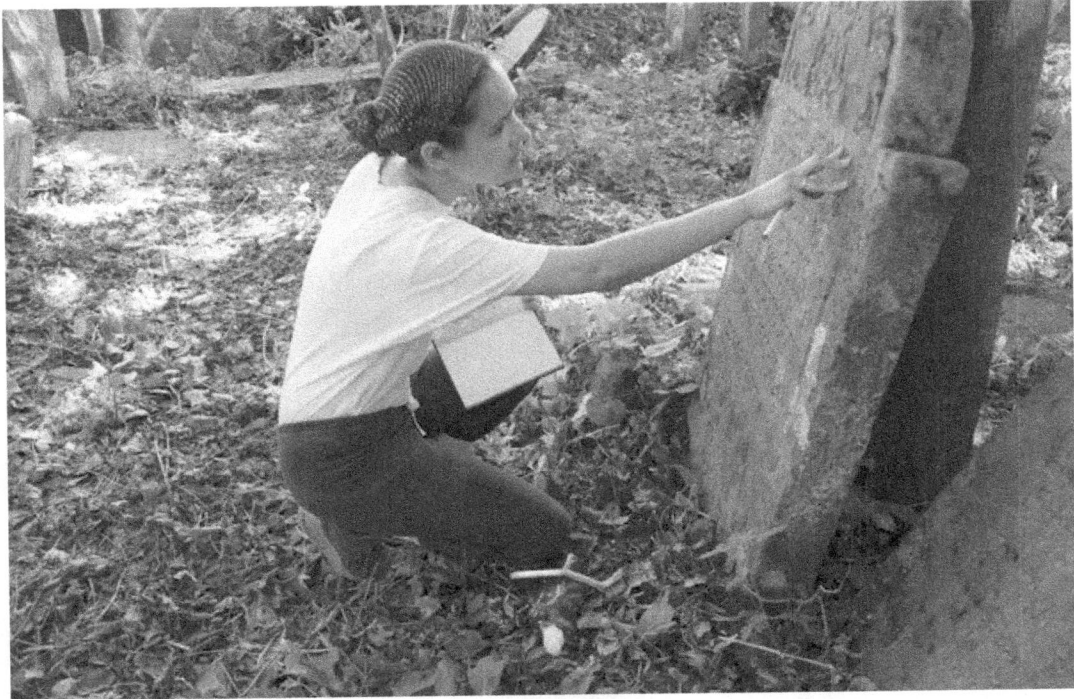

Cleaning and taking notes of inscription on a headstone

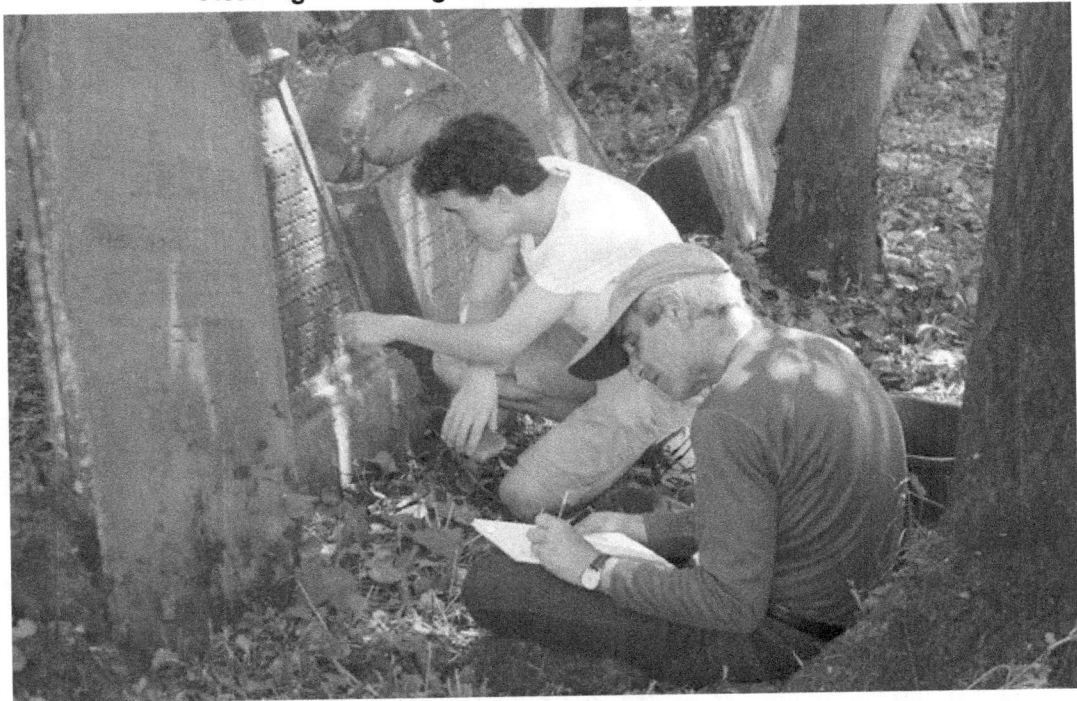

Dartmouth College student and Rabbi Edward Boraz recording and translating a
headstone inscription

Cleaning headstones

Painting the new fence around the cemetery

New Gate at the Korczyna Jewish Cemetery

Project Preservation group in front of new gate at the cemetery

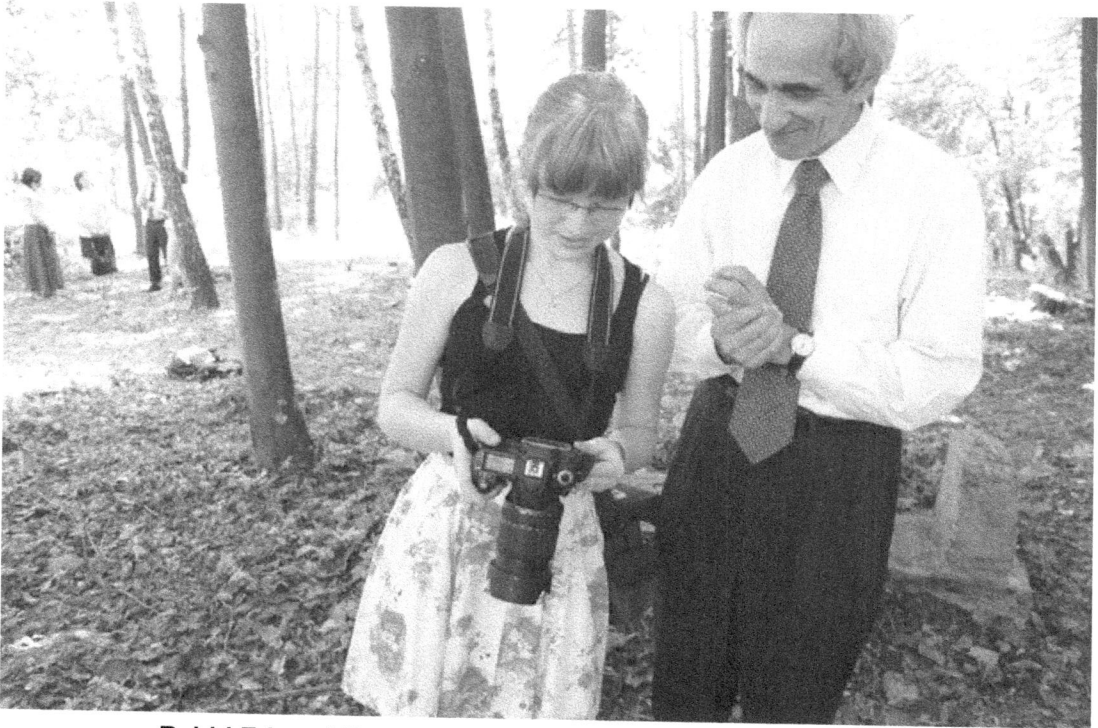

Rabbi Edward Boraz inspecting photographs of the cemetery

Dartmouth College students and local students at the Jewish Cemetery

Dartmouth College students and Rabbi Edward Boraz in front of the cemetery

Dartmouth College students and local students at the Korczyna High School

Newly erected plaque at the entrance to the cemetery

List of Headstones in the Korczyna Jewish Cemetery
Compiled by Project Preservation of Dartmouth College in 2012
Under the Leadership of Rabbi Edward Boraz

Row A

Name	Father's Name	Patronymmic	Hebrew DOD	Date of Death	Location
Alexander Zisya	Dov	Yashtpotz	1st of Sivan 5635	4-June-1875	A21
Ari	Rabbi Eliezer Joshua	Levush	19th of Tevet 5602	1-Jan-1842	A14
Avigdor	Yekutiel Mordechai		7th of Iyar 5638	10-May-1878	A22
Baruch	Tzvi		11th of Kislev 5615	2-Dec-1854	A16
David			11th of Menachem Av 5633	4-Aug-1873	A17
Hayyim	Pinchas [HaLevi]		5th of Nisan 5698	6-Apr-1938	A03
Israel	Yehoshua		15th of Tevet 5699	4-Feb-1939	A05
Joseph Hayyim	Avraham Yoel [Halevi]	Ettinger	9th day of Shevat 5698	11-Jan-1938	A08
Joshua Leib Grin		Grin			A04
Kalonimos	Yechezkel		2nd of Elul 5633	25-Aug-1873	A26
Lieb [Leib] and David	David [father of Lieb]	Kirschner	4th of Tishrei 5703	15-Sep-1942	A01
May this person's soul be Bound					A06
May this person's soul be Bound					A07
May this person's soul be Bound					A11
May this person's soul be Bound					A18
May this person's soul be Bound					A23
Menachem	Rabbi Yosef	Bender	19th of Kislev 5604	12-Dec-1843	A28
Mordechai Nisan	Tuvyah		12th of Tamuz 5627	15-Jul-1867	A27
Rabbi Eleazer	Rabbi Naphtali Yosef		22nd of Elul 5696	9-Sep-1936	A02
Rabbi Meir	Moses		3rd of Heshvan 5607	23-Oct-1846	A13
Rabbi Moses	Rabbi Toviah		5th of Tishrei 5604	29-Sep-1843	A10
Rabbi Yechezkel Michal	Rabbi Dan Yaakov Segal	[Horowitz]	10th of Nisan 5634	28-Mar-1874	A20
Shalom	Yechezkel		10th of Elul 5633	2-Sep-1873	A25
Shimson Tzvi	Yosef	Bender	4th day of Shevat 5597	10-Jan-1837	A09
Simchah [Bonim]	Tzvi		4th of Elul 5601	21-Aug-1841	A12
Unknown	Alexander [HaCohen]	Sender	15th of Tevet 5607	3-Jan-1847	A15
Yaakov	Tuvi		8th of Kislev 5648	24-Nov-1887	A24
Yechezkel	Yitzchak		3rd of Elul 5633	26-Aug-1873	A19

Row B

Name	Father's Name	Patronymmic	Hebrew DOD	Date of Death	Location
Avraham	Yehuda		13th of Tevet 5592	17-Dec-1831	B09
Avraham	[Meir]				B02
Eleazer	Yonatan [HaCohen]	Lippman	28th of Adar II 5603	30-Mar-1843	B10
Ephraim Fishel	Israel Rappaport		3rd of Elul 5691	16-Aug-1931	B07
May his soul be bound					B05
Mordechai					B12
Nachum	Rabbi [...]				B08
Rabbi Asher	Shmuel		1st of Adar 5691	18-Feb-1931	B01
Rabbi Naphtali Yosef	Yaakov Zev		14th of Nisan 5661	03-Apr-1901	B04
Yaakov	Mordechai				B11
Yechiel Mechal	Moshe		3rd of Kislev 5590	29-Nov-1829	B06
Yisrael	Hagaon		1st of Tamuz 5623	21-Jun-1863	B03
Yosef	Yehuda	Bendet			B13

Row C

Name	Father's Name	Patronymmic	Hebrew DOD	Date of Death		Location
Aaron	Rabbi Shmuel	[Epstein]	1st of Kislev 5660	3-Nov-1899		C02
May his soul be bound						C09
May this person's soul be bound						C06
May this person's soul be bound						C07
May this person's soul be bound						C08
May this person's soul be bound						C13
Meir	Rabbi Elazar		5612	1851 or 1852		C14
Mordechai Elazar	Rabbi Asher		4th of Tamuz 5692	08-Jul-1932		C01
Rabbi Mattisyahu	Mordechai Zev [HaCohen]		1st Shevat 5611	4-Jan-1851		C12
Rabbi Samuel	Avraham		1st of Shevat 5630	2-Jan-1870		C04
Rabbi Yehoshua Menachem	Rabbi Israel Segal		15th of Nisan 5610	28-Mar-1850		C11
Shlomo						C03
Simchah Bonem	Eli		4th of Tevet 5634	24-Dec-1873		C05
Yehuda Leib	Yosef		1st of Tevet 5607	20-Dec-1846		C10

Row D

Name	Father's Name	Patronymmic	Hebrew DOD		Date of Death	Location
Avraham Yitzchak	Moshe		5th of Heshvan 5626		25-Oct-1855	D15
Elchanan	Meir		1st of Adar 5654		6-Feb-1894	D06
Elemelech	Mordechai			5609	1848 or 1849	D12
Jacob	Rabbi Shaul		6th of Iyar 5665		11-May-1905	D02
Matisyahu	Asher	Zelig	9th of Kislev 5616		19-Nov-1855	D13
May this person's soul be bound						D17
May this person's soul be bound						D05
May this person's soul be bound						D07
May this person's soul be bound						D08
Mendel	Nachman	Sharut	10th of Shevat 5678		23-Jan-1918	D09
Mordechai Mendel		Mendel	[Adar II 563?]		[1830?]	D10
Moses Yosef	Israel					D16
Natan	Isaac	[Isaac]				D11
Rabbi Moses	Rabbi Eliyahu		12th of Shevat 5609		4-Feb-1849	D14
Yitzchak Isaac	Natan Nehtah	Netah	25th of Kislev 5664		14-Dec-1903	D03
Yoel Eli	[...] ben Zion		24th of Adar 5667		10-Mar-1907	D01
Zakkai Shalom		[Rezakueki nt]	24th of Elul 5664		04-Sep-1904	D04

Row E

Name	Father's Name	Patronymmic	Hebrew DOD	Date of Death	Location
Aharon			1st of Adar II	8-Mar-1886	E09
Ari ben Natan			Adar II		E03
Avigdor	Yehuda		22nd of Av 5633	15-Aug-1873	E27b
Avraham Menacham	Yaakov		1st of Heshvan 5642	24-Oct-1881	E11
Baruch Avraham	Hayyim Asher [HaCohen]		2nd of Tevet 5632	14-Dec-1871	E13
Dov Ber			17th of [...]		E14
Eliezer	Naphtali [Shuvni]	[Shuvni]	9th of Shevat 5647	3-Feb-1887	E07
Eliezer	David		22nd of Elul 5637	22-Sep-1867	E25
Ephraim	Yitzchak Zev		1st of Sivan 5642	19-Mar-1882	E32
Hayiim Shaul			25th of Adar		E19
May this Person's Soul Be Bound					E10
May this Person's Soul Be Bound					E22
May this Person's Soul Be Bound					E23
May this Person's Soul Be Bound					E24
May this Person's Soul Be Bound					E26
Meir	Yehuda		9th of Sivan 5641	6-Jun-1881	E12
Meir Aharon	Menachem Zev		2nd of Iyar 5648	13-Apr-1888	E06
Menachem	Zev		16th of Av 5633	16-Aug-1873	E15
Meshulam [Zisha] [Zusya]	Yosef Bendit	Bendit	1st of Heshvan 5670	15-Oct-1909	E05
Mordechai Tzvi	Yechiel Mechel		1st of Tishrei 5648	19-Sep-1887	E31
Moses Dov	Yaakov		Erev Rosh hashanah 5638	7-Sep-1877	E33
Naphtali	Moses		12th of Adar 5647	19-Mar-1886	E08
Naphtali	Elazar		15th of Av 5638	14-Aug-1878	E16
Naphtali Tzvi	Joseph		25th of Sivan 5642	12-Jun-1882	E21
Rabbi Moses Ari	Rabbi Eliezer		8th of Heshvan 5638	15-Oct-1877	E34
Shalom Yehudah	Kalman	Levush Lazar	26th of Elul 5692	27-Sep-1932	E01
Shimon	Yehoshua				E17
Shlomo Meir	Menachem Mendel		13th of Av 5642	29-Jul-1882	E20
Tuvyah	Nisan		1st of Iyar 5649	1-May-1889	E04
Tzvi Yaakov	Moses Menachem	Horowitz	4th of Pesach 5685	14-Apr-1925	E02
Yehoshua	Avraham [HaLevi]		[...] Adar 5647	Feb or Mar 1887	E18
Yisrael Dov	Pinchas		[4th of Kislev]		E28
Yitzchak	Yaakov		18th of Tevet 564?		E29
Yitzchak	Shmuel		[...] Iyar 5680	Apr or May 1920	E30
	Mordechai		21st of Av 5632	25-Aug-1872	E27

Row F

Name	Father's Name	Patronymmic	Hebrew DOD		Date of Death	Location
[Bintiv] Henne	Mordechai					F40
Eleazer	Yehoel Mechel	Horowitz	9th of Av 5653		22-July-1893	F32
Eliezer Lipah	Moses		24th of Shevat 5654		31-Jan-1894	F06
Elkah				5623	Circa 1873	F23
Esther	Eleazer		3rd of Pesach 5636		11-Apr-1876	F30
Hannah Rachel	Yisrael Dov		19th of Sivan 5663		14-Jun-1903	F12
Hayeh	Y'choel Mechal Segal		17th of Tevet 5640		1-Jan-1890	F16
Hayeh	Alexander	Bender	5th of Elul 5571 or 5591		25-Aug-1811 or 14-Aug-1831	F41
Hindah	Tzvi Yaakov		1st of Pesach 5640		29-Mar-1880	F18
Leah Baylah	Yosef Bendit	[Bendit] Axelrod	2nd of Rosh Hashanah 5655		2-Oct-1894	F15
Malkah	Tzvi Yaakov		4th of Adar 5656		18-Feb-1896	F17
May she be bound in the bonds						F13
May This Person's Soul Be Bound						F01
May This Person's Soul Be Bound						F04
May This Person's Soul Be Bound						F08
May This Person's Soul Be Bound						F10
May This Person's Soul Be Bound						F22
May This Person's Soul Be Bound						F25
May This Person's Soul Be Bound						F26
May This Person's Soul Be Bound						F27
May This Person's Soul Be Bound						F28
May This Person's Soul Be Bound						F31
May This Person's Soul Be Bound						F33
May This Person's Soul Be Bound						F34
May This Person's Soul Be Bound						F35
May This Person's Soul Be Bound						F36
May This Person's Soul Be Bound						F38
May This Person's Soul Be Bound						F39
Nachman	Yisrael		2nd of Sukkot 5654		28-Sep-1894	F07
Naphtali Tzvi	Zev		4th of Kislev 5667		21-Nov-1906	F03
Pesel Dvorah	Yosef Bendit	[Bendit] Axelrod	19th of Tishre 5665		28-Sep-1905	F14
Rabbi Judah	Rabbi Asher	Zelig	16th of Tevet 5643		26-Dec-1882	F37
Rakel	Rabbi Mordechai Macheel [Notarikon]		10th of Iyar 5647		29-Apr-1887	F21
Rekliyon						F24
Sarah Yehudit	Avraham Yehoshua		9th of Shevat 5649		11-Jan-1889	F29
Tzvi	Ari [HaCohen]	Zissel	14th of Shevat 5660		14-Jan-1900	F09
Tzvi Hayyim	Shalom		5th of Heshvan 5651		19-Oct-1890	F05
Yechiel Baruch	Ben Zion		13th of Kislev 5662		24-Nov-1901	F11
Yehudit Rachel			Purim			F19
	David					F02
	Yerush Tzvi		2nd of Shavuot 5612		25-May-1852	F20

Row G

Name	Father's Name	Patronymmic	Hebrew DOD	Date of Death	Location
Dobah	Yisrael Yosef		16th of Adar I 5651	24-Feb-1891	G26
Faige	Mordechai		4th of Heshvan 5642	27-Oct-1881	G20
Gittel	[Leibush]	[Leibush]	1st of Tevet 5639	27-Dec-1878	G22
Hannah Raizel	Moshe		Erev Pesach 5630	15-Apr-1870	G27
Leah	Netah		8th of Shevat 5597	14-Jan-1837	G35
Leibah Tzviyah	Hasid Yosef		12th of Heshvan 5655	11-Nov-1894	G12
May her soul be bound	Yehudah		19th of Shevat 5634	6-Feb-1874	G30
May This Person's Soul Be Bound					G01
May This Person's Soul Be Bound					G04
May This Person's Soul Be Bound					G05
May This Person's Soul Be Bound					G11
May This Person's Soul Be Bound					G13
May This Person's Soul Be Bound					G14
May This Person's Soul Be Bound					G18
May This Person's Soul Be Bound					G19
May This Person's Soul Be Bound					G21
May This Person's Soul Be Bound					G29
May This Person's Soul Be Bound					G31
May This Person's Soul Be Bound					G33
May This Person's Soul Be Bound					G34
May This Person's Soul Be Bound					G36
Natan Yehudah	Tzvi Yaakov		23rd of Shevat 5662	31-Jan-1902	G08
Perel	Moshe David		18th of Tevet		G16
Pinah Hayeeh	Yitzchak		28th of Tishre 5642	21-Oct-1881	G25

Rachel	Rabbi David		10th fo Nisan 5634	28-Mar-1874	G15
Razel	Moshe Yitzchak		9th of Av 5641	4-Aug-1881	G23
Rivkah	Yaakov	Galmodah	6th of Sukkot 5662	03-Oct-1902	G09
Sarah	Meshullam		26th of Sivan 5652	21-Jun-1892	G10
Sarah			15th of Iyar		G17
Sarah Mendel	Tzvi		7th of Tevet 5637	23-Dec-1876	G28
Sarah Rivkah Chayeh	Samuel Hezeel		13th of Tishre 5642	9-Oct-1881	G24
Simah Baylah	Yehudah Lev		11th of Adar II 56??		G32
Yehudah Naphtali	Zev		7th of Pesach 5663	18-Apr-1903	G02
Yisrael	Yaakov		5th of Av 5663	29-Jul-1903	G03
Yonah	Aharon		7th of Pesach 5663	28-Apr-1902	G07
Yosef	Avraham Simchah		22nd of Heshvan 5663	22-Nov-1903	G06

Row H

Name	Father's Name	Patronymmic	Hebrew DOD	Date of Death	Location
Aharon Naphtali	Samuel		1st of Elul 5654	12 or 13-Aug-1893	H20
Alexander	Avraham		20th of Iyar 5657	22-May-1897	H13
Avraham Moshe	Mordechai		4th of Shevat 5653	21-Jan-1893	H21
Avraham Yitzchak	Yaakov		1st of Elul 5670	05-Sep-1910	H01
Avraham Yoel	Moses		11th of Adar 5674	09-Mar-1914	H05
Azriel	Yehoshua		25th of Tamuz 5659	3-Jul-1899	H11
Baylah Ettah	Avraham Yitzchak		23rd of Elul 5653	4-Sep-1893	H24
David	Meshulam [Zisha] [Zusya]		8th of Nisan 5670	17-Apr-1910	H02
Eleazer Lipah	Shlomo		13th of Shevat 5651	22-Jan-1891	H10
Eleazer Lipah	Moshe		7th of Av 5654	9-Aug-1894	H17
Esther Devorah	Rabbi Yoel Ephraim [HaCohen]	Fischel	11th of Iyar 5637	24-Apr-1877	H28
Israel	Pesach		19th of Sivan 5656	31-May-1896	H15
Joshua	Eleazer		6th of Adar 5655	2-Mar-1895	H16
Male Levite					H06
May This Person's Soul Be Bound					H04
May This Person's Soul Be Bound					H07
May This Person's Soul Be Bound					H08
May This Person's Soul Be Bound					H09
May This Person's Soul Be Bound					H14
May This Person's Soul Be Bound					H22
May This Person's Soul Be Bound					H26
May This Person's Soul Be Bound					H27
Rabbi Zev	Rabbi Yoel Ephraim [HaCohen]	Fischel	24th of Adar II 5665	31-Mar-1905	H03
Yitzchak	Yechoel Yaakov		12th of Tishre 5654	22-Sep-1894	H19
Yosef	Yisrael		3rd of Shevat 5654	10-Jan-1894	H18
			Nisan 565?	1890s	H12
	Gedaliaya			5688	Circa 1922	H23
	Rabbi Yisrael Dov		25th of [...] 5640	Circa 1880	H25

Row I

Name	Father's Name	Patronymmic	Hebrew DOD	Date of Death	Location
Avraham	Shmuel		27th of Av 5671	21-Aug-1911	I01
Avraham	David		Shevat 5575	12-Jan to 10-Feb-1815	I32
Avraham [Meier]	Aaron Meir	[Meier]	4th of Adar 5664	20-Feb-1904	I03
Blimah [Blumah]	Moshe				I22
Chayyah Rozah	Naphtali Tzvi		13th of Tevet 5666	10-Jan-1906	I11.2
Devorah	Hayim		5610	Circa 1850?	I07
Dovah	Tuvyah		3rd Heshvan 5640	20-Oct-1879	I30
Faigah	Arin	Hertz	24th of Adar II 5651	30-Aug-1891	I08
Gitel			Heshvan		I29
Hannah	Moshe		9th of Iyar 5660	8-May-1900	I19
Hayeh	Yonah		5th of Tevet 5646	13-Dec-1885	I13.2
Hayeh	Zissah Ari		14th of Adar 5659	24-Feb-1899	I20
Hayeh [Pearl]	Hayim Yisrael	[Pearl]	16th of Tevet 5665	24-Dec-1904	I12
Leah	Eliyahu		20th of Tevet 5669	13-Jan-1909	I06
Malkah	Alexander [Zusyeh]		5th of Tishre		I31
May this soul of this person be bound					I02.2
May this soul of this person be bound					I03.2
May this soul of this person be bound					I13
May this soul of this person be bound					I14
May this soul of this person be bound					I15
May this soul of this person be bound					I16
May this soul of this person be bound					I18
May this soul of this person be bound					I21
May this soul of this person be bound					I25

May this soul of this person be bound					I26
May this soul of this person be bound					I28
May this soul of this person be bound					I29.2
May this soul of this person be bound					I34
Mordechai David					I04
Pearl	Nachum		Nisan 5636	26-Mar to 24-Apr-1876	I35
Rachel	Dov [HaCohen]		Fast of Ester [11 Adar]	4-Mar-1909	I09
Rachel Leah	Shlomo		13th of Nisan 5650	3-Apr-1980	I27
Rebecca	Aaron		Heshvan 5657	8-Oct to 5-Nov 1896	I24
Rosah	Yehoshua		16th of Av 5657	20-Aug-1897	I02
Sanach	Meir		22nd of Kislev 5663	22-Dec-1902	I14.2
Sarah	Moshe Mordechai		3rd of Kislev 5661	25-Nov-1900	I17
Shimon			13th of Tevet 5648	28-Dec-1887	I11
Shprintzah	Yaakov Segal	[Segal]	13th of Av 5629	21-Jul-1869	I33
Tzarnah	Avraham		18th of Kislev 5655	26-Nov-1895	I05
Yaakov			5657	11-Mar-1905	I23
Yacht	Matti [HaCohen]		18th of Tamuz 5666	11-Jul-1906	I10
Yentil			Iyar		I15.2

Row J

Name	Father's Name	Patronymmic	Hebrew DOD	Date of Death	Location
Baylah	Baruch	Gitel	1st of Kislev 5662	12-Nov-1901	J16
Chayeh Rivkah	Yehoshua		6th of Shevat 5675	21-Jan-1915	J10
Ether Etteh	Dov		21st of Shevat 5652	19-Feb-1892	J18
Etta Rosa	Joshua		18th of Iyar 5674	14-May-1914	J11
Ettah	Avraham Moshe		22nd of Adar 5652	21-Mar-1892	J22
Hannah Hayeh	Tzvi		22nd of Adar II 5646	29-Mar-1896	J26
Hava Leah Shevah	Ze'ev		25th of Elul 5629	1-Sep-1869	J06
Hayeh	Joseph		1st of Pesach 5645	30-Mar-1885	J28
Hennah			3rd of Shevat 5675	18-Jan-1915	J09
Hennah	Rabbi Yaakov		4th of Tamuz 5645	17-Jun-1885	J27
Jacob	Ephraim [HaLevi]	Fischel	10th of Sivan 5675	23-May-1915	J04
May his soul be bound					J02
May this person's soul be bound					J12
May this person's soul be bound					J13
May this person's soul be bound					J14
May this person's soul be bound					J19
May this person's soul be bound					J20
May this person's soul be bound					J24
May this person's soul be bound					J25
May this person's soul be bound					J32
Miriam	Nafitali David		28th of Sivan 5673	3-Jul-1913	J08
Naavah	Rabbi Tverchel		5th of [...] 5661	1900-1901	J15
Pearl	Yaakov		13th of Shevat 5654	20-Jan-1894	J21
Raisel	Meir		21st of Shevat 5650	11-Feb-1890	J23
Sarah	Zev Pinchas		9th of Tishre 5661	2-Oct-1900	J17
Sarah Perel	Moshe		2nd of Iyar 5672	19-Apr-1912	J07
Shlomo	Rabbi Shimshon	Gimple	21st of Adar 5677	15-Mar-1917	J01
Shlomo	Dov [HaCohen]		14th of Sivan 5675	27-May-1915	J05
Temmah	Yehudah	Levush	28th of Tamuz 5641	25-Jul-1881	J29
Tzichul	Rabbi [...]				J31
Tzirel Rivkah	Rabbi Natan		15th of Iyar		J30
Yosef	Pesach Avraham		5th of Heshvan 5659	6-Nov-1898	J03

Row K

Name	Father's Name	Patronymmic	Hebrew DOD	Date of Death	Location
[ ]tarim	shin-resh		5650	1890	K14
Aharon	Yaakov Yitzchak				K04
Batyah Velkah	Menachem [HaLevi]		8th of Sivan 5697	18-May-1937	K06
Esther	Yitzchak		19th of Elul 5679	14-Sep-1919	K16
Faigeh Pearl			25th of Iyaar		K10
Frimat	Shmuel Sini		22nd of Kislev		K12
Hai	Eleazer [HaLevi]	Horowitz	last day of Pesach 5676	25-Apr-1916	K07
Hannah	Yechezkel		11th of Kislev 5634	1-Dec-1873	K23
Hindah	Moshe		4th of Tevet		K17
May Her Soul be Bound					K08
May her soul be bound					K11
May this peron's soul bound					K09
May this peron's soul bound					K15

May this peron's soul bound					K19
May this person's soul be bound					K05
Miriam	Yechezkel		Erev Pesach		K22
Moses	Yaakov Yosef		5th of Adar II 5684	11-Mar-1925	K02
Rachel	Ari Lev		5643	1883	K18
Retzah	Meshilam Menachem		5th of Av 5636	26-Jul-1876	K21
Simah Rikil	Tzvi		13th of Iyar 5633	10-May-1873	K24
Vita Leah	Avraham Yehoshua		5th of Adar 5639	28-Feb-1879	K20
Vita Rachel	Tzvi		6th of Heshvan 5676	14-Oct-1915	K13
Yisrael Yitzchak	Menachem		13th of Adar II 5684	19-Mar-1924	K03
Zev [Reich]		[Reich]	5675	1915	K01

Row L

Name	Father's Name	Patronymmic	Hebrew DOD	Date of Death	Location
Basha	Mordechai David		11 Heshvan 5682	12-Nov-1921	L09
Blumah Nichah	Moshe Yosef		23rd of Shevat 5676	28-Jan-1916	L15
Gad Asher	Yaakov Yitzchak		7th of Heshvan 5695	16-Oct-1894	L03
Hai	Abah		11th of Shevat 5658	3-Feb-1898	L20
Hannah	Yisrael Isar		7th of Shevat 5680	27-Jan-1920	L13
Hayiim Tzvi	Netah Yehudah		5th of Nisan 5692	11-Apr-1932	L04
Hayim Eli	Shmuel Ari	Kaufman	14th of Sivan 5696	4-Jun-1936	L01
Libah			1st of Adar 5640	13-Feb-1880	L12
Malkah Tzvi	Tzvi Ari		5th of Tamuz		L07
May this Person's Soul Be Bound					L16
May this Person's Soul Be Bound					L17
May this Person's Soul Be Bound					L18
May this Person's Soul Be Bound					L22
Menachem	Avraham Simchah		1st of Kislev 5695	8-Nov-1934	L02
Miriam	Naphtali Zvi		24th of Sivan 5675	6-Jun-1915	L14
Rachel Rivkah	Yosef Aharon		11th of Tevet 5683	30-Dec-1922	L08
Rivkah	Natan Netah		25th of Adar 5655	21-Mar 1895 or 23rd-Mar-1865	L19
Roseh	Naphtali Yosef		3rd of Iyaar 5686	17-Apr-1926	L05
Sirkah	Hayim Yechiel				L10
Yentah	Menachem Yehoshua		Hoshannah Rabbah 5657	28-Sep-1896	L21
Yocheved Hai	Mordechai		16th of Sivan 5620	6-Jun-1860	L11
	Avraham Yitzchak		16th of Tamuz 5626	29-Jun-1866	L06

Row M

Name	Father's Name	Patronymmic	Hebrew DOD	Date of Death	Location
Baylah	Rabbi Shimon		1st of Pesach 5657	18-Apr-1897	M24
Baylah	Elisha [HaCohen]		21st of Adar 5630 (5640)	22-Feb-1870 or 4-Mar-1880	M34
Blumah	Daniel		8th of Pesach 5645	7-Apr-1885	M27
Breindel	Yosef		21st of Elul 5630	31-Aug-1870	M35
David		Ringelheim			M02
Esther Yenteh	Yitzchak		5th of Shevat 5685	30-Jan-1925	M08
Faigah	Rabbi Eli	Katz	1st of Heshvan 5642	24-Oct-1881	M29
Faigeh	Tanvi		9th of Tamuz 5687	09-Jul-1927	M05
Friedel	Moshe		19th of Shevat 5674	15-Feb-1914	M17
Goldah	Zev Wolf	Wolf	3rd of Tamuz 5675	15-Jun-1915	M14
Hendel	Aaron		4th of Adar I 5643	11-Feb-1883	M28
Henneh Tziah	Yehoshua		22nd of Iyaar 5655	16-May-1895	M23
Leah	Shimon		Tamuz 5640		M31
Libah	Avraham Avish	Avish	28th of Tishre 5646	7-Oct-1885	M26
Malkah	Moshe Avraham		26th of Sivan 5687 [5686 or 5684]	26-Jun-1927 [8-Jun-1926 or 28-Jun-1924]	M09
Malkah Nana	Moshe		11th of Heshvan 5676	19-Oct-1915	M13
May her soul be bound					M15
May her soul be bound			5659	13-Mar-1905	M20
May this person's soul be bound					M01
May this person's soul be bound					M04
May this person's soul be bound					M11
May this person's soul be bound					M18
May this person's soul be bound					M21
May this person's soul be bound					M22
Meital	Aharon		2nd of Adar II 5684	08-Mar-1924	M30
Miriam	Menachem		16th of Adar 5639	11-Mar-1879	M10
Miriam	Joshua		28th of Adar 5675	14-Mar-1915	M06
					M16

Name	Father's Name	Patronymmic	Hebrew DOD	Date of Death	Location
Miriam Raizel	Yosef [HaCohen]		27th of Tevet 5622	30-Dec-1861	M12
Naltah [Z'latah]		Katz	1st of Av 5678	31-Jul-1878	M33
Pearl	Meir		5640	22-Feb-1905	M19
Pearl	Yaakov		18th of Tevet 5640	2-Jan-1880	M32
Sara	Moses		7th of Tamuz		M25
Tovah	Tzvi		5696	1936 or 1935	M07
Yechiel Michal	Zev		4th of Shevat 5696	26-Jan-1936	M03

Row N

Name	Father's Name	Patronymmic	Hebrew DOD	Date of Death	Location
Baylah	Yaakov		1st of Iyar		N15
Devorah Malkah			25th of Av 5668	22-Aug-1908	N31
Esther	Ari		2nd of Pesach 5682	16-Apr-1922	N13
Ettah Malkah	Yechiel Aharon [HaLevi]	Gotwin	5th of Tishre 5698	10-Sep-1937	N01
Fraidel	Zusman		19th of Shevat 5674	15-Feb-1914	N19
Gildah	Rabbi Joshua		9th of Heshvan 5652	10-Nov-1891	N26
Gitel	Mordechai Menachem		27th of Shevat 5674	23-Feb-1914	N17
Gitel	Natan		18th of Tevet 5640	2-Jan-1880	N30
Hannah	Moshe		7th of Tevet 5676	14-Dec-1915	N16
Hannah	Yehudah		5th of Av 5625	29-Jul-1865	N29
Hannah Malkah	Naphtali Yosef		26th of Shevat 5685	20-Feb-1925	N09
Havah Shasah			1st of Shavuot 5655	29-May-1895	N24
Hayeeh Seril	Mattisyahu [HaCohen]		13th of Tevet 5607	1-Jan-1847	N34
Hayeh Sarah		Treitel	14th of Sivan 5608 or 5605	15-Jun-1848 or 19-Jun-1845	N35
Hayyah Blima	Tzvi		Fast of Gedaliah 5655	3-Oct-1894	N25
Henneh	Eli Leib		8th of Tevet 5679	11-Dec-1918	N14
Lavi	Yehudah Livush	Livush	10th of Tevet 5687	15 or 16-Dec-1926	N07
Lebah	Pardesi		25th of Elul 5659	31-Aug-1899	N23
Malia	Mordechai Tzvi	Nadrah?	11th of Iyar 5665	12-May-1908	N22
May her soul be bound					N28
May her soul be bound					N10
Mindle	Aharon Shaul		1st of Tamuz 5682	26 or 27-Jun-1922	N12
Pearl Genendle	Yitzchak		Av 5696	20-Jul to 18-Aug-1936	N02
Rachel Leah	Yosef		7th of Tishre 5686	25-Sep-1925	N08
Ratzah	Hoshea		Eve of Nisan 5607	17-Mar-1847	N32
Rayzel			Adar I 5689	1929	N05
Rivka	Haim Yisrael		25th of Kislev 5674	24-Dec-1913	N18
Sarah	Moshe Natan	Hertzberg Yosele	1st of Nisan 5689	8-May, 11-Apr, or 4-May-1929	N04
Tabah	Shimshon		Erev Rosh Hodesh Heshvan 5610	15-Oct-1849	N33
Toibah Haavah	Yechiel Michal		24th of Kislev 5673	4-Dec-1912	N20
Tovah	Meier		27th of Adar 5687	1-Mar-1927	N06
Yenteh	Avraham Yitzchak [HaLevi]		26th of Sivan 5689	4-Jul-1929	N03
Yuttah	Eleazer Lipah	Katz	9th of Shevat 5638	13-Jan-1878	N27
Zisel	David		4th of Av 5683	17-Jul-1923	N11
Zlata	Menachem		17th of Sivan 5673	17th of Sivan 5673	N21

Row O

Name	Father's Name	Patronymmic	Hebrew DOD	Date of Death	Location
Avraham Simcha	Yitzchak		20th of Nisan 5648	1-Apr-1888	O35
Avraham Yehoshua	Raphael		11th of Heshvan 5661	3-Nov-1900	O31
David	Hayim		1st of Adar 5670	10-Feb-1910	O29
Eleazer Lipah	Ari Lebush	Levush	8th of Av 5625	31-Jul-1865	O02
Eleazer Lipah	Avraham		1st of Av or Nisan 5663	25-Jul or 29-Mar-1903	O22
Fischel	Elimelech	Fischel	13th of Kislev 5670	26-Nov-1909	O26
Gadel	Shlomo Mordechai		1st of Tamuz 5667	13-Jun-1907	O27
Hayim Aharon	Avraham		7th of Nisan 5675	22-Mar-1915	O12
Jacob	Ben Zion		29th of Kislev 5682	30-Dec-1921	O07
Josef Ari	Yaakov		5th of Shevat 5679	6-Jan-1919	O08
May this Person's Soul be bound					O19
May this Person's Soul be bound					O21
May this Person's Soul be bound					O24
May this Person's Soul be bound					O33
Menachem	Avraham David		23rd of Nisan 5683	9-Apr-1923	O06
Mordechai Tzvi	Menachem		5690	1929-1930	O01
Moshe	Naphtali		25th of Elul 5675	4-Sep-1915	O09
Moshe Tzvi	Mordechai		2nd of Iyar 5663	29-Apr-1903	O23
Moshe Yechiel	Simchah Binas		15th of Tamuz 5624	19-Jul-1864	O04
Natan Netah	Shalom Yehudah		25th of Elul 5673	27-Sep-1913	O14

Name	Father's Name		Hebrew DOD	Date of Death	Location
Rabbi Tzvi [HaCohen]	Aharon		5th of Sivan	1-Jun-1911	O17
Shimi	Meir		2nd of Shevat 5677	25-Jan-1917	O28
Shmuel	Moshe Ezrah		10th of Tamuz 5676	11-Jul-1916	O10
Tziporah Maise	Yosef	Bendit	19th of Shevat 5605	27-Jan-1845	O34
Tzvi	Moshe		6th of Nisan 5674	2-Apr-1914	O11
Tzvi	Zev				O18
Yechiel	Eleazer Lipah		4th of Shevat 5664	21-Jan-1904	O25
Yechiel Baruch	Yisrael Dov		4th of Nisan 5672	22-Mar-1912	O15
Yechiel Michal	Zev		9th of Elul 5624	10-Sep-186	O05
Yehoshia	Hayiim [HaLevi]		6th of Tamuz 5684	8-Jul-1924	O03
Yitzchak	Avraham Mordechai		2nd of Pesach 5668	17-Apr-1908	O20
Yitzchak Yaakov	Moshe Menachem [HaLevi]		3rd of Kislev 5675	21-Nov-1914	O13
Yosef	Yekutiel		20th of Tamuz 5658	10-Jul-1898	O32
Yosef Tzvi	Pinchas Yehudah		8th of Tishre 5662	8-Sep-1901	O30
			7th of Elul 5671	31-Aug-1911	O16

Row P

Name	Father's Name	Patronymmic	Hebrew DOD	Date of Death	Location
Alexander	Menachem		27th of Heshvan 5655	5-Nov-1904	P28
Avraham	Yosef		6th of Kislev 5681	17-Nov-1920	P15
Betzalel Yaakov	Avraham David		22nd of Kislev 5689	5-Dec-1928	P07
David Ari	Joseph Yisrael		5th of Tevet 5685	1-Jan-1925	P09
Eleazer	Shmuel		14th of Kislev 5684	22-Nov-1923	P10
Eleazer	Yakov Yitzchak		9th of Sivan 5674	3-Jun-1914	P23
Eleazer	Dov	Lieber	16th of Tishre 5672	8-Oct-1911	P17
Hanah Malkah		[Weinglass]	10th of Shevat 5675	25-Jan-1915	P25
Hayyim Zev	Naphtali Yosef		26th of Heshvan 5677	22-Nov-1916	P16
Malkah Leah	David		13th of [...] 5672	1911 or 1912	P26
May his Soul be bound					P13
May this Person's Soul be bound					P01
May this Person's Soul be bound					P18
May this Person's Soul be bound					P21
May this Person's Soul be bound					P27
Meier	Menachem Mendel	[Finzel] [Finkel]	5th of Nisan 5673	12-Apr-1913	P03
Mordechai [HaCohen]			Tevet 5625	Dec-1864 or Jan-1865	P06
Moses	Gedaliah		2 Shevat 5677	18-Jan-1907	P20
Naphtali Tzvi	Matisyahu [HaCohen]		22nd of Av 5696	10-Aug-1936	P02
Natan Netah	Dov [HaLevi]				P19
Sarah	Hayim Israel		16th of Adar 5683	4-Mar-1923	P24
Yaakov Yitzchak	Eleazer [HaLevi]		6th of Hanukah 5672	21-Dec-1911	P22
Yakov	Mordechai Tzvi		11th of Tishre 5685	9-Oct-1924	P11
Yechiel Aharon	Nisan Mordechai [HaLevi]		25th of Iyar 5691	12-May-1931	P04
Yechiel Michal	Yitzchak		28th of Shevat 5689	8-Feb-1929	P08
Yehuda Tzvi	Yisrael Shimon [HaCohen]	Miroslov	4th of Tevet 5625	2-Jan-1865	P05
Yisrael			Pesach		P14
Zev	Yisrael Meir		25th of Elul 5681	28-Sep-1921	P12

Row Q

Name	Father's Name	Patronymmic	Hebrew DOD	Date of Death	Location
Berachah D'vorah	Arinirch		26th of Adar 5674	24-Mar-1914	Q25
Binah	Moshe		28th of Shevat 5626 or 5686	13-Feb-1866 or 12-Feb-1926	Q17
Dinah	Naphtali	Weber	8th of Elul 5693	30-Aug-1933	Q05
Esther Malkah	Avraham Moshe		13th of Tevet 5656	30-Dec-1895	Q32
Esther Zeldah	Shmuel [HaLevi]		1st of Av 5695	31-Jul-1935	Q03
Etah	Baruch Mordechai		26th of Shevat 5638	30-Jan-1878	Q12
Faigeh	Shimon		9th of Adar 5684	14-Feb-1924	Q19
Fefil	Yitzchak		24th of Tamuz 5696	14-Jul-1936	Q16
Freida	Alexander		5688	1927 or 1928	Q15
Hannah	Naphtali Tzvi		1st of Adar 5667	15-Feb-1907	Q27
Hannah	Alexander	Sheindel	6th of Tevet 5693	4-Jan-1933	Q06
Hayeh Libah		Margolis			Q01
Leah	Yitzchak [HaCohen]		16th of Kislev 5625 or 5688	16-Dec-1927	Q13
Leah	[Yevuel] [Shmuel] [Refuel] Michal		8th of Nisan 5668	9-Apr-1908	Q26
May her soul be bound					Q09
May this person's soul be bound					Q28
May this person's soul be bound					Q31
Miriam Eltah	Meir		23rd of Av 5660	18-Aug-1900	Q30
Miryam Zissel	Tzvi		9th of Tamuz 5694	22-Jun-1934	Q14
Pesel	Yaakov		3rd of Sukkot 5691	11-Oct-1930	Q10

Name	Father's Name		Hebrew DOD	Date of Death	Location
Pesel	Yaakov		26th of Heshvan 5675	15-Nov-1914	Q23
Raisel	Ari		17th of Elul 5679	12-Sep-1919	Q22
Raisel	Avraham Dov		15th of Tevet 5675	1-Jan-1915	Q24
Rivkah Rachel	Yitzchak		Kislev 5684	Dec-1924 or Jan-1925	Q20
Roza	Yechiel Baruch		4th of Kislev 5692	14-Nov-1931	Q07
Sarah	Yosef		7th of Nisan 5665	12-Apr-1905	Q29
Sarah	Naphtali		7th of Heshvan 5692	18-Oct-1931	Q08
Sarah Faigah	Avraham Hayiim		10th of Kislev 5694	28-Nov-1933	Q04
Sarah Rivkah	Naphtali		3rd of Heshvan 5685	31-Oct-1924	Q18
Simah	Mordechai	Berglas	5th of Iyar 5690	3-May-1930	Q11
Tamah	Pinchas		20th of Kislev 5683	10-Dec-1922	Q21
Tilah	Mordechai [HaCohen]		9th of Tevet 5696	4-Jan-1936	Q02

Row R

Name	Father's Name	Patronymmic	Hebrew DOD	Date of Death	Location
Alexander	Alexander		7th of Adar 5692	14-Feb-1932	R17
Ben Zion Dov	Raphael		18th of Av 5689	24-Aug-1929	R21
Faige	Rabbi Moshe Yael		9th of Nisan 5661	29-Mar-1901	R31
Feiga	Meir		25th of Sivan 5690	3-Jun-1930	R11
Hai	Menachem Mendel		9th of Tamuz 5675	21-Jun-1915	R24
Hai [Hayah]	Aharon Shaul		1st of Adar II 5693	28-Feb-1933	R07
Hayiim	Menachem [Nachum]				R14
Hayim	Israel Meir		11th of Sivan 5689	19-Jun-1929	R22
Isaac	Shimi [Shimon]		5th of Av 5694	17-Jul-1934	R23
Joshua	Yosef	Blank	Sukkot 5693	14-Oct-1932	R12
Libah	Avraham Moshe		22nd of Tevet 5664	10-Jan-1904	R27
Malkah	Tzvi		4th of Tishre 5686	22-Sep-1925	R29
Mattai	Yaakov		7th of Adar 5694	22-Feb-1934	R19
May this Person's Soul be Bound					R02
May this Person's Soul be Bound					R03
May this Person's Soul be Bound					R08
Menachem Manis Jeremiah	Avraham	[Manis]	1st of Adar II 5692	9-Mar-1932	R26
Meshullam	Menachem [HaLevi]	Weinstein	18th of Nisan 5691	5-Apr-1931	R16
Mindel	Zev [HaCohen]	Rappaport	25th of Tevet 5692	4-Jan-1932	R05
Mishkat	Shimon Yitzchak		26th of Kislev 5666	24-Dec-1905	R28
Moses Nathan	Avraham [HaLevi]		2nd of Elul 5693	24-Aug-1933	R20
Naphtali		Hirsch	Adar 5691	18-Feb to 18-Mar-1931	R15
Sarah	Shabtai Yitzchak		12th of Tishre 5692	23-Sep-1931	R04
Shaindel	Baruch Avraham	Katz	13th of Av 5692	15-Aug-1932	R06
Shmuel	Shabtai		1st of Iyar 5692	7-May-1932	R18
Yechiel Michal	Aharon [HaLevi]		27th of Heshvan 5689	10-Nov-1928	R25
Yisrael Meir	Naphtali Tzvi		8th of Tevet 5693	6-Jan-1933	R13
Yocheved Zipporah	Eli	Hersh	4th of Tishrei 5698	9-Sep-1937	R01
Yotah	Yechiel Michal [HaLevi]		1st of Elul 5665	1-Sep-1905	R30
Zephtil	Asher Zalkah	[Zalkah]	14th of Kislev 5690	16-Dec-1929	R10
Zlatah	Moshe David	Kirshanter [Kirsanter]	17th of Heshvan 5693	16-Nov-1932	R09

Row S

Name	Father's Name	Patronymmic	Hebrew DOD	Date of Death	Location
Baylah					S6
Hanah Rivkah	Avraham Yehosua	Hesher	26th of Tamuz 5700	1-Aug-1940	S1
Hayeh Libah	Avraham Elikim				S5
May her soul be bound					S2
Raishah	Yehoshua		7th, 17th or 27th of Sivan 5696	28-May, 7-Jun, or 17-Jun-1936	S3
Simah	Hayim Zev		17th of Kislev 5694	5-Dec-1933	S4

Row X

Name	Father's Name	Patronymmic	Hebrew DOD	Date of Death	Location
Bailah Hanah	Menachem Tzvi		1st of Iyar 5679	27-May-1919	X1
Joel	Naphtali	Hertz	12th of Elul		X5
Shmuel	Joseph		17th of Av 5675	28-Jul-1915	X4
Yaakov	Tzvi		Nisan 5674	28-Mar to 26-Apr-1914	X2
Yoel	Eli	Fenig	5th of Av 5689	11-Aug-1929	X3

Sermon Kol Nidre, September 25, 2012

Rollins Chapel

We are all in this Together

The Stories of Yosef Weber

Rabbi Edward S. Boraz, Ph.D.
The Roth Center for Jewish Life
5 Occom Ridge
Hanover, New Hampshire 03755
1-603-646-0361
Rabbi@dartmouth.edu

Introduction

The prophetic reading for Yom Kippur morning is Isaiah Chapter 57:14 through 58:4. There are two sections that I wish to read. The first is as follows:

This is the fast I desire: To unlock fetters of wickedness, and untie the cords of the yoke; to let the oppressed go free; to break off every yoke. It is to share your bread with the hungry, and to take the wretched poor into your home; when you see the naked, to offer clothing, and not to ignore your kin.

If you banish the yoke from your midst, the menacing hand, the evil speech, and you offer your compassion to the hungry and satisfy the famished creature – then shall your light shine in darkness and your gloom shall be like noonday.

I want to read a short story of an aspiring young author by the name of Yosef Weber. He has won literary prizes for his depiction of shtetl life. He is described as *Hasidic*, a pious individual who is grounded in Torah and well respected in his community, yet knowledgeable and engaged in the real world. His story-writing capability is every bit as good as Safron's, Chabon's, Singer's, or Wiesel's.

In Order to Fully Appreciate His Work

The setting is a shtetl and centers on the role of the *kehilla*, the Jewish community's elected leadership and a wheat merchant by the name of Reb Chaim. Everyone in the Shtetl(s) had a vote, but some more than others based on the extent of taxes they had paid the year before. If you paid more, then you had more votes.

The *Kehillah's* primary functions were to levy and collect taxes then use these funds to provide for the poor, for burial in appropriate cases, and to secure the services of both a Rabbi and a Shochet – a kosher butcher. Another important duty was to secure wheat for Passover in order to make Matzah, and that is the subject of matter of Yosef Weber's short story.

The *Kehilah* would do this once a year at the beginning of Adar, about 45 prior to Passover. They would call a town meeting. All the area wheat merchants would be invited. There would be an auction for this contract. The wheat merchant would speculate on the true cost of the wheat against the bid that they would wager. The lower the bid, the better it would be for the Kehillah so as to make it affordable for everyone, for the poor must also have *Matzah*.

For those of you that might have difficulty with this concept because it involves math, the wheat merchant might bid the contract at say 1 zloty (Polish currency akin to a dollar) or so many groshen (pennies) per bushel. Let us say, he would bid 1 zloty ($1.00) per bushel and that the order would be for 50 bushels. He would then go to his own vendors or markets and try to purchase the wheat for less money; an example might be $.50 groshen (half a zloty). Their profit would be 50 groshen, or 100% profit.

Let us begin.

The Story

The Shtetl waited with impatience. With kindness, the first bird of spring announced better or brighter days ahead. The long winter was already on its way out. Odors mixing winter and spring filled the rooms of the house. Ceilings were torn, spider webs everywhere, and water mixed with dust would stream from the walls.

The floor was covered with a thick coat of wet mud where planks disappeared. The small windows sealed with earth after the holiday of Succoth accumulated moisture and turned to a green slime. Through these windows, the mud-covered rays of the outside tried to enter the house.

The mist and the melting snow added a depressive feeling. The old worn clothes itched and scraped the body. The hay of the mattresses was already rotten and spilled from the beds. The air in the room was stifling. Filth surrounded us and the youth was like all youth. How could we escape a bit from the room? However, the holiday of Pesach knocking at the door.

The first day of the month of Adar, between the Mincha and Maariv service, the Shamash of the shul banged his bony hand on the table and announced in the name of the community that after the services there would be an auction for the Pesach flour. The announcement evoked a great deal of joy from the membership; a sort of holiday feeling swept through the air and warmed the entire shul. Happiness was written on all the faces. The hope for spring, flowers, grass and promenades was on everybody's mind. People started talking. It took a while until the congregation finished the Maariv service and quieted down for business. The various shul activities like the Mishnayot study group that met every evening, was suspended due to the Auction. Their tables emptied and orphaned for this evening. The lamps in the area gleamed a bit weaker than other days. Here (in the Bet Midrash, House of Study) sat people in winter evenings who studied and frequently day dreamt. Young boys would spend entire evenings studying the Talmud and often think of their future. Suddenly, the area was deserted.

The services finished, clusters of congregants formed to discuss the matter on hand. Next to the door and near the stove stood a few sacks of flour to show and their owners, the wheat merchants. These merchants discussed all kinds of possibilities and deals in order to form a cartel that would set the price and so they would bid as a unit. However, all efforts to form a cartel failed and the merchants rushed home to bring money for the deposit that would be needed if they won the auction. In another area of the Shul stood the jokers of the crowd who made fun of the way the business session was conducted.

Meanwhile the Shamash was very busy carrying messages back and forth, while merchants grew more and more moody. Next to us stood a group of *cheder* boys listed all the items that their parents would purchase for them for the Pesach holiday: new suits, shoes and hats. Their mouths salivated when they described the taste of the matzos and potato latkes. Profusion of words and noises and above us scattered the smoke of cigarettes and pipes away.

Suddenly, a loud noise was heard. The Shamash banged the wooden hammer on a table and stood up on a bench in the corner of the eastern wall, so as to be closest to Jerusalem, and so that he would tower above the congregation. His glazed eyes looked toward the ceiling and his head tilted to a side that gave him a saintly look. The yellow goat beard completed the picture. He announced that the auction has officially begun. The anticipation of the meeting grew by the minute. Haim, the biggest wheat merchant, moved to the big table covered with a green tablecloth. The movement was difficult and slow since the shul was packed with so many people. The people were jealous as well as respectful of the position of Haim.

Two candelabras stood on top of the table with burning candles. At the head of the table sat the rabbi and next to him the head of the Kehillah. A pen, paper, ink, and the seal of the Kehillah were placed on the table. Alongside of it sat the members of the kehilla board, their faces stern and serious. Haim reached the table and counted his deposit money. Meanwhile two other groups were formed who sent their representatives to the table. The rabbi then spoke at length about the laws of kashrut for Passover, the duties of the mashgichim or religious supervisors to oversee the safekeeping and use of the flour for Passover. The speech was followed by the leader of the kehilla who discussed the financial aspect of the purchase of the flour, the financial situation of the kehilla and so on.

Haim the wheat merchant looked askance at all the other merchants and chewed one wheat kernel after the other. He paced back and forth and seemed to talk to himself in an angry tone; his heavy gray black moustache prevented others from hearing. His eyes half closed and his forehead deep in thought he seemed determined to move ahead. Indeed, he took several steps to the table and announced in his loud and husky voice ninety-four groshen. The audience began to murmur, the faces of the leaders indicated discomfort.

Haim noticed the situation and stated that he could not do it cheaper. The leader of the community signaled to the Shamash to start the auction. The latter immediately began in his melodious tone, ninety-four groshen for the first time and ninety-four groshen for the next time. Suddenly the audience protested vociferously, screams and shouts - a robbery, murder, so expensive, stop the auction! Do not sell to the thief. He will make a fortune. Let the kehilla buy flour. We will bring flour from distant places! This community belongs in Chelm screamed a troublemaker. All other interested merchants added fuel to the incitement of the audience. No one should deal with this dishonest merchant; in all likelihood, we will never get fine flour.

Haim was mad and stormed out of the shul, bunch of beggars, I will show you, he said to himself.

The hammer banged again, the congregational outbursts stopped, silence in the shul. The Shamash voice intoned again, ninety groshen for the first time and the next time and the suddenly - a stern look from the leader of the kehilla stopped the Shamash in mid-air. The latter read the message and pointed to his nose as if to say, I understand and his hand signaled that the bid would fail. The Shamash started again the bid, ninety groshen for the first time and ninety groshen for the next time and *sei gesund* - to your health, he added. The latter remark appealed to the religious people and the atmosphere of the shul calmed down. The audience loosened up and jokes and wisecracks started to make the rounds.

The tension disappeared and joviality returned to the shul. Shlome, a happy Jew with a red nose and a potbelly rubbed his hands and slapped his nearby neighbors saying that happy days were here again. The Shamash's voice thundered again, eighty-five groshen for the first time and eighty-five groshen for the next time and eighty-five groshen for the first time. The audience that protested earlier so vociferously did so not out of stinginess. However, it did not want to be made a fool. The people knew that Haim was going to make money but they wanted it to be fair.

Haim was full of anger, a plague on you he said to himself, even if I have to add to the deal, I will add but the deal will be mine. He ran to the table and shouted eighty-three. The kehilla leader winked to the Shamash to end the auction. The latter started, eighty-three groshen for the first time, eighty-three groshen for the next time and eighty-three groshen for the third time. Mazal Tov to Reb Haim!

The Auction

This is a story about spring and renewal. Despite the poverty of the Shtetl, the mud-floors, the dirt, the rotting hay, there is the smell of spring and Passover. This festival symbolizes the best - a desire for new clothing that no longer scrapes the body, shoes, hats, and most of all ensuring that everyone has Matzah for Passover. The people of Weber's Shtetl see beyond this mud, dirt, rotting hay, and the slimy green oozing from the windows. It is a story about making real the message of Isaiah that we read on Yom Kippur in ways yet to be revealed.

There is communal concern for the poor. The price of the wheat has to be low enough so that the poor will have dignity by being able to purchase the matzah, one law for everyone.

In Shtetl life, nothing is more important than learning and prayer. There, older men study Mishnayot, while the younger students study Talmud. Texts in both provide that if all 612 commandments were on side of the scale and the study of Torah on the other, the two would be evenly balanced. Hence, the significance of suspending the study of Torah in a House of Study so as to take care of the community should not be lost on any of us.

The only thing that is not dispensed with is תפילה – prayer, nothing more than talking to God. When that is finished, a tablecloth is spread, candlesticks are used to provide light, and the town meeting begins. The Rabbi teaches the importance of *kashrut,* because the Auction must begin with an everyday commitment to *kedushah,* holiness. These merchants understand that at the end of the day, everyone has to do the right thing. The hollering, the shouting, calling Chaim a *gonif* (thief), is the "stuff of communities"; not unlike town meetings or some Board Meetings that I have attended. Haim has to have that contract, for he must do good in the world and to accomplish this, he cannot leave the community to its own devices. Profit is neither the motivator nor the leverage in this deal. It is the *mitzvah* of making sure that every single person will have matzah on Passover. No one is going to "outbid" him.

It is pride, ego, even if for a little less money, to do a public *mitzvah* for this little Shtetl. Weber wants us to see that life is a celebration when we care for everyone as a community, even if we call someone a *gonif* or shout and scream at one another.

Weber is teaching us in the Auction that we are all in this world together; rich and poor, healthy and sick, single, married, with children, without children. Weber gives us Haim who has to have that contract because Haim has to be a *macher* in the community. However, what did that mean? It meant helping the community and the poor so they could have Matzah on Passover. This is the world of Yosef Weber and it has become our world tonight on this Yom Kippur.

Yosef Weber and Kol Nidre

Yosef Weber was born in the first part of the 20th century in a town called Brezower, Poland, not far from Korcyna, Poland, the 2012 site for Project Preservation. We discovered this short story at the end of the *Yizkor* (A Book of Remembrance about the Jewish Community of Korcyna, [page 191 in the original Yizkor Book, page 98 in the translation]) that was published some 20 years after its physical destruction.

In the *Yizkor* book, he was described as a kind soul, always ready to help. He personified Torah by always showing respect for each person whom he met. He was well read in religious matters and also had a fine general background. He had a gift to describe types of people, scenes, pictures of daily life, and the ability to write stories.

Thus, in 1929, he entered "The Auction" in a contest sponsored by the Warsaw Yiddish newspaper, Haint (Today). He was awarded 2nd prize for this story and received the sum of 50 zlotys – in today's currency a little under $16.00.

Twelve years later, in 1941, he and his wife were transferred to the Korcyna Ghetto. There, he was forced to serve in the Judenrat. He remained kind to all under the most horrific of circumstances. One year later, in 1942, he and his wife were executed by the Nazis. They may have been shot or sent to Belzec, the death camp that was located nearby. The record is unclear. It hardly matters.

What Matters Tonight

Yosef Weber's work lives on. All of you now know who he is and more importantly, how our ancestors focused on the truly important things in Jewish life; community, respect for all, concern for the poor, and hope for a better tomorrow by ensuring that the community have matzah on Passover. Chaim was a wealthy man, not because he made a good living as a wheat merchant, but because he had to get that contract, at all costs, even if he lost money on the deal.

Tonight, we have performed a mitzvah that is every bit as important as providing Matzah for everyone. Let us read just a bit further from the tomorrow morning's prophetic reading:

From your midst shall arise rebuilders of ancient ruins, you shall restore foundations laid long ago and you shall be called, "Repairers of broken fences, the restorer of lanes for habitation.

Tonight, by hearing the writings of man who would otherwise have been forgotten, as would his community, you have become the rebuilders of the ancient ruins. You have restored the foundations that were laid long ago. You have repaired one of the many broken fences and have restored a lane of habitation that extends from Sinai to this evening; one that no person or people could ever cut asunder.

I beseech the Heavenly Court on this Kol Nidre to find that the prophetic truth of Isaiah fulfilled by this community this evening. And as such, as its Rabbi and advocate, that you 'O God grant favor unto your people; that you O' God set this community astride in the heights of the earth, and allow them to enjoy the heritage of its ancestors, Abraham, Isaac, Jacob, Sarah, Rebecca, Rachel and Leah Amen.

Sermon III Kol Nidre

What Are Ancestors Lived and

Bequethed Unto Us

10th of Tishre

September 14, 2013

Rabbi Edward S. Boraz, Ph.D.
Michael Steinberg '61 Rabbi of Dartmouth College Hillel
The Roth Center for Jewish Life
5 Occom Ridge
Hanover, New Hampshire, 03755
1-603-646-0361
Rabbi@dartmouth.edu

Introduction

This past year, we lost a dear congregant. He had a generous heart, a brilliant mind, and was one of three founding members of the Upper Valley Jewish Community. He was also a Professor of Philosophy for over 40 years at Dartmouth. His name was Professor Bernard Gert, z'l, may his memory be for blessing. He was a moral philosopher. Perhaps the core question to which he tried to address was the following "Is it possible for humankind to develop a morality that is grounded solely on rationality, and not either directly or indirectly derived from a theological framework?" Could there be a universal morality that a society could adopt and work that did not involve God? Of course, never one to shy away from an answer, he not only devoted his academic career to that question, he answered it in the affirmative in his works "Morality" and "Common Morality."

One of the great lessons from his life's work is that there could be two solutions to a moral quandary, each of them being equal in their sensitivity and degree of morality. This is indeed the very essence of the Talmudic discourse.

What then should our morality be based? Where do we turn to find those deep values upon which to return "t'shuvah" our hearts, as religious people, to a life of meaning? How can we be united if moral paths differ from each other?

The Headstones

As many of you may know, our Dartmouth College students spent 5 days in the town of Korcyna. Laboriously, we hand copied the inscriptions of each stone we could locate. I spent this summer engaged in the tediousness of transcribing and translating 540 headstones. Often, I would ask myself, "What is the point of all this? What difference does it make for many seem to contain much the same language and description of the deceased who were buried up to 1938?

One night this summer, from out of those areas of the mind where ones receives a flash of insight that one never had before (perhaps at stone no. 375, 425), the following occurred to me. These stones are telling us something about the about the manner in which our ancestors wanted to be remembered. They are actually teaching the way in which these Jewish communities wanted to remember those who had passed away. These stones were about virtue and character and their relationship to belief and faith.

Our remembrance of the past can be used as a basis for how to live going forward. As descendants of these Jewish communities, these stones speak to us of Jewish virtues upon which to base a life of meaning.

So on this evening, on this Kol Nidre, a prayer about the importance of our words, about promises to God made, broken, and renewed, I want to describe two of the most common phrases; one used for men, the other for women.

A Pure, Upright, and God-fearing Man

The most common phrase for Jewish men is taken from the opening verse in the Book of Job. It reads:

Here lies buried a man - pure, upright and in awe of G-d

There is irony in the selection from Job. He was a man who had everything taken from him that he loved in life and thus began to deeply challenge G-d on the fundamental question of why good people suffer in this world. When we view Jewish history of Europe, even before the tragic events of the Shoah, we see enormous difficulties that include exile, poverty, violence that had government sanction, and anti-Semitism at its height. Instead of selecting a latter passage from Job where there is anger directed at the Almighty, we see this verse on the headstone of such men as Baruch ben Mordechai – a man pure, upright, and in awe of God.

The Hebrew word "Tum" is first discovered in describing Jacob in contrast to Esau. It means purity, simplicity, and innocence. Life is complicated, to be sure. However, Judaism teaches that each of us have a part of our heart that is always pure and can never be defiled. Like Jacob, we are innocent at the core of our being. We know that life at its core is simple, not complicated. The purpose of these Days of Awe is to return - "T'shuvah" to this state of simplicity, to experience yet again that sense of innocence and purity.

Let us now move to the word "Yashar". According to the classic work "The Complete Hebrew-English and English-Hebrew Dictionary by Reuben Alcalay, the Hebrew "Yashar" means upright, just, fair dealing, or honest. Whenever a person receives an *Aliyah* (which means to ascend to the "Torah" and recite the blessings before and after the reading), the person chants these and afterwards, we say "Yashar koach" – which colloquially means – well done! (Alcalay, 972). It really means may you continue in the upright (manner) with strength. "Yashar" is related to living a moral life – a life grounded in the ethical dictates of Torah as we study its meanings and how we live - so that we can be upright and straight in our relationship to others and to God. "Yashar" – despite life's complications we strive to have the "Yashar" be our guide.

Finally, "Yraha alohim" – in awe of God or commonly translated as G-d fearing. Most of us do not have a literal "fear" of God. We rather rely on the commandment of Moses to "Love the Lord your God, with all your heart, with all your soul and with all your might (Deuteronomy 6:4)." We see ourselves as loving a God that is benevolent, kind and compassionate. The Mishneh and Talmud, the great rabbinic works of the 2nd and 5th centuries stated that Job only served God out of love, never from fear (Talmud Sotah 27b). The sculptors of these stones knew that this passage would be understood by the children, grandchildren, and their loved ones; the ones who would care and maintain these people's final resting. The stonecutters knew that when they inscribed these words, the departed one, in good times and in bad, would always be remembered as one who was pure, innocent, strove to be morally upright, and most of all one who loved God (Talmud Sotah 27b).

Sarah bat Chanah (Sarah the Daughter of Hannah)

The descriptive language they used on the headstones for women were distinct from those of the male counterparts. Today, those for the males could just as easily be applied to women in our world and vice versa.

There are four terms that are commonly found at the outset of these beautiful poems inscribed in sacred remembrance:

A woman who was important, humble, *kasher*
And A Woman of Valor

There is paradox to some extent. The term "Khshuv" indicates a woman of importance standing within the community. Because there are so many stones that bear this inscription, it suggests that women played an important role in communal affairs; and indeed as we will see with the phrase "Aishet Chiyal" – a Woman of Valor – this has significant value. But

I think the word can also mean thoughtful. "Tznoha" suggests two qualities. One is chaste. The other is humility. These words suggest that **Sarah** was humble and yet important, a recognized person who was vital to the community and thoughtful.

The term "Kashra" has the root *kasher* – which refers to purity, as the word כ‎ם does for men. It means that she was meticulous in her concerns for leading a religious life that included keeping a Kosher home, going to Mikveh, but not simply as an end in itself. Rather, her concern for these details was bound to her humility and to her modesty. These attributes led her to be seen as an important woman in the eyes of her people and all who mourned her passing.

The last phrase – "Aishet Chiyal" – a Woman of Valor (the word "Chiyal" can mean force, army and also soldier (Alcalay, p 754). It is taken from Proverbs 31 and attempts to address the inquiry of a prince regarding the qualities that one should look for in an "Azrah Knegdo" – a life-long helper – queen or a wife - that stands facing the other. In the context of this passage, he is searching for a princess who one day may become queen.

The real question is what should we, as Jews, should be looking for in not only choosing a partner with whom to build a life, but also how we should. I will simply read the poem. I have added a few words so as to render its meaning more inclusive – that is the underlying Jewish values apply to all such relationships of love.

A woman of valor - who can find, for her price is far above rubies

The heart of her lover safely trusts in her, and so he lacks for nothing

She will do her lover good and not evil all the days of her life.

She seeks wool, and flax, and works willingly with her hands.

She rises also while it is yet night, and gives food to her household

She considers a field, and buys it

With the labor of her hands she plants a vineyard.

She girds her loins with strength, and makes her arms strong.

She perceives that her merchandise is good; her candle does not go out by night

She puts her hands to the distaff, and her hands hold the spindle.

She stretches out her hand to the poor; she reaches forth her hands to the needy.

Strength and dignity are her clothing; and she shall rejoice at the time to come.

She opens her mouth with wisdom;

In her tongue is the Torah of loving kindness

She looks well to the ways of her household

She does not eat from the bread of idleness
Her children rise up, and call her blessed;
Her life's partner also praises her.
Many daughters have done virtuously, but you excel them all.

Conclusion

Let us return to what constitutes morality or the Jewish way in the modern world; especially if we hold it as truth that there can be two opposite solutions to the moral dilemmas, the moral challenges, of our time. These stones of our ancestors give us way to think about our lives and the challenges that we face. Moral decisions, how we wish to act in our own lives, can be centered on virtues by which our Ancestors deeply valued. These would be purity, love of G-d, and trying to live within an upright and honest way. A moral life, which is something I believe we all strive for, must be based on humility, kindness, concern for one's family and those less fortunate who live in our community.

When we act from these virtues, not only can we considered חשובה – important in the eyes of our community, but in the eyes of communities that are yet to be formed in generations the end of time. This is immortality worthy of our consideration and reflection on this Kol Nidre. It is not so much what specifically we do that matters, but more importantly what are the virtues, the ideals upon which are actions are based and how they are then reflected in the actions that follow.

In the end, only God will know what lies deep in each heart, but on Kol Nidre, we "invite" God in to see that the "Tum" – the purity and innocence- is still there. And on this Kol Nidre, we promise God that from this day forward, we will strive for others to show it to others as our ancestors promised you on such a night as this.

Amen

INDEX

Note that this index only covers the original yizkor book contents up to page 247 and does not cover the Appendices.